W9-AWD-166

THE UPSTART GUIDE TO
Buying, Valuing, and Selling Your Business

Scott Gabehart

DEARBORN™
A **Kaplan Professional** Company

This publication is designed to provide accurate and authoritative information in regard to the subject matter covered. It is sold with the understanding that the publisher is not engaged in rendering legal, accounting, or other professional service. If legal advice or other expert assistance is required, the services of a competent professional should be sought.

Associate Publisher: Cynthia A. Zigmund
Managing Editor: Jack Kiburz
Interior Design: Lucy Jenkins
Cover Design: The Publishing Services Group
Typesetting: Elizabeth Pitts

Copyright © 1998 by Dearborn Financial Publishing, Inc.®

Published by Dearborn, a Kaplan Professional Company

All rights reserved. The text of this publication, or any part thereof, may not be reproduced in any manner whatsoever without written permission from the publisher.

Printed in the United States of America
99 00 10 9 8 7 6 5 4 3

Library of Congress Cataloging-in-Publication Data
Gabehart, Scott.
    The upstart guide to buying, valuing, and selling your business / Scott Gabehart.
        p.   cm.
    Includes bibliographical references and index.
    ISBN 0-57410-087-4 (alk. paper)
    1. Sales of business enterprises—United States. 2. Business enterprises—United States—Purchasing. 3. Business enterprises—Valuation—United States.   I. Title.
HD1393.4.U6G33   1997   97-19701
658.1′6—dc21   CIP

Dearborn books are available at special quantity discounts to use as premiums and sales promotions, or for use in corporate training programs. For more information, please call the Special Sales Manager at 800-621-9621, ext. 4514, or write to Dearborn Financial Publishing, Inc., 155 N. Wacker Drive, Chicago, IL 60606-1719.

Table of Contents

Chapter 14 Financing Issues 277

Debt Financing   278
Equity Financing   280
Creative Financing   289

List of Figures

Foreword

I began teaching a series of courses on entrepreneurship in the fall semester 1985 at The American Graduate School of International Management (Thunderbird). While no one seemed to question the incorporation of a business plan project in an entrepreneurship curriculum, it was not universally accepted that the evaluation of an existing business was a necessary part of the subject matter.

Why not? What better device for the aspiring entrepreneur to know the essential "ingredients" of running a going venture? How critical is cash flow? What effect does a reduction in the aging of receivables create? What is the breakeven point? Are we carrying too much inventory? Can we lengthen our payables? How do we compare to industry averages? How do we compare with our competition? Exactly what is our business worth?

It's not just a matter of establishing a value for the stock, there are also the issues of mergers and acquisitions, spin-offs, establishing ESOPs, incentive stock options, private and public issues, LBOs, gifting or transferring stock, tax regulations and consequences, estate planning and insurance coverage, to name a few additional considerations. At the heart of the matter, perhaps, is our ability to discern the relative merits of buying an existing business vis-à-vis creating a new venture.

Further, we need to recognize that it's not just obtaining a value described in dollars and cents—but more importantly, learning the critical factors in buying, creating, operating, and selling a business. For 11 years, I have taught from personally created course notes and illustrative cases. Certainly, books exist on these topics (my bookshelf includes more than 20 such volumes on buying, valuing, and selling businesses). When Scott Gabehart approached me with the idea of writing a book, my immediate reaction was: one more?

Scott, a Thunderbird graduate with a master's in international management (MIM) continued his education by taking course work toward the Ph.D. in economics at Arizona State University, taught and worked in the area of accounting and taught graduate courses in economics and finance at the University of Phoenix. He has worked full-time as a business broker for VR Business Brokers for many years.

His contention was that, while many texts did exist, none had the complete set of ingredients. There was no doubt that he had the knowledge and background since he dealt with the topics of business valuations and acquisitions on an ongoing basis. Despite (or because of) my initially negative reaction to the idea of another book in this area, Scott has written the text before you now. Without question, it's the most complete guide on these topics, considering the qualitative factors on an equal footing with the various quantitative approaches. What makes this book exceptional is that Scott lives in this world on a daily basis and does not observe it from the more distant perspective of a theoretician. His compilation of actual contracts and clauses, for example, is unparalleled in this area.

Read it! Whether you're buying or selling a business, or whether you are just curious as to what factors are important in the valuation of a business, you will obtain useful information that no business owner should do without. I plan on integrating *The Upstart Guide to Buying, Valuing, and Selling Businesses* into the required reading for my course work.

Paul R. Johnson, Ph.D.
Professor of Entrepreneurship
The American Graduate School of International Management (Thunderbird)

Preface/Acknowledgments

Let's face it. It crosses almost everyone's mind at some point or another. Being on your own, owning your own business—what an attractive escape! How many people are tired of working so hard for their ungrateful superiors, not really able to share fully in the fruits of their labor? Being on your own allows you the freedom to adapt your personal skills and intolerances into a way of life that can be both emotionally and financially rewarding.

On the other hand, owning your own business is certainly not a panacea or utopia. It is not normally a "get rich quick" scheme nor can it be accomplished for "no money down." The process of buying a business is, in and of itself, hard work, time-consuming, frustrating, and possibly expensive (all before you even go to work the first day!). It can be, however, an excellent alternative to the confines and rigidities of serving an employer. Whether you are considering this option for the first time or are currently a business owner wishing to sell or expand, the many practical insights contained in this guide are equally valuable.

My goal in writing this guide was to create a comprehensive, user-friendly, and current analysis of buying, valuing, and selling businesses to be utilized by buyers, sellers, brokers, attorneys, accountants, and business consultants. Instead of buying two to six of the books already available, this extensive guide develops all the tools you will need to understand the processes involved in the valuation and sale of a business. Elaborating on both the buyer's (Chapters 1 to 7) and seller's (Chapters 12 and 13) interests and perspectives is a uniquely important feature of this book. Buyers will normally become sellers and sellers often become buyers once again, and many parties are concerned with business valuation (Chapters 8 to 11). Furthermore, it is my experienced opinion that deals founded upon a more complete, mutual understanding are more likely to both "reach the finish line" and "survive the closing." A chapter on financing (Chapter 14) rounds off the comprehensive nature of this publication.

Where appropriate, outside sources of information and guidance are presented, including dozens of current phone numbers for quick contact. Distinctions are made between smaller businesses (privately held) and larger businesses (publicly traded) in many sections, notably the chapters on business valuation (Chapters 8 and 9). An unparalleled variety of sample forms, contracts, and lists of many types are presented in a series of step-by-step analyses as used by experienced brokers and savvy practitioners. The guide thoroughly addresses and explains all the major topics, terms, concepts, and concerns involved in the process of buying, valuing, and selling a business, supplemented by a user-friendly glossary and detailed index. Dozens of sources for current business opportunities are introduced (Chapters 1 and 3), once again with phone numbers or World Wide Web addresses. Use of this guide in conjunction with professional assistance from your broker, attorney, and accountant (Chapter 2) will lead to optimal results. Without doubt, the quality and quantity of actual forms (purchase agreements, listing contracts, confidentiality agreements, addendums, counteroffers, disclosure documents), practical contract clauses and useful analytical tools (worksheet for calculating cash flow, analysis of purchase form, analysis of seller's proceeds form, worksheet for calculating start-up costs, business acquisition criteria) are unsurpassed by any existing publication. For user-friendly access, most of the forms are included in the disk that accompanies the guide. Despite the fact that this is not a "get rich quick" book or a guide to buying a business for "no cash down," I am confident that it will serve you well no matter what your role is in a given transaction.

Acknowledgments

I would like to thank my wife Mitra for her unending patience and goodwill. Special thanks also to Jim Roth and Sam Stapley of Roth and Associates of Scottsdale, Arizona. Finally, thanks to Cynthia Zigmund and the rest of the Dearborn team for making this process as enjoyable as it was.

About the Author

Scott Gabehart is a business broker and managing director of VR M&A, International in the state of Arizona with the VR Business Brokers office in Scottsdale, Arizona (Roth & Associates at www.az-vr-businessbrokers.com).VR is the nation's largest business brokerage firm, having sold more than 30,000 businesses since 1979 (www.vrbusinessbrokers.com).

Scott is a licensed real estate agent with VR as well as a licensed securities representative (Series 7: General Securities) with Fortis, Inc. He has served as secretary of the Valley Board of Business Brokers and is a member of the Institute of Business Appraisers.

In addition to his experience in business brokerage, Scott teaches graduate level accounting, finance, and economics at the University of Phoenix. His academic training includes bachelor's degrees in economics and German, a master's degree in international business from Thunderbird (recently ranked as the number-one graduate program in international business in the United States by *U.S. News & World Report*), and substantial Ph.D. coursework in economics at Arizona State University. Previous work experience includes several years as corporate auditor for Motorola and Schering-Plough corporations.

CHAPTER 1

Choosing the Right Business

Making the decision to own your own business is a difficult and emotional process. Millions of people from diverse backgrounds have chosen this entrepreneurial path via the risky purchase of established businesses or the riskier option of starting a business from scratch. Many factors will affect a person's choice to pursue self-employment and should be formally evaluated beyond the presence of a "gut feel" that this is the right time and the right decision. How do you know that you are ready for this type of venture? How can you know which type of business will suit your skills and desires and help ensure a favorable outcome to your choice? As you move down the path to self-employment, you will ask yourself many such questions. This chapter will alert you to many of the pertinent issues facing the would-be entrepreneur.

For starters, consider the following questions taken from a self-assessment questionnaire found in a book called *Buy the Right Business—At the Right Price* written by Brian Knight and the Associates of Country Business, Inc. (Upstart Publishing Company, 800-245-2665). First-time buyers will find this book extremely user-friendly as it contains dozens of checklists and questionnaires relating to the purchase of a business.

Self-Assessment Questions

1. Are you willing to work long hours with few vacations and irregular time off to achieve your goals?
2. Are you prepared to place the needs of your business before those of yourself and your family if necessary to preserve the health and continuity of your business?

3. Does your need to be independent and in control of your work environment make it difficult for you to be satisfied working for others?
4. Do you feel that you have a great deal of self-discipline? Can you apply yourself to a job that needs to be done even when you don't feel like doing it?
5. Do you have a broad range of business management skills and a high level of information consciousness?
6. When things go wrong, do you pick yourself up promptly and move on to another challenge instead of brooding for a long time and feeling a lot of self-pity?

The stronger your "yes" responses were, the more likely you are to succeed in small business ownership. Here are two more books that might help you assess your entrepreneurial inclinations: *101 Best Businesses to Start* by Sharon Kahn and the Philip Lief Group (Doubleday, 800-323-9872) and *Work with Passion: How to Do What You Love for a Living* by Nancy Anderson (New World Library, 800-423-7087).

As a business broker, I am constantly amazed by the endless variety of ways there are to "make a buck!" As an instructor of economics, I energetically define the attributes of capitalism (free enterprise) that have made it the predominant form of economic system in the world. The essence of capitalism is freedom—economic freedom. Flexible, intelligent, hard working, motivated entrepreneurs are constantly searching for "profitable" processes, services, and products. Quicker, better, cheaper, friendlier—these are the characteristics associated with profitable endeavors. Approximately five million people started businesses in 1997, because they thought they could do it quicker, better, and cheaper. Additionally, close to one million established businesses changed hands. As the economy changes structurally (i.e., from agrarian to manufacturing to service to information based), the core of processes, products, and services changes. Some notable examples of uniquely evolutionary businesses include:

- Fax broadcast companies
- Manufacture of recycled office products (e.g., paper, pens)
- Airbag repair service

All these businesses exist and are profitable today. Technologies and consumer preferences are constantly changing. All companies and many individuals utilize a fax regularly. Fax-based advertising can be highly successful as a result. The trend toward earth-friendly solutions to the usage of scarce resources has accelerated the trend toward recyclable products. Airbags will be standard equipment on all cars before too long, requiring significant monitoring and repair needs. As an entrepreneur, you must be aware of the changes and trends unfolding around you. In economic terms, you could say that *demand* creates or leads to *supply*. Generally, businesses will fall into one of the following categories:

- Manufacturing
- Wholesale/Distribution

- Retail
- Service

In terms of prevalence, two other categories could be added:

- Food related
- Automotive related

Choosing the "right" business is by no means straightforward. First-time buyers seriously may consider many businesses from different categories before landing the "right" one. Honest analysis of your personal strengths, weaknesses, and even hobbies is a necessary step toward making a sound decision. Continuously ask yourself what it is that you do exceptionally well. What are your areas of expertise? What skills do successful business owners have that you don't? What are your bottom-line constraints in terms of time and money? Brainstorming possible business ideas that match your skills and hobbies is also beneficial. It is also useful to categorize business opportunities by type as either established, start-up, franchised, home-based, relocatable, or distressed. Note that crossing of categories and types is common, such as a food manufacturing business or a home-based franchise.

To appreciate the big picture, analyze the grid in Figure 1.1.

FIGURE 1.1 Business Opportunities

TYPE / CATEGORY	Established	Start-Up	Home-Based	Distressed	Franchise	Relocatable
Retail						
Manufacturing						
Wholesale/ Distribution						
Service						
Food						
Automotive						

Within each category and type there are many possibilities in terms of location, products, size, and history. Determining which category and type is appropriate for you is a personal process. Use of a business broker to explain the pros and cons of a given possibility can be enlightening. In addition to understanding the "quirks" of a given category and type, a business broker might know the history of specific businesses. Experienced brokers also will have a "gut" feeling about potential matches between buyers and businesses. Before analyzing the particular categories and the trade-offs between them, let's look at some examples of "trendy" businesses:

- Home health care
- Internet consulting/marketing
- Specialized staffing services
- Family entertainment centers

- Mobile service floor covering
- Disaster restoration/relief
- Mobile blind service
- Family entertainment centers

Many magazines feature current assessments of hot business opportunities, including *Entrepreneur* (800-274-6229), *Small Business Opportunities* (212-807-7100), and *Business Start-Ups* (800-274-8333). To summarize, general choices are between categories of businesses (e.g., retail, manufacturing) and types (e.g., established, start-up). Detailed evaluation of specific choices (i.e., particular business opportunities) will be addressed in later chapters.

Start-Up Businesses

This guide primarily addresses the purchase and sale of established businesses (going concerns). Please note that this is not a get-rich-quick book, nor does it provide extensive insights into the successful day-to-day operation of a business (except of course those decisions that directly impact the value and salability of a business). For a list of several "Owning and Managing" books for several different types of businesses, call Upstart Publishing Company at (800-245-2665). Review the list found at the end of this chapter for quality entrepreneurial assistance. This is not a guide to starting a business from the ground up. Many excellent books have been written in this area; for example, *The Start-Up Guide, The Small Business Survival Kit*, and *Strategic Planning for the New and Small Business* are available through Upstart Publishing Company.

Many people struggle with the choice between starting from scratch and purchasing an established business. Two general options exist that deserve coverage at this juncture:

1. Independently starting a business from scratch
2. Jointly starting a business from scratch with the assistance of a franchiser

The basic choice between an established business and a start-up operation is worthy of personal introspect. Without previous business ownership experience, starting a small, home-based business on your own can be an attractive option, allowing you to "test the waters" and minimize the amount of cash and time required to strike out on your own. On the other hand, purchasing an established company can be attractive if you have not "brainstormed" your way into your "dream" start-up business or if you have ample cash and seek immediate cash flow.

Examine the worksheet in Figure 1.2 to size up the types of cash investments required for a start-up operation. Remember that there is an inherent tendency for experienced and inexperienced entrepreneurs to underestimate the costs involved in opening the doors and keeping them open for the first year.

FIGURE 1.2 Worksheet to Evaluate Start-Up Costs

Start-Up Costs	Estimated Costs
Leasehold Improvements	
1. Redecorating	$ _____
2. Furniture, fixtures, and equipment (FF&E) (e.g., computers, fax, security systems, modem, copiers, pagers, scanners, mobile phones, software)	_____
3. Signs and displays	_____
4. Associated labor costs	_____
5. Vehicles (lease or own)	_____
Deposits, Prepayments, etc.	
1. Rent deposit	_____
2. Utility deposit	_____
3. Business permits and licenses	_____
4. Insurance premiums	_____
5. Equipment lease deposits	_____
6. Service contracts	_____
Inventory	
1. Merchandise	_____
2. Office supplies	_____
Operating Expenses for Six Months	
1. Working capital (cash, accounts receivable, debt service)	_____
2. Labor (employees and self, including payroll taxes, training, recruiting)	_____
3. Utilities	_____
4. Other payments (tradename and trademark search, research fees, bank fees, accounting and legal fees, trade association fees, chamber of commerce fees)	_____
5. Health care and worker's compensation	_____
6. Marketing fees (yellow pages, mailers, brochures, newsletters, business gifts)	_____
7. Travel and entertainment (e.g., gas, tolls, parking, trade shows, vendor meetings)	_____
8. Loan payments (bank and credit cards)	_____
Living Expenses for Six Months	
1. Home and auto	_____
2. Utilities and insurance (home, auto, life, health)	_____
3. Other payments	_____
Total Cash Investment Required	$ _____

Starting from scratch can be as simple as a part-time operation or entail the establishment of a business location through development of a comprehensive business plan. According to Will Davis, it is possible to start a business for less than $1,000. You can purchase his book, *Start Your Own Business For $1,000 or Less* through Upstart Publishing Company. Simpler options might be an extension of a hobby or your full-time profession. A choice between an independent start-up and a franchise start-up would be the purchase of operational materials from organizations that charge only a one-time fee (commonly referred to as business opportunities, as opposed to franchise opportunities). These opportunities are abundant and can be initially evaluated by picking up a copy of one of the magazines listed earlier. Examples include the following:

Service
- Mortgage/utilities reduction
- Specialty advertising

Wholesale
- Book distribution
- Security products

Retail
- Gold related products
- Electronics products

Miscellaneous
- 1-900 phone services
- Inflatable rides/games

All these opportunities are non-franchise, which means there will be no royalty payments on future sales. The costs associated with these opportunities are generally one-time start-up fees or training fees and mandatory purchases of inventory and/or equipment. Total costs for starting these types of operations generally range from about $100 to $25,000. The cost is low, but support will be minimal compared to a franchise opportunity.

If you make the decision to start a business on your own from scratch, you must develop a business plan, obtaining professional assistance if needed. A business plan *should* be prepared for all business ventures, start-up or otherwise. Consider the following:

- *The Business Planning Guide* by David H. Bangs, Jr. (Upstart Publishing Company, 800-621-9621)
- *How to Write a Successful Business Plan*, by Julie K. Brooks and Barry A. Stevens (New York: American Management Association)
- BizPlan Builder (software) from Jian Tools for Sales (800-346-5426)
- PlanMaker (software) from POWERSolutions for Business (800-955-3337)

Free assistance is available from the Service Corps of Retired Executives (SCORE). Call 800-634-0245 for the office nearest you. General issues to be addressed when starting a business from scratch include the preparation of a strategic plan and business plan as well as review of a new company checklist (see Figure 1.4). Please note that *many of the required steps outlined below for starting a business from scratch will also apply to the purchase of an existing business.*

Business Plans

The creation and annual updating of business plans is an integral endeavor of most successful businesses. When the dust settles, your business plan should contain the following key items:

- Clear and concise company mission and description of management team
- Powerful executive summary
- Knowledge and insights into relevant market
- Credible financial forecasts and detailed cash flow analysis

We will conclude our look at business plans by presenting a sample business plan outline in Figure 1.3.

FIGURE 1.3   Business Plan Outline

   I. **Executive Summary**

  II. **Introduction**
   History
   Description of the business
   Goals/objectives/strategies (near-term and long-term)

 III. **Management**
   Managerial skills/requirements/track record and depth
   Organizational chart
   Concise statement of corporate policies and procedures

 IV. **Marketing**
   Industry overview
   Marketing strategy
   Product classifications and descriptions/market niches
   Market demand, competitive analysis and customer profiles
   Anticipated market share
   Price determination (compare to competition)
   Advertising/Promotion
   Distribution

VIII. **Production**
   Anticipated production quantities by category
   Capacity by category (facilities needed)
   Efficiency/productivity
   Make/buy decisions
   Purchasing strategy/sourcing
   Quality statement
   Inventory control and shipping/receiving
   Plant/equipment maintenance and safety

 VI. **Financial**
   Sources and uses of funds
   Balance sheets and income statements (initial and projected for three years)

FIGURE 1.3   Business Plan Outline, continued

       Cash flow analysis (at least until consistently profitable)
       Breakeven and ratio analysis—internal and to industry
       Implementation schedule (Pert chart)

  VII. **Conclusion**

 VIII. **Appendix**

   IV. **Exhibits**

Clearly, choosing to start a business from scratch requires great courage, good planning, and a lot of hard work. The rewards of making a business grow can be substantial—emotionally and financially. The emotional rewards seem to be the driving force behind most small business owners. Control of their destinies, freedom to do as they wish, pride in their products or services, recognition from peers as well as substantial income all can bring a feeling of accomplishment to the owner.

As mentioned earlier, there is an abundance of checklists and questionnaires available to assist would-be entrepreneurs determine their "suitability" for successful small business. There are "many hats" to be worn (chief executive officer and janitor!) by the small business owner. Accounting, advertising, contracts, credit, customer service, personnel, pricing, and taxes must be properly understood to ensure success. If you commit your resources to something as risky as small business ownership, you must strive to increase your understanding of all functional areas, taking remedial steps if necessary.

New Company Checklist

Opening the doors to a new business is much more involved than coming up with an idea and buying some inventory. The *Guide to Establishing a Business* (Arizona Department of Commerce, 602-280-1480) is an easy to read, useful guide that includes the checklist in Figure 1.4.

FIGURE 1.4   Checklist to Establishing a Business (*Most of these steps apply to the purchase of an established business as well.*)

❑ Have you completed your strategic and business planning?

❑ Have you determined the type of business structure your organization will assume?

❑ If so, have you followed the appropriate registration procedures for the organization structure?

❑ If applicable, have you registered your business trademarks and tradenames?

❑ Have you determined whether your business is subject to any special licensing requirements?

FIGURE 1.4   Checklist to Establishing a Business, continued

❑   Have you obtained a federal employer identification number? (Form SS-4)

❑   Will your business be required to obtain a state sales tax license and submit monthly reports?

❑   Will you be required to withhold state and federal income taxes from the compensation paid to your workers?

❑   Will you be required to pay state taxes and submit quarterly reports for unemployment purposes?

❑   Will your business be required to pay federal unemployment taxes and submit quarterly reports?

❑   Will you be required to provide insurance coverage to protect against industrial injuries?

❑   Have you made a thorough review of your insurance needs?

❑   Have you reviewed federal and state labor laws and determined personnel-related policies?

❑   Have you checked the environmental regulations regarding air, water, and solid waste?

❑   Have you consulted your accountant regarding tax planning, management controls, and accounting systems?

❑   Have you obtained state, county, and city operating permits and licenses associated with your business?

❑   Have you made sure your operations are consistent with correct zoning?

❑   Have you checked with utility companies to ensure delivery and to obtain the cost of service extensions and deposits?

Home-Based Businesses

A significant portion of the current entrepreneurial surge is taking place in the comforts of home. Current estimates are that as many as 40 million people are working at home. Besides a flexible schedule and convenient location, overhead is kept to a minimum as thousands of dollars for rent and utilities are saved. The ability to stay close to children is another plus. Inexpensive and powerful technology in the form of computers, fax machines, and modems has dramatically improved the performance of home-based businesses. With voice mail, Web pages, multimailbox answering systems and portable faxes, it is now possible for home-based operations to foster the appearance of size and instant credibility. For a "crash course" in home office management, consider purchasing the videotape *How to Be More Profitable and Productive in Your Home Office* (800-338-7531).

Working at home also presents special challenges. For example, staying focused on business with kids in the house and your favorite TV show on every day requires a unique type of discipline. Saying no to friends and spouses who request special favors is not always easy. Issues like time management, business licensing, neighborhood zoning, tax deductions for the home office, and proper insurance coverage require special attention from the home-based entrepreneur.

Home-based opportunities include numerous franchises, such as a promotional products company called Adventures in Advertising (Bellevue, Wash.), a local business database supplier called Business Information International (Memphis, Tenn.), a computer tutoring business called Computertots (Great Falls, Va.) and a residential cleaning business called Merry Maids (Memphis, Tenn.). Other popular areas include desktop publishing, Internet services, commercial driving, food services, greenhouses, and vending machines. Start-up costs for theses home-based franchises range from $2,000 to $30,000. For additional support, consider purchasing the multimedia kit, *Starting Your Home-Based Business* (Upstart Publishing Company). The magazine *HomeBusiness Journal* (315-865-4100) is dedicated to the home business. Finally, consider contacting the following organizations for current information available for the home-based business owner:

- American Association of Home Based Businesses (301-963-9153)
- Home Executives National Marketing Association (HENMA @ 708-761-1322)

Distressed Companies

Yet another type of business deserving special attention is the so-called distressed company. They may also be referred to as "turnarounds." This particular option is quite risky and is not recommended for the first-time business owner. The attraction to this type of opportunity lies in the likelihood that either a favorable price, friendly terms, or both can be worked out. Owners of businesses who are on the brink of bankruptcy are more likely to accept creative offers than a solidly profitable one. Extreme caution must be exercised when attempting to purchase distressed companies. Determining precisely how troubled the company is may not always be straightforward. If you choose to actively look for this type of opportunity, consider seeking information from the following sources:

- *Local auctioneers.* These liquidators of bankrupt firms will consider preliquidation offers for the entire assets of a troubled company. Check your local Yellow Pages.
- *Dun and Bradstreet and other credit agencies.* Believe it or not, you can obtain lists of companies with faltering credit credentials. Invaluable source of partners or acquisitions.
- *Public records.* Investigate the public records available at your county clerk's office for recorded tax liens. Inability to pay state and federal income taxes is frequently the cause of sale or liquidation.
- *Bankruptcy court.* The federal bankruptcy courts will provide you with a list of frequently used attorneys, who will be in touch with current and pending cases. Check your Yellow Pages for bankruptcy attorneys.

- *Business brokers*. Last but not least, contacting several of these professionals might pay off. They certainly are aware of failing or nearly insolvent firms, but will or cannot always disclose such information.

The key concept to grasp is that there is no such thing as a bad business. Practically every business has valuable assets that can serve a new owner well under the right terms and conditions. Businesses become insolvent for many reasons, some of which will not apply to new ownership. Squabbling partners, absentee owners, and insufficient working capital are all reasons businesses fail and become available. Another tool for spotting distressed companies is to walk through major shopping centers and downtown areas and look for unusually low inventory levels, broken windows, burnt out signs, or a generally rundown appearance. To help confirm your hunches, try to discover the troubled firm's corporate name (or dba) and check with Dun and Bradstreet (800-362-2255) for a report on its history, payment record, and liens and judgments. TRW, Trans-Union, and Equifax will also provide credit reports. Finally, two companies offer useful information regarding bankruptcy filings. Federal Filings, Inc., a Dow-Jones subsidiary, (800-487-6162) will follow any bankruptcy you ask for. Adar Group (508-477-5000) can also assist clients in locating these opportunities as well.

Franchises

This option is a hybrid between a start-up operation and a seasoned business. If you buy a franchise, you become licensed to market the franchiser's goods or services in a specific area for a specific period of time. Most franchises in the United States are so-called business-format types, requiring franchisees to conduct business in the format required by the franchiser, which can range from nonrestrictive to quite detailed. This format offers not only a trade name and a logo, but a complete system for conducting business. The franchisee will receive assistance with site selection, personnel training, advertising and promotions, various start-up issues, and purchase of inventory in exchange for an up-front franchise fee and ongoing royalty payments. Because of the wide-ranging issues covered in a franchise agreement, special care must be taken when evaluating franchise opportunities. The two most important documents are the Uniform Franchise Offering Circular and the Franchise Agreement. *Obtaining experienced legal counsel is highly recommended.* You can request a free copy of the *Consumer Guide to Buying a Franchise* (Federal Trade Commission, 202-326-2222). This easy-to-read booklet lays out several issues regarding the purchase of a new franchise.

As another preliminary step, consider purchasing one of the following books, available from the Franchise Times Library (510-839-5494). *The Original Franchise Match* evaluates more than 2,000 different franchise opportunities, matching them with your available investment and personality. *Understanding an Offering Circular and Negotiating a Franchise Agreement* analyzes 62 different legal/business issues open to negotiation with the franchiser. *The Franchise Fraud* challenges and exposes many myths depicting the safety and certainty of franchise investments.

General Information

Franchising will offer you the freedom to own, manage, and direct your own business. However, there are responsibilities as well, which will be spelled out in detail in the franchise agreement. Franchisers, seeking to maintain consistency, will typically control the following areas, to one degree or another. Careful scrutiny of the franchise agreement is critical!

Location

Many franchisers require preapproval for franchisee outlet locations. Given their experience and understanding of relevant consumer demographics, this can increase your chances for success. On the downside, they may not approve your location choice.

Control of Offered Goods/Services

Food related franchisers, for example, may require strict adherence to preapproved menus or vendors. Service franchisees, on the other hand, may be prohibited from offering similar or complimentary services, which might be deemed highly profitable. The goal, once again, is to maintain uniformity and consistency from one franchise to another—at the possible cost of losing additional sales. Uniformity in exchange for flexibility is the basic tradeoff.

Design and Decoration Requirements

Most franchisers will strictly control the appearance of a unit to preserve consistency. Additionally, the franchisee must agree to make periodic upgrades, changes, or additions without reimbursement from the franchiser.

Operations

Strict controls regarding store hours, signage, uniforms, advertising, and financial reporting exist for most franchisees. Only approved vendors may be used in certain franchises, possibly inhibiting variety and raising costs. Occasionally, restrictions will exist that prohibit sales being made outside a stipulated territory.

None of the above restrictions should be taken lightly, as the franchiser will normally possess the right to terminate or not renew the franchise agreement. After the original franchise term expires, there is no guarantee that a renewal will be granted. If a renewal is granted, it may be under vastly different terms and conditions.

The start-up aspect to a new franchise is clear. After site selection, you will begin your business from scratch (no existing customer base). However, the fact that the franchiser will train you in almost every aspect of the business sets you quickly in motion toward an on-going concern. Hopefully, there will be benefits from name and brand recognition as well. Training is included in the franchise purchase price and should be taken seriously. You will receive guidance for personnel training, advertising, maintaining books and records, customer service, purchasing, and other operational areas.

In addition to the up-front franchise fees, which range from $5,000 to $500,000 (see *Entrepreneur* for the Franchise 500), you will likely be paying an ongoing royalty fee. This fee is typically a percent of gross sales, typically between 2 and 8 percent. Naturally, the franchise will reserve the right to audit your books. Payment of the royalty finances the ongoing provision by the franchiser for training, research, and general business support. Support staff should be available during business hours to assist franchisees with almost every concern that will arise.

Often there will be another cost in the form of an advertising fee, also typically a percent of gross sales. This can be extremely valuable for a Burger King franchise in a city with several restaurants, but not as valuable if you are the lone franchise in a newly developed area separated from the main market regions. This element of your purchase can be negotiable. Make sure that you receive your fair share of the benefits generated by the franchiser's advertising. Remember, you won't get what you want unless you ask! There is always the reality of relative bargaining strengths, and you need to develop a feel for what is negotiable and to what degree. You will have more bargaining power with a relatively new franchiser than a proven, well-established one.

Due Diligence Procedures for Franchises

Buying a franchise requires a slightly different approach than buying a nonfranchise business. The due diligence process is generally comprised of the following:

1. Evaluate your personal style and preferences.
2. Review franchise guides; attend franchise expo.
3. Carefully analyze uniform franchise offering circular and franchise contract.
4. Consult franchise owners, successful and otherwise!
5. Meet with franchiser at corporate headquarters.
6. Obtain legal counsel before signing anything.

Step 1

This first step is comprised of the general decision to strike out on your own and a second decision regarding the restrictions that come with franchising. The franchise option is a hybrid of self-employment and obligations to the franchiser. Are you comfortable with restrictions such as operating hours, product lines, insurance requirements, store design, and reasonable entry by franchiser personnel? Working within the confines of a franchise is not agreeable to those who not only seek total independence but dread the idea of paying 5 to 8 percent of their sales to the corporate office.

Step 2

If the franchiser-franchisee relationship is acceptable to you, the next step is to investigate available franchises. There is a franchise (several thousand) for almost every type of market and business. The Annual Franchise 500 published in *Entrepreneur* (800-274-6229) comprehensively ranks opportunities by category. After reviewing these lists, you might purchase a guide to franchises (e.g., *Bond's Franchise Guide* or the *Franchise Handbook*, published quarterly by Enterprise Magazines, Inc.), to obtain additional information. These guides are available at your local bookstore or by calling the International Franchise Association at 202-628-8000.

Another excellent opportunity to become acquainted with the many available options is to attend trade shows held throughout the year in major cities across the country. The publication *Business Opportunities Journal* publishes a comprehensive list of upcoming trade shows each month. Call 800-854-6570 for the latest edition.

Step 3

Once your search has been narrowed, the real work begins. First, you need to review the *Uniform Franchise Offering Circular* (UFOC), which is a legally mandated publication for every franchise (no exceptions) and is similar to a prospectus distributed for new security issues (stocks and bonds). It discloses important information about the franchise including required investments, backgrounds of key principals involved, and audited financial statements. Although franchisers are not required to distribute their UFOC to all who request it, the *Franchise Rule* does stipulate that it be turned over at

- any meeting "in person" between franchiser and potential franchisee to discuss the purchase sale of a franchise, *or*
- ten working days prior to signature on a binding contract or prior to making payment for the franchise.

The practical result of these rules is that prospects cannot be required to put money down until at least ten working days have passed (cooling off period) since being introduced to the franchise. This requirement applies to cash payments of all types, including good faith deposits.

Although the information contained in the UFOC is required by law, it is not audited or otherwise verified by governmental authorities. Analyzing past and present lawsuits will provide great insights into the type and magnitude of problems the franchiser is experiencing. In fact, it is wise to make a written request to the franchiser for details regarding lawsuits that have arisen since the printing of the offering circular, determining the frequency and type of disputes.

Each UFOC will contain a written description of franchise offering and franchiser, audited financial statements, and a sample franchise agreement. Look for the following general types of information: date of formation and backgrounds of key operating officers; detailed breakdown of all required investments and fees; restrictions on product offerings; commitments made by franchiser; past or current lawsuits; exposure to bankruptcy proceedings (franchiser, officers, and directors); advertising and promotional programs; current and former franchisees, including terminations, nonrenewals and projected franchisees, and financial statements of franchiser. In new UFOCs, if a franchiser has agreed to a lower initial fee during the past year, it must be disclosed. Finally, note that franchisers are not required by law to make any claims regarding earnings potential. To establish the average level of sales and profits, you may need to call the current franchisees. If earnings claims are made, they must be made according to strict Federal Trade Commission (FTC) guidelines, satisfying the following general standards:

- A reasonable basis must exist to support the accuracy of the claim.
- The franchiser must present documentation supporting the claim at the time the claim is made.
- Earnings claims must be differentiated by geographic location (e.g., New York versus Peoria).

The greater the percentage of revenues generated by royalty payments (as opposed to initial franchise fees), the more likely the franchise has proven the test of time.

The most important document of all is the franchise agreement (franchise contract). It is imperative that you seek qualified legal help to review and propose changes to this binding commitment. Specifically, there will be two separate documents to review and sign: a purchase contract and a franchise agreement. The purchase contract will cover price and terms, services to be provided, and the franchise package. Some franchisers will extend credit to qualified borrowers, or you may seek out a bank loan. There will be a brief description of the services to be provided by the franchiser, broken down into what are called *initial* services (before the location is opened) and *continuous* services. Also attached to the purchase contract will be a complete list of equipment and inventory included in the sale. If the purchase of the franchise is made on credit, expect the lender to place a lien (UCC-1) with the appropriate state and county authorities.

The franchise agreement outlines in great detail all the rights and obligations of both the franchiser and franchisee. When reviewing the UFOC, try to answer the following questions:

Franchise Fees
1. What are the total investment costs?
2. What are the royalty payments? When are they due?

Franchisee Rights
1. Which trademarks, trade names, patents, copyrights, secret methods, formulas, recipes, etc. are included and what steps has franchiser taken to protect same?

2. Is absentee ownership allowed?
3. What territorial limitations exist? Are any additional locations planned by franchiser nearby?
4. Are there special purchase discounts available for key product lines?
5. Can franchisee purchase product outside of approved/recommended suppliers?
6. What constitutes a breach of contract? What is *cure period*?
7. Can franchisee operate under any type of business entity (e.g., sole proprietor or corporation)?

Franchisee Obligations
1. Who controls the hours of operation, product offerings, and pricing?
2. Is there a franchise operations manual that must be followed?
3. What is the advertising fee? Must advertising be approved by franchiser?
4. What type of insurance coverage is required?
5. Is the franchisee prohibited from owning or operating another business?
6. Is it possible that the franchisee will be required to remodel or redecorate at some point in the future without being reimbursed by franchiser?

Franchiser Obligations
1. How much training will be provided to owners and employees? Included in franchise fees?
2. What is the nature of support to be provided after the purchase? How long is franchise period?
3. Under what conditions can franchiser enter premises and review books, records, and operations?
4. Can the franchiser own and operate its own units? Within what proximity to existing locations?

Assignment/Transfer/Renewal/Termination
1. Can the franchise be sold or otherwise transferred? What is approval process and transfer fee?
2. Does franchiser have right of first refusal upon sale of franchise?
3. What are the renewal procedures and fees?
4. Under what circumstances may the franchiser terminate the franchise agreement? Vice-versa?
5. What is meant by *just cause* or *reasonable cause*?

Step 4

One of your most valuable tools is to speak freely with existing and departed franchisees. Make sure you contact a mixture of successful and not so successful owners. Another set of inquiries should by made to suppliers that have terminated their relationships with the franchiser. Finally, check with the better business bureau and the regional office of the FTC for any complaints. When interviewing franchise owners, consider asking the following questions:

1. Why did you buy this franchise? How long have you owned?
2. Are you satisfied with the franchise overall? Has franchiser lived up to commitments?
3. Did you receive adequate training?
4. What were the total costs incurred to purchase the franchise and then get it up and running?
5. How long did it take for you to turn a profit? What are current monthly sales and profit?
6. Are the products purchased through the franchiser good quality and priced fairly?
7. Approximately how many hours per week do you work? Is your spouse or family involved?
8. If you had to do it all over again, would you buy this franchise?

Step 5

If steps one through four check out favorably, you may want to invest the time and money to visit the franchiser's headquarters in person to evaluate its staff and other resources. These relationships can be critical to your success. Although it is possible to sign on without meeting the franchiser in person and touring its offices, this is ill-advised.

Step 6

Franchise opportunities offer a special combination of start-up thrills and proven business techniques. Choosing the right franchise in a given price range is easier said than done. By following the advice in this chapter, your odds for a successful purchase and profitable investment are improved. *Above all else, locate and consult a qualified, experienced franchise attorney before you take the plunge.* Make sure that he or she is experienced and ask for several references including a list of the specific franchise agreements the attorney has negotiated (ask for company names as well to see if they are similar to your present prospects).

Relocatable Businesses

Another type of business worthy of discussion is the *relocatable business*. A relocatable business is formally defined as a business for sale that can be moved and operated without loss of customers. A bimonthly newsletter called appropriately

Relocatable Business can be purchased for $85 (six months) or $150 (one year) from Business Listing Services, Inc. (Highland Park, Ill., 800-927-1310). This publication lists names and phone numbers of owners and/or brokers. Examples from a recent edition (priced between $5,000 and $10 million) include:

- Travel Service— booking bike tours
- Publishing—rock bands
- Wholesaler—"new age" items
- Manufacturing— artificial turf products
- Mail Order— name brand cotton clothes

Review

There is an entire range of possibilities for getting into business for yourself. Starting a business with no history is riskier, but the returns can be higher. Buying an established, profitable business will cost you more, but at a lesser risk. Franchise opportunities and distressed businesses lie somewhere in the middle of these two extremes.

Business Categories

The other major decision relates to the category of business you wish to enter. Retail, distribution, manufacturing, service, food, or automotive are the major sectors. The "right" choice is personal in nature and depends on many factors. We are now ready to review the major categories of businesses.

Retail

Retail businesses will typically be located in a high visibility area, strip mall, or conventional mall and are most dependent on the old adage "location, location, location." A typical due diligence procedure for this type of business is to visit the location at different times of the day over several days to monitor traffic levels at the store and center. Common types of small, entrepreneurial retail businesses include (Standard Industrial Classification [SIC] Codes 52–59):

- Gift stores
- Framing stores
- Clothing
- Health products
- Computer software
- Florists
- Hardware stores
- Auto parts

Of course, some businesses such as mail stores are hybrids, offering services (copies, mail box rental) as well as retail items (stationery, keys). The exact combination is determined by trial and error as well as owner preference. As you drive around any town, it is obvious that retail businesses are everywhere. Getting the product, whatever it is, to the end customer is what any economy is all about. Approximately 32 percent of the U.S. Gross Domestic Product is based on retail trade. Retailing is a dynamic part of our free enterprise system that changes right along with consumer tastes and preferences. What's "hot" today will probably fade over time. If the products don't change, the advertising methods or service approach will. Consider the following characteristics of retail businesses:

- Demographic trends are important (e.g., immigration and aging are significant trends).
- Business hours are long, often more than 70 hours per week.
- Inventory and accounts receivable are important assets, working capital requirements are significant.
- Employees are typically unskilled, earning near minimum wages.
- Pricing is seasonal, cyclical, and a key determinant of success.
- Value shopping and price shopping are trends (most value, least time).
- Focusing on a particular product (niche) is replacing the general retailer.
- Computerized inventory and sales management systems are prevalent and required for full efficiency.
- Mail order, home shopping, and Internet shopping must be part of the retail business of the future.
- Ordering by fax is a growing trend as is electronic checkout (no clerks).
- Both casual attire and wellness products are popular items.
- Approximately 40 to 50 percent of total sales and profits occur during the holiday season.

Automotive and food businesses can also be categorized as service businesses, but this distinction in and of itself is not that important. When purchasing any retail business, pay close attention to inventory and accounts receivable. When valuing a retail business, the purchaser must determine how much of the inventory on hand is actually salable at retail prices. Most brokers will value inventory at cost, without trying to micromanage the true current value. If the inventory is not salable, this should enter into the final price and terms. If credit is granted by the retailer, careful examination of the accounts receivable aging schedule and historic bad debt expenses is critical. Remember that recognizing a sale and collecting cash can be totally different events. In practice, there are trade-offs between overgenerous credit (bad debts) and stingy credit (lost sales). Another major due diligence concern is that when you are attempting to verify sales, *for any category or type of business, you must check and cross-check* and fully explain any discrepancy between: gross and net sales (adjusted for returns and allowances) per financial statements; gross and net sales per federal tax returns and state and local sales tax reports. These numbers should be matched against cash deposits into checking or savings accounts and credit card reports (or cash into the owner's pockets!). Somehow, they should all add up in a credible fashion. A similar analysis should be conducted regarding expenses. See Chapters 3 and 6 for more details. Also turn to Chapter 10 for rules of thumb for retail businesses. Important considerations in valuing retail businesses are:

- Average markup? Gross margin, cost advantages?
- Seasonality factors. Reliance on one brand?
- Accounts receivable and inventory aging. Terms offered to customers?
- Location, lease, general appearance?
- Bargaining power of suppliers? Payment terms?

Watch out for obsolete or slow-moving inventory. You should not have to pay for these products. Also determine if recent sales figures include aggressive inventory clearance sales, where the products were sold at or near a loss to boost reported sales.

Manufacturing Businesses

As a business broker, I am aware of many otherwise intelligent people who want to buy a small manufacturing business. This includes people who unfortunately are not qualified to do so (financially, emotionally, or operationally). Beyond the apparent charm of earning a living the old-fashioned way, by producing something, there can be nice profits involved. The more specialized the product, the more difficult entry into the industry is. This will generally mean more robust sales and profits and a more attractive business. Consider the following list of prominent industries:

- Food products
- Textiles
- Electrical equipment
- Chemicals and metals
- Furniture items
- Apparel goods
- Paper products
- Recreational products

Operating a manufacturing business is, in many ways, the most complex of options. There will likely be a larger payroll and the associated personnel issues to deal with (front and back office). Regulatory concerns such as the Environmental Protection Agency (EPA) and Occupational Safety and Health Administration (OSHA) are heightened. There will be substantial investments in inventory and customer credit (accounts receivable), which will grow faster than profits, requiring access to additional financing (working capital) as needed. Many manufacturing companies experience cash flow difficulties from their first day in business forward. They will typically sell for higher multiples of cash flow than other categories as a result of higher asset values. Preliminarily, you should investigate the following issues, asking the seller these questions directly in person or even in writing:

- What is the size of the market? SIC code?
- What additional products could be added to increase sales?
- Are technical skills significant?
- Specifically, what regulatory bodies are aggressively involved?
- Are the employees unionized or otherwise organized?
- Is the equipment current and in good working order? How advanced is the computer aided design?

- What are the credit terms offered to customers versus payment terms for purchases of inventory? Is there a just-in-time inventory program in place?
- What is the current accounts receivable aging versus historical bad debt expense?
- Have there been significant events, recent or expected, that will seriously impact business costs or sales?
- What percent of total sales do the four top customers comprise? Are they under contract terms?
- How long is the seller willing to train and/or stay involved in the business?
- Are any of the procedures, processes, or products patented? Any patents pending?

Under an asset purchase (as opposed to a purchase of stock), the seller will typically keep the accounts receivable and cash balances, and pay off all the payables, delivering the business free and clear of all debts (unless otherwise agreed upon). Depending on the significance of work in progress, the seller may or may not include it as part of the selling price. A business might be offered for sale for X dollars plus work-in-progress. If this is a large dollar figure, it should be addressed early on and included as part of the original offer or counteroffer.

It is no surprise that the fastest growing manufacturing areas are technology-based. Paying close attention to export potential is increasingly important. Reduced barriers to trade, countries experiencing wholesale conversions to capitalism and free trade, and greater governmental support for exporters has helped facilitate this global expansion. Consider reading the following publications: (1) *Exporter's Guide to Federal Resources for Small Business* (Superintendent of Documents, Washington, D.C. 20402, order number 045-000-00263-2) presents and describes all major federal programs designed to assist business owners that export, including contact persons. (2) *Import/Export Can Make You Rich*, (Prentice-Hall, 1988) is a step-by-step guide to importing and exporting, answering many practical questions commonly asked in this area. Also consider contacting the American Association of Exporters and Importers, (11 West 42 Street, New York, N.Y. 10036, 212-944-2230). With members in every sector of international trade, it maintains contacts with all major government agencies and offers numerous publications. As always, useful information about a particular industry can be found in the Yellow Pages under headings such as export financing, export representative, international trade, and foreign trade consultants.

One final fact related to manufacturing and industrial businesses is that more than 90 percent of all purchases are initiated by the buyer, not the seller. The most widely known and utilized buying guide is the *Thomas Register of Manufacturers*, which features product and service sections, company directories and distributors. This multivolume publication is available at most larger public libraries.

Wholesale/Distribution Businesses

There are many variations within this category, but the common link is the role of serving as a middleman between buyer and seller (SIC Code 5000 to 5199). Wholesalers and distributors avoid maintaining a finished showroom, utilizing less expensive warehouse space and reduced staff relative to retail businesses. Wholesalers, distributors, and manufacturer's representatives are all basically the same type of business. They can be as basic as one person working out of a home office or as complex as a large distributor of imported products across the country. The most important factor to consider is the transferability of new accounts. Being able to maintain the existing client base will typically require the sincere assistance of the seller. As a buyer, make sure that you are comfortable with the seller's pledge to make appropriate introductions. Also look for "easy operations," rapid turnover of product, and accelerated payment terms. If the products are extremely technical and difficult to understand, the appeal is limited. A seller guarantee (minimum level of sales) coupled with an earn-out clause would be ideal. Other key considerations are:

- How quickly do you pay for product versus how quickly will your customers be required to pay?
- What are profit margins?
- What additional lines might be available to facilitate growth?
- Are any permits, certificates, or licenses required to do business?
- Are customer relationships contractualized? Have attorney review them.
- How involved is the delivery process? Are trucks involved in the sale?
- Are the operations computerized? Has the Internet been pursued as a marketing tool?
- What is the extent of slow-pay and uncollectible debts?
- Who are the key customers? What percent of total sales do the top three and ten customers comprise?

In between the extremes of manufacturing operations and full blown wholesalers are manufacturers' representatives or agents. Agents are independent contractors who work on a commission basis for more than one company. Commonly referred to as outside sales agents, their "connections" can be sold as a business. The following areas of our economy are thriving with wholesalers and distributors of all sizes:

- Electrical components
- Communications equipment
- Groceries, beer, and wine
- Lumber and hardware materials
- Paper and packaging products
- Computer supplies/goods
- Auto parts
- Drugs and toiletries

Service Businesses

Approximately two-thirds of our entire economy is service-based. Fostered by improvements in technology and a surge in outsourcing, the service sector of the U.S. economy continues to grow. The largest categories are health care, consulting and business, household and personal services. The Bureau of Labor Statistics estimates that many of the fastest growing companies over the next decade will be service-based. Consider the following list as an overview of the service sector of our economy (SIC Code 7000 to 8999):

- Hair salons
- Printing
- Residential cleaning
- Computer repair

- Automotive repair
- Entertainment
- Health care
- Rental businesses

Of the four major categories of businesses (manufacturing, retail, wholesale, and service), service businesses are the least likely to end up in bankruptcy. According to Ralph Heins, a business broker with John Hall and Associates in Phoenix, Ariz. (602-844-5900), "service businesses offer the highest return for the smallest capital investment of all business categories." The essence of these businesses is the provision of a service to customers. Based on price, quality, reputation, and overall customer relations, service businesses seek to differentiate themselves from the normally intense competition that exists.

Similar to manufacturing, service industries that are experiencing the most rapid growth are linked to the rise in business spending for computers and telecommunications. Computer services, data processing, and electronic information services are three leading growth areas for the service sector, according the *U.S. Industrial Outlook*, published by the U.S. Department of Commerce. Many of the leading service franchises today are home cleaning businesses, reflecting demographic changes in our economy.

An interesting franchised business-to-business service company is called the Business and Marketing Store, located in Tempe, Ariz. This company is presented to would-be owners as a "one-stop marketing and advertising headquarters," featuring many different franchise opportunities rolled into one, including high-speed and full service copy shop and printer, advertising specialty store, direct mail company, business form store, graphic and design shop, and advertising consultant. When you consider that printing franchises today require a minimum investment of approximately $150,000, the $15,000 franchise fee for the Business and Marketing Store coupled with the Danka copier program makes this an attractive franchise option. According to Peter Nowell, president, the keys to success for this operation are a commitment to hard work, a good credit history, and a successful marketing background. Peter may be reached by phone (602-968-1902).

When evaluating a service business in general, it is important to identify and evaluate the key services. The following general questions will help you preliminarily evaluate a service company:

- What are the major services offered? By percent of sales?
- How does this company differentiate itself from the competition?
- Is there a seasonal or cyclical nature to the business?
- Are special licenses or training required?
- Are there existing contracts that can be transferred to a new owner?

Favorable attributes include: easy to run, no special skills required, high and growing demand, absentee owner or owner who only manages. A difficult task is to evaluate the degree to which existing customers will continue their allegiance when ownership changes. Many service businesses reach profitability based upon the personal relationships cultivated by the owner. The transferability of these relationships is difficult to quantify and predict.

Service business will, on average, sell for lower multiples of cash flow than manufacturing or retail businesses as a result of two primary factors:

1. Lack of hard assets (equipment and inventory)
2. Personal nature of the business

The key problem in establishing value is related to the personal relationships between the seller and customers. As a result of this situation, many service businesses will be sold on an *earnout* basis, which couples the actual sales performance of the business under new ownership with the final purchase price. Later chapters will describe the complexities of such an arrangement for both the seller and the buyer.

Food Businesses

It is no secret that everyone must eat to survive. This simple fact explains the prevalence of food-related businesses in our economy (SIC Codes 2000 to 2099, 5140 to 5149, 5400, 5410, 5490, and 5800). The future belongs to those who can accurately predict the dynamic changes that will take place in each and every segment of our economic system. Concerning the present and future of food-related markets, two major trends take center stage. As time goes by, greater portions of food budgets will be allocated to:

- Eating out
- Health foods and dietary supplements

The first trend is a result of a curious mixture of the two wage-earner family and higher disposable income coupled with the struggle to work enough hours to make ends meet. The second trend is a function of both greater consumer awareness and the trend toward eating out. Both of these trends have resulted in an explosion of related business opportunities, notably franchised operations. Other noteworthy characteristics of the food service industry include:

- Easy, low cost entry
- Dramatic failure rates

For the cost of a lease deposit, minimal inventory, and other start-up expenditures, it is quite easy to enter the premises of a restaurant that has recently shut down. It is this easy entry that attracts would-be entrepreneurs with the proper motivations but improper business training. Furthermore, it is the easy entry factor that leads to the high failure rate—easy come, easy go! To grasp the vast array of food-related operations to choose from, review the following list:

- Restaurant or café
- Deli or sandwich shop
- Yogurt shop or ice cream parlor
- Bar or lounge
- Pizza shop
- Donut shop
- Fast food
- Drive-In

Regardless of your preferred format, a dramatic proliferation of franchise opportunities in the food arena has made this option difficult to ignore. In fact, many food-related franchises can be purchased for less than $50,000. For a comprehensive introduction to the many food-related franchises, see the annual Franchise 500 issue published by *Entrepreneur* magazine. For a review of affordable franchises, see the August 1996 edition of *Income Opportunities* magazine. When evaluating established food-related businesses such as restaurants, delis, ice cream parlors, or bars the following questions should be addressed as part of a preliminary review:

- What is the seating capacity?
- What is food and drink cost as a percentage of sales?
- Can the hours be profitably expanded? Do they deliver or offer takeout?
- What is the cost, age, and condition of the equipment included in the sale?
- Is there a full kitchen? What equipment is owned versus leased?
- Is there a liquor license involved?
- Who are the key employees? Are they likely to stay if needed?

Experienced owners will focus immediately on food costs, labor costs, and lease payments as a percentage of sales to assess the performance of the business. Given a good location and quality atmosphere, seasoned practitioners can attempt to increase sales (advertising) and reduce expenses (labor and food). Careful control of inventory is critical. Evaluating the quality of employees is a critical yet intangible area to address. Treating employees fairly and paying above market wages can improve results dramatically in this labor-intensive business. According to Reuel Couch, a business broker specializing in the sale of restaurants, many people truly believe that they have what it takes to successfully run a food establishment, only to be disappointed by their actual performances. Great care must be taken in finding the right restaurant or bar for you. Experienced brokers, such as Reuel (BIS, The Restaurant Brokers, 602-491-0123, Tempe, Ariz.), can help you make a wise decision in terms of choosing the best opportunity and not overpaying for it (franchises tend to sell for the highest percentages of gross revenues, approximately 40 to 80 percent; bars will sell for 50 to 70 percent of gross sales; restaurants with a license to sell beer and wine will go for 35 to 50 percent).

Automotive Businesses

Just as everyone must eat to survive, most everyone must drive to survive! Automotive manufacturing, distribution, retail, and repair and service companies (SIC Code 3710, 5010, 5510 to 5599, 7510 to 7549) make up a substantial part of our economy. As they relate to small businesses, automobile repair and service companies permeate the economic landscape. Increases in technological complexity make it more difficult for owners to do their own repairs at the same time that car owners are hanging on to their cars for a longer period of time, increasing dollar expenditures toward repairs. According to Paul Gallo, owner of VIP Realty in Tempe, Ariz., automotive repair/service businesses offer attractive returns to investors as a result of the unique characteristics of their services. Mr. Gallo, in addition to being a successful business broker, is a landlord who has rented space to dozens of different automotive-related businesses. He believes that one of the major attractions to owning this type of business is that the consumer is not driven by finding the lowest price all the time, but is motivated by finding the best value over time. This gives auto repair owners the chance to secure customers for life without fear of losing them to a lower bidder down the street.

Key automotive segments include:

- Auto repair, general
- Auto sales, new and used
- Auto transmission sales or service
- Gasoline or service stations
- Auto lube and tune
- Auto muffler or brake shops
- Auto parts and tires
- Auto paint and body shops

These opportunities are available as either independently owned shops or franchises. Each of these areas is unique, requiring specialized review and due diligence. For example, consider a few of the appropriate questions to ask for the following areas.

Gas and Service Stations
1. Is it full service or self-serve? How many pumps? Average markup per gallon?
2. Does the oil company offer rebates for volume?
3. What is the age and condition of the storage tanks? Have they or will they be replaced?
4. Has a Phase I, II, or III environmental audit been performed recently?
5. How long does franchise agreement last? What is transfer fee?
6. Does the oil company have the right of first refusal upon sale? Is lease with third party? Does the business cater to a special niche?

General Repair
1. Does the business cater to a special niche? Could new owner increase sales or cut expenses?
2. Is the equipment state of the art? Are technicians certified?
3. What is the cost of goods, labor, and rent as a percent of total sales?
4. What has been the extent of advertising efforts? What percent of sales?

5. How long has the current owner been active with the business? How long for sale?

Franchise opportunities. Franchise opportunities can be found in virtually every automotive segment. Despite high royalties, rents, and competition, franchises continue to proliferate across the nation. Even with obligatory payments as high as 13 percent of total sales (royalty plus advertising), franchise names and systems remain attractive options. Consult the *Entrepreneur* magazine Franchise 500 for ideas.

Why Businesses Fail

More businesses fail than succeed. It is appropriate to end our first chapter on this sobering note to keep balance in our analysis. Understanding why businesses fail can help avoid such a devastating outcome.

Ignoring Reality

When contemplating the purchase of an ongoing concern or establishing a business from scratch, emotions run high. Make sure you know as much as possible about the business you are committing to and listen to those who criticize or doubt the choices you are making. Entrepreneurs are naturally optimistic, but they must also be realistic!

Insufficient Start-Up Capital

You must be honest as to how much money is required to either start from scratch or continue operating a going concern. Entering a business venture with sufficient cash is critical for both peace of mind and optimal performance. Don't ignore the fact that you will likely need funds for living expenses for a certain period of time.

Lack of Operating Cash Flow

If a business cannot generate sufficient sales revenues to cover operating costs, it will starve. Even a rapidly growing business needs additional cash infusions to finance new inventory and credit sales. One of the leading reasons that I am asked to help owners sell their growing, profitable businesses is that they are undercapitalized and cannot perform to the company's peak level of sales and cash flow. Plan for the worst and have alternative sources of additional financing lined up and ready to tap.

Poor Pricing

Pricing is as much an art as it is a science. The tendency is to underprice, failing to account for all costs associated with providing a good or service. Both fixed (rent, utilities, insurance) and variable (labor and inventory) costs must be covered, leaving enough to pay for debt service, the owner's salary, and a return on investment. Avoid overly generous or too strict credit policies as both can destroy a company's profitability.

Poor Management

This catchall category includes the inability to delegate authority and motivate employees, lack of a realistic business plan, and simply a lack of effort on the part of the owner to go the extra mile. Take the time to write a detailed business plan—no exceptions! You must realistically outline planned expenditures, revenues, and marketing efforts, and analyze your competition carefully.

Bad Service

If you do not treat the customer properly, you will have no customers. To a great extent, the "customer is always right" and you can't let your ego stand in the way of this. As your business grows, you are likely to play an increasingly secondary role with customers, highlighting the need for quality employees.

Other Factors

Other causes for business failures are poor strategic planning (long term), overoptimistic sales forecasts, failure to analyze the competition, and failure to pay all taxes. One often overlooked or underestimated area is marketing. Don't forget that you need to create customer awareness and bring them to your doors. As much as 50 percent of your time should be spent cultivating customers and executing advertising programs. Once you get the customers, give them a reason to return! Consider tapping any one of the following sources before you take the plunge:

- Business courses at your local community college or university
- SCORE (800-634-0245)
- Local and U.S. Chamber of Commerce, Small Business Institute (202-463-5970)
- U.S. Small Business Administration (202-205-7714)
- Association of Small Business Development Centers (703-448-6124)
- National Association for the Self-Employed (NASE) (800-232-6273)
- Video Learning Library (800-383-8811)
- Center for Entrepreneurial Leadership, Inc. (816-932-1000)

Congratulations! You have made it through the first chapter and have most likely made significant progress toward your goal of evaluating the many pros and cons of self-employment and entrepreneurship.

CHAPTER 2

Using Professionals

Now we turn to the procedural matters associated with the purchase or sale of a business. The decisions regarding whether and how to use professionals are critical. Business brokers, certified public accountants, business appraisers, attorneys, escrow companies, bankers, business consultants, and leasing consultants all can play important roles. However, the parties referred to here have specific interests in each transaction. Keeping this in mind will help you make the best decision as to how to accept or reject their advice. In the end, there is no substitute for your ability to size up these individuals in each situation and judge whether they are credible and capable of truly working with your best interests in mind. As you read this chapter, *conceptualize your efforts as an attempt to build a team of professionals, who, for a fair price, will help you find, evaluate, purchase, operate, and ultimately sell a business.* Even if you have the skills to perform all the necessary steps on your own, the benefits of qualified assistance in the form of differing interpretations of complex situations will normally outweigh the costs.

Business Brokers

For many small business sales, a business broker is involved (see VR's Web Page at www.vrbusinessbrokers.com for an excellent overview of common business brokerage issues). Normally, the broker represents the seller and will be paid by the seller. Although most brokers will behave professionally, deal with all parties fairly, and disclose all material facts, there will be differing degrees of professionalism and performance. If you would like a broker to represent you (buyer's broker), you might be required to pay him or her separately from the purchase price of the business. If you do, the fees paid are tax-deductible, representing an often ignored benefit. Although practices vary from state to state, it is possible to have the broker represent the buyer and be paid by the seller (typically through a co-broke arrangement).

From the seller's point of view, several factors should be considered when selecting a broker. Realizing that their services can be invaluable (or worthless), caution must be exercised during the selection process. Friends, peers, accountants, and attorneys are all good sources for referrals. One pitfall is the high-pressure tactics of certain business brokerage houses. You need to choose not only a qualified broker, but also an upstanding brokerage firm. In high-pressure firms, agents (brokers) must obtain a minimum number of listings each month or they are at risk of losing their positions. Such pressure will often lead to unrealistic valuations to get the listing and subsequent abuses to get the business priced in line with market values. Generally, the broker's duties to the seller (client) include the following:

- Act primarily for the client's benefit, showing good faith and loyalty
- Disclose all material facts and maintain complete confidentiality
- Obey lawful instructions of seller and present all offers on a timely basis
- Properly handle all monies received

The agent must also deal with the purchaser (customer) on a fair basis and disclose all material facts. Each state has its own real estate department, which regulates the activities of agents or brokers. Most business brokers will be licensed by these departments, although this is not always the case. It can be comforting to know that the agent or broker you are working with is licensed and subject to training requirements and disciplinary proceedings.

Disclosure of agency is mandatory for licensed business brokers who handle real property. The important question is: who do the agents represent? The seller, purchaser, or both? Many states now allow *dual agency*, which can quickly become treacherous territory. Most brokers will choose to represent one side or the other. As concerns the purchaser's interests when working with a broker owing allegiance to the seller, the question is whether or not the broker must disclose information relating to the seller's insolvency, for example, or any other possible negative attributes. Most states will hold that the agent should inform the buyer of any and all materially adverse circumstances, regardless of agency obligations, but this area is subject to potentially vague and costly legal interpretations.

A second disclosure relates to the existence of any lien/encumbrance on property being transferred (real or personal) in connection with the transaction. This disclosure protects the purchaser and should be made by the seller and/or the seller's agent as soon and as frequently as possible. If the broker knows that a supplier will be filing a lien for nonpayment shortly after the scheduled closing date, this must be disclosed. Escrow companies routinely conduct a Uniform Commercial Code (UCC) search to locate any recorded liens or encumbrances. If they were not previously recorded or will be recorded only after closing, and the seller or broker is aware of them, they must be disclosed.

If a purchaser feels uncomfortable working exclusively with an agent who represents sellers, there are alternatives. One is to request buyer agency, which entails primary allegiance to the buyer. Agency issues are the source of numerous complaints handled by real estate departments, many of which end up in court causing great grief for all parties. Typical complaints include agent acting as dual agent without proper and timely disclosure; no disclosure or disclosure of agency made after negotiations had begun to unfold; and buyer perception of buyer agency contrary to agent's alleged disclosure. If a purchaser chooses buyer agency, written disclosure is required. Informing all parties on a timely and documented basis is the key to proper results. A buyer's broker agreement is included in the end of this chapter.

As a buyer's agent, payment for services can be received from either the buyer or the seller. If the buyer hires the broker as an exclusive agent to find a suitable business, and the chosen business was not already listed, the buyer might agree to pay 10 percent of the purchase price to the broker at closing. Having the buyer agree to pay the commission makes it easier for the broker to approach potential sellers (the broker does not have to negotiate a commission) and arrange for preliminary introductions. If the located business is already listed with another broker, the buyer's broker will normally co-broke and receive half of the commission paid by the seller. It is also possible that the broker will be paid by both the seller and purchaser.

Beyond referrals, you might select a broker that has been advertising heavily in the business opportunities section of your local paper. If you are interested in a small manufacturing company, find and interview such a candidate. For larger transactions, you might want to turn to investment bankers or M&A specialists such as VR M&A, International (800-770-8762, ask for me or Steve Crisham). VR M&A specializes in the sale of middle-market opportunities. These intermediaries can also be found in the Directory of M&A Professionals (New York: Dealers Digest, Inc.). When evaluating brokers, you should interview at least two candidates from different firms. The following list of questions is quite comprehensive and may be modified.

Broker Interview Questionnaire

1. How long have you been a business broker/M&A specialist? At least two years full-time experience in qualifying buyers, soliciting offers, writing contracts, and closing sales is critical. Trust your intuition as well. A "green" business broker who has owned, operated, and sold numerous businesses similar to yours in the past might be well qualified. The two-year rule improves the odds of hiring a broker who can go the distance.

2. Are you a member of professional brokerage organizations? This question targets the broker's experience and commitment to the profession. Several organizations and professional qualifications exist, such as the following:

- International Business Brokers Association (IBBA). A leading organization that sponsors conventions, seminars, and workshops year-round while promoting professional standards and valuable networking opportunities.

Members take coursework leading to the designation of Certified Business Intermediary (CBI). (703-437-4377).

- Institute of Business Appraisers (IBA). This group tests the individual's understanding of business appraisal. Members are not generally business brokers, but provide appraisal services (561-732-3202).
- State or Local Brokerage Associations. The Valley Board of Business Brokers (VBBB) is an MLS-type group of business brokers. Members are subject to continuing ethical standards. They will also receive valuable training and co-broke opportunities.
- National Association of Securities Dealers (NASD Series 7). Many M&A specialists offering a company's stock for sale carry this designation. Very few business brokers have this securities license, but it should be viewed as a plus.
- Various Trade Associations. Brokers specializing in the sale of restaurants might belong to the American Restaurant Association. Membership can indicate a commitment to the industry.
- International Association of Merger and Acquisition Professionals. Located in Northbrook, IL (708-480-9037).

3. Is the broker licensed by the state real estate department/commission?
Whereas few business brokers possess a securities license from the NASD, few M&A specialists will have real estate licenses. Legally, to sell real property, an intermediary must be licensed. Generally, business brokers will (should) have real estate licenses if they are handling the transfer of a lease or the sale of buildings or land.

4. How many deals have you closed in the past year? What types and sizes?
It is quite easy to exaggerate one's past sales due to the difficulty involved in verifying the claims. Ask the broker to substantiate these claims. The acceptable range could be two to nine. More is generally better, but frankly it is possible to be selling too many businesses. A broker selling two or three per month is successful, but may not be able to pay full attention to less important deals. M&A specialists, on the other hand, may only complete one to three deals per year. If they are not credible to you, they will probably not be credible to other parties (e.g., buyers, sellers).

5. What is your closing to listing ratio?
This question can be used to gain further insight into the broker's background and to facilitate comparison from one candidate to the next. Only one out of six or seven businesses listed for sale nationwide actually sells.

6. Will you willingly co-broke with other agents?
Unless the sale involves overwhelming confidentiality concerns, the answer should be a strong yes. Your chances of selling for top dollar in a timely fashion are improved dramatically through offering of co-brokerage fees. You would like to see your broker co-broking with other, qualified, registered, and professional brokers. Experienced brokers not only know the importance of a confidentiality agreement, they also know who the qualified brokers are through past experiences.

7. What is your marketing strategy? Marketing strategies will vary from one business to the next, including:

- Preparation of a generic one-page profile and detailed company analysis
- Networking by broker with other qualified agents
- Advertisements in local business opportunities section (at least twice per month)
- Letter and phone campaign to potential suitors (while maintaining confidentiality)
- Advertisements in pertinent trade journals or magazines and the Internet

Ask the broker or M&A specialist to declare specifically how much money will be spent on advertising and compare your results from one candidate to the next. Although contacts with other brokers is equally important, committing to these expenditures is necessary for a balanced, full exposure effort.

8. How do you qualify buyers? This is one of the most important functions fulfilled by intermediaries. Sellers must continue to run their business and do not have the time to entertain prospects that are lacking proper qualifications. Also, buyers must be screened to protect the seller's confidentiality. All prospects must read, review, and sign a nondisclosure (confidentiality) agreement. No exceptions. Practically, the main purposes of a confidentiality agreement are:

- To register with the broker, protecting his or her right to earn a commission
- To require the prospect to maintain confidentiality
- To agree to work only through the broker and to not approach any employees, suppliers, customers, or the owner without the broker's knowledge and approval
- To agree not to circumvent the broker for purposes of avoiding a commission
- To acknowledge that information is being sought to evaluate the business for purposes of buying the business, not to gain competitive insights
- To agree that all documents received by prospect will be returned to the seller
- To acknowledge that the prospect is not an agent for the IRS or other tax authority
- To agree to allow seller to investigate background of buyer

Legal ramifications for failing to adhere to the agreement should be spelled out. They should be signed by principals only, not by fiduciaries such as accountants or attorneys working on behalf of the principals. All principals should sign (e.g., both a husband and wife should sign). The owner should control who receives the confidential information, if desired. It is possible to limit the distribution of detailed information contingent upon review by the seller of the buyer's background. It may be a competitor that the seller wishes not to deal with under any circumstances. Or, the owner may simply defer this decision to the broker, relying on his or her judgment.

The primary documents that a broker can request from buyers are a resume and a personal financial statement (see Figure 2.3 for a sample personal financial statement). At a minimum, the following should be addressed:

General Questions for Buyer
- Are you involved with this type of business right now? Previously?
- What other management experience have you had? Can you provide references?
- How long have you been looking for a business? Describe your ultimate business.
- Have you made offers to purchase recently? Why did the deals fail?
- Who will be involved in the decision-making process? Spouse, partner, attorney?
- When can you commit to the purchase of a business? Have you quit your job?

Financial Questions for Buyer
- What amount of personal income do you require on an annual basis?
- What are your cash resources for down payment, closing costs, and working capital?
- Have you filled out a personal financial statement carefully and included bank references?
- Would you be willing to pledge additional personal collateral to secure financing?
- Can you describe your credit history? May we obtain a copy of your credit report?

The broker must ensure that the buyer is "for real," capable of running the subject business and able to finance the purchase and working capital requirements—all before the seller is contacted and an appointment scheduled. The larger the business, the more important this initial screening is.

9. Which business valuation techniques do you use? If you have read Chapter 8, you are aware of the variety of techniques available to value a business. The value of a business broker includes the fact that he or she should have a "finger on the pulse" of the market and therefore be able to accurately assess the approximate current market value of your business. In fact, you should ask specifically what sources of current comparable sales figures the broker has access to and how they might impact the valuation results. You should expect qualified brokers or specialists to answer that they use a variety of techniques based on cash flows, asset values, future earnings, and comparable sales.

10. What price do you think you can get for my business? Most experienced brokers can generate an approximate valuation if they have an income statement from the past 12 months, quickly calculating adjusted cash flow (ACF), estimating the value of the assets, and making assumptions about future growth. You need to test the broker's skills and confidence and begin to determine if you can sell your business at a price sufficient to justify your decision to sell.

11. How long will it take to sell the business? This question will elicit an interesting array of responses, ranging from "I have a highly interested and qualified buyer right now" to "the average business takes six months to a year to sell." The answer to this question depends upon several factors, including the skill and aggressiveness of the broker; the quality, type and trend of the business being sold; and advertising at the right place at the right time (luck!). It is not uncommon for businesses to be on the market for several years. All things considered, you should be prepared to wait for a full year, but if a particular broker can convince you that he or she is better than the averages, maybe they are!

12. Are your commissions negotiable? Commissions are generally calculated as a percentage of the final selling price. For smaller businesses, up to a sales price of about $500,000, you will be asked to pay between 10 and 12 percent. The stronger your business is and the easier it is to sell, the more likely the broker will be to negotiate downward. The dilemma that you might face is that some of the most qualified and successful brokers will not negotiate their commission at all, but they could be worth it! Additionally, most brokers will have a minimum commission of between $8,000 and $12,000 (also negotiable). For businesses larger than $500,000, the applicable percentages will decline and the applicable minimum commissions will rise. The Double Lehman Index is often used by professional M&A firms to structure commission arrangements for larger transactions. This formula works as illustrated below:

12 percent for the first $500,000
10 percent for the second $500,000
8 percent for the second $1,000,000
6 percent for the third $1,000,000
4 percent for the fourth $1,000,000
2 percent for any amount more than $4,000,000

The seller might ask the broker up front to accept a reduced commission if the seller accepts a lower than asked for purchase price. This may be addressed when the listing agreement is signed or in the middle of a transaction when the seller is considering acceptance. It is quite common for a seller to agree to a deal if the commission is reduced to a certain amount less than originally stipulated. Depending upon circumstances, a broker may or may not agree to this request. Another less common approach is to ask the broker to carry the commission if the seller agrees to carry the purchaser with a promissory note. In other words, if a business is sold for $200,000 with $100,000 down and the balance paid back monthly for five years, the commission would be paid in similar fashion (half at closing and the balance paid in monthly installments over five years). Most brokers, however, will insist on being paid completely at the time of closing.

13. Are there any up-front or retainer fees? Once again, there is a difference between business brokers and investment banking firms. Most business brokers are not owed a single penny until the business is legally sold or the commission is otherwise earned (such as if an offer mirroring the seller's asking price and terms is received and the seller backs down from the deal). Occasionally, business brokers will charge and business owners will agree to pay a small fee of between $500 and $2,000 for a comprehensive business evaluation. Normally, this payment will be credited toward the commission payable at closing if the business is subsequently sold.

On the other hand, M&A specialists (also called middle-market firms) will always charge either up-front or retainer fees. One successful middle-market firm charges close to $35,000 to perform its valuation and market the business. This money is nonrefundable in the event the business does not sell, but will be credited against the commission earned if the business is sold. Other firms will charge less than this, but will not credit the amount against the future commission.

14. Will you consider less than a sole and exclusive listing? There are different levels of commitment between the seller and the broker, each associated with pluses and minuses. The broker will almost always request a *sole and exclusive* listing (see Chapter 13 for a sample Sole and Exclusive Agreement) that gives the broker the exclusive right to receive and the owner the obligation to pay a commission within the time period of the agreement regardless of who locates the buyer. Note also that most listing contracts have a clause that carries responsibility for payment of commission beyond the expiration of the contract for a period of up to two years for those buyers introduced to the business by the broker.

In general, this aspect of utilizing a broker is similar to working with residential real estate agents. The sole and exclusive agreement locks you into working with the chosen broker no matter what happens over the period of the agreement. Whether the broker, you, or a cousin locate the buyer, he or she has earned the commission. If you sign a sole and exclusive, you are basically locked in for the duration, so do your homework carefully. If the broker you are working with will not agree to an arrangement less than a sole and exclusive, you might ask for the right to rescind the contract halfway through the specified length (or with 30 days notice) if you are not satisfied with his or her performance.

Another way to protect yourself is to include specific performance criteria, which if not met, will allow you to terminate the relationship. Examples include requiring the broker to run one ad every other week, mail 100 letters within two months, or present an average of one qualified buyer each week by the third month. Before signing a listing contract, read every portion carefully and consider consulting your attorney for feedback. The best relationships with brokers are ones of trust and mutual respect.

When reviewing the contract, pay close attention to the section or sections that spell out the conditions under which a commission is due and payable to the broker. In many contracts, it will seem like a commission is due under questionable circumstances. Remember that the precise conditions of the contract are just as negotiable as they are for any other contract. Contracts that are prepared by brokers will tend to be tilted strongly in their favor. Consider the following:

Seller agrees to pay broker a commission if any of the following five conditions occur:

1. Broker locates purchaser who is ready, willing, and able to buy business on the offered price and terms.
2. Seller unnecessarily delays or stops completion of the sale after having agreed to by signing this document.
3. Seller removes the business from sale or otherwise intends to unilaterally rescind this agreement.
4. Seller sells, trades, leases, gives away, or otherwise transfers ownership within a three-year period after the end date of this agreement.
5. Seller sells or otherwise transfers business, accepts deposits, or places advertisements during the sole and exclusive period with or without the assistance of the broker.

Obviously, you cannot expect a broker, who will only be paid if the business is sold, to work diligently toward the sale of a business only to have the owner do an "end-round" to avoid the commission. Nonetheless, it is the seller's prerogative to carefully review and amend the agreement to the mutual satisfaction of both parties. Let's review the five conditions.

Condition 1: If the broker finds a buyer who writes an offer that "mirrors" the price and terms on the listing contract, a full commission is due and payable, whether closing occurs or not. The seller can protect his or her interests in this situation by incorporating an additional clause into the listing contract stating that the sale of the business is contingent upon the seller's review of the buyer's credit and background. Even without this clause, you could refuse to sell to someone because of insufficient skills, but an unscrupulous broker could taunt you with a lawsuit in an attempt to settle for a sizable payment. If it were an offer that mirrored the offering terms, you would find yourself in a difficult position. Before you get the wrong idea, most brokers are professional and ethical and will not force you to sell your business against your will. This illustrates once again why it is important to choose a broker with high ethical standards. The integrity of the broker is equally if not more important than the specific verbiage placed into the listing contract.

Condition 2: This clause is intended to strengthen the broker's position, in light of having committed to perform work and pay for advertising without receiving any compensation to do so. If a broker is going to work for you on a commission basis, he or she needs to know that you will help and not hinder the process for any reason. Occasionally, sellers will enter into a sole and exclusive agreement with best of intentions only to stumble across a buyer on their own. If the seller feels that the buyer they have located as a result of their own efforts is legitimate, they might hamper the broker by failing to provide necessary financial documents, missing appointments with broker-generated prospects, or a host of other delaying tactics. By holding off the broker's candidates, the seller hopes to wait until the listing expires and sell to their buyer without paying the commission. The broker's basic problem here is that it would require a costly legal suit to try and prove that the seller has hindered the sale.

Condition 3: This clause strongly supports the broker's efforts to sell your business on a commission basis. The message, once again, is if you are serious about selling and are willing to take the broker's time and advertising money up front, you cannot change your mind about selling. If the sellers are worried that they may not actually want to sell, they should be honest with the broker beginning with the first meeting. Sellers can request a short-term agreement for two, three, or six months if they are uncertain. Then, it is up to the fully informed broker to decide if he or she wants to risk limited time and money on such a wavering seller. Most professional, ethical brokers will agree to let the seller out of a contract for legitimate reasons, such as the arrival of the busy season (e.g., the holiday season for retailers), the end of the lease for the seller's premises where the seller cannot continue to operate the business, or the onset of serious, debilitating illnesses. *The best of brokers should not be considered adversaries, but partners.* They want to help you sell your business and expect your honest cooperation.

Condition 4: Because the listing agreement is almost always prepared by the broker, there is normally a bias in the broker's favor. Most agreements will spell out in detail the conditions for which a commission is due and payable, but will devote little or no content to specifying the conditions that would amount to a breach of contract (lack of performance) for the broker, such as insufficient advertising or failing to locate and present qualified buyers. Most brokers would not be adverse to including specific numeric goals to be met in order for the agreement to continue in force. At a minimum, these goals or requirements would probably boost your broker's attention toward your business and improve the odds for a successful closing. However, as with all benchmarking and goal setting, time can be wasted by trying to reach the goal without providing genuine and productive efforts. For example, if the listing agreement requires that at least three qualified buyers tour the business within the first six months, the broker might arrange for a tour with a buyer, qualified on paper only, simply to meet the requirement and keep the listing in force. As concerns clause 4 specifically, the intent is fairly obvious. If the broker presents a qualified buyer who for some reason chooses not to proceed during the period of the listing agreement, but follows up and makes an offer to purchase six months after the expiration, the broker has clearly been the *procuring cause* and is entitled to be paid. How long does a broker "own" a buyer or seller? Just as covenants not to compete (noncompete agreements) cannot be overly restrictive in terms of geography or duration to the point where they preclude the seller from earning a living, obligations to pay a commission cannot be overly aggressive.

Condition 5: This condition truly makes for a "sole and exclusive" arrangement for the broker, restricting the seller from attempting to sell or actually selling without the assistance of the broker.

15. *How many members of your firm will be assisting you?* This question will help you get a feel for the cooperative nature of the agents working for the firm. The lead broker is by far the most important, but any affirmative response to this question is welcome. You truly are hiring a team of brokers. If it is a legitimate, respectable firm with a history, it will also have a listing in the Yellow Pages.

16. How will communications be handled? You should expect regular contact (weekly) for a sole and exclusive listing. Brokers will feel less obligated to communicate with you under exclusive or open listings. Lack of contact may mean that the broker is busy closing other deals. Although this could be favorable in general, it does not help you presently. It may also mean that you are not a priority to the broker. In any case, do not hesitate to call the broker at any time!

17. Can you provide a list of references? Although most sellers do not like to discuss something as personal as the sale of a business with strangers, current references should be asked for and made available. References from larger businesses are more difficult to obtain, as their sale tends to be more confidential. You must ask for references, if for no other reason than to establish that they exist!

You may also check to see if they are members of the better business bureau. When interpreting complaints, judgment must be used to establish who was truly at fault (many complaints do not relate to unethical, unprofessional, or illegal acts). If the broker holds a real estate license, you may wish to check with the state real estate department as well.

18. What is the standard length of your contract? Are there cancellation provisions? Both of these conditions are very important to the broker and the seller. Most brokers would prefer a one-year, noncancelable sole and exclusive listing agreement, whereas most sellers would prefer a shorter term of three to six months, cancelable unilaterally upon notice. These areas generate great stress between the broker and seller. The more profitable and well established your business is, the more likely you are to receive concessions from the broker. I am comfortable with a six month listing and a unilateral 30-day cancellation right. These concessions comfort the seller and help establish an atmosphere of trust and cooperation (not every broker is quite so accommodating!). Inflexible brokers might be some of the best in the business, but I feel strongly that goodwill and trust is preferable to force.

The Listing Contract

All the issues previously discussed must be addressed contractually. Owners of small businesses with sales of less than $5 million will sign listing contracts with business brokers. Owners of larger "small" businesses with sales of more than $10 million (middle-market companies) generally will sign agreements with M&A firms. Finally, attorneys will facilitate the sale of your business on an hourly basis or for a flat fee.

Key issues include retainer fees, exclusivity, commission, contract length, and determination of whether or not to sell stock or assets. For smaller businesses, an asset sale is most probable. As the size of the business increases, the likelihood of the sale of stock increases. For stock sales, there is some question as to who is legally capable of facilitating such a sale. Business brokers with only real estate licenses cannot always sell the stock (securities) of a business and an M&A specialist with a securities license cannot generally sell real property (land and buildings). In practice, both can and do occur.

A problematic scenario occurs when a business broker lists a business as an asset sale only to end up with an agreement that calls for the sale of stock (per legal counsel). The issue is whether the broker is qualified or if he or she is acting illegally as an unregistered broker-dealer (securities). Historically, the "Sale of Business" doctrine has served to protect the unlicensed business broker by holding that the sale of a majority interest in a closely held business involves primarily a sale of assets. The Securities and Exchange Commission (SEC) has reaffirmed this principle on numerous occasions. The SEC has historically maintained that parties who merely bring prospects together (earn a finder's fee) and do not actively participate in determining the value or negotiating the sale of securities and who do not share in the generated profits or losses are not securities brokers and therefore need not register as a broker-dealer.

Laying out terms and conditions in the listing agreement that will apply to and reappear in the purchase agreement is a sound approach. This serves notice to the broker that certain issues are important to you and should be handled as directed. One area worthy of such coverage is the handling of earnest checks. When there are multiple offers and counteroffers, this becomes critical. Although this is addressed primarily in the offer to purchase, you can influence the broker by writing instructions into the listing agreement. For example, you can request that the broker present only offers with earnest check deposits equaling some minimum amount, forcing the broker to be firm with buyers. Alternatively, you could request that these deposits be placed immediately into escrow with a certain percentage to be nonrefundable. You can instruct the broker to present this request as a type of processing fee, reimbursing you (and probably the broker) for your time and efforts. Frankly, requesting nonrefundable escrow deposits before due diligence is completed will not be well received. This approach will work only if your business is highly attractive and it is a seller's market. As a bargaining chip, however, if you coach the broker to request this nonrefundable deposit (even in anticipation of a quick rejection by the buyer), it might create an aura of value. The point is that by inserting instructions to the broker into the listing agreement, you are taking control of this life-shaping transaction.

Many different clauses can be placed into the offer for purchase agreement, which will strengthen the deal from the seller's perspective. *As a seller, you must take the time to control the process to your best ability and avoid complete and unequivocal reliance on your broker.* Placing the broker on notice that you have a good understanding of the processes involved will encourage him or her to work harder and smarter to represent your interests.

Finally, if a corporation is involved, most brokers will require that you provide them with a notarized corporate resolution to buy or sell, similar to the one found in Figure 2.4.

Accountants

Accountants can assist in establishing and confirming value, interpreting financial statements, reviewing purchase contracts, facilitating due diligence, and helping a new owner become fully operational in terms of tax registration, use permits, and other governmental requirements. They may also lead you to suitable businesses for sale. After a purchase is completed, consider retaining the seller's accountant, who can offer unique support based upon knowledge of the firm's history. However, it might be wise to utilize an independent accountant for due diligence and valuation advice as existing accountants may have a small motivation to prevent the deal from closing and possibly losing a client. *Accountants' key roles will normally be in providing advice concerning tax issues and performing miniaudits of target acquisitions.*

Make sure that accountants take the time to actually verify sales and expenses for at least a few sample periods (months). They will too often rely on their "gut feelings" after only a cursory review of the financial statements and a brief analysis of the seller's accounting procedures. Be prepared to pay for a minimal audit of sales and expenses. Ask them to explain in detail the experience they have had in valuing businesses and performing due diligence investigations for businesses similar to the one being bought or sold. Ask them specifically what they would do if they had four hours to investigate a business. Compare their responses to the due diligence steps outlined in Chapter 6. Don't hesitate to ask for references.

Following the purchase, accountants can help you with establishing an accounting system, preparing cash projections, strategic and tax planning, cost reduction techniques, acquisition services, integrated computer systems, and pricing and breakeven analysis. As a final suggestion, consider offering your chosen accountant an equity position in your firm in lieu of up-front and monthly fees. Creating a mutual interest in this fashion is worthwhile if it can be worked out properly!

Attorneys

Perhaps the most controversial group of professionals involved in facilitating the sale of small businesses is attorneys. In most states, business brokers possess the legal authority to write contracts and the use of standard, time-proven, boiler-plate contracts generally is sufficient for smaller transactions. However, *attorneys should be consulted to review purchase contracts and make suggestions that seek to protect or strengthen the interests of one side or another.* In states where business brokers are given the authority to write contracts, the role of attorneys might be to review the contract and perfect the language. Their goal should not be to renegotiate price and terms. By the time the agreement is signed and received by the attorney for review, there has already been a meeting of the minds and further substantive changes or additions might damage the chances of closing. *Changes should be made only to strengthen the existing agreement or to address pertinent legal issues and wording.* A major deal breaker occurs when attorneys on both sides get involved bringing up new issues and additional negotiations. The dilemma here is they might be raising legitimate concerns or they might be unnecessary and ultimately destructive. The realization that attorneys have little or no exposure to liability if they recommend against a deal and possibly great exposure if they give a green light sheds additional light on this predicament.

It may be wise to consult your attorney *before* you list a business for sale and *before* offers are written by brokers in order to receive specific advice as to what should or should not be included in a listing or offer. A business broker will generally be qualified to write clear, concise, legally valid, and enforceable contracts. The specialized contract writing skills of a business broker represents a significant portion of his or her expertise and value. If the broker actively participates in the negotiations between buyer and seller and constructs the agreement, the role of the attorney can be secondary.

Nonetheless, an excellent contingency for both buyer and seller to be placed in the offer to purchase is the right to attorney review. There should be a reasonable time constraint on this contingency (as there should be for purchaser due diligence and attorney review), but it is a prudent way to reduce the tension associated with such a major event. Attorneys might suggest specific changes after reviewing a purchase agreement that has already been signed by seller and buyer. See the chapters on buying and selling for precise and detailed clauses that enhance the buyer's or seller's position.

In addition to utilizing attorneys to review purchase contracts, they may be used for any or all of the following services:

- Smoothly transferring ownership of business and all assets
- Legally establishing existence of business (e.g., S-corporation or C-corporation, LLC)
- Reducing tax liabilities annually and upon sale of a business
- Obtaining transaction privilege tax license and federal taxpayer identification number
- Reviewing existing employment/service contracts of target acquisition
- Drafting a nonbinding letter of intent
- Performing proper environmental due diligence reviews
- Protecting intellectual property rights
- Obtaining operating licenses, such as liquor licenses
- Evaluating stock versus asset sale
- Filing for immigration visas relating to business acquisition (gold card)
- Formulating exit and estate planning strategies
- Reviewing franchise offering circulars and agreements
- Handling various breaches of contract by buyers or sellers

When you are evaluating and interviewing attorneys as you build your team, consider asking the following questions:

- Describe your experience handling listing agreements and purchase contracts.
- How many years have you been performing this kind of work? What types and sizes?
- Can you provide current references?
- Have all the deals you worked on made it to closing? If not, why not?
- What are the total fees for the typical transaction?
- Have there ever been complaints lodged against you with any public or private agency?

Some of the most important questions cannot really be answered until a transaction is unfolding. Does the attorney listen to you? This is critical owing to the many unique details and characteristics of each deal. Is the attorney willing to see you on short notice? Does he or she return calls promptly? Beyond any doubt, the most critical element of all is the amount of relevant experience the attorney possesses in the purchase and sale of small businesses. Find the right attorney and he or she will serve you well. If you seek to educate yourself, there are numerous self-help legal guides that can provide useful information and support covering many legal issues. For example, *The Legal Guide for Starting and Running a Small Business*, by Fred Steingold (800-992-6656).

Methods that serve to reduce overall legal fees, known as *alternate dispute resolutions*, are worth investigating as you find yourself entering into various contractual arrangements (e.g., confidentiality agreement, purchase agreement, promissory note). There are three possibilities, as follows:

1. Mediation—results in a nonbinding, voluntary settlement arranged through an independent third party
2. Arbitration—results in a specific, detailed binding (or nonbinding) decision laid down by an independent third party after hearing and evaluating all relevant facts
3. Mini-Trial—results in a nonbinding settlement mediated by an independent third party who listens to the relevant facts presented by attorneys from each side.

These methods will typically lead to quicker, less expensive outcomes than court battles. Including arbitration or mediation clauses in contracts between buyers, sellers, brokers, and other parties is increasingly common. See Chapters 4 and 5 for sample arbitration clauses. For information regarding arbitration, call the American Arbitration Association (New York, N.Y., 212-484-4000).

Escrow Companies

After agreement has been reached on price and terms and due diligence has been favorably completed, most business sales are formally completed with the assistance of an escrow company. After contingency removal forms are signed, escrow is opened via escrow instructions from the broker and the escrow company's work begins. There will be constant communication between the broker, buyer, seller, and escrow company as information is transmitted, reformulated, and otherwise processed. The basic goal of the escrow company is to ensure that the business can be and is legally transferred to the benefit of both parties.

In most states, escrow companies are used as an independent third party, representing neither the buyer or seller, to prepare all the official closing documents, including the bill of sale, promissory note, and covenant not to compete. They will also conduct a UCC search against state and local public records to verify the existence or nonexistence of liens, judgments, or other encumbrances against the assets of the business being sold. Ensuring compliance with the state Bulk Sales Act is another important service. The closing will not be allowed unless the assets can be delivered free and clear of all debts or to the mutual satisfaction of the buyer and seller. The escrow company will also ensure that corporate resolutions are executed, new liens recorded, and future note payments received. Upon receipt of the final payment toward a seller's carry-back note, the escrow company will release the lien and transfer the original bill of sale to the new owners of record.

Escrow companies will provide these valuable services based on a fee structure that depends on both the size of the business and the number of services selected by the buyers and sellers. The processing of note payments, for example, is optional, and will add to the closing costs accordingly. Additional fees may be charged for rush orders. It is a matter of mutual agreement between buyer, seller, and broker as to which escrow company will be utilized. Please be aware that not every escrow company can handle business closings properly. There are many peculiarities involved that require specialization. Perhaps more important than the fees they charge is their level of experience and expertise. Average closing fees for small businesses will range between $800 and $2,000, with the expense normally split between buyer and seller (although this is negotiable). As part of their services, escrow companies will make sure that the following matters are addressed:

- All prorations are properly calculated as of closing (e.g., rent, property tax, equipment lease)
- Corporations are legally authorized to buy and sell (notarized corporate resolutions)
- Seller's and buyer's corporations are in good legal standing
- All recorded liens, judgments, and encumbrances are known to buyer and properly disposed of
- All property tax (real and personal) payments are current
- All future note payments are properly calculated, collected, and disbursed
- Default notices are officially mailed and processed
- Inventories are counted prior to escrow
- All closing documents are properly prepared and signed

- Broker is relieved of liability regarding presentation of information by seller (broker's disclaimer)
- New liens against assets of business sold via promissory note are recorded (UCC-1)
- All necessary steps are taken to process the sale of real property, if involved

Business Appraisers

Business appraisers are professionally trained arbiters of value. There are appraisers specializing in many different areas, including real estate, equipment, art work, as well as businesses. Business appraisers, on average, put more time and effort into valuing a going concern than a business broker or accountant would but may not actually produce a better valuation. They are not normally utilized for the sale of typical-sized small businesses (sales of up to $1 million), where valuation results are reached by the seller or buyer primarily in conjunction with the efforts of a qualified business broker who can be relied on to be in close contact with current market values. Business appraisers become involved for a variety of reasons, particularly to resolve legal and tax-related disputes involving divorce, partnership, or corporate dissolution, bankruptcy, Employee Stock Ownership Plans, and other similar purposes. They will also tend to be involved more with larger businesses, typically corporations, posting sales of more than $2 million annually. Professional appraisers are certified by one of several organizations. Two of the leaders in business valuation are: The American Society of Appraisers (ASA) (800-272-8258) and The Institute of Business Appraisers (IBA) (561-732-3202).

The ASA is multifaceted and can recommend specialists for real estate, equipment, intangible assets, or businesses. The IBA specializes in businesses only. Certified appraisers must meet background, training, and continuing education requirements. They are also bound by strict ethical and professional standards regarding the appraisal process. A very useful, free pamphlet *Reviewing a Business Appraisal Report* is available from Willamette Management Associates (503-222-0577).

Most small business owners are not routinely aware of business appraisers in their area. The best approach to selecting an appraiser is to once again rely on the recommendation of your trusted colleagues, accountant, broker, or attorney. If you are going to pay $1,000 to $10,000 for this service, the appraiser should obviously be properly skilled and experienced. If no acceptable recommendations are forthcoming, you can call the professional organizations listed previously and ask for appraisers in your area. The Yellow Pages are another source for finding the appropriate appraiser.

As a final point, it is possible to obtain a rough estimate on the value of your firm by a certified appraiser without having to pay the fees for a complete, formal report. Hourly consulting services are available to provide these rough approximations. If you do not need a full-blown, formal assessment, the quick version can serve you well.

Sample Forms

The last section of this chapter comprises four useful forms and a list of equipment appraisers. Figure 2.1 is a buyer's broker agreement that allows the broker to work for and be paid by the buyer. Figure 2.2 is a confidentiality or nondisclosure agreement to be obtained by a prospective purchaser. Figure 2.3 is a basic personal financial statement to assist the seller in evaluating credit extension. Figure 2.4 is a corporate resolution to allow the broker the right to sell a business. Figure 2.5 lists major equipment appraisers.

FIGURE 2.1   Buyer's Broker Agreement

BUYER'S BROKER AGREEMENT

THIS AGREEMENT is made by and between

_____, Broker
(Broker's full business name)

hereinafter referred to as Broker, and _____

hereinafter referred to as Buyer.

Buyer hereby retains Broker to seek out a business or property to be purchased by Buyer (in exchange for the agreed upon fees listed below) in the City (Town) of

_____, in _____county, in the

state of _____, as herein described:

_____

_____

_____

to be used as:

_____

_____

_____under terms

and conditions acceptable to Purchaser.

If Buyer, or any other person acting for Buyer or in Buyer's behalf, purchases any property (real or personal), during the life of this contract or within two years thereafter, which was first introduced or submitted to Buyer by Broker during the duration of this contract, and the description of which was submitted to Buyer in writing, either personally or by mail posted prior to the termination date of this contract, Buyer agrees to pay to Broker a commission of _____% of the purchase price.

If Buyer, or any other person acting for Buyer or in Buyer's behalf, obtains an option to purchase any such business or property, during the duration of this contract or within two years thereafter, which was first introduced or submitted to Buyer by

---

FIGURE 2.1   Buyer's Broker Agreement, continued

Broker during the life of this contract, and the description of which has been submitted to Buyer in writing either in person or by mail posted prior to the termination date of this contract, Buyer agrees to pay Broker the sum of $_____ as a commission and further agrees to pay Broker _____ (%) of the purchase price minus the amount previously paid to Broker of obtaining said option, should Buyer either exercise said option, or purchase said property, or assign said option within one year after termination of this contract, or purchase the business or property within one year after the expiration of this option so obtained, whichever is later.

In consideration of Buyer's agreement as set forth above, Buyer agrees to pay Broker a retainer fee of $_____, which shall be subtracted from any commission due to Broker should Broker be successful in obtaining a satisfactory business or property, otherwise said fee is to be retained by Broker for services rendered.

The duration of this contract shall be from the _____ day of _____, 19_____, through and including the _____ day of _____, 19_____.

Dated this _____ day of _____, 19_____.

Broker   Buyer(s)

_____   _____
(Agent for Broker)   Address and Phone Number

_____   _____

FIGURE 2.2   Confidentiality Agreement

CONFIDENTIALITY AGREEMENT

The undersigned parties understand and agree that:

1. Information provided on any business is confidential, and that any information disclosed to others may be damaging to the business and their owners. We agree that we will not discuss any information, including the name of the business, to anyone other than advisers, agents, accountants, attorneys, and affiliates, who also agree to the same confidentiality. We agree that all copies of materials and data provided shall be confidential and shall be returned to the seller within seven days.

2. We will not contact the business owner or their landlords, employees, suppliers, or customers except through the Broker. All correspondence, inquiries, offers to purchase, and negotiations relating to the purchase of any business presented by the Broker will be conducted exclusively through the Broker.

3. Our intent is to purchase a business and not for purposes of gaining information for business competitors, the Department of Internal Revenue, or any other governmental or taxing agency.

4. We will not circumvent the Seller and Broker by obtaining property leases, customers, employees, vendors, or any portion of these businesses using the knowledge gained through disclosure of information from the broker.

5. All information about the business is provided by the Seller and is not verified by the Broker. We understand that purchasing a business represents investment risks and we should obtain professional assistance from independent accounting, legal, and financial advisors to verify said information prior to entering into an agreement to purchase any business. We will not rely solely on the unaudited information provided by the Broker. Broker has no knowledge to the accuracy of said information and makes no warranty, or guarantee, expressed or implied, as to the accuracy of such information.

6. If we enter into an agreement to purchase a business, we will provide a personal and/or business financial statement(s) and resume and we authorize the Seller to obtain, through standard reporting agencies, financial and credit information about myself and/or the companies or affiliates we represent for the seller extending credit to us. The information will be held confidential by the Seller and Broker.

7. The Broker is not an agent for me, but is an agent for the Seller and has a contract providing a fee to be paid to the Broker by Seller upon sale, trade, lease, or transfer of the Seller's business or property. We will not be responsible for the fee to the Broker if we purchase the business through the Broker. If we should

FIGURE 2.2   Confidentiality Agreement, continued

circumvent the Broker and become a manager, trade, purchase stock, or otherwise become connected with the business, a full commission is owned by me to the Broker. Any changes in representation by the Broker must be in writing and shall be disclosed to all parties involved.

We, the undersigned, understand, acknowledge, and agree that this agreement is legally binding upon the undersigned, and all others involved in the analysis and evaluation of this information in connection with the possible purchase of the Business, and agree that the Business will have the right to apply any court jurisdiction for a restraining order or such other relief as may be appropriate to reinforce the terms of this agreement and may look to the undersigned for any compensatory or punitive damages, including court costs and attorney's fees that may result from any breach of this agreement.

_____   _____   _____
Principal Signature   Date   Principal Name (print)

_____   _____
Social Security Number   _____

                                                _____
                                                Principal Address

_____
    Agent for Broker

Note: The confidentiality agreement in Figure 2.2 is a contract between the buyer and the broker, but could be modified to represent an agreement between a buyer and a seller. Consult your attorney for proper instructions in this regard. As always, it is important to obtain approval from your attorney before signing any documents.

FIGURE 2.3   Personal Financial Statement

PERSONAL FINANCIAL STATEMENT

Date _____

Name _____

Address _____

City _____

State _____ Zip _____

Phone (Res.) _____   (Bus.) _____

Assets	Amount		Liabilities	Amount	
Cash on hand in banks			Notes payable to banks		
U.S. govt. securities— see schedule			Secured		
Listed securities —see schedule			Unsecured		
Unlisted securities —see schedule			Notes payable to relatives		
Accounts and notes receivable due from relatives and friends			Notes payable to others		
Accounts and notes receivable due from others—good			Accounts and bills due		
Accounts and notes receivable—doubtful			Accrued taxes and interest		
Real estate owned —see schedule			Other unpaid taxes		
Real estate mortgage owned			Mortgages payable on real estate—see schedule		
Automobiles			Chattel mortgages and other liens payable		
Personal property			Other debts—itemize		
Other assets—itemize					
			Total Liabilities		
			Net Worth		
Total Assets			**Total Liabilities & Net Worth**		

FIGURE 2.3 Personal Financial Statement, continued

Source of Income		Personal Information	
Salary	$	Business or occupation	
		Age	
Bonus and commissions	$		
Dividends	$	Partner or officer in any other venture	
Real estate income	$		
Other income—itemize	$	Married	Children
		Single	Dependents
Total	$		

Contingent Liabilities	General Information
As endorser or comaker	Are any assets pledged?
On leases or contracts	Are you defendant in any suits or legal actions?
Legal claims	Personal bank accounts carried at
Provision for federal income taxes	Have you ever taken bankruptcy?
Other special debt	Explain:

FIGURE 2.4   Corporate Resolution

CORPORATE RESOLUTION

THIS IS TO CERTIFY THAT at a meeting of the Board of Directors, _____, an _____ corporation, which meeting was properly and duly called in accordance with official bylaws on the _____ day of _____, 19_____, at which at least a quorum of the Board of Directors was present, the following resolution was adopted and the same has not been altered, amended, or revoked:

RESOLVED, that _____ the _____ of this corporation is hereby authorized to execute and deliver, in the name of and on behalf of the corporation, a listing contract agreement with _____ and any other documents that may be deemed necessary in authorizing _____ to sell, for a commission, the BUSINESS known as _____ which is owned by the corporation, without further act or resolution of this board.

THE UNDERSIGNED PRESIDENT AND SECRETARY certify that they are the President and Secretary, respectively, of this corporation, and that as such officers, have possession of the corporate books and records of the above named corporation. The undersigned further certify that the authority conferred by the above resolution is not inconsistent with the Charter or Bylaws of this corporation, nor the laws of the State of Arizona.

IN WITNESS, WHEREOF, the President and Secretary of the Corporation have signed this resolution on this _____ day of _____, 19_____.

ATTEST:

_____   _____

President   Secretary

STATE OF _____

COUNTY OF _____

On the _____ day of _____, 19____, before me, the undersigned Notary Public, personally appeared, _____ who acknowledged _____ to be the Secretary of _____, a Corporation, and the _____ being duly authorized to do so, executed the foregoing instrument for the Sole Purpose contained therein, by signing the name of the Corporation by _____ as Secretary.

IN WITNESS WHEREOF I have hereunto set my hand official seal.

_____, NOTARY PUBLIC

Note: Similar resolutions must be executed to legally effect the sale or purchase at closing as well. In other words, a resolution is necessary to authorize the broker to sell the business for a commission and a second resolution is required to legally consummate the purchase (corporate resolution to buy) and sale (corporate resolution to sell).

FIGURE 2.5   Short List of Major Equipment Appraisers

Arthur Andersen & Company (Houston, Texas, 713-237-2323)

Business Advisory Services (Seattle, Wash., 206-223-5400)

William F. Comly & Son, Inc. (Philadelphia, Penn., 215-634-2500)

Coopers & Lybrand (Chicago, Ill., 212-259-2753)

William Kasper & Associates (Escondido, Calif., 619-746-1927)

Note: For a complete listing of appraisers in your area, consult your Yellow Pages under appraisers, making sure that you choose one who is qualified (certified) to appraise the particular type of asset for which you seek assistance. Home appraisers cannot typically appraise business assets properly. See the book called *Cashing Out* by David Silver (Dearborn Financial Publishing, 1993) for a thorough list of appraisers.

The Buying Process

The processes involved in buying a business, when considered all at once, are numerous and require a balanced and prepared approach to be fully, efficiently, and effectively implemented. For purposes of this guide, these processes or steps will be presented and analyzed as follows:

Chapter 3
Step 1: Decide to buy
Step 2: Choose type and category of desired businesses
Step 3: Interview and select team of professionals
Step 4: Locate and preliminarily investigate opportunities

Chapters 4 and 5
Step 5: Write offer or letter of intent

Chapter 6
Step 6: Negotiate final price and terms
Step 7: Perform comprehensive due diligence

Chapter 7
Step 8: Address preclosing issues
Step 9: Orchestrate successful closing
Step 10: Deal with transition issues

Well, you have made up your mind. You would like to go out on your own and buy a business. You are seeking job security, financial growth, and the ability to control your own future. Many obstacles lie ahead on this chosen path—financial, physical, and psychological. How do you begin? What type and category of business do you buy? How do you determine its value? What strategy should you use in the negotiation process? How do you protect your interests contractually? Whom can you turn to for help?

Step 1: Decide to Buy

At this point, I would recommend that you peruse Chapter 1 again for a review of the variety of business opportunities available. There are distinct pros and cons of starting a business from scratch versus buying an ongoing concern or buying a franchise versus any independently operated business. If you are a first-time buyer, it is critical that you learn and understand as much as possible about what makes a particular type of business successful as well as the myriad facets of the buying process.

As you venture down this road, you should be comforted by the fact that people from all backgrounds are taking their destiny into their own hands by starting or buying a business. There are approximately 20 million businesses (IRS data) in the United States, with more than 99 percent of these small businesses having less than 500 employees. As corporate America downsizes, "small business America" is upsizing, producing almost all the net job creation during the late 1980s through the mid 1990s, currently employing three out of five Americans!

According to Jim Roth, owner of the VR Business Brokers office in Scottsdale, Ariz. (602-949-8612 and http://www.az-vr-businessbrokers.com), this downsizing trend will continue through the end of the decade and into the 21st century. Jim, a former executive from a Fortune 100 corporation, remains in close contact with upper management personnel from many large corporations who continue to feel the insecurity associated with these major restructurings and rightsizings. He is convinced that more and more of these highly motivated, highly skilled employees will be taking the entrepreneurial plunge in search of greater control over their destinies.

Step 2: Choose the Type, Category, and Size of Desired Business

One of the many keys to successfully owning and operating a small business is to carefully choose the "right" one. To begin with, there is the choice regarding the type and category of business that best fits your disposition and background. Chapter 1 provides an overview of these options. Additional sources that might provide useful insights include the following: *Fired Up! From Corporate Kiss-Off to Entrepreneurial Kick-Off*, by Michael Gill and Sheila Patterson (Viking Press, 800-253-6476) and *Honey, I Want to Start My Own Business*, by Azriela Jaffe (HarperBusiness, 800-236-7323).

There is an abundance of questionnaires found in other books and magazines at bookstores and libraries that try to assist prospects in the determination of their suitability for small business ownership and their chances for success. The questions in

Chapter 1, which test your temperament relating to the risks and challenges of entrepreneurship, are one such example.

One of the most useful steps that you can take to facilitate the beginning stages of your search is to develop specific criteria to be applied against each possible acquisition. Naturally, individuals will select and prioritize their own criteria. General categories for consideration include:

- Miscellaneous Considerations
    1. Close to friends/relatives/schools/hospitals
    2. Abundance of outdoor activities
    3. Allows family to work together
    4. Favorable climate
- Geographic Proximity
    1. Metropolitan/country atmosphere
    2. Particular region, state, or city
    3. Located no more than 30 minutes from home
- Business Criteria
    1. Sales of at least $_____ and adjusted cash flow (ACF) of at least $_____.
    2. Business in operation for at least _____ years with same owner for at least _____ years.
    3. No more than _____ full-time employees
    4. Open for business for no more than _____ hours per day and week
    5. Purchase price no greater than $_____ and down payment no greater than $_____
    6. Working capital requirements no greater than $_____
    7. Sales made on cash basis primarily (no significant credit)
    8. Capable of _____ percent growth per year for _____ years
    9. Seller agrees to remain involved after sale, at least _____ weeks/months
    10. Gross profit margin of at least _____ percent
    11. Lienable assets of at least $_____

All the criteria outlined above can easily be individualized. Knowing what you want in terms of available types and categories of businesses is a good first step. For example, narrowing your search to independent retail gift shops or franchise hair salons will allow you to focus on the specific types of criteria.

Whether you are looking for a start-up, franchise, relocatable business, or a more traditional ongoing concern, an excellent place to begin your search is with a business broker. Ask your friends or associates if they can recommend a broker to you. If this doesn't work, look in your Yellow Pages under business brokerage. Many smaller communities will not have a separate listing for business brokers, which means you will need to look under real estate brokers. If you call a real estate office, make sure that the person you work with is experienced in business brokerage (preferably full-time for several years).

Business brokers may also be found in the classified section of your local newspaper, generally under the business opportunities heading. Realize that many brokers will not devote complete time and energy to a buyer who is calling every broker in town. Remember that most brokers will be working for and will be paid by the seller. Their highest allegiance, therefore, is not to the buyer. Hiring a broker to work for you (buyer's broker) is a viable option and was introduced in Chapter 2.

As introduced in Chapter 1, there are several magazines, newspapers, guides, and trade shows that feature a wide variety of options (also see Appendix B for a comprehensive list of Web sites relating to buying, valuing, and selling your business). Examples include:

- *Today's Business Owner* Magazine (VR Business Brokers, 800-377-8722)
- *The Franchise Handbook* (414-272-9977)
- *Income Opportunities* Magazine (800-289-7852)
- *Business Opportunities Handbook* (414-272-9977)
- *Relocatable Business* (800-927-1310)
- *National Business Exchange* (805-375-0755)
- M&A Marketplace (http://www.webcom.com/cfnet/)
- *The Wall Street Journal* (classified section)
- Nation's List International (800-525-9559)
- Business Exchange Network (510-831-9225)
- Great Western Business Services (800-999-SALE)
- International Business Exchange (512-310-2966)

To locate smaller (sales less than $3 million and cash flow less than $500,000), established, single-owner types of businesses in your area, however, your best bet is the local Sunday newspaper's classified section. Not every newspaper will have extensive business opportunity listings, but all major metropolitan areas will list hundreds of opportunities and contacts. Another option is to look in trade journals for specific types of businesses (e.g., restaurants in *Restaurant Business* (212-986-4800) or *Foodservice Product News* (212-206-7400).

As of December 1996, the magazine *Today's Business Owner* (VR Business Brokers) can be purchased at participating Barnes and Noble superstores across the country. This magazine presents hundreds of established businesses for sale of all types and sizes, listed by region. Phone numbers for the appropriate offices are also available. These ever-changing listings can also be accessed online at http://www.vrbusinessbrokers.com.

If you are seeking larger (sales more than $3 million and cash flow more than $500,000), privately held companies, the trade associations, *The Wall Street Journal* and the M&A Marketplace are good sources. Another avenue for larger acquisitions is through VR M&A, International. Stephen Crisham, president, has participated in and coordinated all facets of dozens of middle market transactions, working closely with local professionals throughout the nation. Having responsibility for the state of Arizona, I will be happy to discuss these opportunities with you (voice mail 602-509-6995), or you may contact Mr. Crisham directly (800-770-8762).

Step 3: Interview and Select Professional Team

Look to Chapter 2 for a thorough review of the wide variety of professionals who can assist in the purchase of a business. Clearly, selecting a business broker, accountant, and attorney are the most important choices to be made. Not only are they productive sources of leads to help you find the right business, but they can help educate you about the entire process and make sure that your interests are protected.

Step 4: Locate and Preliminarily Investigate Opportunities

Broker Meeting

The first meeting will normally be a "getting to know you" session. You can query the broker's background and the broker will ask you questions regarding your work experience, financial resources, credit history, motivations, etc. The focus of the broker's questions will be the extent of your business skills and financial resources and your degree of motivation to buy a business. Your answers will naturally influence how much effort the broker expends in assisting you with your search. *If you are serious about buying a business, make sure the broker is fully aware of this.* Bring a copy of your current resume if you have one, or prepare a one-page summary of your relevant experience. Also, be painstakingly accurate regarding the amount of cash you possess to finance a deal. Be precise as to what form the cash is comprised of (e.g., liquid assets such as CDs and money market funds or less liquid assets such as stocks and treasury bills). If your money is tied up in a pension fund that will require time to access, make sure you disclose this. Most brokers will ask buyers to fill out a personal financial statement (see Chapter 2). According to Anthony Baio, broker with VR Business Brokers (602-949-8612), being forthright about your capabilities (operational and financial) is the most important aspect of this initial interview. Buyers have a tendency to overstate or understate their true cash availability, either out of pride (overstate) or fear of the seller using this fact against them (understate). Misstating the true cash picture can be a waste of everybody's time, including yours! A good broker will begin to educate (or refamiliarize as the case may be) you as to the general steps involved in buying a business. A broker can assist you with the following key steps:

1. Find suitable opportunities, visit locations, and meet with owners
2. Review preliminary financial and nonfinancial information
3. Estimate value, make offer, and negotiate final contract
4. Conduct due diligence review and facilitate closing and transfer of ownership

Within each of these areas, there are often bewildering details and disagreements. The broker should assure you that you can, in effect, make an offer to buy a business without risking anything but your time. Offers are normally made contingent upon many factors, notably a favorable review of the company's books, records, and operations. Any personal checks or money orders written by the purchaser toward the purchase of a business should be made out to either the escrow company or possibly the broker's trust account (under no circumstances should the check be made payable to the seller or the broker personally). These checks normally should be held by the broker uncashed until all contingencies are removed.

The broker should ask you to sign a confidentiality agreement, also known as a nondisclosure agreement (see Chapter 2). If you are not asked to sign such a form, this is an indication that you may not be dealing with a professional intermediary. The main purported purpose behind the confidentiality agreement is to protect the seller and the confidentiality of the sale and all information provided to the buyer. As you can imagine, most sellers do not want their employees, customers, and suppliers to know the business is for sale and minimizing the spread of such knowledge is critical. Other purposes exist as well, such as protecting the broker's right to be paid a commission. By signing the form, the buyer is in effect registering with the broker. Note that the standard nondisclosure form also clearly states that the broker's primary allegiance is to the seller.

The broker should have at least two specific opportunities to introduce to you at this first meeting, providing you with a one-page profile of the business, which outlines the relevant history, financial performance, assets, lease information, and employee data. After reviewing these profiles, there may be a business that you would like to investigate further. If you express genuine interest in a particular business, there may be a comprehensive package of information available (10 to 20 pages) filled with much of the data that you would need to plan your due diligence efforts. If you remain interested, ask the broker to arrange for a preliminary meeting. This will normally occur at the preferred time and location of the seller, who might be fearful of the employees discovering that the business is for sale. The seller must, however, recognize the buyer's need to evaluate the business as thoroughly as possible, including exposure to the operation when it is running at full speed. If it is a retail or service business where customers are routinely walking in and out, it may be possible to *anonymously visit* the business as a customer, being careful not to arouse the suspicion of curious employees or customers.

Owner Meeting

Handle this first meeting with great care. If the seller is impressed with your background and presentation, you are more likely to get a better price and terms and even an elevated commitment to help during and after the transition phase. Research the industry, local competition, and the business itself. Punctuality is a must, and at the appropriate time and manner, schmoozing can strengthen your position and the likelihood of reaching agreement on price and terms. You want the seller to want to sell the business to you above all other purchasers. Despite the gravity of your decision to buy, you must not lose sight of the fact that the seller has spent many long years building this enterprise and is truly selling a part of his or her life!

During your tour, an important check on the fit of the business is to visualize yourself running the business for up to 12 hours per day, six days per week for years to come. Does it feel right? If the thought of being there and taking care of all the daily problems is a positive one, then continue onward. If not, carefully determine why. Establish what it is that doesn't feel right and use this insight to refocus your sights. Also visualize the changes you might make to improve sales and reduce expenses, and ask the owner what changes he or she would make.

In general, you are looking for a *credible reason for sale; timely response from seller to offers/counteroffers; appropriate training commitment; thorough and accurate books and records; reasonable covenant not to compete; acceptable lease terms; and price and terms that allow servicing of debt, earning of a living wage, and a return on the down payment investment.* One practical problem concerns the attempt to get as much information as possible from the seller before you write a formal offer. Some sellers are quite cooperative in this regard, others are not. Larger, more confidential business opportunities will be more challenging when it comes to gleaning information prior to making an offer. If it is a business that you are genuinely interested in, be prepared to write an offer, turn over an earnest check, and wait. Once there is agreement on price and terms (a signed contract), you should have plenty of time to review the company and industry (due diligence). The dilemma is that you may not feel comfortable making an offer until you know more about the business, but the seller will not divulge detailed, confidential information to every prospect who simply asks for it.

Introduction to Adjusted Cash Flow (ACF)

Of all the procedures involved in analyzing, valuing, and buying a business, this is certainly one of the most important and controversial. Cash flow means different things to different people. Proper education in this area is absolutely necessary for all would-be entrepreneurs. Generally speaking, *adjusted cash flow (ACF) is a measure of the pretax cash benefits accruing to a single owner-operator over a period of time, typically one year.* Consider the following concepts that are similar in nature but quite different in practice:

Gross revenues. A measure of total sales, gross revenues contribute to but are distinct from cash flow in a business brokerage context. When you multiply the quantity of units sold (Q) times the prices per unit sold (P), you obtain gross revenues or gross sales.

Net income (earnings after taxes or EAT). This measure is most useful for publicly traded companies that pay dividends. Dividends typically are paid only if a company earns a positive net income. The calculation of net income per GAAP is based on accrual accounting, which recognizes revenues earned and expenses incurred as they happen, regardless of when cash flows in or out. *Net income is first and foremost an accounting measure, which may be significantly different from cash flow.*

Adjusted cash flow. This is the generally accepted measure of cash flow used when evaluating the purchase of most businesses. It is an attempt to measure the total pretax cash benefits accruing to an owner-operator of a business. The significance of this measure lies in its usefulness as a gauge of the true financial success of an ongoing concern. Note that larger businesses will be valued based on uniquely defined measures of cash flow, such as *net free cash flow* (NFCF), as presented in Chapter 9. Beginning with the net income figure on an income statement, certain adjustments are made to reflect the true cash benefits accruing to a single owner-operator. When measuring cash flow based on this procedure, we are attempting to generate a number that is useful in a comparative fashion. All other things being equal, a company with $100,000 ACF is preferred to one with $70,000 ACF. To make these comparisons possible, we adjust the cash flow figures to reflect the efforts of a single owner who is working the business full-time (roughly 50 to 60 hours per week).

Another issue concerns family members (teenagers, college students, elder aunts, uncles, and parents). If they are paid for work beyond their value, cash flow should be adjusted upward. Determining the precise hours and wages involved is often difficult, but should be addressed. It is often difficult for a buyer to know for sure how much time relatives are spending at the business. A common tool in this situation is to watch the business from a distance over a several-day period. This effort on the part of the buyer can pay off in terms of a clearer understanding of who is doing what and how often.

It is also possible for the company's cash flow to be overstated if family members are helping but not receiving compensation. This is common for businesses that seem to be losing money. A spouse might be spending five to ten hours per week (without compensation) paying bills, sending out collection notices, and preparing the financial statements. If this information surfaces, cash flow should be adjusted downward. Also be sure to understand exactly how many hours the owner is working. If the owner is working excessive hours, you should adjust the cash flow figure for hiring additional help. Also, be aware that family employees are occasionally paid "under the table" to avoid payment of significant payroll taxes.

Precise examples for calculating ACF are found in Chapters 8, 9, and 10. *ACF represents the pretax cash benefits accruing to a single owner-operator from the operation of a business before debt service and owner's compensation.* There may be minor differences of opinion as to what constitutes ACF, but the general thrust is indisputable. ACF is typically calculated as the sum of the following items:

	Net income
+	Owner's salary
+	Owner's payroll taxes
+	Owner's benefits (e.g., auto payments, health insurance, travel)
+	Noncash expenses (e.g., depreciation and amortization)
+	Interest expense
+	Nonrecurring, extraordinary expenses
−	One-time, nonrecurring revenues

When evaluating items like owner's perks and one-time expenses and revenues, different approaches might be taken. Being consistent in your calculations from one business to the next will allow you to effectively compare apples to apples. Once again, *ACF represents the amount of cash available to pay income taxes, pay the owner a salary or dividends, retire debt, replace worn out equipment and, hopefully, earn a return on the initial cash down investment.* As you gain experience, you will see how logical the concept is. A common difficulty is being able to accurately evaluate expenditures that may actually be personal expenses (e.g., supplies relating to the owner's hobby). While the general concept is easy to grasp, there are awkward complications. Properly tracking the work and wages of family members is just one example. Another example involves the allocation between cost of goods sold on the income statement and ending inventory on the balance sheet. In this case, the issue concerns how much expense should be recognized (which decreases net income and ACF) for the inventory sold during the year. Under an accrual basis of accounting, typically either first-in, first-out (FIFO) or last-in, first-out (LIFO) will be used to attach costs to the units sold. For small companies that utilize a cash basis, the cost of goods sold might be greatly overstated to the extent that inventory was purchased and expensed, but not sold. A true ACF would be adjusted for this, realizing that some of the purchases of inventory simply increased stock (as opposed to being sold) and should be accounted for accordingly (as an asset, not an expense). In this case, ACF should be increased by an appropriate amount. Note the central role that ACF plays in the Analysis of Purchase Form in Figure 3.1, which you may find useful.

FIGURE 3.1   Analysis of Purchase Form

Analysis of Price and Terms

Line 1:	Total Sales Price	$_____
Line 2:	Down Payment	$_____
Line 3:	Additional Working Capital Infusion	$_____
Line 4:	First Year's Total Cash Investment (2+3)	$_____
Line 5:	Balance Requiring Financing (1–2)	$_____
Line 6:	Length of Note	_____ years
Line 7:	Interest Rate	_____ %
Line 8:	Monthly Payment Amount	$_____
Line 9:	Total Annual Note Payments (Line 8x12)	$_____

Analysis of Adjusted Cash Flow (ACF)

Line 10:	Adjusted Cash Flow (ACF)	$_____
Line 11:	Total Annual Note Payments (from Line 9)	$_____
Line 12:	ACF After Note Payments	$_____
Line 13:	Return on First Year's Investment (12÷14)	_____ %

FIGURE 3.1 Analysis of Purchase Form, continued

Analysis of Stabilized ACF

Line 14:	Desired Owner's Wages	$_____
Line 15:	"Stabilized" ACF (ACF after owner's/manager's salary)	$_____
Line 16:	Total Annual Note Payments (from Line 9)	$_____
Line 17:	Stabilized ACF After Note Payments	$_____
Line 18:	Return on First Year's Investment (17÷4)	_____ %

Lines 1 and 2 can be filled in with either an asking price and down payment or an offered price and down payment. Line 14 can be filled in using either the owner's required salary and perks or a manager's salary. Chapter 6 contains two useful worksheets for calculating ACF.

CHAPTER 4

Preparing Offers or Letters of Intent

Step 5: Write Offer or Letter of Intent

If your interest in a business continues to grow after a thorough preliminary review and a meeting or two with the seller, it is time to take the more serious step of writing an offer or preparing a letter of intent. These efforts are an attempt to discover if there can be a meeting of the minds with the seller regarding price and terms.

Letter of Intent

Some buyers utilize a letter of intent (see Figure 4.1) to facilitate the purchase of a business. Corporate buyers, buyers in states that rely on attorneys to draw up contracts (rather than brokers), and those that have heard of this vehicle and appreciate its simplicity are the major users of letters of intent. According to Sam Stapley, designated broker with VR Business Brokers in Scottsdale, Ariz. (602-949-8612), a letter of intent is basically a gentleman's agreement that allows the buyer to comfortably look closer at a business before committing to a binding contract.

Letters of intent are generally nonbinding, unless specifically stated otherwise, even though they call for written acceptance by the seller. They are often used to avoid the active involvement of a broker in the sales process. *Their attractive features can at the same time be their greatest weaknesses.* First, because they are often general in nature, many issues are left open to confusion and potentially untimely bickering. Being completely nonbinding and normally without an earnest deposit, it is perhaps too easy for the buyer to "get a look" and take the business off the market. Many brokers believe that it is in the best interest of the seller and the deal in general to prepare a standard offer for purchase contract. Purchase offer forms address most of the significant issues involved in buying or selling a business. For buyers concerned about the binding aspect of an offer, a standard offer for purchase/purchase agreement form allows for contingencies. They may be "boiler-plated" contingencies (such as due diligence) or written in per addendum (such as bank financing). Although legal interpretations as to when such an agreement becomes binding will differ, the general feeling is that a deal is *not* a deal until all contingencies are removed (nonbinding until all contingencies are removed). Therefore, a standard *offer for purchase is also nonbinding until the business is thoroughly examined, contingencies are removed, and escrow is opened.* Please review the letter of intent in Figure 4.1.

FIGURE 4.1   Letter of Intent

LETTER OF INTENT

Dear Sir:

1) The purpose of this letter is to inform you of our interest in acquiring the stock and/or assets of your company _____. We intend to purchase your business via a formal purchase agreement, incorporating the key elements listed below:

2) Price to be $_____ consisting of $_____ cash in certified funds at closing as a down payment and a $_____ note payable over ___ years at ___ percent interest.

3) The intent is to acquire all assets and assume all liabilities listed on the balance sheet at the time of closing. The specific assets and liabilities will be listed in detail and included as part of the formal purchase agreement. Certain assets and liabilities may not be included as part of the sale.

4) Purchaser reserves the right to obtain a portion of the down payment from outside financing sources and to obtain these funds by using the company's assets as collateral.

5) The offer is contingent upon a complete and satisfactory due diligence review of the company's books, records, and operations, with such review expected to be finished within ___ days. The formal purchase offer will contain standard seller warranties and representations concerning the business. In order to draft such a formal offer, we are requesting access to the following information to be reviewed by our advisers:

1. _____ 4. _____
2. _____ 5. _____
3. _____ 6. _____

FIGURE 4.1 Letter of Intent, continued

6) Seller agrees to continue operating business in a normal fashion by meeting all financial obligations and maintaining the cash balances and net worth amount within ___ percent of the levels as of the day this letter of intent is signed by seller. Seller promises to notify buyer if there are any material changes, current or anticipated, to company's financial and operating position.

7) All expenses incurred by either party concerning this review period shall be borne exclusively by the party incurring such expenses. Seller agrees to provide full access to company information for the buyer's auditors and legal staff.

8) Please note that this letter attempts only to outline our intent to evaluate your company in good faith, as described above, and is not meant to be a legally binding agreement.

We look forward to working further with you and successfully concluding a deal.

Buyer: _____ Date: _____   Seller: _____ Date: _____

Although the buyer is obligated to nothing, the seller has promised to provide substantial proprietary information, a truly lopsided situation. Fortunately for the seller, there is no commitment to take the business off the market, which means that new prospects and offers can be entertained. It is fairly common for the buyer to request that the seller remove the business from the open market during the due diligence period. Unless a buyer agrees to a partially nonrefundable escrow deposit, sellers will feel justified in continued showings of the business. If the buyer resists allowing the seller to continue working with the new prospects, the seller might agree to inform the buyer of any offers that come through during the due diligence period and possibly give a formal *right of first refusal*.

Offer to Purchase

A more comprehensive document than the letter of intent, the offer to purchase (also called purchase offer, purchase contract, contract to purchase, purchase agreement, sales contract, etc.) is also more commonly utilized. There are infinite numbers of actual contracts, containing various clauses, contingencies, conditions, covenants, representations, and warranties. Brokers will use standardized contracts that have proven the test of time while attorneys utilize a series of paragraphs. Their agreements are also standardized to the extent that they will tend to use the same paragraphs from one deal to the next, making adjustments as necessary. Neither format is preferable, as it is the content that matters above all else. Buyers will try to control the format and content right from the start. Sellers have been known to respond to initial offers with counteroffers that are of a completely different type of format, trying to gain control themselves. The outcome is a function of the relative expertise and bargaining strength of each side. Every purchase contract should contain at least the following components:

1. Type of sale (asset versus stock)
2. Price, down payment, and terms of repayment
3. Buyer and seller contingencies, with deadline for removal
4. Covenants, indemnifications, warranties, and representations (buyer and seller)
5. Miscellaneous conditions and definitions
6. General list of liabilities/contracts/other obligations to be assumed by new owner
7. General list of all assets to be included in the sale (tangible and intangible, as per IRS Form 8594). Assets specifically excluded should also be accounted for.
8. Miscellaneous schedules, documents, and attachments
9. Closing date

At this point, it may be wise to review the purchase agreement in Figure 4.2 at the end of this section. Presently we are focusing on the many contractual clauses that are most applicable to the buyer, but obviously both parties must agree to all provisions. Peruse Chapter 13 for seller-oriented clauses. Let's discuss the components listed above.

Stock versus Asset Sale

One of the first decisions to be made by the seller of corporations (S or C) is whether to sell the company's stock or its assets. Material differences exist between a stock sale and an asset sale. Although the great majority of smaller transactions are completed as asset sales, primarily as a result of buyers wanting to avoid unknown liabilities and wanting to redepreciate the fixed assets, most larger transactions occur as sale of corporate stock. Deals can be made or broken depending upon a party's strong preference for one structure or the other. Chapter 13 contains a condensed review of the advantages and disadvantages of each option to both the buyer and the seller. It is the seller who faces the immediate tax liability associated with the sale of the business, so more times than not this decision will be more pressing to the seller. The seller is also interested in being released from liabilities associated with past actions. Additionally, the seller normally has only one level of tax to pay if the stock is sold (capital gain). If assets are sold, there may be a tax on the sale of the assets first and then on the liquidating dividends. Buyers, on the other hand, do not easily accept the idea of assuming all liabilities, known and unknown, no matter how detailed the seller's covenants, representations, and warranties are. The ultimate decision is dependent on relative bargaining strengths and other factors such as price, seller financing, and employment contracts.

Our present focus is on contractual issues surrounding a sale of stock, culminating in review of a comprehensive contract for the sale of such stock. *The majority of contingencies, conditions, covenants, warranties, representations, and miscellaneous terms that apply to an asset deal also apply to a stock deal.* Noticeable differences between the asset sale and stock sale in terms of the final purchase agreement concern:

- Precise description of shares being transferred
- Amount of assumed liabilities, inherited cash (bank accounts), and accounts receivables
- Expanded covenants covering changes in corporate, financial, or legal structure prior to closing
- Presence of stock pledge agreement (regardless of other security interests)

Please be advised that attorney guidance is probably even more important in this realm than that of the sale of assets. A detailed agreement is shown in Figure 4.2. Your attorney may not find all clauses necessary to your situation. Selected commentary will follow.

FIGURE 4.2   Corporate Stock Sales Agreement
(Exhibits referred to in Figure are not included in Figure)

CORPORATE STOCK SALES AGREEMENT

THIS AGREEMENT is made and entered into on _____, 19_____, between *name of authorized officer(s)* of *selling company, Inc.*, (hereunder referred to as seller) and *name of authorized officer(s)* of *buying company, Inc.* (hereinafter referred to as buyer). Seller is desirous to sell to buyer and buyer is desirous to purchase from seller, all shares of *selling company, Inc.* (hereinafter referred to as *SCI*) under the terms contained in this agreement.

WHEREBY seller is owner of all issued and outstanding shares of stock for *SCI* and is desirous of selling/transferring all such shares to the buyer, with the goal that upon completion of said sale, buyer will be sole and controlling shareholder of all issued and outstanding shares of stock for *SCI*, and as an inducement for seller to join in agreement with buyer, *name of authorized officials* hereby agree to personally guarantee certain obligations of *SCI* as described herein and in exchange for good and valuable consideration of the many arrangements, conditions, stipulations, terms, covenants, warranties, and representations contained herein, the following articles are jointly and reciprocally agreed among the parties:

FIGURE 4.2   Corporate Stock Sales Agreement, continued

(Article 1)

Description of Total Purchase Price

The purchase price paid to *SCI* by buyer for all shares of *SCI* shall be based upon the following asset values and assumed liabilities. Buyer agrees to pay seller for the purchase and redemption of all said shares a sum equaling the original cost of all inventory in stock at time of closing (as described below and listed on Exhibit 1) plus an additional *$150,000* from which all existing, assumed liabilities at closing (Exhibit 2) shall be deducted (also described below). For example, if inventory shall be $75,000 and total assumed liabilities equal $45,000, the total, final purchase price shall be $150,000 + $75,000 − $45,000 = $180,000. Additionally, certain liquid assets, personal artifacts, and automobiles will be transferred to seller from *SCI* (as described below ad listed in Exhibit 3). As concerns calculation of inventory cost, *SCI* and buyer agree to hire an independent third party (the Inventory Counters, Inc.) to tally such values on the day prior to closing. Invoice cost properly adjusted for relevant trade discounts and purchase discounts plus delivery costs shall serve as the calculation formula. Based upon the experienced, professional judgment of said third party, reductions from cost may be made for merchandise deemed to be damaged or otherwise unmerchantable, with such inventory being returned to *SCI* (partial values may be utilized). Such determination by third party shall be fully binding without recourse by *SCI* or buyer. Fees incurred regarding inventory counting shall be split 50-50 between *SCI* and buyer.

As concerns existing liabilities to be assumed by buyer, this shall be deemed to mean all financial obligations, debts, and liabilities of the buyer that exist or accrue at the time of closing (transfer), which includes, among others, the following:

1. Accounts payable to vendors
2. Wages and payroll taxes payable
3. Rents payable (real and personal property)
4. Notes payable (banks and nonbanks)

Any and all such obligations of all types, sizes, and descriptions, whether collateralized or unsecured, presently due or due in the future, fixed or variable, known or contingent (known and unknown), primary or secondary, disputed or uncontested, are to be included in this corporation and listed on Exhibit 2. Exceptions include any obligations that are deemed to be 100 percent covered by insurance policies and any fees relating to late payments that are incurred after ownership is transferred.

As concerns those assets that are to be transferred to the selling corporation (*SCI*) and its principals as of the day of closing, they shall include the following, and be listed with sufficient detail on Exhibit 3:

FIGURE 4.2   Corporate Stock Sales Agreement, continued

1. *All paintings and decorative memorabilia contained in corporate offices*
2. *Two automobiles (1997 Mercedes Benz and 1996 Chrysler Minivan)*
3. *All cash on hand (petty cash) and in accounts (passbook savings account, checking accounts, and five certificates of deposit)*
4. *All company receivables of all types*

Payment of Total Purchase Price

As concerns actual payment of the total purchase price, such payments shall be structured as follows in accordance with the provisions of the above paragraphs:

1. *$75,000* down payment at closing, in the form of a certified check or cash, payable to *SCI*
2. *$105,000* approximate seller carry-back note, to be adjusted as of closing for actual inventory and transferred liabilities.

Further adjustments (prorations) to be made at closing include the following:

1. Rent
2. Utilities
3. Accrued payroll (wages and taxes)
4. Personal property taxes
5. Prepaid expenses (e.g., insurance, maintenance contracts)
6. Transfer taxes
7. Other

Said carry-back balance to be evidenced by a signed promissory note, payable monthly over *five* years, at *10* percent interest, as clarified in Exhibit 4. This note will be secured via a chattel security agreement (lien) against all transferred assets, to be perfected via UCC-1 filing and as otherwise required (Exhibit 5). Additionally, buyer will personally guarantee said note payment (Exhibit 6) and execute a stock pledge agreement (Exhibit 7) covering all issued and outstanding shares by buyer relating to purchase of *SCI*.

(Article 2)

Closing Date

The delivery to buyer of certificates for the shares of *SCI* sold hereunder by *authorized officer(s)* and the payment of the initial installment of the purchase price thereof by buyer to seller will be at noon on _____ 19__(hereinafter referred to as the "closing date") at the offices of _____, located in

_____.

FIGURE 4.2   Corporate Stock Sales Agreement, continued

(Article 3)

Delivery of Certificates

Seller hereby agrees to sell and transfer and the buyer agrees to purchase all shares of stock in *SCI* (common shares, evidenced by stock certificate #1). Accordingly, on the closing date, seller shall deliver to buyer the certificates evidencing shares of *SCI* agreed to be sold hereunder, duly endorsed for transfer, and buyer shall pay seller the sum of *seventy-five thousand dollars ($75,000)* representing the initial installment of the purchase price to be paid for said shares by buyer. Said shares will be immediately pledged to seller as collateral for promissory note. The balance of approximately *one hundred and five thousand dollars ($105,000)* will be paid by buyer to seller in the amounts and dates indicated in Article 1 after which time seller shall deliver to buyer all such certificates of shares stated therein, reflecting payment in full.

(Article 4)

Representations/Warranties

Seller warrants, represents, and agrees as follows:

a) Seller has full and absolute title to all shares of *SCI* (all classes) to be sold pursuant to this agreement.

b) Seller warrants that there are no existing outstanding subscriptions to sell additional shares, no outstanding proxies, assignment of rights or any other type of transfer mechanism. Seller's title to said shares is free and clear of any lien, charge, pledge, encumbrance, or sequestrations while said shares constitute all of the outstanding shares of *SCI* and by sale said shares hereunder, buyer will receive good and marketable title thereto, free from any liens, charges, or other encumbrances.

c) *SCI* is a corporation duly organized, registered, and existing by virtue of the laws of the State of _____ and is accordingly in good standing.

d) All required tax returns, past and present, have been properly filed and paid.

e) *SCI* has free and clear title to all assets included in sale (unless clearly described on Exhibit 8).

f) The current property lease (shown at Exhibit 9) is in full operational force and effect, without modification and without breach of any kind. There are no current or anticipated eviction proceedings or other planned actions that might harm buyer's future interest in said lease.

g) All existing security interests, lease-option arrangements, liens, and encumbrances are described in full in Exhibit 8. The UCC-1 statements referred to remain in full force without current or impending default or proceedings to terminate, repossess, or foreclose on related assets.

FIGURE 4.2   Corporate Stock Sales Agreement, continued

h) There are no current or pending governmental audits or lawsuits against the business (except as described in Exhibit 10).

i) That all contracts entered into by corporation are cancelable at will, without penalty and excepting property lease and secured assets listed on Exhibits 8 and 9.

j) All information presented in all Exhibits referred to above are true and accurate to the best knowledge of the seller.

k) Said outstanding shares of said corporation have heretofore duly been issued and are valid, fully paid, and no assessment is outstanding against the same or any part thereof

l) *Name of authorized officer* is presently the President of *SCI* and is fully authorized to execute all documents required to transfer shares.

m) On _____ 19_____ *SCI* shall have the amount of inventory necessary for the normal operation of a _____ in accordance with the inventory to be taken on the day prior. Seller makes no representations or guarantees as to the exact dollar amount of inventory to be in existence on the day prior to closing except that it shall be between *$65,000* and *$85,000*.

n) All representations and warranties of seller contained in this agreement shall survive the closing, shall remain in full force and effect, shall not merge or terminate, and shall inure to the benefit of buyer and his representative successors and assigns.

(Article 5)

Books and Records

During the period from the date of this contract to the date of closing, seller shall allow buyer and buyer's accountant and lawyer access to *SCI's* records, files, financial statements, all tax returns, and other requested documents and computer records, provided that buyer's investigation shall not unduly interfere with seller's normal operations. Buyer agrees not to disclose, share, sell or use at any time or in any way information obtained regarding *SCI* which was acquired in connection with this purchase agreement. Buyer to take all necessary and reasonable steps to prevent any other persons from acquiring confidential information obtained from *SCI*.

(Article 6)

Licenses

Buyer shall obtain all required approvals from the proper authority facilitating this change in corporate ownership. Buyer agrees to bear all related costs to obtain said approval. Seller agrees to cooperate in signing all required paperwork relevant thereto.

FIGURE 4.2   Corporate Stock Sales Agreement, continued

(Article 7)

Covenants

Between the signing of the contract and *closing date SCI* will not:

a. conduct any liquidation or going out of business sales, transfer, sell, or otherwise dispose of any corporate property or assets material to the operation of its business other than in the ordinary and normal course of day to day business

b. create, participate in, or agree to the creation of any liens or encumbrances on its corporate property, with the exception of those created in the routine day to day operations of the business

c. enter into any leases, contracts, or agreements of any kind or character or incur any liabilities except those to which it is presently committed (Exhibits 2, 8, and 9) or those arising in the ordinary and normal course of business as previously conducted

d. make any payments, liquidating dividends, or distributions to any officers, shareholders, or employees, except dividends, wages, and salaries made to employees in the ordinary and usual course of the business as normally conducted

e. make any changes to the bylaws, articles of incorporation, or board of directors

f. amend or repeal its articles of incorporation or bylaws or reissue any treasury shares

Note: any of these restrictive covenants may be overridden with the signed approval of buyer

(Article 8)

Successors and Assigns

The contents of this agreement shall inure to the benefit of and bind the successors and assigns of buyer and seller and their heirs, executors, administrators, successors, and assigns.

(Article 9)

Life Insurance

Buyer shall pay life insurance premiums in support of buyer's life with all proceeds payable in the event of buyer's death during the life of this purchase contract. The amount of insurance coverage (Keyman Policy) shall decline in proportion to the remaining outstanding balance of the promissory note owed by buyer.

(Article 10)

Seller Warranty and Indemnification

Seller hereby represents and warrants to buyer that only those liabilities listed on Exhibit 3 shall require assumption. If any additional debts, liabilities, or other

FIGURE 4.2   Corporate Stock Sales Agreement, continued

obligations arise or are claimed to exist by creditors subsequent to closing, then the buyer shall have all available rights to indemnify as against seller pursuant to agreement outlined in Exhibit 11 (indemnity agreement). If seller refuses to sign and/or fully indemnify buyer per said agreement, the buyer (or buyer's corporation) may choose to reduce or eliminate the remaining note payments owed to seller for such undisclosed liabilities (right of offset).

(Article 11)

Covenant Not to Compete

In partial exchange for the valuable consideration received by seller for the sale of this business, seller hereby covenants not to compete with buyer in accordance with the noncompete agreement attached to this contract (Exhibit 12). It is agreed and understood that the consideration therefore shall be *ten* dollars only.

(Article 12)

Familiarization Clause

Seller hereby agrees to hand over all corporate records (including but not limited to sales invoices, tax returns, purchase orders, insurance policies, corporate records and minutes, and all written and computer documents. In addition to turning over such materials, seller agrees to cooperate fully in familiarizing buyer with all material aspects of the day to day operations of the business for a period of *two weeks, full-time (40 hours per week)* and then by phone for up to *five* hours per week for *three* months.

(Article 13)

Officer Resignations

Seller agrees to provide buyer with signed resignations of all departing officers and directors (as noted in Exhibit 13), leaving buyer as sole shareholder and causing buyer to change officers and directors and report such changes to the appropriate state agency.

(Article 14)

Finder's Fee

Buyer and seller acknowledge that _____ (broker) has facilitated the consummation of this transaction by introducing the parties and has earned a finder's fee to be paid solely by seller at time of closing.

(Article 15)

Miscellaneous

The following miscellaneous terms, facts, conditions, and comments are hereby acknowledged and understood by buyer and seller:

FIGURE 4.2   Corporate Stock Sales Agreement, continued

1. This contract represents the entire understanding between the parties and any subsequent changes to this agreement must be mutually agreed upon and in writing.
2. This contract is executed with copies, all of which shall have the full force of law similar to the originals.
3. Buyer and seller agree to undertake, execute, and complete all actions and paperwork reasonably necessitated to live up to the provisions and goals of this agreement.
4. Time is of the essence in carrying out the terms and conditions of this agreement.
5. In the event that there is a major casualty to the business (causing harm equal to 15 percent or more of the business assets), buyer shall have option to terminate this agreement.
6. Buyer and seller agree that in the event of any disputes regarding this agreement, the rules and procedures of the American Arbitration Association will be followed with the findings to be binding for both parties. The place of arbitration shall be _____.
7. In the event that any provisions of this agreement are found to be invalid or unenforceable in any court of competent jurisdiction, the validity and enforceability of the remaining provisions or portions thereof shall not be affected thereby, remaining in full force and effect.
8. Compliance by buyer and seller with any of the provisions of this agreement may be waived by the other party. No waiver of any provision shall be construed as a waiver of any other provisions. All waivers must be in writing and notarized.
9. This agreement may be executed in several counterparts, all of which together shall constitute one agreement, binding on all parties hereto.
10. All risk of loss or damage to the assets being sold herein or to the company premises shall be seller's responsibility prior to closing with such responsibilities passing to buyer as of closing.

(Article 16)

Notices

All notices required or permitted to be given hereunder shall be in writing and shall be sent by registered mail to the following locations:

Buyer _____

Seller _____

Addresses may be changed via written notice (registered mail).

FIGURE 4.2 Corporate Stock Sales Agreement, continued

(Article 17)

Withdrawal of Offer

In the event that buyer is unable to satisfactorily prove/verify the amount of sales, cash flow, and assets presented in the offering memorandum provided by broker, buyer may unilaterally withdraw from all obligations under this contract, or attempt to renegotiate for a different price and/or terms.

Comments Regarding Stock Sales Agreement

Many of the terms, conditions, contingencies, warranties, covenants, and representations contained in an asset sale are precisely the same as in a stock sale. Major differences were mentioned in the beginning of this section. Consider the following comments:

1. Stock sales almost always require a "formula" price, owing to the final adjustments of inventory and liabilities. Although inventory is commonly adjusted for an asset sale, many times it is simply ignored for smaller stock and asset sales after agreeing upon an acceptable value. Large inventory values require careful scrutiny and professional counting. Exact balances on assumed liabilities are also required.

2. Given the requirement for key officers of a small corporation to personally guarantee many of the corporate obligations, it is important for the seller to terminate, eliminate, or otherwise escape from these potential burdens. Many creditors are not willing to release the principal and seek to strengthen their position by requiring the new party to personally guarantee the debt as well (leased equipment, for example). If the secured party will not release the seller immediately, it is prudent to ask for release after the new principal proves his willingness and ability to pay (e.g., six months or one year later). At a minimum, the seller should seek indemnification and warranties from the buyer regarding those liabilities.

3. Although this particular sale is of existing shares, there are circumstances where the new owner is better served by asking the seller to retire the existing shares and issue new shares to the buyer to consummate the deal. This is done for legal reasons (relating to unknown liabilities, for example), which are worth discussing with your attorney.

4. The word "material" is a disaster waiting to happen. As any good contract writer will tell you, precise and clear verbiage is ideal. Defining material to be 5 percent or more of sales, net income, or ACF is better than simply using the word material.

5. The words "indemnify" and "indemnity" are also used frequently. As described later, the indemnification section of an agreement establishes the liability of each party to the other related to problems or disputes that arise prior to and then subsequent to the closing and describes the options available to each party if either chooses to recover damages.

6. A distinction worthy of clarification is between the buyer (seller) and the buyer's (seller's) corporation. Legally speaking, buyer and seller individually are separate entities from their corporations. Complicated legal concepts, personally executed documents, and the reality of case law often blurs this distinction and in many cases requires a current and qualified interpretation by legal counsel. Even corporate guarantees may be vulnerable to personal liability where the "corporate veil" can be pierced.

7. In a stock purchase, there is no allocation of the purchase price. The buyer simply assumes all assets and liabilities as they are. For tax purposes, the buyer will inherit the existing status of depreciation schedules and net operating losses. The gain or loss on the subsequent sale of stock is a capital gain or loss (not ordinary income). *Consult your tax professional for pertinent advice regarding the sale of stock in small businesses.* The Revenue Reconciliation Act of 1993 created a special tax provision that reduces the capital gains tax in half if the stock is held for five or more years (C-corporation only).

8. There is a fluid market in most large metropolitan areas for the purchase (discounting) of seller carry-back notes. Note buyers are looking for "seasoned" paybacks (timely payments for at least one year) and high returns (they will pay the seller as little as 50 percent on the dollar). The buyer will be affected by who owns this "paper," who may not be as lenient or understanding if payment difficulties arise. It may be in the interest of the buyer to obtain a "right of first refusal" on the sale of this paper.

9. Contrary to Article 8 regarding successors and assigns, which amounts to the buyer or seller being able to "assign" all rights and responsibilities to third parties without approval of the other party, it may be wise to deny or restrict such assignment rights. Consider the following:

> The rights of the seller under this agreement are not assignable or transferable without buyer's written consent. No party other than the seller shall be a third party of any obligation, agreement, or promise of buyer hereunder. No assignee or successor in interest of seller shall be a third party beneficiary of any such obligation, agreement, or promise. Any attempted assignment by seller without the required consent shall be void.

> One reason for this restriction is that the buyer may not want to deal with a third party regarding the note payments (particularly if there is an earn-out provision, which generally requires cooperation between the parties). The buyer may feel that he has more control (negotiating power) over the seller than over a new party or the buyer may seek to keep the seller involved in the business.

10. Arbitration is increasingly popular among even sophisticated parties who seek to minimize legal fees. Many options exist. Consider the following clauses:

Jurisdiction of Disputes "Any controversy, dispute, or claim arising out of or relating to this agreement, or the breach thereof, that cannot be resolved amicably by the parties shall be settled by arbitration in accordance with the Rules of the American Arbitration Association, except that whether or not arbitration has been requested or is in process, nothing herein shall prevent any Party from pursuing equitable remedies, including interim relief, in any court of competent jurisdiction, and except as may be unanimously otherwise agreed by the parties.

(i) The place of arbitration shall be _____ unless in any particular case the parties agree upon a different venue. There shall be three (3) arbitrators of all disputes arising under this Agreement. All of the three arbitrators shall be picked by the American Arbitration Association in accordance with its rules, interpreted to give effect to the provisions of this Agreement.

(ii) The parties will proceed with the arbitration expeditiously and will conclude all arbitration proceedings in order that a decision may be rendered within 180 days from the service of the demand for arbitration by the initiating Party unless the Party requesting arbitration also requests immediate arbitration, in which case the arbitrators shall use their best efforts to render their decision within 60 days after the appointment. Subject to the foregoing time limitations in connection with the arbitration the parties shall be afforded reasonable opportunity for deposition and document discovery, subject to limitations determined by the arbitrators. The dispute shall be resolved by majority vote of the three arbitrators, if three are acting. Such decision shall be expressed in writing, including the reasons for such decision in reasonable detail.

(iii) The award of the arbitrators shall be final and binding upon the parties and judgment thereon may be entered in any court having jurisdiction thereof. In the event that the arbitrators determine by majority vote that the claim or defense of any Party involved in the arbitration was frivolous (i.e., without justifiable merit), the arbitrators may by majority vote require that the Party at fault pay or reimburse the other Party for any or all of the following: (1) all fees and expenses of the arbitrators, (2) the reasonable attorney's fees of such other Party, and (3) any other reasonable out-of-pocket expenses incurred by such other Party in connection with the arbitration proceeding. The arbitrators shall determine and decide all issues that arise in carrying out the purposes and intent of the foregoing unless specific provision is made herein for resolving such issues.

11. Let me stress two important concepts. First, get it in writing! There are rare circumstances where verbal agreements will suffice (legal, valid, and enforceable), but it is recommended that all agreements be in writing. Additionally, any changes to a contract should require written documentation and possibly notarization with witnesses. Any changes made to an existing contract in the form of handwritten, additional verbiage should be initialed and dated by all relevant parties (i.e., buyer, seller, broker). Second, inserting the phrase "time is of the essence" in your contract will eliminate the possible ambiguity that clever lawyers can manipulate.

12. As discussed in Chapter 13, the sale of stock is governed by federal statutes relating to the SEC. The sale of stock for most small businesses will be considered an exempt transaction, but larger transactions may require careful consideration and specific attorney advice. The following warranty is contained in the escrow paperwork prepared for presumably exempt stock sales:

> The undersigned buyer and seller hereby warrant that they have obtained a legal opinion that the sale of the corporate stock by seller to buyer is an exempt transaction pursuant to _____(insert relevant state law)_____, same being a sale by bonafide owners of stock as an isolated transaction directly to buyer and buyer understands and agrees that he has examined the books of the corporation and that the stock sold hereunder need not be qualified by description or qualifications. Buyer and seller hereby indemnify and save harmless escrow agent against any responsibility or liability regarding the transfer or sale of said stock.

Price, Down Payment, and Repayment Terms

The successful completion of every deal begins with agreement on price and repayment terms. The buyer naturally seeks the lowest price while the seller seeks the highest. The buyer begins by making an offer based on his or her preliminary review of the presented data, including the seller's asking price and terms. Most buyers will not make an offer (even with a risk-free, refundable escrow deposit) until they have seen current financial statements. After one or two meetings with the seller and time to review the presented data, an interested buyer will make a formal offer. This offer is made assuming that all the presented financial statements are accurate. If they ultimately prove to be inaccurate, the buyer's earnest check is fully refundable (unless otherwise agreed upon). The offer will outline the full price, timing, and amount of down payment and precise terms of repayment. The full price is normally stated in terms of cash payments, but may include stock or other types of consideration such as land, real estate, or note assumptions.

The exact final price may be indeterminate in the case of an *earn-out*. Typical earn-out arrangements include linkage of all future payments to future actual gross sales revenue, booked; future actual taxable income, per Schedule C; or future actual number of customers served. The idea of linking future payments to the success of the business is appealing because it allows the buyer to make payments in proportion to the realized performance of the company. Acquisitions that are high risk to the buyer may be salable only under such terms. Second, it creates added incentive on the part of the seller to help the new owner succeed. The main difficulty is choosing a repayment mechanism that is fair to the seller (see Chapter 7 for detailed commentary).

More common than the earn-out is a standard seller's carry-back note. A deal may be struck, for example, based on a down payment of $50,000 coupled with a promissory note of $100,000, payable monthly for six years at 10 percent per annum. The buyer must personally guarantee this note and possibly offer specific collateral beyond the assets of the acquired business. Buyers will try to secure seller financing without personally guaranteeing the debt, but most sellers are not impressed with corporate guarantees (corporations can easily be sold, liquidated, shuffled, recapitalized, or terminated). Only large, publicly traded companies are relied on for this type of guarantee and even then key officers may be asked to sign personal guarantees.

Promissory Note, Bill of Sale, and Chattel Security Agreement

An important aspect of buying or selling a business concerns the willingness of the seller to offer terms. Buyers seek financing from the seller to maximize the size of business purchased (and its corresponding ACF) and to keep the seller interested in the performance of the business subsequent to closing. Offering terms increases the likelihood that the business will sell and may enhance the final, realized compensation to the seller. Given the low level of market interest rates in existence today, a 9 or 10 percent return on lent money is also attractive. Finally, selling a business with an installment note can generate favorable tax consequences for the seller (i.e., spread out the capital gain over several periods). If you are looking for a more "solid" or "fixed" payback schedule, but still seek some flexibility in the timing of the repayment, consider the following options:

Variable Rate Note

Similar to the home loan variety, this arrangement ties the actual interest rate charged on outstanding balances to major bellwether interest rates, such as the prime rate listed in *The Wall Street Journal*. This mechanism ensures that the seller doesn't get stuck with below market returns and the buyer doesn't get stuck with above market rates.

Balloon Payment Note

This mechanism reduces the required monthly payments for a predetermined period of months or years, allowing the new owner time to accrue sufficient cash balances from operations or from outside sources. One scenario provides for interest-only payments for a six to twelve month period with the entire principal balance to be paid in full via subsequently obtained bank financing. This allows the buyer time to obtain a bank loan without having to postpone or delay the closing. This setup requires great trust on the part of the seller in the buyer's ability to obtain this outside financing. To protect the seller's interest, the buyer must be willing to lose his or her down payment if the attempt to obtain this outside financing fails.

Principal Reduction Note

The concept here is based on the seasonal nature of many businesses (e.g., retail stores during the holidays, accounting practices during tax season, and pool service companies during the summer). This scheme calls for periodic (annual, biannual) lump-sum reductions in principal in addition to the appropriate monthly interest and principal payments.

There are many possibilities regarding the scheduling of note payments from the buyer to the seller. Tailoring your specific needs to a given format is worth consideration. *In practice, however, most notes represent straight amortization, fixed rate loans, payable in equal monthly installments over a definitive period of time.*

Promissory Note

The primary document evidencing the credit extended by the seller and assumed by the buyer is the promissory note, which is a legal IOU executed by the buyer (borrower, debtor, maker) in favor of the seller (lender, creditor, payee). Promissory notes take many forms depending on the needs of the parties and the aggressiveness of the attorneys and brokers. I have seen deals proceed to the actual closing before both parties recognize that more detailed terms are required to complete the financing arrangements. Brokers or attorneys should ensure that the seller's interest is protected and the buyer's position is not compromised *before* reaching the closing!

If the actual purchase agreement is silent as to specific terms and conditions for the promissory note, and an escrow company is being utilized, the escrow company will infuse certain basic terms and conditions as it prepares the note. Importantly, however, the escrow company may not spell out the details covering prepayment, late payment penalties, or default conditions. It is then left to the buyer, seller, broker, and other representatives to clarify these issues. This is wisely accomplished prior to rather than during the closing. Precise definitions, conditions, and preferably descriptive examples for all the following areas should be incorporated into a promissory note:

Key Areas Addressed in Promissory Note
- late payment dates and penalties / prepayment conditions
- default conditions and related remedies; reentry rights in the event of default
- amount and type of collateral and guarantee (personal and/or corporate)

- relationship between note payments and lease payments (e.g., cross default clause)
- clearly defined payment structure (e.g., interest only, straight amortization)
- interest rate equal to at least the U.S. Treasury rate for similar term debt instruments
- acceleration clause (due on sale clause)/transfer or assignment rights (right of first refusal)

A sample promissory note and related guaranty statement is shown in Figure 4.3.

FIGURE 4.3   Promissory Note

PROMISSORY NOTE

For good and valuable consideration received, I (we) hereby jointly and severally promise to pay to the order of _____, located at
_____ , the amount of _____ dollars ($_____), plus interest at the per annum rate of ___ percent, on all unpaid balances. The following terms and conditions shall apply:

Payments

Monthly payments in the amount of $_____ each, due on or before the ____ day of each month, beginning on _____,19__ and each month thereafter, until all interest and principal are paid in full. In any case, the entire principal balance together with all accrued interest shall be due in full on or before _____, 19__. There will be no penalty for prepayments of principal.

All principal and interest payments to be paid in legal tender of the United States of America. The payers and endorsers hereof waive grace, presentment, demand, notice of dishonor and protest, and all notices thereto, and further agree to remain bound, excepting any extension, modification, or other concessions by holder (lender) or upon discharge or release of any obligor hereunder or part of this note, or upon substitution, exchange, release, or dismissal of any collateral granted as security for this promissory note, until this note is paid in full. Any such changes or modifications must be in writing and notarized.

Security

This note is formally secured by a chattel security lien, executed against all the assets of the business noted above, including all tangible and intangible assets, unless specifically excluded per the purchase contract, and as described per Attachment A to said contract. Borrower hereby further agrees to personally guarantee all obligations under this note, as per Attachment B to said purchase contract.

FIGURE 4.3   Promissory Note, continued

Acceleration

All outstanding principal and interest shall be considered fully due and payable immediately upon the occurrence of any of the following events, which shall be deemed as a default on the part of the borrower:

1) Monthly payment is not received within 10 days of due date referred to above
2) Breach of conditions outlined in the chattel security agreement, personal guarantee, stock pledge agreement, or any other security related provision
3) Death, dissolution, or liquidation of the undersigned, or any related guarantor or endorser
4) Filing of bankruptcy (voluntary or involuntary) or formal assignment of rights for the benefit of other creditors

Default

In the event of default as described above, the borrower hereby agrees to pay all reasonable legal and court fees related to collection efforts. Payments owed but not paid within ten days of due date shall be subject to an additional late fee equal to 10 percent of such payment. All payments will be mailed to the official address of lender as listed below, unless designated in writing otherwise (notarized).

Modifications

Any and all changes/modifications of terms granted by holder shall be binding and valid provided such changes are in writing and notarized. Each of the signed parties below (lender, borrower) hereby irrevocably grants the other party a specific power of attorney to make such changes/additions/modifications on its behalf.

Miscellaneous

This promissory note will take effect as a formal, sealed, instrument to be construed, interpreted, governed, applied, and enforced per the laws of the state of _____. As indicated in a previous paragraph, this note is secured by the referenced chattel security agreement.

City: _____   Creditor(s) (lender): _____

State: _____   Borrower(s) (debtor): _____

Date: _____

   Acknowledged, under oath, before me on the ___ day of _____, 19__.

By: _____

_____
Notary Public

Note: Consult with your attorney before utilizing this promissory note or any portion thereof.

Most business sales on terms are anchored by some type of collateral, including in order of prevalence, the following: security interest in the assets of the business (chattel security agreement); personal guarantee by the buyer (borrower); pledge of specific, additional collateral. Normally, the buyer (principal shareholder of a corporation) will be asked to personally guarantee the debt after agreeing to pledge all the assets of the acquired business. Occasionally, specific assets such as common stock, buildings, and even personal residences will be pledged to strengthen the personal guarantee, in which case a separate pledge document will be prepared and executed. As concerns a buyer's personal residence, sellers are well advised to investigate the applicable state homestead laws, which serve to protect an individual's equity in a personal residence from attack by creditors (amounts and terms of protection vary state to state, but can be higher than $150,000!). Once again, attorney advice is warranted. As concerns the personal guarantee, it can be found in the terms and conditions of the promissory note itself or as a supplement thereto. It is commonly referenced in the purchase agreement as well. Buyers will attempt to guarantee the loan through their corporations, but most sellers will balk at this idea. Any type of bank financing will require a personal guarantee. Consider the guaranty agreement in Figure 4.4.

FIGURE 4.4 Guaranty

GUARANTY

The undersigned parties (purchasers of _____ for _____ dollars, as evidenced by the purchase agreement signed both ways on _____) do hereby jointly and severally guarantee all payments associated with the promissory note dated _____ and agree that those payments may be accelerated as described within the terms and conditions of the promissory note.

City: _____

State:_____

Date: _____

Guarantor(s): _____

_____

Acknowledged under oath, before me on the _____ day of _____, 19__.

_____
Notary Public

Bill of Sale

The formal document representing ownership of a business and its assets purchased by the buyer is the bill of sale. According to commercial law, a bill of sale is required for the sale of most personal assets, and once again the Uniform Commercial Code plays a prominent role. The bill of sale serves to transfer the ownership of the personal assets to the new owner. Typically, a complete, signed list of assets is attached to the bill of sale. This is another reason why it is important to create a comprehensive list of assets included in the sale of any business. If the business is sold with seller financing through escrow, the bill of sale will be held by the escrow agent until the final payment is received. The escrow company will also file the UCC-1 financing statement on behalf of the seller to "perfect" the seller's interest and ultimately remove this lien by filing a UCC-2 termination statement at the same time it forwards the original bill of sale to the buyer. At this point, the buyer owns the business free and clear. Examine the simple bill of sale in Figure 4.5.

FIGURE 4.5   Bill of Sale

BILL OF SALE

KNOW ALL MEN BY THESE PRESENTS: That I (we), the undersigned seller, for and in consideration of _____ Dollars ($_____), paid by _____, the buyer, receipt of which is hereby acknowledged, do hereby sell, assign, and convey to the buyer, all rights, title, and interest in and to the following personal property:

_____

_____

_____

_____

Dated this _____ day of _____, 19___.

                                        _____

                                        Seller

                                        By: _____

                                        Authorized Agent

State of _____

County of _____

     Subscribed and sworn to before me, the undersigned Notary Public, this

_____ day of _____,

19_____, by _____.

My Commission Expires: _____

_____   Notary Public

Chattel Security Agreement

With seller financing, there is a need for the sellers to legally protect their interests in the business and its assets. While the promissory note is evidence of the liability and the bill of sale is evidence of ownership of the assets, the bill of sale cannot be transferred to the new owner until the note is paid in full. During this interim period, sellers legally perfect their interests in these assets by executing a chattel security agreement (lien). The term *chattel* is a synonym for personal property. Additionally, a UCC-1 form, filed at the appropriate county and state offices, represents a legal, formal claim against the assets of the business as described in the chattel security agreement. Upon final payment, it is the responsibility of the seller (creditor) to remove the lien and give the original bill of sale to the newly unencumbered owner. The chattel security agreement is simply evidence that the assets of the business are encumbered by the seller until the note is paid off. This lien will prevent the new owner of the business from using these already liened assets as collateral for additional financing. More importantly, it will prevent the new owner from selling the business to a third party before the original seller has been paid in full. Review the following chattel security agreement in Figure 4.6 and related UCC-1 statement in Figure 4.7, which are standard fare for seller financed business sales.

FIGURE 4.6   Chattel Security Agreement

CHATTEL SECURITY AGREEMENT

---

1. Creation of Security Interest
   The undersigned Debtor grants to the undersigned Secured Party a security interest in the property described in Section 2 (Collateral) to secure all Debtor's present and future debts, obligations, and liabilities of whatever nature to Secured Party (Obligations).
2. Description of Collateral
   Collateral to include all assets referred to in purchase agreement dated _____ and Bill of Sale executed on _____, including, but not limited to all personal property, inventory, equipment, documents, files, intangible assets, assets, accounts, trade name, and contract rights that debtors currently possesses (see attached equipment list as well). This security interest is intended to secure all payments for debtor to creditor relating to the promissory note dated _____.
   Debtor warrants:

   (a) Ownership—Debtor is the owner of the Collateral free of all encumbrances and security interests (except Secured Party's Security Interest).

FIGURE 4.6 Chattel Security Agreement, continued

(b) Purchase Money—If checked here, the Collateral is being acquired by Debtor with the proceeds of a loan from Secured Party (said proceeds will be used for no other purpose).

(c) Use and Address—The Collateral is used or bought for use primarily for the purpose indicated below:

_____

_____

Business and the address of Debtor's principal place of business, or if none, Debtor's residence, is shown below Debtor's signature.

(d) Mobile Equipment—If any Collateral is equipment of a type normally used in more than one state, Debtor's chief place of business (if other than that below Debtor's signature) is: _____

(e) Location of Collateral—The Collateral will be kept at the address below Debtor's signature or, if not, at:

_____

(No. and Street)   (City or Town)   (County)   (State)

and such location shall not be changed without the prior written consent of Secured Party.

(f) Fixtures—If the Collateral is to be attached to real estate, the street address and legal description of such real estate is: _____

_____

and the name of the record owner of such real estate is: _____

_____

(g) Changes of Address—Debtor shall advise Secured Party in writing of any changes of address in a timely fashion. Debtor warrants that his principal place of business is stated by signature below and that all records relating to this security agreement are maintained on those premises.

4. Persons Bound

    All parties signing this Agreement, other than the Secured Party, are Debtors, and the obligations hereunder of all Debtors are joint and several. This Agreement benefits the Secured Party, its successors and assigns, and binds the Debtor(s) and their respective heirs, personal and representatives, successors, and assigns.

5. Other Provisions

    This Agreement includes all the provisions on the reverse side (additional security agreement provisions).

    Dated this _____ day of _____, 19_____

_____   _____
Secured Party   Debtor

FIGURE 4.6   Chattel Security Agreement, continued

Debtor

By _____

Authorized Signature   Debtor

Address: _____   Address: _____

Additional Security Agreement Provisions

Maintenance of Collateral. Debtor agrees to perform all acts that secured party deems necessary or desirable to protect his interest, including tasks related to financing, continuation amendments, and termination statements. Debtor shall maintain the Collateral in good condition and repair and not permit its value to be impaired, keep it free from all liens, encumbrances, and security interests (other than those created or expressly permitted by this Agreement); defend it against all claims and legal proceedings by persons other than Secured Party; pay and discharge when due all taxes, license fees, levies, and other charges upon it; not sell, lease, or otherwise dispose of it or permit to become a fixture of an accession to other goods except as specifically authorized in this Agreement or in writing by the Secured Party; not permit it to be used in violation of any applicable law, regulation, or policy of insurance. Loss of or damage to the Collateral shall not release Debtor from any of the Obligations.

Insurance. Debtor shall keep the Collateral and Secured Party's interest in it insured under policies with such provisions, for such amounts, and by such insurers as shall be satisfactory to Secured Party from time to time, and shall furnish evidence of such insurance satisfactory to Secured Party. Debtor assigns (and directs any insurer to pay) to Secured Party the proceeds of all such insurance and any premium refund and authorizes Secured Party to endorse in the name of Debtor any instrument for such proceeds or refunds and at the option of Secured Party, to apply such proceeds and refunds to any unpaid balance of the Obligations whether or not due and/or to restoration of the Collateral, returning any excess to Debtor. Secured Party is authorized in the name of the Debtor or otherwise, to make, adjust, settle claims under and/or cancel any insurance on the Collateral.

Inspection of Collateral. Secured Party is authorized to examine the Collateral wherever located at any reasonable time or times, and Debtor shall assist Secured Party in making any such inspection.

Maintenance of Security Interest. Debtor shall pay all expenses and, upon request, take any action reasonably deemed advisable by Secured Party to preserve the Collateral or to establish, determine priority of, perfect, continue perfected, terminate and/or enforce Secured Party's interest in it or rights under this Agreement.

Authority of Secured Party to Perform for Debtor. If Debtor fails to act as required by this Agreement or the Obligations, Secured Party is authorized, in debtor's name or

FIGURE 4.6   Chattel Security Agreement, continued

otherwise, to take any such action including without limitation signing Debtor's name or paying any amount so required, and the cost shall be one of the Obligations secured by this Agreement and shall be payable by Debtor upon demand with interest at the highest legal rate applicable from the date of payment by Secured Party.

Default. Occurs if one or more of the following events transpires:

Nonperformance. Debtor fails to pay when due any of the Obligations, or to perform, or rectify breach of, any warranty or other undertaking by Debtor in this Agreement or the Obligations;

Inability to Perform. Debtor or a surety for any of the Obligations dies, ceases to exist, becomes insolvent or the subject of bankruptcy or insolvency proceedings;

Misrepresentation. Any warranty or representation made to induce Secured Party to extend credit to Debtor, under this Agreement or otherwise, if false in any material respect when made; or

Insecurity. Any other event that causes Secured Party, in good faith, to deem itself insecure, as evidenced by:

1. An assignment, composition, or similar device for the benefit of creditors.
2. An attachment or receivership of assets not dissolved within 30 days.
3. The filing by (or against) debtor or any guarantor of a petition under any chapter of the Federal Bankruptcy Code.

All of the obligations shall, at the option of Secured Party and without any notice or demand, become immediately payable; and Secured Party shall have all rights and remedies for default provided by the *relevant state* Uniform Commercial Code as well as any other applicable law and the Obligations. With respect to such rights and remedies:

a) *Assembling Collateral.* Secured Party may require Debtor to assemble the Collateral and to make it available to Secured Party at any convenient place designated by Secured Party.

b) *Notice of Disposition.* Written notice, when required by law, sent to any address of Debtor in this Agreement at least ten calendar days (not counting the day of sending) before the date of a proposed disposition of the Collateral is reasonable notice.

c) *Expenses and Application of Proceeds.* Debtor shall reimburse Secured Party for any expenses incurred by Secured Party in protecting or enforcing its rights under this Agreement, including without limitation reasonable attorneys' fees and legal expenses and all expenses of taking possession, holding, preparing for disposition, and disposing of the Collateral. After deduction of such expenses, Secured Party may apply the proceeds of deposition to the Obligations in such order and amounts as it elects.

FIGURE 4.6   Chattel Security Agreement, continued

d) Waiver. Secured Party may permit Debtor to remedy any default without waiving the default so remedied, and Secured Party may waiver any default without waiving any other subsequent or prior default by Debtor.

e) Other Action. Take any other action that Secured Party deems necessary or desirable to protect the collateral of the security interest.

f) Course of Dealing. No course of dealing or delay in accelerating the obligation or in taking or in failing to take any other action with respect to any event of default shall affect Secured Party's right to take such action at a later time. No waiver as to any one default shall affect Secured Party's rights upon any other default.

g) Concurrent Rights. Secured Party may exercise any or all of its rights on default concurrently with or independently of and without regard to the provisions of any other document that secures an obligation.

Nonliability of Secured Party. Secured Party has no duty to protect, insure, or realize upon the Collateral. Debtor releases Secured Party from any liability for any act or omission relating to the Obligations, the Collateral, or this Agreement, except Secured Party's willful misconduct.

Waiver of Defenses Against Assignee. Debtor shall not assert against any assignee of Secured Party's rights under this Agreement or any of the Obligations any claim or defense Debtor may have against Secured Party.

Charging Debtor's Credit Balance. Debtor grants Secured Party, as further security for the Obligations, a security interest and lien in any credit balance and other money now or hereafter owed Debtor by Secured Party or any assignee of Secured Party and in addition, agrees that Secured Party may, without prior notice or demand, charge against any such credit balance or other money any amount owing upon the Obligations, whether due or not.

Applicable Law. This agreement shall be governed by and construed under the laws of the *relevant state.*

Notices. All official communications relating to this agreement shall be in writing and shall be deemed delivered if mailed, postage prepaid, to a party at the principal place of business specified in this agreement.

Successors and Assigns. This agreement shall inure to the benefit of and shall bind the heirs, executors, administrators, legal counsel, successors or assigns of the parties. Obligations of the debtor, if more than one, shall be joint and several.

WHEN RECORDED RETURN TO:

FIGURE 4.7 Uniform Commercial Code Financing Statement (UCC-1)

UNIFORM COMMERCIAL CODE FINANCING STATEMENT (UCC-1)

Effective Date	County and State of Transaction
Debtor (Name, Address, and Zip Code)	Secured Party (Name, Address, and Zip Code)
Assignee of Secured Party (Name, Address, and Zip Code)	Record Owner of Real Property, If Not Debtor (Name, Address, and Zip Code)
Counties Where Collateral Is Located	❏ Products of Collateral are also covered. ❏ Proceeds of Collateral are also covered.

Financing Statement covers the following types of items of property:

and all accessions to, and spare and repair parts, special tools and equipment and replacements for, and all proceeds of the foregoing.

If collateral is timber to be cut, crops growing or to be grown, minerals or the like, accounts to be financed at the wellhead or minehead of the well or mine, or goods that are or are to become fixtures, the real property to which these are affixed or concerned is legally described:
❏ This Financing Statement is to be filed in the office where mortgage on the real property would be recorded.

This Financing Statement is filed or recorded without Debtor's signature to perfect a security interest in collateral that:
❏ Is already subject to a security interest in another jurisdiction when it was brought into the state or which Debtor changed location to this State;
❏ Are proceeds of the original collateral described above in which a security interest was perfected;
❏ Is no longer effective due to lapse of the original filing;
❏ Was acquired four months or less after Debtor has changed its name, identity, or corporate structure.

Signature of Debtor   Signature of Secured Party or Assignee

Contents of Standard Purchase Offer

Let's return now to the basic contents of a standard purchase offer (additional clauses can be found in Chapter 7, transition issues; Chapter 13, selling a business; and the previously presented stock sales agreement in this chapter). It seems that every broker and every attorney utilizes a unique purchase contract. The reason is that purchase contracts are, to varying degrees, comprised of the following contractual components, each of which has an endless array of possibilities:

- Contingencies
- Conditions
- Covenants
- Indemnifications
- Representations and warranties

Each of these contribute important substance to a contract. Within each category, there will be a seemingly endless variety of specific examples. Understanding their unique nature will facilitate construction of fair, legal, valid, and enforceable contract to the benefit of all parties.

Contingencies

Properly written offers should contain one or more contingencies to be removed prior to placing the earnest deposit check at risk (prior to opening escrow). *Contingencies* are often considered the same thing as conditions, but as used in the process of buying a business, they refer to events or outcomes (positive or negative) that must occur for the deal to proceed (for there to be a formal meeting of the minds) toward closing. In fact, contingencies are often referred to contractually as *conditions precedent,* with the time dimension corresponding to closing (i.e., a condition that is satisfied preceding closing). *The most common contingency found in a purchase offer requires a satisfactory review of all books, records, and operations by the purchaser prior to legally consummating the transaction.*

Contingencies should be brief, clear, and easily interpreted by all parties. They should also be written with an appropriate time constraint (allowing for extensions based upon mutual agreement) or be of a self-liquidating nature. A contingency removal form similar to the one in Figure 4.8 is normally utilized.

FIGURE 4.8 Contingency Removal Form

CONTINGENCY REMOVAL FORM

As concerns the signed purchase agreement between buyer (_____)
and seller (_____) dated _____ for that business known as:

_____

and located at

_____ ,

(City, County, State, Zip)

the buyers signing below hereby formally "remove" the contingency included in said
purchase offer and described below, being fully satisfied as to its current status.
Buyer agrees that once all contingencies are removed, escrow shall be opened and a
closing date scheduled.

The contingency which reads:

_____

_____

_____

_____

is hereby satisfied.

Buyer: _____ Date: _____ Buyer: _____ Date: _____

The contingency removal form can be utilized for seller contingencies by simply changing the required signature. Let's review some of the common contingencies.

Buyer Contingencies

As concerns the buyer, every offer should have the following four contingencies at a minimum, while recognizing that every deal requires attention to specific details.

Books and Records
Offer is contingent upon favorable review of books, records and operations by seller. Buyer to verify gross sales equal to _____ for the year ending _____.

Legal Counsel
Offer is contingent upon favorable review of purchase contract and all related documents by buyer's legal counsel. Buyer's counsel to approve/disapprove of said documents within _____ days from submission by seller or seller's counsel.

Some variant of the two clauses above should be included in every offer to ensure that the business is performing as presented and that the contract is legally valid, enforceable, and otherwise proper. *The role of the attorney should be to perfect the language as opposed to renegotiate the deal.* It can be risky to sign a contract and then request material changes to its content. Obtain attorney guidance as much as possible before you sign the offer to avoid this conflict. Any escrow deposits turned over to the broker should also be given on a contingent basis, as follows:

Escrow Deposit
> Broker is directed to hold earnest deposit uncashed until all contingencies are removed. The escrow check is to be placed into escrow if and only if all contingencies are removed.

Instruct your broker that you wish to see all three of these clauses in every offer. If the broker resists, you might seek out a new broker. Other common buyer contingencies address the property lease and bank financing.

Lease
> Offer is contingent upon landlord acceptance of new owner in the form of a lease assignment, sublease, or new lease to the complete satisfaction of the buyer.

For many businesses, there will be no sale if the lease is not properly transferred. Many businesses have no value without such a lease (e.g., retail shops). A diligent broker will take the time immediately after a business is listed for sale to query the landlord to uncover any problems (such as late payments, notice of default, sale of property, or bankruptcy of land owner) and to verify that the transfer/assignment will not be unnecessarily withheld.

Adding detail can strengthen a given clause. In our current example, satisfaction of the lease contingency is left to the buyer alone. Many contracts will be more specific and demanding requiring the seller to *warrant* (promise) that a lease can be delivered under the terms of the existing lease, as follows:

> Seller warrants delivery of lease for a period of at least _____ years together with assignment of existing terms and conditions.

Although this clause is not written in the standard form of a contingency (i.e., contingent on, it amounts to the same thing and places the burden on the seller). Sellers place themselves in an awkward position if they warrant that the buyer will be a residing tenant for an extended period of time after closing. Most sellers will try to avoid making commitments that are beyond their control. *The new lease or assignment should be completed and signed by all parties prior to or at closing.* See Chapter 7 for more insights into lease transfers and assignments, including sample lease assignment, intent to lease, and lease amendment forms.

If the buyer is purchasing the real estate instead of entering a lease, there should be a cross-contingency stating that the purchase of the business is contingent on closing the sale of the real property and the purchase of the real property is contingent on the closing of the business sale. Consider the following contingency concerning bank financing:

Bank Financing

Offer is contingent on buyer applying for and receiving funding for a bank loan in the amount of $x at no more than y percent, payable over at least a two-year period. Buyer to present evidence of formal loan commitment within two weeks of providing banker all required documents. Seller to cooperate fully in turning over requested information needed to make the loan application.

Requiring a formal bank commitment within two weeks strengthens the seller's position and would not normally be willingly offered by the buyer, but asked for in a counteroffer from the seller. Even the best written contracts will be worthless if the other side is unable to live up to the terms. You may end up fully protecting your interests but wasting all your time and money!

A common concern of the seller arises when bank financing is combined with seller financing. Banks will rarely (almost never) accept a backup position to the seller in the event of liquidation. Banks will try to not only collateralize heavily (both the assets of the business and personal assets of the owner), but also assume first position among creditors. Banks are more likely to lend to buyers if the seller remains involved (receiving note payments), but they will not let the seller take the priority interest in the assets of the business if bankruptcy occurs.

When writing an offer with contingencies, the buyer will probably prefer to have an open-ended time frame for removal. If the buyer is rushed, mistakes in judgment as to what should be reviewed might occur. Further, if you are required to remove contingencies within a prescribed period of time, and you can't or don't remove them, the seller rightly has the option to move on to another buyer. Depending upon your financial strength, the seller's motivations, and the existence of other buyers, this may or may not matter. Ideally, however, you want as much time as you need to complete your review and address other contingencies. Your progress will also depend on whether or not the seller has requested and the buyer has agreed to allow continued showings and the acceptance of backup offers. If the seller is allowed to continue showing the business, buyers will normally move quicker to complete their review. In almost every case, experienced sellers will require that contingencies be removed within a maximum time frame, such as two to four weeks.

As you might imagine, there are many "variations on a theme" to the major contingencies listed above. Consider the following clauses:

Inspection Clause (Books and Records)

This contract is contingent upon buyer's final inspection of seller's financial records relating to said business within _____ days from signed mutual acceptance. In the case that buyer fails to notify seller in writing (certified or registered mail) of his disapproval within _____ days, it shall be deemed that buyer has approved subject records and this contract shall continue in full force and effect unless seller has obstructed buyer's ability for reasonable review. Seller hereby agrees to make all required documents readily available to buyer during this _____ day period.

This clause places the responsibility for completing the review squarely on the shoulders of the buyer, who must respond in writing to reject the business as presented. Failure to respond in writing could lead to loss of the escrow deposit. Now we move from *generally required* to *specifically optional* contingencies, of which there may be one or many.

Franchise Approval

Offer contingent on formal approval by franchiser of franchise transfer to buyer at no cost to buyer on or before one week prior to scheduled closing date per purchase contract.

This is another example of a contingency that is beyond the direct control of the buyer and seller. It might help to include wording to the effect that both parties agree to prudently and diligently assist in processing the application for transfer. It is wise to move quickly because the franchiser will normally possess two to four weeks (per the original franchise agreement) for processing.

Liquor License

Offer contingent upon buyer successfully obtaining appropriate (legal and formal) liquor license transfer. Buyer and seller to make immediate application, within five days of signed purchase contract, for said transfer. License transfer fee to be paid by buyer.

This is an example of a multifaceted clause that includes a contingency (formal approval of transfer), a covenant (apply within five days), and a condition (transfer fee paid by buyer). Similar clauses can be utilized for all licenses and permits, such as the following:

License/Permit Transfer

In the event that this agreement is subject to the transfer or acquisition of any license, permit, interim appointment, bond, or any document requiring the approval of a third party or governmental agency, buyer and seller agree that all necessary steps to expedite such transfers or acquisitions of such documents will be taken by buyer and seller as required.

Given the extreme importance of contingencies, great effort is expended in placing them into the contract and removing them. Normally, the seller has taken his business off the market while contingencies are being removed, so expect pressure to remove them quickly. A separate clause (condition) might be included to stress their importance, such as:

Reasonable Efforts

Buyer shall make every reasonable effort to promptly remove all contingencies contained within this contract on or before _____, 19__. If said contingencies are not removed, this agreement is null and void and of no further force.

Nothing irritates a seller more than a buyer who is unreasonably slow at removing contingencies, particularly inspecting books and records. Nothing irritates a buyer more than a seller who is unreasonably uncooperative in providing access to documents needed for such a review. Mutual trust and respect will work wonders for most transactions.

Trial Period

Seller represents that he has been grossing $_____ per month, and that during a trial period of ___ working days he will prove a gross volume of $_____ with a variance of plus or minus ___ percent. If this trial period verifies the represented sales, purchaser hereby waives further proof of income. If the business should be closed any day or days during the trial period for any reason, then an equivalent number of days will be added from the previous or subsequent week wherein buyer was present at business location and observed the actual sales. During this trial period, seller or seller's agent will remain with buyer to familiarize buyer with normal business operations.

Seller Contingencies

Just as buyers are provided with insurance in the form of standard contingencies, sellers seek similar protection. Seller contingencies are not as numerous as buyer contingencies, but they are equally as important. Acceptance of a signed offer should include the following contingencies (or you need a new broker!). See Chapter 13 for a thorough review of pro-seller clauses.

Legal Counsel

Acceptance of offer is contingent on favorable review of all purchase offer related documents by seller's legal counsel.

Buyer's Background

Acceptance of offer is subject to favorable review by seller of buyer's background.

These contingencies are general in nature, without deadlines for removal. From the seller's point of view, this is preferable. By making acceptance contingent on favorable review of buyer's background, seemingly anything unfavorable would allow the seller to back out of the deal, if so desired. If the seller were providing credit (seller financing), review of the buyer's credit report would be mandatory, and would be related to the buyer's background. Consider the following slightly different approval clause:

Seller's Approval of Buyer's Financial Condition
Offer is contingent on seller's approval of buyer's financial statement and credit report. Failure to provide seller with these documents within ____ days from mutual signing of this contract shall render said contract null and void and cause earnest deposit to be returned to buyer. If seller fails to notify buyer in writing (certified or registered mail) within ____ days of receipt of financial statement and credit report, approval of said documents shall be implied and this contract shall continue in full force and effect.

Note that contingencies may be removed either via a formal contingency removal form or by an appropriately worded clause attached to an amendment, as follows:

Buyer's Acknowledgment
Buyer acknowledges having personally investigated to his or her full satisfaction, or having had reasonable opportunity to investigate, all aspects of the company and the assets being sold hereunder, including but not limited to the company premises, all utility services and systems available to said premises and all improvements and fixtures situated thereon; all equipment, tools, inventory parts, appliances, and other tangible assets included in this sale; any underlying encumbrances or applicable lease options, licenses, uses, variances, permits, covenants and/or restrictions pertaining to company premises or any of the assets included in this sale; and any other items or intangible rights included in this sale. Buyer acknowledges having thoroughly reviewed to his or her satisfaction, or having had reasonable opportunity to review, all of seller's financial records pertaining to the operation of the company and its business; and buyer acknowledges having finally relied upon personal judgment and decision in entering into and consummating this purchase and sale. Buyer is satisfied that he or she personally has the financial resources and business acumen to successfully operate the company. Buyer acknowledges and understands that future profits from the operation of the company are in no way guaranteed by seller.

Conditions

These are events or nonevents that must or must not occur on, before, or after a certain time. A common condition of sale is that inventory in the amount of x will be included in the purchase price, with counting and inspection to occur the day of closing. This condition effectively terminates at closing. Another condition concerns training, where the seller agrees to train the buyer in all aspects of the business for 40 hours per week for two weeks. This condition survives the closing, but terminates two weeks after. Review the following common conditions:

Inventory

> On the day prior to closing, buyer and seller agree to meet and jointly take inventory, which in no case shall be less than $_____, as measured by cost. If the inventory on hand is greater (less) than $_____, the down payment and purchase price shall be adjusted upward (downward).

This clause is written plainly and avoids reference to "delivered free and clear" of any liens, attachments, or encumbrances. All states have bulk sales laws per the UCC that prevent the "bulk transfer" of inventory from the seller to buyer without full payment to suppliers. Larger businesses and companies with significant inventory (retail and manufacturing companies) are subject to these laws. Accordingly, purchase contracts will also contain a bulk sales clause, which amounts to a condition of sale/warranty. Consider this:

UCC—Bulk Sales Transfer

> Pursuant to state laws, and in compliance therewith, seller shall, at the date of possession, execute and deliver to buyer an affidavit warranting that as of the closing, the company shall have no creditors.

This particular clause is brief, amounting to an "end run" around the requirement that all creditors be notified in writing of the pending sale (if the law applies) to give them the opportunity to make their claims against the seller for any nonpayment and possibly file a lien against the seller in the event of nonpayment (which would preclude the closing from taking place). There are numerous circumstances under which the bulk sales law is not applicable and a signed waiver by buyer and seller would be satisfactory for purposes of consummating the sale. The clause above would be acceptable if the law were being waived, but there is no clear indication that this is the case.

Assumption of Liabilities

> Upon consummation of the transaction outlined herein and as a condition concurrent to the closing, buyer agrees to assume and indemnify seller against all liabilities presented on Exhibit _____. Except as described on this Exhibit, buyer is assuming no other liabilities of any type.

Buyers will often agree to assume certain liabilities as part of the purchase price. The general rule, however, is that the business and all assets will be delivered free and clear of any debts, liens, or encumbrances. Typical exceptions occur when the buyer agrees to continue making payments on leased equipment. Credit card processing contracts, maintenance agreements, and service contracts are also commonly assumed. Whether they are assumed or not, disposition must be in writing. Consider the following clause:

Buyer Not to Assume Encumbrances

If for any reason the buyers are not approved by the beneficiaries of the encumbrances herein, seller agrees to remain responsible for said encumbrances as guarantor for the buyers. If for any reason the beneficiary's statements are not received by the close of escrow, the escrow agent is hereby instructed by the buyer and seller to accept the balance given by the seller as the amount owing. The seller warrants that the given balances will be correct.

A related topic involves the existence of unknown, overlooked, or intentionally hidden liabilities that are due after the closing. The buyer can seek protection against these unknown liabilities in many different ways, creating "layers" of protection. First, the seller must warrant that the business is delivered free and clear, except as otherwise disclosed on an attached exhibit. Second, purchasing the business with seller financing provides leverage in the event that these overlooked debts come due after the close. Third, the buyer might require (negotiate) the establishment of a *set-aside* fund, or possess a *right of offset,* both of which give the buyer contractual rights to make good on these unknown debts with the seller's funds. The set-aside fund will be placed into an interest-bearing escrow account and administered by a third party. These funds, under predetermined and mutually agreed upon conditions, can be used to make good on these overlooked debts. Exactly how much to put into such an account and for how long is a matter of negotiation. As to the precise terms of how the funds will be disbursed, attorney advice in this regard is highly recommended. Common situations involve constraints on the amount per claim (only claims greater than $x) and the total amount of claims. *The right of offset option is a contractual mechanism whereby the buyer has the right to withhold or reduce the monthly note payments to the seller under acceptable and appropriate conditions.* Surprisingly, most smaller deals close without any of these formal protections.

Miscellaneous Conditions

Review the purchase contract presented in the next chapter for a comprehensive set of clauses.

Extended Closing

If both parties agree, closing may be extended beyond _____. Such agreement must be in writing.

Work in Progress

On or before close of escrow, an accounting of all work in progress shall be made utilizing the percentage of completion method as mutually agreed upon by buyer and seller. Upon completion of each contract, the net profit from each contract shall be divided between seller and buyer in proportion to the percentage of completion of each contract. Example: job is 80 percent finished at close of escrow, seller gets 80 percent of net profit, buyer gets 20 percent of net profit.

Incorporation by Buyer

It is hereby acknowledged and agreed that BUYER may elect to incorporate. In such event, the new corporation shall become the BUYER, and BUYER shall cause the corporation to ratify all of the terms and conditions of this Purchase Contract and Receipt. Further, BUYER hereunder shall continue to be personally liable for the performance of the Agreement, covenants and agreements, and the payment of any unpaid balances owed to SELLER hereunder.

Telephone Numbers and Yellow Page Ads

The SELLER herein agrees to assign all telephone numbers to the BUYER that are listed for the Company in all White or Yellow Pages of all phone books.

Company Records

At time of possession, Seller shall deliver to Buyer all customer accounts, records, and documents pertinent to the operation of the Company, including copies of any documents necessary to enable Buyer to conduct the Company's business with its suppliers and customers.

There is no area as sensitive as earnest deposits and backup offers. Consider the variations between the following clauses.

Escape Clause

It is agreed that in the event seller receives a bona fide, noncontingent offer on the assets of the subject business during the term of this agreement, seller agrees to give written notice of such an offer to purchaser, and purchaser shall have _____ days from receipt of such notice to remove all buyer's contingencies contained herein. In the event buyer is unable to remove all said contingencies within a _____ day period, this agreement shall be rendered null and void and earnest check shall be immediately returned to buyer.

One Backup Offer

It is agreed that seller has accepted a contingent offer from a third party for the purchase of subject business. In the event that seller or third party negotiates the removal of the contingencies contained in said offer within the time periods allowed, this agreement shall be rendered null and void and earnest funds returned to buyer. However, in the event that said contingencies are not removed within the time periods allowed, this agreement shall become effective immediately. For all purposes herein, the date of mutual acceptance shall be the date on which this agreement becomes effective as provided in this paragraph.

Please recognize that based on the previous clause above, there is no deal until acceptance is communicated to the buyer. In the event that counteroffers have been made on outstanding deals, the following clause might be appropriate.

Executed Counteroffer

It is understood that seller has executed a counteroffer to a third party for the sale of subject business. In the event that said counteroffer is accepted and seller and said third party negotiate the removal of the contingencies contained in said counteroffer within the time periods allowed, this agreement shall be rendered null and void and earnest check returned to buyer. However, in the event that said counteroffer is not accepted nor the contingencies removed within the time periods allowed therein, this agreement shall become effective immediately upon communication to buyer of such fact. For all purposes herein, the date of mutual acceptance shall be the date on which this agreement becomes effective and was so communicated as provided in this paragraph.

Buying Business "AS IS"

Buyer acknowledges and agrees that the assets listed on Exhibit A are hereby sold and transferred "AS IS" with all faults. All implied warranties including the implied warranty of merchantability and the implied warranty of fitness for a particular purpose are hereby disclaimed. Seller makes no express warranty of any kind in connection with such assets. Buyer further acknowledges that he has had an opportunity to inspect the assets and that he has conducted such inspection to his/her satisfaction.

Notices

All notices required to be given hereunder shall be in writing and either delivered or sent certified mail, return receipt requested and postage prepaid, to the parties at the following addresses: _____

_____

Only One Spouse

Escrow agent is hereby authorized and instructed to accept any one of the signatures of the sellers, if more than one, and any one of the signatures of the buyers, if more than one, for the purpose of consummating the deal contemplated by this escrow in strict accordance with its terms with the exception of all documents drawn in connection with these instructions, without liability on the part of the escrow holder for so doing.

Please be aware that even though all parties are not required to sign the closing documents, they are required to sign the purchase contract and its attachments and amendments. As always, situation-specific legal advice is prudent.

Corporate Purchase

Buyer agrees to supply escrow agent with corporate resolution authorizing purchase of subject business and its assets by corporation to be created by purchaser under the terms and conditions outlined herein, and shall designate _____ as authorized signatory to execute all documents as required to complete the purchase of subject business.

See Chapter 2 for a sample corporate resolution form, which can be utilized to authorize the hiring of a broker for commission or the purchase or sale of a corporation.

Contact with Seller's Customers

As soon as possible following the Close of Escrow, Seller shall contact each of its customers to inform them that their accounts have been transferred to Buyer. Such contact shall be made in writing in a form to be jointly determined by Seller and Buyer. It shall inform Seller's customers that their existing contracts will be honored by Buyer and will provide Seller's customers with the name of a contact person designated by the Buyer who will be able to answer questions and will provide all necessary additional information to Seller's customers to enable them to become customers of Buyer with no interruption in service.

Employees

All employees of the business herein sold shall be terminated from employment by Seller as of the date of Closing and shall be reemployed by Buyer or his nominee as of said date on an *at will* basis. Seller shall use its best efforts to see that its employees will continue employment after this sale and agree to be reemployed by Buyer following the Closing.

Default and Remedies

In the event of any anticipatory or other breach of this Agreement by any party hereto, or upon the failure of this transaction to close due to the wrongful actions or failures to act of either party hereto, then this agreement shall be deemed to be in default.

In the case of SELLER breach, BUYER may immediately cease performance and avail itself of any and all remedies available hereunder or at law for such breach or default, including, in the case of default by SELLER, BUYER'S right to specific performance. Any earnest money deposits shall be refunded to the BUYER.

In the case of BUYER breach, SELLER may retain the earnest money deposit as liquidated damages and immediately cease performance and avail itself of any and all remedies available hereunder or at law for such breach or default.

Sale by Buyer

BUYER and SELLER hereby agree that BUYER shall have, subsequent to the closing, the right to sell the Company or any portion thereof, provided, however, that any such sale shall not detrimentally affect any security interest in the Company at the time of such proposed sale, and further provided that BUYER obtain from SELLER SELLER'S written consent authorizing any such sale. SELLER'S consent shall not be unreasonably withheld.

Covenants

This next contractual component, the *covenant,* is a type of promise made by one party to another. It is possible to describe a clause as both a covenant and a condition or a term. It is best to think of covenants as promises to do or not do something during the period of time between the signing of the contract and the closing (with the notable exception of a covenant not to compete, which clearly stays in force past the closing date). Covenants serve to protect the buyer from material, legal, operational, and financial changes in the operation of the business pending closing. The seller is obligated to continue running the business in a fashion that could be considered as the normal course of business.

Probably the most important covenant is the *covenant not to compete,* whereby the seller agrees not to directly compete with the buyer for a certain period of time within a certain geographical area. Although this obligation extends beyond closing, it is still referred to as a covenant. Properly written covenants include descriptions of prohibited activities and remedies available to the buyer for breach of the covenant. Naturally, if the buyer defaults on the note payments to the seller, the covenant should be considered null and void and the Seller released. Chapter 7 contains a thorough discussion of covenants not to compete.

Many different covenants can be included in a purchase agreement, such as a promise by the seller not to do any of the following between the signing of the agreement and closing: take on new debt, sell new shares, amend bylaws or charter, or default on existing contracts. Affirmative covenants would be to run the business as usual, maintain inventory levels and staffing, and account for work in progress. Note the similarities between covenants and contingencies. The major difference is that contingencies must be formally satisfied or the contract is immediately null and void. If a covenant is violated, it may require legal action to remedy. Consider the following covenants:

Pre-Closing Conditions

Prior to the Close of Escrow, the SELLER agrees that the business of the Company will be conducted only in the ordinary course. No increase will be made in any employee's compensation, no contract or commitment will be entered into with respect to the business without the BUYER'S prior written consent, and SELLER will use its best efforts to maintain the business intact and to preserve for the BUYER the goodwill thereof. The purchase of inventory as is the customary and normal course of this business is permitted.

Conduct of Business

From the date of this Agreement through the Closing Date, Seller will not operate its business other than in the ordinary course or make distributions or payments of any kind whatsoever to any party or owner or partner of Seller or make any expenditure, payment, transfer, or use of cash of any kind or incur any liability or obligation in excess of $1,000 without the prior written consent of Purchaser. During the period from the date of this Agreement to the Closing Date, Seller will preserve intact all rights, privileges, franchises, and other authority adequate for the conduct of the Seller's business and operations, and Seller will maintain satisfactory relationships with any and all suppliers, contractors, distributors, customers, and all others having business relationships of any kind with Seller.

General Covenants

Seller shall:

1. take all steps to preserve the integrity and value of the company assets;
2. preserve insurance coverage of all types and amounts currently in force; and
3. maintain and prepare the financial records and financial statements in accordance with GAAP and/or as historically prepared (consistency in preparation).

Off the Market

As discussed, Seller agrees to cease all communications with third parties regarding the sale of the business, whether for the sale of assets or stock or whether formal or informal. Seller further agrees to halt solicitation of new prospects.

In practice, most covenants are seller covenants. Here are a few buyer covenants or joint covenants:

Contingency Release Clause

Buyer shall make every reasonable effort to promptly remove all contingencies contained within this contract. In any case Buyer shall have until _____, 19__, to remove all of Buyer's contingencies.

Confidentiality

Buyer and all parties related to Buyer, including employees, consultants, associates, principals, officers, and other professionals are bound to confidentiality regarding any and all financial and ____ details discussed during due diligence. Buyer agrees to sign separate nondisclosure agreement and be responsible for other parties that gain access to company information. Furthermore, in the event that the sale is not completed, Buyer agrees to return all documents related to the sale of the business within one week of decision to halt the purchase.

Indemnification

This portion of a purchase contract describes the conditions and procedures whereby buyer or seller may claim damages in the event of a breach of the many representations and warranties included in the purchase contract. The bulk of protection here is for the buyer. This is the process of *holding harmless* another party from a particular liability. It is common to see buyers and sellers selectively cross-indemnify one another. Sellers will indemnify buyers against any undisclosed or unknown liabilities, and buyers will indemnify sellers against future claims by creditors or shareholders. Within the standard purchase agreement, indemnifications are often combined with warranties and/or representations, as follows:

Indemnification

Seller does hereby indemnify Buyer and hold it harmless from and against all debts, claims, actions, cause of action, losses, damages, and attorney's fees, now existing or which may hereafter arise, pertaining to Seller's operation and ownership of the Company prior to the date of possession, except to the extent Buyer has assumed, in writing, such responsibilities, liabilities, or other debts hereunder. Buyer does hereby indemnify and hold Seller harmless in similar fashion for all aspects of the ownership of the Company and the operation of its business for the period following date of possession.

Warranty Against Liabilities

Seller warrants and represents that all outstanding liabilities of the Company will be paid in full on or before the date of possession and that Buyer will receive possession and control of the Assets of the Company, free and clear of any such liabilities, claims, or encumbrances, including but not limited to any sales, withholding, payroll, or other taxes.

The clause presented above can also be expanded into a type of *right of offset* clause by adding this last sentence to the paragraph:

SELLER and BUYER agree that should any debts or liens owed by the SELLER prior to close of Escrow remain unpaid after the close of Escrow, then the BUYER, at his option, may pay these debts and deduct the costs from the Promissory note or funds held in escrow. Such action causes no default in the terms of the promissory note.

Please note that further examples of all contractual components are found in the stock purchase agreement presented earlier in this chapter and the asset purchase agreement presented in the next chapter. Ask your broker or attorney for sample contracts to gain further insights.

Representations and Warranties

Although they are technically different, it is common to find representations and warranties lumped together in Purchase Contracts. Collectively, they represent an attempt to force the buyer and seller to truthfully and accurately present information. The idea is that the buyer and the seller are relying on each other in material ways. Signing off on representations and warranties, which are *binding* claims made to the other side, opens the door for legal action in the case of fraud, misrepresentation, deceit, or even mistake. There will be a greater variety of seller representations and warranties than for buyers, which are generally limited to their legal and financial abilities regarding purchase of the business. Although some sellers will try to limit their representations and warranties and even attempt to sell their business "as is" (like a used car), this will not normally suffice. Minimal warranties and representations include:

- All liabilities owed are presented in the purchase agreement.
- Seller has full legal authority to sell assets of the company.
- Seller is not presently or expected to be prior to closing in default on any contract, agreement, lease, or other legal commitment.
- All leases covering real and personal property are in good stead.
- All required tax returns have been filed.
- No undisclosed liens, attachments, guarantees, or litigation exists.
- All financial data presented is accurate.

This portion of the purchase agreement can generate tension between buyers and sellers because detailed representations raise the seller's potential liability and create circumstances whereby the buyer might cease making payments on a carry-back note. Specific examples of seller representations and warranties include:

Close Without Tax Release
Seller warrants that he has no sales tax number or employees for the location being sold, and Buyer, relying on Seller's warranty, joins with Seller in instructing escrow agent to close without releases from the appropriate state taxing agencies.

Permits and Certificates
Seller warrants and represents that all permits, licenses, and certificates required by any governmental agency or body having jurisdiction over the Company and its business that are necessary to continue the operation of the Company in its present premises will be current and valid as of the date of possession.

Trial Period

Seller hereby represents that he has been generating gross sales of $_____ per week, and that during the agreed upon trial period of ___ working days (5 working days per week) Seller will prove gross revenues of $_____, plus or minus ___ percent.

Note: The trial period representation above is normally associated with a condition similar to the one below.

If the efforts of Seller during the trial period above prove accurate, Buyer hereby waives the need for further proof of income.

Now we turn to buyer representations and warranties:

Good Standing

Buyer represents and warrants that as of the date of closing Buyer will be a valid, duly organized corporation in good standing with proper authority to enter into this transaction consummating the sale of the corporation.

General Representations

Buyer is not or will not be subject to any agreement of any kind that would be breached by consummation of this sale. Relevant documents reflecting such agreement include but are not limited to bylaws, judgments, decrees, indentures, leases, mortgages, or liens.

Contingency Removal

Buyer and Seller warrant that all contingencies as stated in the purchase contract and receipt have been satisfied and hereby instruct Escrow Agent to proceed with the closing of escrow.

This warranty and the representation below (prepared by escrow company) are examples of *joint* buyer and seller clauses:

The parties agree that there are no representations between them, or by the broker, that are not specifically set forth, and they further agree that this escrow supersedes and voids any prior agreements, whether written or verbal.

Given that each deal is unique, buyers, sellers, attorneys, accountants, and brokers must choose on a case by case basis which clauses are necessary to properly consummate a transaction. The clauses provided in this guide are wide ranging but certainly not all-inclusive. Review them and use them as your broker or attorney see fit. Consider using the following documents:

• Certificate of Warranties and Representations

- Seller's Disclosure Form (personal property, i.e., the business)
- Seller's Disclosure Form (real property)

Certificate of Warranties and Representations

Different types of deals (stock versus asset), different types of businesses (child care versus manufacturer of semiconductors), and different types of purchasers and sellers (sole proprietor versus corporation) will lead to different disclosures, warranties, and representations. You need legal assistance to maximize your protection. Consider the examples in Figure 4.9, 4.10, and 4.11, each of which may appear in the body of the purchase contract or in a separately signed Certificate that is referenced to the purchase contract.

FIGURE 4.9   Certificate of Warranties and Representations

CERTIFICATE OF WARRANTIES AND REPRESENTATIONS

I.   This Certificate of Warranties and Representations supplements the purchase contract dated _____ between _____ (Buyer), an _____ corporation and _____ (Seller), an _____ corporation, for the purchase of the business being acquired thereunder and is a part of the due diligence review by Buyer as provided for under the contract.

II. As additional consideration to Buyer, Seller, and Seller's shareholders, _____, jointly and severally, represent and warrant to Buyer that the following statements are true and correct upon which Buyer may rely without further investigation or inquiry:

A. Seller is a properly organized and validly existing corporation in good standing in the State of _____, and has the authority to own its properties and carry on the business in which it is now engaged.

B. Seller has no control of or interest in any other corporation, association, or business organization.

C. The copies of the Articles of Incorporation and Bylaws of Seller, which shall be certified by the Secretary of each corporation and delivered to Buyer, are complete and correct and have not been amended except as certified to by the Secretary.

D. Seller's stock records are substantially complete and correct. The shareholders are the 100 percent owners of all the issued and outstanding stock of Seller.

E. The minute book of Seller contains all recorded proceedings of the shareholders and directors.

FIGURE 4.9   Certificate of Warranties and Representations, continued

F. None of the business conducted by Seller requires that Seller be licensed or qualified as a foreign corporation doing business in any other state except as set forth on the Disclosure Statement attached hereto as Exhibit I.

G. The entire authorized and issued capital stock of Seller consists of the voting common stock set forth on the Disclosure Statement, and there are no other series of common or preferred stock, including any loans to any shareholders that could be classified as a second series of stock pursuant to the Internal Revenue Code of 1986, as amended, and its regulations thereunder.

H. All stock issued and outstanding by Seller has been validly issued and is fully paid and nonassessable.

I. The Disclosure Statement contains a true and complete list of the directors and officers of Seller.

J. Seller and the Shareholders have the full right and power to enter into the contract.

K. None of the employees of Seller belong to or are part of any organized labor organization or union, and no stockholder, director, officer, or principal executive of Seller is affiliated with such an entity.

L. No stockholder, director, officer, or principal executive of Seller owns, directly or indirectly, any interest in, or as a director, officer, or employee, of any corporation, partnership, firm, association or business organization, entity, or enterprise that is a competitor, potential competitor, or supplier of Seller or in any way associated with or involved in the businesses conducted by Seller; provided that ownership of not more than 5% (five percent) of the capital stock of any corporation listed on a national securities exchange shall not be deemed to be ownership of an interest in such corporation for the purpose of this section. No stockholder and no director, officer, or employee owns, directly or indirectly, in whole or in part (other than such parties' ownership interest of Seller), any property, assets, or right, tangible or intangible (including but not limited to any trademark, trade name, copyright, or trade secret), that Seller is presently using or the use of which is necessary for its business.

M. There are no other material liabilities of Seller that are not set forth in Seller's Financial statements disclosed herein except for current liabilities incurred after the date of Seller's last financial statement in the ordinary course of business reflected in the journals and ledgers of Seller.

N. Exhibit II includes the following financial statements: The Balance Sheet and Statement of Income of Seller and for the calendar years ending December 31, 1997, 1998, and 1999, and the most current of such statements for Seller. These statements on consistent with past accounting procedures, practices and principles, and present fairly the financial condition of Seller and the

FIGURE 4.9 Certificate of Warranties and Representations, continued

results of its operations as of the dates set forth thereon, and for the periods covered therein.

O. None of the rights of Seller under any agreement, leasehold interest, license agreement, or any other contract will be impaired by the consummation of the transaction contemplated by the contract. All of the rights of Seller will be enforceable without the consent or agreement of any party except or set forth in the Disclosure Statement.

P. Except as set forth in the Disclosure Statement, neither Seller nor Shareholder is in violation of any outstanding judgment, order, injunction, award, or decree specifically relating to it and is not in violation of any federal, state, local, or foreign law, ordinance, or regulation that is applicable to its business or assets, including without limitation environmental laws and occupational health and safety laws. Seller has all permits, licenses, orders, approvals, authorizations, and concessions required by any regulatory body.

Q. The Disclosure Statement includes a description of the premises, building, structure, and lease terms, and conditions for the lease to which Seller is a party and a list of all material contracts, agreements, concessions, commitments, and leases relating to or affecting Seller, together with all amendments and supplements thereto and modifications thereof. For the purposes of this paragraph, "material" shall mean a total expenditure or income of $5,000 or more during the period of the contract. Seller shall deliver to Buyer true and complete copies of all such material contracts, agreements, concessions, leases, commitments, amendments, supplements, and modifications thereof. All of the agreements are legally valid and binding, in full force and effect, and will not be affected by this Agreement.

R. The Disclosure Statement contains a description of all machinery, equipment, vehicles, and other tangible personal property owned by Seller. The Disclosure Statement also includes a description of all intangible personal property owned by Seller, including any trademarks, trade names, or other intangible rights. Such rights are owned by Seller free and clear of any security interest, lien, or encumbrance except as specifically set forth on the Disclosure Statement.

S. Except as set forth in the Disclosure Statement, there are no claims, litigation actions, investigations, or proceedings existing or pending or, to the knowledge of any director or shareholder, threatened, and no order, injunction, or source is outstanding against or relating to Seller or its assets or business, and neither Seller nor the Shareholder know or has reasonable basis for knowing any information that may result in such a claim, litigation action, investigation, or proceeding.

FIGURE 4.9 Certificate of Warranties and Representations, continued

T. Seller is not presently in default, or alleged to be under or in breach of any term, provision, or clause of any agreement, license, lease, commitment, instrument, obligation, or contract except or disclosed on the Disclosure Statement. To the best knowledge of Seller and to shareholders, no other party to any agreement, license, lease, commitment, instrument, obligation, or contract to which Seller is a party is in default hereunder or in breach of any term or provision thereof, except for delinquent accounts receivable and as disclosed on the Disclosure Statement. To the best knowledge of Seller and the Shareholders, there exists no condition or event that, after inquiry or lapse of time or both, could institute a default by Seller or any other party to such agreement, license, lease, contract, instrument, obligation, or contract.

U. The Disclosure Statement specifically lists all employee health programs, and benefits, if any, and seller has no contract of any kind (written or oral) relating to employees, including any employment contract, union contract, pension, profit sharing, retirement, bonus, stock option, group life, or accident insurance or any employee benefit plan except as set forth in the Disclosure Statement. Seller carries adequate insurance coverage for its assets and businesses, including casualty, general liability, and all related risks. All such policies of insurance are in full force and effect.

V. Except as set forth on the Disclosure Statement, all of the real property, equipment, furniture, and fixtures, leasehold improvements, and tangible assets used by Seller are in good operational condition and repair, and are capable of being used for their intended use in the ordinary course of business.

W. All federal, state, and municipal tax returns and reports required by law to be filed by Seller have been filed, and all taxes shown thereon to be due and paid. Seller does not have any tax liabilities, including without limitation federal income taxes, state income, or franchise taxes, real and personal property taxes, sale and use taxes, worker's compensation or contributions, and unemployment insurance payments, other than as shown on the Disclosure Statement and those that have accrued since the date of this signed certificate in the ordinary course of business for which returns or

FIGURE 4.9   Certificate of Warranties and Representations, continued

payments are not yet due. Seller has not executed or filed with any taxing authority any agreement extending the period for assessment or collection of any federal or state taxes.

X. Copies of Seller's federal and state income tax returns for the years ending 1997, 1998, and 1999, have been given to Buyer. Seller has not filed any amended return for these years.

Y. Seller and shareholders acknowledge and agree that the representations and warranties made herein or in any agreement, instrument, certificate, disclosure statement, or other document delivered in connection herewith shall survive a closing indefinitely. No investigation or lack thereof, by Buyer or any of its agents shall be deemed to constitute or imply a waiver of any representation or warranty of Seller or shareholders.

Z. No representation or warranty made by Seller or the shareholders and no statement contained in any exhibit, certificate, Disclosure Statement, or other document delivered to Buyer pursuant to or in connection with this transaction contemplated hereby contains, or will contain, any untrue statement of material fact or omits, or will omit, to state a material fact necessary to make the statements contained therein, in light of the circumstances in which they are made, not misleading.

The parties set forth below acknowledge and agree that the above warranties and representation are true and correct and shall be true and correct on the date of closing of the acquisition between Buyer and Seller.

Seller(s) _____   Date _____

For proper effect, obtain a notarized copy of the Certificate of Warranties and Representations. If real property is involved, many new issues and concerns arise, as addressed in the disclosure statement in Figure 4.10. You should consult a licensed real estate agent (most business brokers are licensed agents) or an attorney to cover all bases. Only experienced attorneys are aware of current legal developments. Review and utilize these forms (Figures 4.10 and 4.11) when purchasing a business that comes with real property!

FIGURE 4.10 Seller's Disclosure Statement

SELLER'S DISCLOSURE STATEMENT

Business/Personal Property

This disclosure statement refers to the business known as _____
and located at (address) _____.
The seller provides the information for the purpose of it being disclosed to a buyer
knowing that the buyer may rely on it in deciding whether to purchase the business
and that it may influence the price and terms offered for the business by the buyer to
the seller. Use addendums as needed.

A. Regulations

Are there any matters in progress or unresolved with any agency of the following
type involving the business, its operations or assets? Are there any threatened or pending claims against the business or its agents involving any regulation, ordinance, law,
or rule administered by any agency of the following type? Answer yes (y) or no (n).

_____ Building Department
_____ Department of Agriculture
_____ Department of Employment/State or Federal
_____ Environmental Agencies/State or Federal
_____ Fire Department
_____ Health Department
_____ Internal Revenue Service/State or Federal
_____ OSHA
_____ Police Department
_____ State Alcoholic Beverage Department
_____ State Tax Authorities, Income, Sales, etc.
_____ Zoning Commission

If yes, or any other, explain:

_____

B. Required Licenses, Permits, and Certificates

List all required licenses, permits, and certificates: _____
_____

C. Environmental

Does the business have any problem or potential problem in areas regulated by
any of the following? Answer yes (y) or no (n). If state regulations apply, please note
as such.

_____ Clean Air Act
_____ Clean Water Act
_____ Federal Comprehensive Environmental Act

FIGURE 4.10 Seller's Disclosure Statement, continued

_____ Federal Water Pollution

_____ National Environmental Policy Act

_____ Noise Pollution Control

_____ Occupational Safety and Health Act

_____ Resource Conservation Recovery Act

_____ Response, Comprehensive Environmental Act

If yes, or any other, explain:

_____

Does your business include the handling or disposing of any hazardous water? Yes or

No _____

If yes, or any other, explain: _____

D. Legal Considerations

Is the business affected by any of the following? Answer yes (y) or no (n).

_____ Back Wages Due or Claims for the Same

_____ Claims for Unfair Labor Practices

_____ Other Pending or Outstanding Problems or Concerns

_____ Outstanding Contracts or Agreements

_____ Outstanding Lease Agreements (other than on the premises)

_____ Pending Litigation

_____ Product Liability Exposure

_____ Union Problems or Demand for Unionization

_____ Unpaid Medical or Other Insurance Premiums

_____ Unresolved Insurance Claims

If yes, or any other, explain:

_____

E. Existing/Pending Contracts

List all existing or pending contracts: _____

_____

The information above is not part of any contract, nor is it a contract between a buyer and seller. It is a disclosure only, made by the seller.

The seller certifies below that the above is true and accurate to the best of the seller's knowledge.

Owner name and title _____ Date _____

Signed by _____

The undersigned purchaser hereby acknowledges receiving a copy of this Seller Disclosure

Purchaser name and title: _____ Date _____

Signed by _____

FIGURE 4.11 Seller's Property Disclosure Statement

SELLER'S PROPERTY DISCLOSURE STATEMENT

Real Property

Property Address _____

Business Name _____

I. Title/Zoning/Building Information

Yes No Unknown

❑ ❑ ❑ 1. Owner's name _____
               Approximate year built _____ Date Purchased _____
               If vacant, how long? ____

❑ ❑ ❑ 2. Do you know of title problems (for example, basements, use restrictions, lot line disputes, liens, encroachments, access, other? If yes, explain _____

❑ ❑ ❑ 3. Zoning classification of the property _____
               Not known _____

❑ ❑ ❑ 4. Do you know of zoning problems/violations? Explain _____
               _____

❑ ❑ ❑ 5. Do you know of any building code or sanitary code violations?
               Explain _____

❑ ❑ ❑   a. Have you or others done any work on the property, e.g., building, plumbing, electrical, or other improvements?
               Describe _____

❑ ❑ ❑   b. If work was done by others, were they licensed to perform the work?

❑ ❑ ❑   c. Were permits required?
❑ ❑ ❑   Were they obtained?
❑ ❑ ❑   d. Was work completed? Explain _____

❑ ❑ ❑ 6. Is any portion of the property in a flood plain/way? Explain
               _____

❑ ❑ ❑ 7. Are there any property tax penalties or other citations against the property?

❑ ❑ ❑ 8. Are there any pending legal disputes concerning the property, proceed or existing homeowners'/owners' association or government, assessments, tax reclassifications, utility, mechanic-man's or materialman's liens that could affect title to the property or the consideration to be paid? Explain _____
               _____

❑ ❑ ❑ 9. Are you currently contracted to convey any right, title, or interest in the property? Explain _____

FIGURE 4.11 Seller's Property Disclosure Statement, continued

Yes	No	Unknown	
❑	❑	❑	10. Are you aware of any other information concerning your property that might affect the decision of a buyer to buy, or affect the value of your property, or affect its use by a buyer, e.g., rights-of-way, the land or buildings? If so, describe ____ _____
❑	❑	❑	a. Are all fences or walls solely owned?
❑	❑	❑	b. Are all fences or walls jointly owned? If no, explain below.
❑	❑	❑	11. a. Is there a homeowners'/owners' association governing this property?
❑	❑	❑	b. If yes, is there a fee? How much $_____

For additional information or further explanation (indicate #), describe below or add attachment:

_____

_____

II. Systems/Utilities Information

Yes	No	Unknown	
❑	❑	❑	12. Heating/Cooling Systems
❑	❑	❑	a. Heating _____ Type _____ Age _____
❑	❑	❑	b. Cooling _____ Type _____ Age _____
❑	❑	❑	c. Identify unheated and/or uncooled rooms _____
❑	❑	❑	d. Known problems in system(s) _____
❑	❑	❑	13. Type of hot water heater _____ Age ____
❑	❑	❑	14. Are there any domestic hot water problems? Explain ____ _____
❑	❑	❑	15. Are there any plumbing system problems/leaks/freezing? Explain _____
❑	❑	❑	16. Are there any bathroom ventilation problems? Explain ____ _____
❑	❑	❑	17. Type of sewage system (sewer, septic, cesspool, etc.) _____ Public ____ Private ____ Planned and approved sewer system _____ If private, (a) Name of service company _____ (b) Date last pumped _____ Frequency _____
❑	❑	❑	18. Are there any sewage system problems? Explain _____ _____

FIGURE 4.11 Seller's Property Disclosure Statement, continued

Yes	No	Unknown	
❑	❑	❑	19. Are there any electrical system problems? Explain _____ _____
❑	❑	❑	20. Water Source: Public __ Private __ If private, well location or company name _____
❑	❑	❑	21. Are there any water pressure problems? Explain _____ _____
❑	❑	❑	22. Are there any drinking water problems? Explain _____ _____
❑	❑	❑	23. Appliances: Are all appliances that are being included in working order? Explain _____
❑	❑	❑	24. Are there any systems/appliances included that have been disconnected or are nonfunctional? Explain _____
❑	❑	❑	25. Is there a security system and/or fire-smoke detection system? Explain _____
❑	❑	❑	26. Are there any existing leased equipment or systems? Explain _____

For additional information or further explanation (indicate #), describe below or add attachment:

_____

_____

III. Building/Structural/Improvements Information

Yes	No	Unknown	
❑	❑	❑	27. Are you aware of any earth movement or settlement problems? Explain _____
❑	❑	❑	28. Has there been major damage to the property or any structure on the property? Explain _____
❑	❑	❑	29. Roof type _____ Age _____ Are there any roof leaks or other roof problems? Explain _____
❑	❑	❑	30. Are there any interior walls/ceiling/doors/windows/floors problems? Explain _____ Type of floor under carpets/linoleum? _____
❑	❑	❑	31. Chimney/fireplace problems? Explain _____ a. Date last cleaned _____
❑	❑	❑	b. Fireplace tools and equipment included?
❑	❑	❑	32. Is the wood/coal stove in compliance with local installation regulation? Explain _____

FIGURE 4.11 Seller's Property Disclosure Statement, continued

Yes   No   Unknown

❑   ❑   ❑   33. History of wood infestation insect or pest problems? Explain

_____

❑   ❑   ❑   34. Is the property insulated? Type _____
Location _____

❑   ❑   ❑   35. Other building, structural, or modification problems? Describe

_____

❑   ❑   ❑   36. Are there any door window openings that may interfere
with ingress or egress in case of an emergency?

❑   ❑   ❑   37. Is there a landscape watering system?
❑ electrical   ❑ manual   ❑ both
Are there any problems? Explain _____

❑   ❑   ❑   38. If applicable, are there any known problems with the pool, hot
tub, spa, sauna, or the mechanical systems? Explain _____

_____

❑   ❑   ❑   39. If applicable, are there any governmental or zoning ordinances
that may affect a Buyer's future use and enjoyment of the pool,
hot tub, spa, or sauna? Explain _____

For additional information or further explanation (indicate #), describe below or add
attachment:

_____

_____

IV. Rental Information
Yes   No   Unknown

❑   ❑   ❑   40. Is the property currently occupied by a tenant? If yes, what is
the expiration of rental agreement? _____

❑   ❑   ❑   41. Have there been promises or representations that the tenant
has the right of renewal or option to purchases?

❑   ❑   ❑   42. Are security deposits or prepaid rents being held? By whom
and how much? _____

For additional information or further explanation (indicate #), describe below or add
attachment:

_____

_____

V. Environmental Information
Yes   No   Unknown

❑   ❑   ❑   43. Is any portion of the property situated on a sanitary landfill?

FIGURE 4.11 Seller's Property Disclosure Statement, continued

Yes   No   Unknown

❑   ❑   ❑   44. Are there any hazardous materials on the property, such as asbestos, dumps, pesticides, radon, lead based paint, underground fuel storage tanks, or leaks? Explain _____

_____

❑   ❑   ❑   45. Are there any hazardous materials in close proximity to the property, such as asbestos, dumps, pesticides, radon, lead based paint, underground fuel storage tanks, or leaks? Explain: ____

_____

❑   ❑   ❑   46. Is any of your property within an area currently designated by any government agency to be environmentally damaged, e.g., Superfund or wetlands area or WQARF or CERCLA sites? Explain _____

❑   ❑   ❑   47. Is your property subject to any known or proposed noise, such as airports or freeways? Explain: _____

❑   ❑   ❑   48. Are there other known neighborhood noises, nuisances, or pollutants? Explain: _____

For additional information or further explanation (indicate #), describe below or add attachment:

_____

_____

This statement is a disclosure of Seller's knowledge of the conditions of the property as of the date signed by Seller and is not a substitute for any inspections or warranties the purchaser may wish to obtain. Any changes to the above will be disclosed by Seller to Buyer prior to closing. Seller/Buyer hereby acknowledges receipt of a copy of this Disclosure. Property inspection reports may be purchased. Buyer is encouraged to obtain a property inspection by an independent third party and to investigate warranty issues.

_____		_____	
Seller	Date	Buyer	Date
_____		_____	
Seller	Date	Buyer	Date

Schedules, Exhibits, Other Attachments

This area varies widely depending upon complexity. Common examples include:

- Allocation of purchase price (Form 8594)
- Contracts to be transferred/assumed, including leases for real and personal property
- Equipment and inventory list (separate list for excluded assets)
- Personal property (and real property) lease agreements/transfers/assumptions
- Financial statements, tax returns, and assumed liabilities
- Personal guarantees and pledge of collateral
- Litigation summary and disclosure of potential liabilities

Escrow Documents

Escrow services were reviewed in Chapter 2. Their first involvement occurs when the buyer has removed all contingencies contained in the purchase contract and places his or her escrow/earnest deposit at risk by *opening* escrow. Once escrow is opened, the escrow agent will *search the public records for liens and encumbrances, prepare escrow documents such as the bill of sale and promissory note, follow the bulk sales law, and calculate closing related prorations.*

Here are a few important ideas. First, realize that an attorney can perform the same work, but not normally as an independent third party. Second, there may be conflict between the purchase agreement and the escrow instructions. The escrow instructions are prepared based on a combination of information provided by the broker, information contained in the purchase contract, and information deemed important by the escrow company and thus included. To prevent potential disputes, clauses may be inserted into the purchase agreement (granting superiority to this agreement) or in the escrow instructions (granting superiority to the instructions). Compare the following:

I. In the event of any conflict between the terms and conditions of these Escrow Instructions and Purchase Contract and Receipt, the terms and conditions of these Escrow Instructions shall prevail and shall constitute an amendment to the Purchase Contract.

II. Closing of this transaction shall occur on or before _____, 19__ (herein referred to as Close of Escrow) unless mutually extended in writing by the parties hereto. The parties designate _____ to act as Escrow Agent for this sale, and each party agrees to pay one-half of the Escrow Agent's fees and expenses in connection with its services. This Purchase Contract, when fully executed by the parties hereto, shall constitute the escrow instructions, except in the event that Escrow Agent shall desire to draw up separate escrow instructions using the same terms and conditions herein, provided; however, that *in the event of any discrepancy between the terms and conditions of such escrow instructions and the provisions of this Purchase Contract, the latter shall control.* For purposes of establishing the date of the Note and the dates on which payments thereunder shall be due, the date of Close of Escrow shall be deemed to be the date of delivery of possession (unless designated otherwise in writing by both parties) of the Company and Assets to Buyer and shall be the date of proration of rent, taxes, assessments, insurance, utility charges, and all other charges, fees, or prepaid expenses pertaining to the Company premises, the Assets being purchased hereunder, and of the operation of the Company.

The first clause giving precedence to the escrow instructions was prepared by the escrow company while the second was prepared by the broker. Supplemental escrow instructions can include as many as 25 additional clauses, which must be agreed on before closing. Situations have occurred where *both* of the above clauses were signed off on! Consider the following escrow-related clauses:

UCC-1

Upon opening and acceptance of this escrow, Escrow Agent shall conduct a UCC-1 search to determine whether any recorded liens are in existence against the Business or any of its assets and shall report its findings to BUYER, SELLER, and BROKER prior to closing of this sale. BUYER and SELLER hereby acknowledge receipt of the UCC lien and judgment search, which shows the following:

A UCC-1 financing statement recorded with _____ in Docket No. _____ with _____ as the *Debtor* and _____ the *Secured Party* has been paid in full and shall be released through escrow.

BUYER and SELLER hereby agree and understand that BUYER shall take possession of the business at the end of the business day of _____, 19__.

BUYER and SELLER hereby agree and understand that the maintenance contract on the _____ has been paid in full by the SELLER and SELLER shall have contract transferred into the BUYER'S name—outside of escrow.

Credit Statement

BUYER shall deposit with the escrow holder, for immediate submission to the seller or his agent, a credit statement/report. Buyer does covenant to the Seller that investigation of it will not reveal anything to adversely affect the credit of the Buyer.

Bulk Sales Waiver

BUYER and SELLER hereby instruct Escrow Agent that no compliance is to be made with regards to notification of creditors under _____ nor has any consent been obtained from said creditors should consent be required. Escrow Agent is instructed and authorized to proceed with the closing of the escrow without said compliance or consent and is hereby relieved of any responsibility or liability with regards to said compliance or consent.

Notice to Creditors

It is expressly agreed that the actual close of escrow shall be upon the published closing date of escrow as published in the Notice to Creditors of Bulk Transfer _____. Escrow Agent is instructed to pay a brokerage commission to _____ for services completed, payable at closing and chargeable to both parties. The parties agree that payment of this commission is not contingent upon the performance of any act, condition, or instruction in the Escrow Agreement.

Preparation of Documents

BUYER and SELLER acknowledge that the following documents were not prepared by Escrow Agent:
1. Promissory Note
2. Employment Contract

BUYER and SELLER hereby indemnify and save harmless *escrow agent* from any and all responsibility or liability in connection with the validity or sufficiency of such documents.

The typical scenario (three times out of four) involves the buyer and seller reading the escrow paperwork *for the first time* at the close of escrow. My advice is to absorb the expense involved with early preparation of closing documents to allow sufficient time for meaningful review. Common areas covered in the escrow paperwork are buyer and seller authorizations (payment of escrow fees, whether closing occurs or not), ramifications of canceling escrow (written notice required, handling of escrow funds, return of documents), escrow company disclaimers (no responsibility for sufficiency of title, no coverage for steps taken outside of escrow, not liable for performance of buyer), and closing costs/prorations (fee split, prorations included and excluded).

CHAPTER 5

The Purchase Agreement

Now we will examine a thorough, user-friendly, standardized purchase agreement. The title of this document implies that it is multifaceted. *It is an offer to purchase, which if signed both ways, becomes a purchase agreement after contingencies are removed.* Execution of this form is the first step in the formal purchase and sale process, as most deals contain one or more counteroffers. Here we go!

Sample Purchase Contract

Paragraph (1) in Figure 5.1 lays out what assets are included in the purchase price. Tangible assets as well as intangible assets such as trademarks and the trade name are included in this sale. If the seller wishes to exclude assets, there should be clear reference in the purchase agreement or in an addendum. Normally, an asset list is attached to the purchase contract. Its importance lies in its comprehensive nature and its use as an attachment to the bill of sale. Furthermore, it will describe the collateral for seller financing and will be part of a UCC-1 financing lien. Items (2) through (17) deal with the purchase price/financing terms. As this contract is written, *the total purchase price can be paid through the following channels:*

- Earnest deposit (held uncashed until contingencies are removed)
- Additional deposit (between original offer and closing)
- Balance of down payment (at closing in certified funds)
- Assumption of debt (e.g., equipment note, previous seller's carry-back)
- Seller financing

Down payments, assumption of existing debts and new seller financing collectively make up the entire purchase price. Let's discuss each of these components. Number (2) is the total purchase price and will equal number (16). Number (3) is the original escrow deposit check, which is normally attached to the offer and held by the broker until agreement is finalized and contingencies are removed. Normally, a personal check (4) payable to the escrow company is used. If not, it should be payable to the broker's trust account (never written to an individual person). Strict, demanding sellers may require a certified check, but this is uncommon for smaller businesses. Additional deposits (7) or the balance of the down payment (6) brought to closing must be certified funds to guarantee timely closing. It is best to use a local bank as the escrow company may require several days to process an out-of-state check. Wire transfers are equally attractive. Assumption of debt (9) can take many forms, such as an equipment loan or previous seller carry-back note. These amounts may be included in the actual purchase price, but not all assumptions are labeled as such. The point is *that the total consideration paid for the business includes assumed debts.*

In terms of the form, another type of debt assumption to be entered here (12) is bank financing. If the buyer is applying for a bank loan, a contingency will also be entered in section (21), similar to the clause found earlier in this step. Assumption of debt, therefore, can be either existing debt payments to be taken over by purchaser or new debt payments arising from external financing. Assumption of debts requires time and effort and is subject to creditor approval. The original debtor will normally remain liable, but this may be subject to negotiation.

When it becomes clear that the deal will proceed to closing, begin working on these assumptions immediately. Creditors do not normally have the same sense of urgency as the buyer, seller, and broker. Finally, the purchase price could be financed through (13), (14), (15) seller financing (seller carry-back note). In this particular contract, the seller is protected by contingency #4 in area (19), which gives the seller the right to review the buyer's credit history. Overall, *the total purchase price (2), (16) is equal to earnest deposits, additional down payments, assumption of existing and new debt and seller financing. Much of the wrangling that occurs deals with finding an agreeable mix of these components.* In practice, the seller will likely counter the price, down payment, or repayment terms while the buyer may revise the originally agreed upon terms after performing a complete due diligence. If the buyer and seller wish to implement an earn-out agreement, a detailed addendum would be required.

Numbers (18) to (21) address some of the most important areas of any purchase agreement—contingencies and conditions. Important and unique covenants, indemnifications, warranties, and representations may also surface in this section of the contract, commonly referenced to formal, multipaged addenda. Number (18) affects the flow of negotiations and reflects the seriousness of buyer and seller. The first offer is normally written by the buyer, who seeks to control the time dimension. Number (18) puts a deadline on the buyer's due diligence. The buyer will want ample time to perform due diligence and remove contingencies, requesting as much as 30 days. The average due diligence period for privately held companies is two to four weeks. An attentive seller will try to shorten this considerably. As always, relative bargaining strengths will determine the final outcome.

Sections (19), (20), and (21) address important contingencies referred to in Chapter 4. Generally, all contingencies must be removed before escrow can be opened and the buyer's money placed at risk. Professional brokers will require the buyer to sign off on each contingency (contingency removal form, as presented earlier). The broker should also obtain a signed *authorization to close* form, capturing the unequivocal desire of both sides to close the deal.

Area (21) is a catch all for any contingencies, conditions, or clauses not addressed properly elsewhere. Both sides will want certain additions, requiring signed addendum(s) or amendment(s). Every deal results in differing contingencies, conditions, warranties, and other clauses. Being aware of the many options will lead to a stronger, clearer, more beneficial contract.

Numbers (22) and (23) address the time given to the seller to accept the offer. If not accepted (signed by seller), the offer is withdrawn and the escrow check returned. This form establishes a specific cutoff time and date (e.g., 6 PM on 7-05-96, or a time based on presentation of the offer). Most offers establish a specific cutoff date, such as 6 PM three days after the offer is written and signed. A less common approach is to stipulate that acceptance occur upon presentation, effectively forcing the seller to decide on the spot. This is a risky strategy that may jeopardize the deal. Most sellers do not react favorably to such pressure. Most sellers will counter the offer regardless of the cutoff time. In general, the seller has three options:

1. Accept as written
2. Present counteroffer
3. Reject offer through silence

Acceptance of the original offer is rare, but motivated sellers without previous offers may have no choice. They fear a negative response to a counteroffer, which is a rejection of the original offer. On the other hand, if the seller is offended by the offer, he or she may feel it is not worthy of a counter. The message from the seller may be that the buyer must do better to get the seller's attention. *Most common by far is the counteroffer, which might address the price, down payment, repayment terms, and a host of conditions, contingencies, and other clauses.* Any component of the original offer is subject to counter. The requested changes may be legitimately desired or part of an overall negotiating strategy. For insights into negotiating techniques, see Step 6 in Chapter 6.

Numbers (24) and (25) also have important implications. The role played by escrow companies is both critical and complex. The critical aspects involve assurances that the business is sold/purchased in a legal fashion. The services of escrow companies are described in Chapter 2. Even in a large community like Phoenix, Arizona, there is little choice when it comes to selecting an escrow agent. In fact, this metropolitan area has only one experienced company. Beyond choosing an (30) escrow agent, this paragraph stipulates a closing deadline. The actual closing date cannot be ensured until all contingencies are removed. Establishing a deadline, however, serves the important function of creating a goal. Removal of contingencies (18) should correspond to the closing deadline (25). *The typical sequence of events leading to closing is: offer, counteroffer, acceptance, due diligence, removal of contingencies, opening of escrow and deposit of escrow funds, preparation and review of closing documents, final deposit of certified funds into escrow, modification and signing of escrow paperwork and distribution of funds, formal passing of ownership and filing of liens and transition events such as training, and payments against note or earn-out arrangement.*

FIGURE 5.1   Offer to Purchase/Earnest Receipt/Purchase Agreement

---

OFFER TO PURCHASE/EARNEST RECEIPT/ PURCHASE AGREEMENT

---

(1) As of _____ at ___ AM/PM, _____ hereafter known as buyer, hereby offers and agrees to purchase all of the assets of that business known as _____ with an address of _____.
Unless specifically excluded per written addendum, this purchase includes all assets, tangible and intangible, including but not limited to any furniture, fixtures, equipment, inventory, trademarks, copyrights, trade names, patents, and leases subject to the terms and conditions presented in this agreement, including the allocation of purchase price contained below:

Purchase Price $ (2) payable as follows:

Earnest Funds $ (3) received at time of offer in the form of (4) payable to (5) . Broker shall hold said funds uncashed until all contingencies are removed and escrow is opened. Seller acknowledges that any such check received by broker is subject to collection.

Balance of Down Payment $ (6) deposited with escrow holder at closing in certified funds

Other Deposited Funds $ (7) other down payment related deposits of any type

Total Down Payment $ (8) as of close of escrow

Assumption of Liability $ (9) (or paid through seller), payable at $ (10) per month, including (11) % interest as per promissory note. Before/after assumption, buyer may negotiate with creditor to secure more favorable terms.

Assumption of Liability $ (12) (or paid through seller), payable at $___ per month, including _____% interest as per promissory note. Before/after assumption, buyer may negotiate with creditor to secure more favorable terms

Remaining Balance $ (13) to be paid to seller as evidenced by buyer's secured promissory note, payable at $ (14) or more per month including interest

and principal from close of escrow for (15) months, with said interest at (15) %
per annum. Any unpaid indebtedness referred to under assumption of liability is
approximate, with any differences to be paid to seller such that entire purchase price
is paid. UCC-1 financing statements to be filed with the proper authorities

Other Terms _____

**TOTAL $ (16) **

Acceptance: When signed by buyer, this form combined with an earnest check
becomes an offer on the part of the buyer to purchase the above business subject to
the terms and conditions stated herein and should the seller fail to accept this offer by
signing page 3 of this document prior to 6:00 PM (22) 19__, or within (23) days
of presentation to the seller, whichever comes last, the buyer shall withdraw this offer
and said earnest deposit will be returned by broker immediately to buyer. Time is of
the essence in terms of performance per this agreement.

Escrow/closing: For the purpose of completing this transaction, the parties hereby
appoint (24) of (24) as escrow agent to receive, deposit, and distribute funds for
the parties and facilitate closing through preparation and execution of escrow instructions and documents evidencing the terms and conditions of this sale on or before 6:00
PM on (25) 19__. Buyer and seller hereby agree to each pay one-half (½) of the
escrow/collection agent's fees and expenses. Upon removal of contingencies in writing,
buyer and seller do hereby jointly and severally, acknowledge, direct, and authorize broker to deposit earnest money and hold same in the escrow account. Buyer and seller
agree to execute all documents necessary to consummate this transaction.

Contingencies: This agreement is subject to and contingent upon the buyer's
written removal of contingencies on or before (18) days from signed, mutual
acceptance of this agreement. Earnest funds to be returned to buyer if contingencies
are not removed. Offer contingent upon the following events :

(19) 1. Buyer reviewing and approving the books, records, and operations of the
business.
2. Buyer proving/verifying business income and cash flow
3. Buyer examining and approving condition of all furniture, fixtures, and
equipment
4. Seller investigating and approving buyer's credit history and credit references.
5. Seller's and buyer's legal counsels reviewing this agreement to perfect the
language (not to change the basic agreement).
6. Buyer's receiving a valid assignment of the existing lease, sublease of the
existing lease, or a new lease with a base rent of $ (20) per month for a
period of _____ years, with additional terms of _____.
7. Additional contingencies and conditions (21)

_____

_____ (see addendums) _____

_____

Purchase Price Allocation: Buyer and seller agree to allocate the foregoing purchase price on or before the time of closing. Said allocations shall be attached to this agreement and be made an integral part hereof. Major categories for allocation include:

Furniture, Fixtures, and Equipment	_____	Covenant Not To Compete	_____
Inventory	_____	Trade Name	_____
Real Property	_____	Consulting Agreement	_____
Leasehold Improvements	_____	Customer Accounts	_____
Leasehold Interest Rights	_____	Goodwill	_____

Inventory: It is agreed by buyer and seller that the on-hand inventory of marketable inventory (not damaged, obsolete, or excessively slow-moving) at seller's original cost shall be approximately $_____. On or near the day of closing, both buyer and seller shall jointly count the stock on hand to establish its value. Any amount greater than or less than the dollar value referred to above shall be added to/deducted from the total purchase price per the promissory note. The amount of inventory included in the sale shall not exceed $_____ or drop below $_____. If the buyer is paying all cash, the funds brought to escrow shall be adjusted accordingly. Buyer and seller may agree to use an independent, outside agency to count and value the inventory, whose final calculations shall be considered binding upon both parties.

Familiarization: Seller, at no expense to buyer, shall familiarize and acquaint buyer with all material aspects of the company's operations from the date of possession or as otherwise agreed for a period of _(32)_ .

Covenant Not to Compete: The seller and seller's company officers/directors agree not to compete, directly or indirectly or in any manner, or engage in the _(33)_ business(es) within _(34)_ (miles or area) of the business purchased nor aid or assist anyone else, except the buyer, within these limits. Furthermore, the above parties will not solicit in any manner any past accounts or employees of the business nor have any interest, directly or indirectly, in such a business, except as employee of the buyer, for a period of _(35)_ consecutive years from close of this sale. Should buyer resell business during this period, the seller/officers/directors agree to continue to be bound by this covenant for the agreed upon duration.

(36) Accounts Receivable, Accounts Payable and Cash: Any and all accounts receivable, accounts payable, and cash existing as of closing are and shall remain the sole property and responsibility of the seller. Any and all accounts receivable, accounts payable, and cash that shall accrue immediately from and after the closing shall become the sole property and responsibility of the buyer. Unless otherwise agreed, seller agrees to deliver business free and clear of all debts.

(37) Arbitration: In the event of any dispute arising between the buyer, seller, and/or broker under this agreement, it is agreed that the matter shall be submitted to arbitration in accordance with the existing rules of the American Arbitration Association. Parties may be represented by legal counsel. Buyer shall not have the right to demand arbitration if it is in default for the payment of any money owed Seller, but shall be permitted to make payments into an escrow account pending disposition of the dispute. Such arbitration shall be pursued in the city and state of _____ and shall be expeditiously completed such that a final and binding decision can be reached within 180 days. Should arbitrators determine by majority vote that the claim made is frivolous, the other party shall be reimbursed all arbitration fees, reasonable attorney fees, and other reasonable costs.

(38) Authority/Consent: No approval, notification, permit, license, authorization, or other action by, to, or from, or filing with any governmental authority or any person or entity having a contractual relationship with seller or other interest in seller or seller's company assets is required in connection with the execution, delivery, and performance of the seller regarding seller's obligations under this agreement (no third party consent required). Both buyer and seller have full power and authority to enter into and conclude the transaction described herein.

(39) Bill of Sale: At close of escrow, seller shall deliver title of the assets to buyer by bill of sale, including but not limited to those assets listed in Exhibit A for which seller warrants that he has good and marketable title, free and clear of all liens and encumbrances, except as disclosed therein. Seller may use the proceeds of the sale to satisfy outstanding debts/liens.

(40) Binding Effect/Assignment: This agreement shall bind and inure to the benefit of the successors, assigns, personal representatives, heirs, and legatees of the parties hereto and upon execution by all parties this agreement shall be absolutely binding and fully enforceable.

(41) Business Deposits: Any and all amounts currently on deposit for the benefit of the business for utility services, lease, taxes, insurance, etc., are and shall remain the sole property of the seller and shall be reimbursed to seller at close of escrow.

(42) Business Premises and Records: Until possession is transferred, seller agrees to maintain the business premises, including heating, cooling, plumbing and electrical systems, built-in fixtures, together with all other equipment and assets included in this sale, in working order and to maintain and leave the premises in a clean, orderly condition (if prepared, see seller's disclosure statement for more warranties and representations made by seller). Furthermore, immediately after closing, seller shall deliver to buyer all customer accounts and records, and any other documents pertinent to the operation of the business that seller may have. Such records shall include copies of those documents necessary to conduct business with suppliers and customers of the business.

(44) Business Trade Name: Seller hereby grants buyer, effective with the closing of escrow, any and all rights held by seller in the trade name, _____ _____, and hereby waives any rights thereof, and shall not after the closing, make use of such name directly or indirectly.

(45) Chattel Security Agreement: At the close of this sale, buyer and seller shall enter into and execute a chattel security agreement giving seller a lien on all assets included in this sale, as more fully described in Exhibit A, until the promissory note owed to seller hereunder has been paid in full.

(46) Choice of Law: This agreement shall be governed/construed under state laws of _____.

(47) Conduct of Business: From the date of this agreement through the closing, seller will not operate business other than in the ordinary course or make distributions or payments of any type to any party, including owners and partners, or make any expenditure, payment, transfer or use of cash of any kind or incur any liability or obligation in excess of $_____ without the prior written consent of buyer. During said period, seller will preserve all rights, privileges, franchises, and other authority adequate for the conduct of the seller's business and operations. Finally, seller agrees to maintain satisfactory relationships with suppliers, contractors, distributors, customers, and all others having relationships with the seller and/or business.

(48) Counterparts: This agreement may be executed in several counterparts, all of which together shall constitute one agreement binding on all parties hereto.

(47) Default and Remedies: In the event of any anticipatory or other breach of this agreement by any party hereto, or upon the failure of this transaction to close due to the wrongful actions or failures to act of either party hereto, then this agreement shall be deemed to be in default.

In the case of seller breach, buyer may immediately cease performance and avail itself or any and all remedies available hereunder or at law for such breach or default, including, in the case of default by seller, buyer's right to specific performance. Any earnest money deposits shall be refunded to the buyer.

In the case of buyer breach, seller may retain the earnest money deposit as liquidated damages and may immediately cease performance and avail itself of any and all remedies available hereunder or at law for such breach or default.

(48) Equipment: Seller warrants that, at the time possession is delivered, all equipment will be in working order and that the premises will pass all inspections necessary to conduct such business. Possession date shall be at settlement/close of escrow.

(49) Further Assurances: After closing, seller agrees to execute and deliver as needed, or cause to be executed and delivered, such documents to buyer and take other such actions as buyer shall reasonably request in order to vest more effectively in buyer good title to the assets as provided herein. Both buyer and seller agree to take such steps as reasonably requested by the other party to more effectively consummate the transactions contemplated in this agreement.

(49) Headings: The headings of each section in this agreement are inserted for convenience only and do not constitute an integral part of the agreement.

(50) Incorporation of Parties: Buyer or seller may elect to incorporate prior to closing such that the new corporation shall become the buyer or seller, and buyer and seller shall cause corporation to ratify all the terms and conditions of the agreements and the payment of any unpaid balance owed to seller herein.

(51) Indemnification: Seller does hereby indemnify buyer and shall hold and save harmless from and against all debts, claims, actions, cause of action, losses, damages, and attorney's fees, now existing or that may hereafter arise from or grow out of past seller's operation and ownership of the business prior to the date of possession, except to the extent buyer has assumed such responsibilities, liabilities, or debts hereunder. Buyer does hereby indemnify and hold seller harmless in similar fashion for all aspects of the ownership of the business and the operation of its business for the period following date of possession. Seller and buyer agree that should any debts or liens owed by the seller prior to close of escrow remain unpaid after the close of escrow, then the buyer, at his option, may pay these debts and deduct the costs from the promissory note or funds held in escrow. Such action causes no default in the terms of the promissory note.

(52) Notices: All notices and other communications under this agreement shall be in writing and delivered via registered mail (return receipt requested) or by recognized overnight courier to the addresses below (unless changed by written notice prior to change of address):

If to buyer: _____

        Phone : _____   Fax : _____

If to seller: _____

        Phone : _____   Fax : _____

(52) Pending Litigation: Seller represents and warrants that there is no action, litigation, arbitration, or other legal proceeding pending or threatened, to the knowledge of the seller against or relating to the business or any of the assets of the business in any court or before any federal, state, or other governmental agency or authority, which would materially and adversely affect the business or assets of the business being sold (except as disclosed in writing per the seller's disclosure statement or attached hereto as an addendum).

(53) Permits and Certificates: Seller warrants and represents that all permits, licenses, and certificates required by any governmental agency or body having jurisdiction over the business that will be necessary to continue the operation of the business in its present premises will be current and valid as of the date of possession. Seller further warrants that the business will be in full compliance with all applicable laws, rules, and regulations of such governmental bodies or agencies.

(55) Fees and Expenses: Seller and buyer shall bear his or her own costs and expenses in connection with the negotiation and preparation of this agreement and the consummation of the transactions contemplated herein, e.g., attorney and accountant fees. Escrow fees to be split equally between buyer and seller and seller agrees to pay broker's commission in full.

(56) Risk of Loss or Damage: All risk of loss or damage to the assets being sold herein or to the business's premises shall, if occurring prior to date of possession, be seller's responsibility, and buyer shall assume all such risk of loss or damage following time of possession.

(57) Sales by Buyer: Buyer and seller hereby agree that buyer shall have, subsequent to the possession date, the right to sell the business or any portion thereof, provided that such sale shall not detrimentally affect seller's security interest in the business at the time of such proposed sale. Buyer shall be required to have written approval of seller prior to reselling or otherwise transferring interest in the business to another when seller has security interest, which approval shall not be unreasonably withheld.

(58) Severability: Any provision of this agreement that is illegal, invalid, prohibited, or unenforceable in any jurisdiction does not preclude the validity of all other provisions.

(59) Telephones: Seller agrees to transfer to buyer seller's interest and right to the phone numbers currently used in the business. Buyer agrees to reassign all telephone numbers used in the business to the seller or its agents or assigns in the event that buyer breaches any terms of this purchase agreement and seller retakes possession of the business under any circumstances.

(60) UCC-1 Search: Upon the opening of this escrow, the escrow agent shall promptly conduct a UCC-1 search to determine whether any recorded liens are in existence against the business or any assets of the business and shall report its findings to buyer, seller, and broker prior to close of escrow.

(61) Uniform Commercial Code—Bulk Transfer: Pursuant to _____, and in compliance therewith, seller shall, at the time of closing, execute and deliver to buyer an affidavit warranting, as of the closing, that the business shall have no creditors, unless set forth herein.

(62) Waiver: Compliance by any party with any of the provisions of this agreement may be waived by the other party. No waiver of any provision shall be construed as a waiver of any other provision. Any such waiver must be in writing and notarized.

(63) Warranty Against Liabilities: Seller warrants and represents that all outstanding liabilities of the business excepting as specifically set forth herein, shall be paid in full on or before close of escrow and that buyer shall receive possession and control of the assets of the business free and clear of any liabilities, claims, or encumbrances, including but not limited to any sales tax, withholding tax, payroll tax, or any other taxes. Seller warrants that any financial information provided to buyer is true and correct and is a fair and accurate presentation of the operation of the business.

(64) Miscellaneous Acknowledgments: Seller acknowledges that broker has made no representations concerning the credit-worthiness or ability of buyer to complete this transaction and relies solely on buyer representations and seller's independent investigation of buyer. Buyer hereby acknowledges that buyer is relying solely on buyer's independent inspection of the business, personal examination of the equipment, fixtures, inventory, leasehold improvements, and other assets of the business, and the representations of seller, not the broker, with regard to the prior operating history of the business, the value of the assets being purchased, and all other material facts of seller in making this offer.

This is a legally binding document that must be read carefully and in consultation with an attorney and other advisers. The buyer hereby agrees to purchase and the seller agrees to sell the business on the terms set forth above. Any subsequent changes to this contract must be in writing.

Dated and Accepted This _____ Day of _____ 19__ At _____ AM/PM

Buyer _____

Buyer _____

Address _____ Phone _____

SELLER'S ACCEPTANCE

I/we accept this offer to purchase and agree to sell the business and its assets (or stock) on the terms and conditions stated herein. Upon written acceptance, this contract shall be fully binding and enforceable.

Dated and Accepted This _____ Day of _____ 19__ At _____ AM/PM

Seller _____

Seller _____

Address _____ Phone _____

It is rare for an initial offer to be accepted as written. Counters should be made on a document similar to the one in Figure 5.2. When executing a counteroffer, which is formally referenced to the terms and conditions of the initial offer, only the points that specifically contradict the initial offer must be addressed. In other words, all terms and conditions of the original purchase will stand as valid unless they are specifically overruled by the counteroffer (e.g., a higher price or down payment). The seller might agree with all verbiage in the original offer except for one or two things. Only these items must be addressed. The counter "flows" with the original offer, as would a counter to the counter (counteroffer number 2), etc.

FIGURE 5.2   Counteroffer

COUNTEROFFER

Counteroffer Number _____

As concerns the purchase offer signed and dated _____ between _____ as buyer and _____ as seller, all of the terms, conditions, covenants, contingencies, indemnifications, and representations and warranties are accepted *except* as follows:

_____

_____

_____

_____

_____

_____

_____

_____

_____

_____

In the event that the buyer (   ) or seller (   ) fails to accept this counteroffer in writing on or before _____, 19____ at _____ AM/PM (circle one), this counteroffer shall be considered null and void and all earnest funds are to be promptly returned to the buyer.

Buyer: _____ Date: _____ Seller: _____ Date: _____

Buyer: _____ Date: _____ Seller: _____ Date: _____

CHAPTER 6

Final Negotiations
and Due Diligence

Step 6: Conclude Negotiations

This chapter illustrates scenarios that may unfold as a deal progresses through due diligence and toward closing. Many individuals in many different ways will contribute to or hinder this process. *Deal breakers* can materialize out of nowhere to the surprise of all parties. Each participant to a transaction (buyer, seller, spouses, brokers, CPAs, attorneys, escrow agents, landlords, government officials, lessors, partners, parents, competitors, suppliers, customers, employees, to name a few!) will have conflicting interests. There are often more than a hundred conditions (pre- and post-closing) and contingencies (self-liquidating and not) to be negotiated before a deal is completed. This guide would not be complete without addressing the many different negotiating tactics and principles that exist. Before proceeding, consider the following key elements/steps to a successful sale:

- Promote a cooperative relationship within an informal environment for the first meeting.
- Understand the other party's needs and express your needs without being demanding.
- Be firm but flexible, and assume the other party is interested in closing.
- Move as quickly as possible without giving the impression of desperation.
- Try not to get overly bogged down on disagreements; focus on areas of agreement.
- Avoid impossible (unrealistic) positions.
- Always put it in writing as soon as possible.

Deal-Breakers

Events that destroy deals can occur at any time, even before the business is formally listed for sale! Either the buyer or seller may be the primary cause. Family members or representatives/agents of the buyer and seller may be the culprits. It may simply be a matter of troubled chemistry between the principals. On a more impersonal level, maybe the problem is the economy (it's doing too well or not well enough)! Or perhaps the impediment is congress and the president, who are dragging their feet on reducing the capital gains tax. The following is a list of parties that may claim the title of *deal-breaker* (either side): family members, brokers, accountants, attorneys, landlords, business associates, bankers, or any and all terms, conditions, and contingencies in the contract. Any one of them could be the primary or contributing cause of a deal falling apart. *Above all, the key to overcoming hurdles is a cooperative and mutually respectful relationship between buyer and seller.* This is a common characteristic of most deals that make it to the finish line. After agreeing on price and terms, all contingencies must be removed (i.e., the real work begins!), leaving plenty of room for disagreement and wrangling. If the spirit of cooperation and respect continues, differences can be overcome. Let's trace a hypothetical deal from beginning to end, illustrating three outcomes: favorable, tolerable, and deal-breaker!

Listing Appointment

The seller has called a local business broker into his place of business to query the broker on the salability of his business. *Favorable:* Seller is highly motivated to sell and wants to know from the broker what a fair price is to facilitate a quick sale. *Tolerable:* Seller claims he is in "no hurry" to give the business away and wants a lot of cash at a high multiple of ACF. *Deal-Breaker:* Seller wants all cash at the highest possible multiple ACF. Seller states that he doesn't really want to sell, but he has heard there are a lot of cash buyers coming to town. *Not!*

Buyer Interview with Broker

Favorable: Buyer is articulate, friendly, and has ample cash balances. Buyer also has owned and operated several businesses in the past 15 years. *Tolerable:* Buyer is courteous but hesitant. Has access to cash through family members and has a sound resume with management experience. *Deal-Breaker:* This person has *no* cash, has never owned a business, and is looking for someone desperate to sell and take over the payments. *Not!*

Buyer Interview with Seller

Favorable: Both buyer and seller arrive on time and warmly converse about their love of golf before discussing business. During interview, both sides determine the other is a person worthy of proceeding further. *Tolerable:* Buyer or seller is 25 minutes late, but calls to give warning. Upon arrival, seller initially is unresponsive but gradually forgives buyer. Buyer asks questions politely, without offending seller. *Deal-Breaker:* Buyer *and* seller are 20 minutes and 40 minutes late respectively. Buyer unintentionally insults seller's punctuality, after violating the nondisclosure agreement by discussing the potential sale with two employees before the seller's arrival. Buyer tells seller he is only interested in purchasing the accounts, not the hard assets, at a discounted price. *Not!*

Buyer Offer to Seller

Favorable: Buyer offers 90 percent of asking price and 100 percent of cash down requested by seller. Buyer asks that 5 percent of the cash down be placed into a special escrow account for six months to protect against unforeseen/overlooked liabilities/expenses. *Tolerable:* Buyer makes offer for 75 percent of asking price and 75 percent of cash down requested. Buyer requests that up to one-third of the future note payments be tied to actual performance of the business after closing. Offer is also contingent on purchaser obtaining back financing at a maximum of 11 percent interest (current SBA rate is 12 percent). *Deal-Breaker:* Buyer offers full price, but only 20 percent down with future note payments tied dollar for dollar to after-tax income above current levels. Buyer's offer is also contingent on obtaining a bank loan (home-equity) within ten days (buyer wants to own business during upcoming holiday season because 40 percent of sales occur in November and December). Seller must agree to train seller full-time for 60 days without further compensation. *Not!*

Seller Counteroffer to Buyer

Favorable: Seller accepts buyer's price and terms but makes acceptance contingent on seller review of purchaser's background and credit history. Seller also tightens up due diligence period to two weeks from one month. *Tolerable:* Seller rejects purchaser's offered price and terms and counters at one-half the difference between original asking price and purchaser's offer. Seller accelerates due diligence and closing dates and requests that the business continue to be shown in order to accept backup offers. Seller requests purchaser to personally provide recent credit report and a list of references (banking and professional). *Deal-Breaker:* Seller rejects offer without formal counteroffer. Seller verbally requests 100 percent cash and a closing date within three days. Broker is asked to inform purchaser that seller has serious doubts regarding purchaser's ability to successfully operate business. *Not!*

Due Diligence Review by Purchaser

Favorable: Purchaser receives all requested information on a timely basis and is able to visually confirm the presented level of sales. Purchaser and seller are working closely together and begin to brainstorm new ideas to improve the business in the future. Serious discussion of possible partnership relationships take place. Families meet one another for dinner at the seller's house. *Tolerable:* Purchaser obtains requested data at an acceptable pace, but tension is emerging over its credibility. Seller seeks to reassure purchaser, who is anxious to move the process forward. Purchaser inadvertently discloses his intention to buy business to a highly valued employee, who fortunately had already been informed by seller. *Deal-Breaker:* Seller holds back information after hearing from several sources that the purchaser has frequently made solid offers only to revise them downward after due diligence is completed with the hope of wearing the seller down. Buyer reacts angrily and begins talking to employees about how he would run the business. Seller's review shows two bankruptcies and recent charge-offs. Buyer harasses seller for information by calling him at home and offending his wife. *Not!*

Purchaser's CPA Review of Books

Favorable: CPA reviews all provided information promptly and tells purchaser that the business appears solid and the price is fair. CPA interviews seller regarding accounting procedures, important customers and suppliers, recent trends, etc., and encourages purchaser to move forward. *Tolerable:* Seller and seller's CPA are slow to provide requested information. Statements from the previous year are available, but up-to-date statements are still being prepared. The seller has multiple businesses, all of which are lumped together on a Schedule C, causing audit difficulties. Ten days pass and the purchaser begins to worry that maybe sales or profitability have declined. There are also indications that the cost of goods has increased significantly. The delay in providing information has cooled the purchaser's interest (as well as the spouse's, who is very concerned about the investment). Purchaser submits a new offer at a slightly lower price. Seller counters again between originally agreed on price and purchaser's new offer, which is accepted. *Deal-Breaker:* Seller originally claims sales of $250,000 and ACF of about $90,000. As purchaser's CPA becomes involved, seller becomes defensive and instructs purchaser and purchaser's CPA that all the information they need is available without the tax return. As it turns out, not only are the tax returns confusing (multiple businesses on one Schedule C), they are significantly different from what was originally claimed (sales, net income are lower). Seller reaffirms original claims, but cannot prove them. Purchaser's CPA gives a "thumbs down" and purchaser revises offer downward, asking that 50 percent of this lower down payment be held in escrow for six months, pending actual sales and profits (earn-out arrangement). This revised offer, after commissions and closing costs, requires *seller* to bring several thousand dollars to the table. *Not!*

Attorney Review for Purchaser

Favorable: Attorney reviews agreement and makes numerous suggestions to solidify purchaser's interests, including: (1) Seller warrants that all equipment leases have been disclosed; offer is contingent on purchaser assumption/transfer of said leases. (2) Covenant not to compete to be extended to eight miles for four years. (3) Promissory note to include clause allowing prepayment without penalty. *Tolerable:* Attorney review leads to the following recommendations: (1) Covenant not to compete to be extended to 15 miles and five years. (2) Promissory note to be secured by assets of acquired company primarily. Purchaser's assets from another separately owned corporation will also serve as collateral. (3) Purchaser agrees to bulk sales waiver as seller covenants that all debts of business will be paid in full as of closing. Further, 10 percent of down payment to be held in separate escrow account for four months, to pay all overlooked, outstanding liabilities incurred prior to close. *Deal-Breaker:* (1) Covenant not to compete to be for a five-year period for a 25 mile radius around location. Further, this covenant is to be structured as a separate payment in the form of a consulting agreement (immediately tax deductible for buyer). Seller to pay relevant payroll taxes on these payments. (2) Promissory note to be guaranteed by business assets only (no personal guarantee). (3) Purchaser to receive as part of purchase price all outstanding receivables and cash balances (checking accounts) of at least $25,000 with existing financial institutions. *Not!*

Attorney Review for Seller

Seller's attorney proposes the following changes. *Favorable:* (1) Promissory note signed by purchaser to be guaranteed both corporately and personally (both spouses). Default to occur if payment is not received after ten days of due date. (2) Seller may accept backup offers during due diligence period. (3) Training period to be for a total of 80 hours within one month of closing. Times to be mutually agreed upon. Purchaser acknowledges that seller has other obligations and cannot be available at all times. *Tolerable:* (1) Allocation of purchase price to be changed as follows: inventory reduced from $25,000 to $15,000, equipment increased from $70,000 to $95,000, and the covenant not to compete is reduced from $50,000 to $35,000. (2) Purchaser agrees to maintain inventory at or above a value of $100,000 (valued at original cost). (3) Purchaser and seller agree that seller may continue to show the business during the due diligence period. If seller receives legitimate offer to purchase with no contingencies, buyer will have *two* days from notice (registered mail) of such offer to remove all remaining contingencies. If these contingencies are not removed within this period, the agreement will be nullified and earnest money returned to purchaser. *Deal-Breaker:* (1) Late fees of $500 per event plus accrued interest of 21 percent APR computed continuously will be levied against late payments on promissory note, which will be personally guaranteed by purchaser. Also, purchase agreement is subject to both evergreen and cross-default clauses. (2) In the event purchaser seeks to sell business before note is paid in full, purchaser will notify seller immediately. Sale of business to a third party must be approved by seller, unless seller is paid in full prior to or at closing of sale. (3) Purchaser to obtain *key-man* insurance policy to match the amount of the outstanding loan balance until note is paid in full. Also, purchaser will maintain liability insurance in amount of $1 million.

After Contingency Removal, before Close of Escrow

Favorable: Buyer and seller are in regular contact planning anxiously for the closing and the subsequent transition period. Families get together for Sunday barbecue. Seller is happily sharing information about the business that will ensure future success. *Tolerable:* Buyer realizes that escrow deposit is now nonrefundable, but is under pressure from spouse regarding suitability of the business and its price. Seller is concerned about sharing too much information with buyer regarding customers and suppliers prior to closing. Buyer wonders if seller is hiding something, and seller wonders if buyer will make it all the way to the closing. *Deal-Breaker:* Buyer leaves town after having placed only $2,000 out of $10,000 total earnest deposit into escrow. Buyer promises to wire the balance on arrival at his destination. Seller has spent five full days preparing analyses and reviewing books and records. After buyer delays sending the remaining $8,000 in certified funds, seller states that he no longer wishes to sell to buyer and wants the $2,000 as liquidated damages. Buyer refuses to release $2,000, and seller hires an attorney to sue broker for failing to obtain sufficient down money and to sue buyer for breaking the contract. Buyer files countersuit alleging misrepresentation on the broker's part and fraud on the seller's part. *Not!*

After Escrow Preparation of Closing Documents, Before Closing

Favorable: Buyer, seller, and attorneys/CPAs review prepared documents and notice that the lien search was for the seller's name only, not the company name. New search is completed without surprises. Also, buyer and seller discover that their escrow fees include preparation of a promissory note, which was already completed by buyer and seller outside of escrow. Escrow company reduces charges appropriately. *Tolerable:* Buyer notes that the seller's corporate resolution to sell is completed under a different corporate name, which turns out to be the parent corporation of the corporation being sold. Buyer is curious as to why this was not previously disclosed and calls for new search and an additional corporate resolution. The new search establishes that liens exist on the parent corporation that must be explained and/or terminated. *Deal-Breaker:* Seller's attorney is dissatisfied with the terms and conditions of the escrow prepared promissory note and prepares one in its place, which requires execution of a personal guarantee, UCC-1 filing against the assets of the business, a pledge of the buyer's mutual fund investments, and a lien against the buyer's home. Buyer's attorney belatedly informs the buyer that he is taking a great risk by waiving the bulk sales law and recommends that the closing be delayed accordingly. Buyer also asks seller for permission to accept backup offers during this period of delay. Seller responds by agreeing only if the purchase price and down payment are reduced by 30 percent each. *Not!*

At the Closing

Favorable: All parties convene early for a closing scheduled at 8:30 AM, allowing time to handle any last minute problems. The closing is also scheduled for the last day of the month to facilitate prorations and final employee payroll commitments. Buyer brings correct amount in cashier funds from a local bank and seller *brings the other spouse* and the keys to the business. After all the paperwork is signed, *hugs* and warm wishes are exchanged before heading to a celebration lunch. *Tolerable:* Buyer arrives 45 minutes late to a closing scheduled for 4 PM on Friday. Escrow company personnel are weary after a long week and suggest that the closing be rescheduled for Monday, but seller and buyer convince escrow agent to complete the closing. As the paperwork is being signed, the buyer notices that the lien search results do not include the company's corporate name, only the seller's personal name was searched. It is also determined that the buyer's corporate resolution was not properly prepared. Given the need to correct these deficiencies, the closing is changed to the *following Tuesday* to finish signing documents and transfer ownership. New escrow worksheets and new checks must be cut, and the seller's plans for a getaway vacation are dashed. *Deal-Breaker:* Buyer requests postponement of scheduled closing as he awaits funding from "Uncle Charlie." He offers to close with only 25 percent of the agreed on down payment, but seller refuses. During this delay, the seller receives an unsolicited offer to buy his business for about 33 percent more than the current deal, all cash. Although the seller agreed in writing to an extension, he refuses to proceed with the original buyer, who shows up for the rescheduled closing alone. Buyer files suit against seller, who has subsequently agreed to sell to the new buyer. *Not!*

Deal-Breaker Summary

It should be clear by now that a deal can collapse for a multitude of reasons. The fundamental causes revolve around credibility, trust, and timing. *An open and constructive relationship is the glue that holds most deals together.* If the seller consciously or even subconsciously fails to disclose a material fact, it will likely surface during due diligence. Even if done unintentionally, the buyer begins to wonder what else might be wrong. Another example is a buyer who pledges to secure bank financing only to repeatedly ask the seller to carry the balance without attempting to get the bank loan. *Surprises and misrepresentations are deal killers. If disclosed, problems can be handled. If not, watch out!*

A second problem revolves around *buyer's remorse*. If, after due diligence, the buyer expresses remorse in the position that the business cannot support the down payment and purchase price, man the battle stations! If there is valid reasoning for this proposition, and the seller is sufficiently motivated, there may be no harm. If the cash flow and other presented facts turn out to be accurate, there is no ethical basis for maneuvering toward a lower price at this juncture. A similar possibility occurs if the seller feels like he or she has settled for an insufficient down payment or price (seller's remorse), causing the seller to be uncooperative in handing over financial documents and answering due diligence questions.

Negotiating Techniques

Volumes have been written on negotiating skills covering both general and situation-specific techniques. The fact is, though, you cannot be something you are not. *Every person has his or her own unique style and habits, and it is not always wise to go against these natural tendencies.* Generalization of techniques is not always useful. There are, however, basic realities associated with the negotiation process worthy of discussion. First, always put yourself in the shoes of the other party. The person selling was likely a buyer not too long ago. Practically every buyer becomes a seller and most sellers have been buyers. Try to bargain with the other side's position in mind.

The second point is that if you don't ask for it, you won't get it. Dr. Chester Karrass, a popular teacher of negotiating strategies, has said "In business, you don't get what you deserve, you get what you negotiate." The premise of his seminars is that negotiation is a business tool and must be practiced for maximum results. As concerns the particulars of buying a business, if you don't start with a lower price than you are willing to pay, you might be giving money away. If you don't ask for two months training, you might not even get one month. If you don't ask the seller to finance 90 percent of the purchase price, you might settle for a greater down payment than hoped for. As a seller, if you don't ask for $200,000, you won't get $200,000. If you don't ask for 50 percent down, you probably won't get 50 percent down.

It is equally important not to ask for too much. If a seller is overpriced, this will scare off qualified buyers before they can see the strengths of the business. For those who take a look despite the high price, credibility might have been damaged. Maintaining credibility is essential for the longevity of the negotiating, closing, and transitioning periods. If credibility is lost, goodwill folds right behind it, likely leading to ill will, claims of misrepresentation, and possibly legal actions. Remaining realistic and credible fortifies any deal and should be a priority. If you try to "steal" a business by offering an offensively low price, be ready to move on to the next deal (you probably won't receive a counter, but you might receive some choice words from the seller). It is one thing to try to get the best deal you can and quite another to lowball with the hope of taking advantage of the seller's position.

Buyers must beware certain tactics used by sellers and brokers. The "I don't really want to sell" routine may or may not be true. If it is true, your bargaining abilities are limited. If it is not true, it is typically an attempt to let the buyer know the business is prospering. If the business is listed with a broker, this claim should be discounted immediately.

Another common comment is "there is a lot of interest in this business," implying that if you don't make a generous offer now, you will lose your chance! This may or may not be true. Real estate laws prevent brokers from blatantly playing one buyer off the other, but it still occurs. The truth is, however, that many buyers wait too long to make an offer and lose their chance to buy a quality business. You must be prepared to counter the seller's counteroffer. Similar to a chess match, think a few steps ahead. The seller might be highly motivated and accept your first offer. But if he is not, be prepared to respond, paying close attention to the sellers "hot" buttons. What is most important to them—price or terms? Time of closing or training period? Listen carefully to what the seller is saying, verbally or otherwise. When making your original and/or subsequent offers, place a time limit on the response period. Anywhere from "upon presentation" to one week can be reasonable. *Sellers (and buyers) have three general options after reviewing an offer/counteroffer: accept in full, accept partially with counteroffer, or reject—no response.*

Be prepared to make concessions without compromising your bottom-line position regarding what you think the business is worth and what you can afford. Another common request by the seller is the right to accept backup offers (particularly if the seller feels that the buyer is "bottom fishing"). Try to make progress at each stage of the negotiating process. Be prepared for "three steps forward and two steps back." Making compromises on what seem like small items to you might be quite important to the seller (and vice versa). Depending on your personal style and whether or not an intermediary is involved, you may want to personally present your offer. I prefer to get the two sides together as soon and as often as possible, unless there is obvious friction between them. For events as large as buying/selling a business, both sides should get along to ensure long-term success. Other brokers want to stay in control of the deal at every step of the way, intentionally keeping the two sides apart.

Considering that it will take a buyer months to find the right business and take the seller months to sell a business (if at all), the next piece of advice can be difficult to live by. When a buyer finds what seems to be the right business or a seller is hypermotivated to sell, it can be difficult to walk away. *As soon as you find yourself prepared to move on at any cost to your interests, you probably will. You don't have to buy this business. You don't have to sell right now. Stay in control.*

Another tactic is to *ask for concessions you don't really want or expect.* When making an offer, ask for extended training, early possession, all closing costs paid by the seller, and a brand new $10,000 sign to be included in the sale. By placing these demands, you allow sellers to feel like they have the upper hand. You might be thinking that this is not honest or ethical (you have a point!). The reality is that building trust and mutual respect does not preclude each side from trying to get the best deal possible. When the seller asks to strike these provisions, maintain your persistence as best you can, perhaps acting surprised. This works equally well for the seller, who can request that the buyer make a separate balloon payment of $10,000 after one year, keep the seller's brother-in-law employed (with a raise), and allow the seller to shop with 50 percent discounts for the next five years, etc.

Rarely should you accept the first offer/counteroffer. Unless timing is a dominant priority, try to do better. If the seller accepts the first offer (less than full-price), the buyer might wonder if there is something wrong. If the buyer accepts the first counter, the seller might believe that he or she could have done much better. However, if it is a fair offer or counteroffer, it should be accepted as is. All this advice is person-specific and situation-specific. The better prepared and knowledgeable all parties are, the better the chances for true success—the purchase and sale of a business at a fair price and fair terms for both sides. As a buyer or seller, you may be asked to make concessions "on the spot." A useful response is to state that the decision is not yours, thereby placing responsibility on a third party. It is easier to compromise with people who are not physically present. When an agent is negotiating a commission, they will often say that they have no authority to offer a reduced commission. If this falls on deaf or angry ears, the agent can offer to consult with the owner (without making any promises, of course).

Negotiations Summary

Negotiations for the purchase or sale of a business are multifaceted. Utilizing a formalized negotiating approach is not always possible. Circumstances change over time and the chemistry between the buyer, seller, broker, and other parties is not easily analyzed by a standardized approach. It may also be futile to negotiate a deal utilizing tactics that are better suited to a personality differing from yours. On the other hand, there are tactics and approaches that can work. For further insights, consider consulting one or two books offering such strategies and advice, such as *The Art of Negotiating,* by Gerard I. Nierenberg and *Friendly Persuasion,* by Bob Woolf.

Most deals that make it to the closing are based upon mutual respect and trust. When these fade away, so do the chances for a deal. There will be trials and tribulations, progress and setbacks. You should not necessarily expect that the other party will like you, but hopefully he or she will trust and respect you.

Step 7: Perform Comprehensive Due Diligence

This step comprises activities reflecting different levels of expertise and different goals. I have witnessed due diligence periods amounting to a handful of questions that were completed in 30 minutes. Due diligence periods associated with larger acquisitions may take several months and involve many different analyses, including reviews of the general areas listed below:

- General Review of Company and Industry
- Quantitative Analysis of Company
- Valuation Results
- Prove Income, Expenses and Verify Licenses, Permits, Leases, Contracts, etc.
- Miscellaneous

A condensed business review form, worksheet for calculating ACF, and expense analysis form are presented at the end of this chapter to facilitate due diligence. *After completion of some or all of the due diligence procedures associated with the above areas, you will have a choice. You may either proceed with the closing or reassess your commitment to purchase.* Assuming that your offer was made based on the seller's presentation of ACF and assets equal to a certain value, you are within your rights to either withdraw completely from the deal or revise the offer based on new findings. The seller is under no obligation to accept your revised offer, but you should offer only what you believe the business justifies. More precisely, your offer should be based on the amount of debt service and owner's benefits supportable by the cash flow. A good place to begin your due diligence review is to assemble the documents needed to properly complete this effort. The following list can be scaled down as needed:

Document Checklist

❑ All financial statements and tax returns from past five years (at least three) including income statement, balance sheet, and statement of cash flows (if available)

❑ Any interim financial statements (e.g., for the last completed month of activity)

❑ All supporting footnotes, disclosures, and supporting tables relating to financial statements (e.g., depreciation schedules, inventory, costing methods)

❑ All sales tax reports for past three years (if applicable)

❑ Corporate resolution to sell (if applicable)

❑ Corporate bylaws, articles of incorporation, board minutes, shareholder agreements (if stock purchase), classes of stock, dividend history

❑ Franchise agreement (if applicable)

❑ Property and equipment lease agreements, names and phone numbers of lessors

❑ Names and phone numbers of seller's key advisors (i.e., attorney, CPA, broker)

❑ Copies of company policies and procedures (e.g., personnel, manufacturing, pricing, credit, warranty)

❑ Seller's disclosure form for business and real property (comprehensive)

❑ Contracts with employees, customers, suppliers, maintenance and security companies

❑ Copies of loan agreements/other debt obligations to be assumed by purchaser

❑ Any reports/findings/fines made by regulatory agencies

❑ List of customers (accounts receivable aging) and suppliers (accounts payable balances) when appropriate

❑ Appraisals, deeds, etc., related to real property

❑ Copy of most recent business plan/business profile

❑ Samples of product brochures and other promotional materials

❑ Complete list of FF&E to be included in sale along with any associated liens or encumbrances

❑ Outside, independent appraisal of business value

❑ Business insurance policies

❑ Results of any tax related audit (federal, state, or local)

Your review can be as involved and complicated as you desire. There are many different types and levels of analysis and valuation. I have seen buyers who are so confident in the seller's credibility that virtually no due diligence investigation occurs. I have also seen buyers that will avoid hard decisions because of a "lack of data." "I really need last month's financials before I can make an offer" is a surprisingly common hang-up. It is highly unlikely that one month's performance will make a difference. If you find yourself making excuses over and over again, even when the business meets most of your criteria, then maybe you should reconsider your plans. Careful quantitative analysis is important, but so are your intuition, "gut feelings," and willingness to take risks and work long hours. Analysis can be categorized as follows:

- *Financial versus Nonfinancial* (e.g., cash flows versus key employees or ratio analysis versus regulatory concerns)
- *Historical versus Projected* (e.g., tax returns versus pro forma projections or actual sales tax reports versus projected sales levels)
- *Analysis by Area* (e.g., the Four Ps of Marketing [product, price, promotion, place])
- *Analysis by Functions* (e.g., accounting, finance, management, marketing, production, purchasing, and distribution)
- *Analysis by Source of Data* (e.g., financial statements, tax returns, business plans, internal company reports and documents, and outside, independent reports [appraisers, brokers])
- *Analysis by Purpose*
  - to secure bank loan (working capital, equipment, outright purchase) or equity funding
  - to estimate company value (cash flows, assets, growth rates)
  - to project short-term cash flows and working capital needs
  - to perform breakeven or "what if" analysis (sensitivity analysis)
- *Analysis of Strengths, Weaknesses, Opportunities, and Threats* (SWOT)

A thorough business evaluation should address ten areas and can be completed by reviewing some or all the documents listed above. For support, turn to the list of industry and firm data sources, ranging from sales forecasts (Predicast) to comprehensive listings of recently merged or acquired companies (SDC Database), found in Chapter 10 in the section on market comparables. The following ten areas should be addressed:

1. Industry review (by SIC code) and investigation of competition
2. Company review, including supplier, employee, and customer interviews (as allowed)
3. Review of pertinent regulatory issues and concerns
4. Cash flow analysis—past and projected ACF
5. Financial statement analysis (ratio, trend, common size analysis, and breakeven analysis)
6. Asset valuation—tangible and intangible, real and personal
7. Overall valuation results—cash flow based, asset based, and industry rules of thumb
8. Verify/audit cash flow (revenues, expenses, and taxable income)
9. Interview seller's outside advisers (CPA, attorney, insurance agent, banker, landlord)
10. Preparation of a minimal business plan

Note: numbers 4, 5, and 7 above will be best completed by using a computerized spreadsheet such as Lotus or Excel. More complicated, larger acquisitions would be facilitated by prepackaged software programs like Cashé (800-993-3600). This highly rated package will generate pro forma financial statements, comprehensive cash budgeting reports, and business valuation results. Two more useful software packages are Alcar and Ronstadt's Financials. Alcar (708-967-4200) is relatively expensive and used by many large corporations. Ronstadt's (800-347-0545) is less expensive and designed primarily for smaller companies and new ventures. Both packages feature additional modules/templates that can be ordered if needed.

Business Evaluation Procedures

For our present purposes, we will utilize *business evaluation procedures* (BEPs) as our recommended standard for reviewing acquisitions. Before studying these detailed procedures, let's review our basic goals:

Goals of Business Evaluation Procedures

- Establish a thorough understanding of all aspects of the business.
- Prove the accuracy of the seller's presentation of business.
- Discover any past, present, or anticipated problem areas or contingent liabilities.
- Establish the probable value of the business using different valuation techniques.
- Anticipate the likely future course of the business under new management.
- Utilize findings to successfully negotiate finance and structure acceptable price and down payment.

Recommended Business Evaluation Procedures

The framework for business evaluation procedures in Figure 6.1 is comprehensive in nature and not all areas will apply to every business. Using this outline to consistently evaluate your targets will improve the chances of making the right choice at the right price. As you review this outline, you may notice that it addresses many of the same areas found in a business plan. As discussed in Chapters 1 and 14, creating a quality business plan is a must for both good planning and obtaining outside financing. Following these procedures will lead to added substance to any business plan.

FIGURE 6.1   Business Evaluation Procedures

I.   **General Overview**
   A. *Background and History*
      1. Founder of company/ownership history
      2. Years in operation and current owner/ownership history
      3. Significant changes over time (e.g., industry, products, location)
   B. *Other Ownership Structure*
      1. Current owner's business form (e.g., corporation, partnership)
      2. Key shareholders/partners
      3. Willingness of current owners to participate in transition/remain involved with company
      4. Review of corporate articles of incorporation, bylaws, board minutes (especially for stock sale)
      5. Loans to/from key shareholders
      6. Other
   C. *Location and Lease*
      1. General demographics of customer base
      2. Nearness to major transportation links (e.g., major intersections, freeway, airports)
      3. Traffic counts
      4. Amount, type, and duration of property lease
         a) Monthly payment/amount per square foot compared with similar properties
         b) Lessee pays common area maintenance (CAM) charges (triple-net?) beyond monthly payment
         c) Expiration date of current lease—options to renew?
         d) Cooperative spirit of landlord (i.e., can lease be favorably renegotiated, assigned, transferred?)
      5. Other
   D. *Asset Structure*
      1. Breakdown between fixed assets (property, plant, and equipment [PP&E]) and other assets
         a) FMV
         b) book value
         c) liquidation value
         d) replacement cost
         e) original cost

FIGURE 6.1 Business Evaluation Procedures, continued

    2. Breakdown between tangible and intangible assets, real versus personal assets (allocation of purchase price)

    3. A/R, WIP, and prepaid assets included in sales price?

    4. Analysis of inventory—replacement cost, FMV and extent of obsolescence, and slow moving stock

E. *Product/Service/Markets/Customers*

    1. Major product lines

    2. Past, present, and future product/service lines by percent of total sales

    3. Major competitors by line

    4. Basic advertising strategies by line

    5. Location of customer base—local, regional, national, international?

    6. Complementary or new product lines forthcoming?

F. *Strengths/Weaknesses/Opportunities/Threats* (may not be able to assess until after entire analysis is complete)

    1. Strengths

    2. Weaknesses

    3. Opportunities

    4. Threats

G. *Reason(s) for Sale*

    1. Initial/primary

    2. Secondary or hidden

    3. How long on the market—any other offers?

II.   **Sales and Marketing**

A. *Detailed Breakdown of Key Products/Services*

    1. Description/importance of each area

       a) Significant trends for each area

       b) Major customers for each area

       c) Credit terms offered to customers

       d) Collection procedures

       e) Warranty and return policies

    2. Sales generated by inside versus outside salespeople by product/service line

    3. Is demand driven by necessity or created through advertising?

    4. What is the seasonal component of the sales mix efforts?

    5. Other

B. *General Marketing Strategies*

    1. Does company have a written marketing plan?

    2. Sales Force

       a) Inside salespeople (employees)

       b) Outside salespeople (e.g., independent reps, distributors)

       c) Compensation packages (e.g., commissions, incentives)

       d) Competence of sales managers

    3. Other

C. *Advertising/Promotional Policies*

    1. Major ad programs (salespeople)

       a) Direct mail

       b) Catalogs

FIGURE 6.1   Business Evaluation Procedures, continued

  c) Salespeople/?

  d) Print, radio, TV

  e) Internet/WWW

 2. Overall expenditures

  a) As percent of sales, compared to industry average

  b) Breakdown, trend of expenditures

  c) Analysis/monitoring of effectiveness of expenditure

  d) Other

 3. Recent changes in above programs/expenditures? Why?

 4. Future mandatory advertising/promotional expenditures

  a) Yellow Pages

  b) Other contractual obligations

D. *Pricing Strategies*

 1. Luxury versus value pricing

 2. Rebates, discounts, terms

 3. Competitive or seasonal factors (e.g., excess demand or input strategy)

 4. Frequency of price changes, pricing control of employees/distributors, etc.

E. *Linkages to Customers*

 1. How are products introduced to end customers?

 2. Are there any contracts with customers?

 3. Any current or estimated future obligations regarding warranties

 4. Amount/percent of sales to repeat customers

F. *Description and Analysis of Key Customers*

 1. Describe the customer base or target markets (e.g., industrial, individuals, service companies)

 2. What percent of sales come from each of the top three, five, and ten customers

  a) Is their repeat business significant and/or increasing?

  b) How long have they been customers?

  c) Will a new owner likely cause them to leave?

  d) What is the credit history of these key customers?

  e) What is the financial condition of these key customers?

  f) Review a current A/R aging schedule and historic bad debt expenses. Are they in decline, stable, or increasing?

 3. What is the geographic scope of the customer base?

  a) Local only

  b) Regional

  c) National or international

 4. Have there been any transportation/delivery-related problems?

 5. What is the decision-making environment of the company personnel responsible for placing orders for the products/services (e.g., purchasing agents, CEOs, or other professionals)?

 6. Has one of the top five customers been added only recently, or is it expected that one of these customers will be leaving soon?

G. *Proprietary Trademarks, Trade Names, Patents*

 1. List and analyze each one.

 2. Determine expiration dates of patents.

 3. Verify registration of each of the above.

FIGURE 6.1   Business Evaluation Procedures, continued

H. *Past and Future Anticipated Growth Rates by Product Line*
   1. Past growth rates
   2. Estimated future growth rates
      a) Seller's estimate by product
      b) Your estimate by product/service line
      c) Status of research and development (R&D) or product planning efforts (e.g., committees, reports)

I. *Analysis of Key Competition*
   1. Who are the industry leaders/key local competitors for the target business?
      a) Who is considered to be the major competitor? Where are they located?
      b) Interview at least one owner/top executive of a similar business.
   2. What is the key advantage of the target company over the competitors? (location, pricing, product features, availability, innovation)
   3. Does there appear to be active competition (price wars) or active collusion (similar and stable pricing)?
      a) Is market potential growing, stable, or declining?
      b) Are there any apparent or expected legal or technological changes that will reshape the industry?
      c) What expenditures on new equipment, R&D, or regulatory compliance measures will maintain or improve the company's relative position in the market?
      d) Are there any barriers to entry preventing the excessive penetration of new competition (technology, permits, high cost, captive customers or suppliers, brand preferences)?
      e) Is it easy for customers to switch from a competitor's product to this company's product and vice versa? Does switching lead to additional costs for the customer?

III.   Management Structure and Key Personnel
   A. *Organizational Chart* (if available)
   B. *Analysis of key management positions and other personnel*
      1. Key managers/personnel by area and responsibility
      2. Key managers/personnel by salary/benefits
      3. Recent promotions/dismissals/wage reviews
      4. Intent of key managers/personnel under new ownership
      5. Personnel files for those managers intending to stay with new ownership
   C. *Extent of union organization?*
   D. *Employment contracts/bonus plans*
   E. *History of outside monitoring*
      1. Workers' compensation payments
         a) As payroll tax
         b) As claims
      2. Unemployment claims
      3. EEOC
   F. *Extent of written personnel policies*
      1. Adequacy
      2. Compliance
      3. Sick pay
      4. Hiring procedures
      5. Training

FIGURE 6.1   Business Evaluation Procedures, continued

G. *Owner's role in business*
1. Current
2. Willingness to participate after closing

H. *Retirement/medical benefits*
1. Pension obligations
2. Employee stock ownership plans
3. Extent of medical coverage
4. Cost to employees/business

IV. **Facilities, Production and Distribution**

A. *Estimated FMV and supporting documentation for all real and personal property.* Description, age, square footage, and estimated or appraised value (also compare to real and personal property tax statements)
1. Real estate—buildings and improvements
2. Real estate—land
3. Personal property—fixed assets
   a) Equipment
   b) Chattel improvements
   c) Furniture and fixtures
   d) Autos

B. *Miscellaneous*
1. Purchasing procedures and inventory flow/control
   a) Documented procedures
   b) Just-in-time strategy, supplier relationships
   c) Interface between sales, production, and distribution
2. Equipment maintenance contracts/amount of deferred maintenance
3. Quality control procedures/policies/inventory
4. R&D efforts
5. Regulatory?
   a) OSHA
   b) EPA
   c) Fire department
   d) Other
6. Other

V. **Financial/Quantitative Analysis**

A. *Overall reliability, amount, and credibility of presented information*
1. Audited, reviewed, or compiled statements
2. Responsiveness of seller to requests for information

B. *Review, compare, and analyze income statement and balance sheets for past five years* (at least three)
1. Prepare common-size statements
2. Calculate and interpret ratios of all types
   a) liquidity
   b) solvency
   c) activity
   d) profitability

FIGURE 6.1   Business Evaluation Procedures, continued

3. Perform trend analysis of common size statements and ratios

4. Compare common size results and ratios to industry standards by SIC code

   a) Robert Morris and Associates

   b) Dun and Bradstreet

   c) Almanac of Business and Industrial Ratios

   d) Other

C. *Perform breakeven and sensitivity* (what-if) analysis for past year and the next five years

   1. Breakeven sales in dollars

   2. Breakeven sales in units

   3. Breakeven including target profit

   4. Breakeven (sensitivity analysis) assuming variations in:

      a) Sales price per unit

      b) Fixed costs per period

      c) Variable costs per unit

      d) Salaries to owner

      e) Minimum acceptable profit levels (if profits included in breakeven analysis)

D. *Calculate cash flow (ACF) based on the formula found in Chapters 3, 9, and 11* (historical and pro forma)

E. *Verify/prove accuracy of financial statements*

   1. Compare income statement to federal and state tax returns.

   2. Compare income statement to state and/or municipal sales tax returns.

   3. Select monthly statements, if available, from the last complete month and from one month of the previous four years (include a December statement, a January statement, and a statement for the highest and lowest level of sales).

      a) For each of the selected months trace and verify the reported sales to original sales invoices, sales journal, bank deposits, charge slips, and/or withdrawals as well as to the monthly sales tax reports if applicable.

      b) For each of the selected months, trace and verify the reported expenses to the check register, canceled checks, invoices, loan papers, depreciation schedules, and other supporting documents.

   4. Thoroughly examine bank reconciliation statements for each of the selected months.

   5. Explain to your full satisfaction any variations between the financial statements, tax returns, bank statements, and other pertinent documents.

F. *Estimate immediate and future working capital needs*

   1. How much cash is needed to operate business at current levels of sales, expenses, and debt, assuming business is purchased without ownership of existing accounts receivable?

      a) Inventory purchases

      b) Payroll obligations

      c) Miscellaneous expenditures

      d) Extension of credit to customers (e.g., ten days, one month, three months)

      e) Retirement of debt (principal plus interest)

   2. How much additional cash will be needed to finance additional sales?

      a) Inventory purchases

      b) Payroll obligations

      c) Miscellaneous expenditures

      d) Extension of credit to customers (e.g., ten days, one month, three months)

      e) Retirement of debt (principal plus interest)

FIGURE 6.1   Business Evaluation Procedures, continued

3. Which financial institution will make working capital loans for this business? What are the likely terms, conditions, and interest rates?

4. Other

G. *Analysis of tax issues*

1. Federal and state income taxes

    a) Past

    b) Future new ownership structure (S-corporation, limited liability company, partnership, or sole proprietor)

2. Sales or excise taxes

    a) State

    b) Local

3. Payroll taxes

    a) FICA

    b) FUTA

    c) Workers' compensation

    d) Other

4. Property taxes

    a) Real property

    b) Personal property

5. Capital gains taxes

    a) For seller upon sale (stock versus assets)

    b) For buyer upon future sale (stock versus assets)

    c) Pros and cons of asset versus stock sale

    d) Impact of financing on tax liability

6. Other taxes

VI. **Valuation Techniques**

A. *Methods*

1. Cash-flow based

    a) Discounted cash flow

    b) Capitalization of earnings

2. Asset-based

    a) Adjusted book value approach

    b) Sum of the assets approach

3. Combination methods

    a) Excess earnings method

    b) Industry rules of thumb

    c) Other

B. *Range and weighted average of above methods* (see Chapters 9 and 11)

It is recommended that you complete the due diligence review with the assistance of a qualified accountant, making sure he or she has completed similar reviews in the near past. The business review form in Figure 6.2 provides a thorough but reasonable overview of a subject acquisition.

FIGURE 6.2   Business Review Form

BUSINESS REVIEW FORM

Business Name and Owner: _____   Phone _____

When was business founded? _____ Years owned by current owner? _____

Partnership—Corporation—Sole Proprietor (Circle One) Who are the partners, officers, or owners?

_____

Is the business trade name registered with the state? _____

Do you own any patents/copyrights/trademarks? _____

Describe the company's products or services: _____

What is the reason for sale? _____

Which markets do you serve? _____

Who is your competition? _____

What are your competitive advantages? _____

How do you obtain new customers? _____

What type of customers do you have? _____

What kind of advertising? _____

Who are your key customers? _____

What are the hours of operation? _____ to _____ Day(s) closed? _____

Are your employees aware that you want to sell the business? _____

Who are key employees? _____

What do they do? _____ Salary? _____

Do they know business is for sale? _____

How many employees? Full-time _____ Part-time _____

Any family members paid by the business? _____ Salary? _____

Any one time/unusual expenses? _____

Must liabilities be assumed? _____ Terms and conditions? _____

What is the fair market value of furniture, fixtures, and equipment? _____

    Leased equipment? _____ Leasehold improvements? _____

What is the difference between market value and current payoff for leased equipment? _____

Any automobiles/trucks? _____

What assets are not included? _____

Are any items dated, consigned, borrowed, or floored? _____ Value $_____

Is inventory seasonal? _____ What is your average markup? _____

FIGURE 6.2 Business Review Form, continued

Lease Information:

Square Footage _____ Expiration Date _____ Security Deposit _____

Fixed Rent _____ Taxes _____ Percent of Sales _____ Increases _____

Other _____ CAM _____ Renewal Options _____

Landlord _____ Who to contract _____

Telephone _____

May we contact landlord or his representative? _____ Why not? _____

Is lease assignable? _____ Landlord's consent required? _____

Reasonableness clause? _____

General Information:

Owner's duties? _____

Are there any necessary repairs that need to be made? _____

Does new owner need special skills or background? _____

How long would it take someone else to learn this business? _____

Is your business seasonal? _____ Which months have the greatest sales? _____

Who is your attorney? _____ Phone _____

Who is your accountant? _____ Phone _____

Are following current: Taxes: Income? _____ Withholding? _____ Sales? _____

Rent? _____ Licenses? _____

What is the trend of your gross sales? _____ Why? _____

What will you do if I buy your business? _____

Why should I buy this business? _____

Remarks _____

_____

Finally, please review the two worksheets in Figure 6.3 and 6.4 to be used for calculating adjusted cash flow (ACF).

FIGURE 6.3   Adjusted Cash Flow Analysis

Business Name: _____ Period: _____

From Income Statement:

1. Owner(s) salary (including payroll taxes) if on P&L   +   _____
2. Discretionary expenses, if on P&L
    Auto expense   +   _____
    Travel and entertainment   +   _____
    Insurance: auto, health, life   +   _____
    Interest   +   _____
    Other _____   +   _____
3. Nonrecurring (one-time) expenses (explain) _____   +   _____

    _____

4. Noncash expenses
    Depreciation/Amortization   +   _____
5. Expenses not included on income statement (explain) _____   –   _____

    _____

6. Total adjustments $ _____
7. Net profit (loss) from income statement $ _____
8. Adjusted Cash Flow (ACF) $ _____

The parties signing below warrant that they are the owners of this business and that the above numbers are true and accurate to the best of their knowledge.

_____   _____
Owner   Date   Owner   Date

FIGURE 6.4   Expense Analysis Worksheet

Business Name: _____
For the Period Of: _____
Net Profit (Seller's Books): $ _____

Item	Original Amount	Amount of Adjustment	Explanation
Addback:			
Depreciation	$_____	$_____	_____
Amortization of write-offs	$_____	$_____	_____
Debt service (loan interest)	$_____	$_____	_____
Owner's salary	$_____	$_____	_____
Manager's salary (if absentee)	$_____	$_____	_____
Discretionary			
Expenses & Benefits:			
Promotions	$_____	$_____	_____
Personal insurance	$_____	$_____	_____
Travel and entertainment	$_____	$_____	_____
Personal auto	$_____	$_____	_____
Other (describe)	$_____	$_____	_____
Other (describe)	$_____	$_____	_____

FIGURE 6.4   Expense Analysis Worksheet, continued

Expenses Buyer May Eliminate:

Equipment rental	$_____	$_____	_____
Discounts and refunds	$_____	$_____	_____
Bad debt write-off	$_____	$_____	_____
Gifts/donations	$_____	$_____	_____
Extra employees, relatives, etc.	$_____	$_____	_____
Other (describe)	$_____	$_____	_____
Other (describe)	$_____	$_____	_____

Total Adjustments Made $_____

Total Cash Flow (net income + adjustments) $_____

Seller hereby verifies that the expenses as adjusted in the above worksheet accurately reflect the true cost of conducting this business, and that the accompanying explanations are correct.

_____   _____
Seller   Date

CHAPTER 7

Addressing Pre-Closing and Transition Issues

Step 8: Address Pre-Closing Issues

After due diligence is completed as part of Step 7 (review of books, records, and operations), other pre-closing issues can be attacked in order to open escrow and move toward closing. In practice, Steps 7, 8, and 9 will tend to overlap. Our focus in Step 8 is to grasp the variety of tasks to be completed before closing can occur. It is wise to attach time constraints and share responsibility for their completion. To this end, a comprehensive pre-closing worksheet is presented. To begin with, the following events should be driven by time constraints:

- Removal of contingencies (e.g., due diligence review, satisfactory lease assignment, bank financing approval)
- Opening of escrow
- Addressing of pre-closing issues
- Closing of escrow

Major contingencies involve financial and operational due diligence, lease assignments, and outside financing/bank loans. Deadlines for their removal should be agreed on by both sides during negotiation of the purchase contract. If additional time is needed, the deadline may be extended in writing via an addendum, shown in Figure 7.1.

FIGURE 7.1   Addendum/Amendment

ADDENDUM/AMENDMENT

Addendum/Amendment (circle one)

To a certain contract dated _____ 19_____, identified below

between: _____, as Buyer

and: _____, as Seller

for that business known as:

_____

and located at:

_____

(City, County, State, Zip)

This Addendum / Amendment (circle one) is executed this _____ day of

_____, 19_____, and shall constitute an integral part of the Offer for

Purchase/Purchase Agreement executed by the undersigned on the date thereof (addendums and amendments should be numerically numbered by date of occurrence):

_____

_____

_____

_____

_____

_____

_____

_____

_____

_____

_____

_____

_____

_____

_____

_____

_____

_____

Buyer: _____   Date: _____   Seller: _____ Date: _____

Buyer: _____   Date: _____   Seller: _____ Date: _____

Note: The addendum in Figure 7.1 can be utilized to amend either the purchase contract or the listing contract for any issue, not just removal of deadlines.

Lease Contingencies

There are two types of leases involved in the sale of most businesses: a building/property lease and an equipment lease(s). Assignment, transfer, or assumption must occur to the satisfaction of the new owner or there will be no closing. Ideally, after the business is listed for sale, the owner and/or business broker will contact the landlord or lessor directly and disclose the intent to sell. Early disclosure allows the seller time to accumulate all required forms and paperwork. Many sellers (tenants) do not want the landlord (lessors) to know the business is for sale until there is a serious buyer with agreement on price and terms. Whether the landlord is informed before or after agreement for sale is reached, most lease assignments/transfers require landlord approval. They may decline the assignment to buyers (tenants) not deemed financially or operationally qualified. At a minimum, they will require the original tenant to remain on the lease until the original term expires (most sellers are uneasy about this, but it is generally unavoidable).

It is critical that all parties review all the fine print contained in the lease, not just the assignment/transfer clauses. As a purchaser (potential tenant), you might consult a leasing specialist to review the terms and conditions, but don't expect too much bargaining power (unless the economy is weak, the center is empty, and the existing lease is about to expire). Whether you are assuming the terms and conditions of the existing lease or negotiating from scratch, it is important to understand the varieties of lease arrangements that exist. Property leases are likely to be one of the following:

- Full-service or gross lease
- Modified gross lease
- Triple net lease

In the Phoenix area, triple net leases are the most common followed by some variant of the modified gross lease. Primary differences revolve around questions of who will pay property taxes, property insurance, maintenance and repairs, utilities, and janitorial expenses. The unique aspect of the triple net format is that the tenant is responsible for paying all the operating expenses of the property, whereby the landlord receives a *net* rent. Importantly, tenants may be responsible for an additional payment beyond the payments made throughout the year (a liability for the buyer as of year end) or, less likely, tenants may be the recipient of a refund due to overpayments.

There are many variations, including a modified gross lease where the landlord is responsible for the external repairs and the tenant is responsible for internal repairs. Provisions may limit what the landlord or the tenants pay for any given expense category. Seemingly small items can become bothersome if not clearly understood early on.

Only the landlord (often a management company) can legally effect the transfer/assignment or write a new lease. Whether it is transfer/assignment *or* a new lease, the wording of the contingency normally requires that it be acceptable to the purchaser of the business (new lessee). The lessor's willingness to proceed quickly is a major concern. The purchaser will seek at least preliminary approval for the transfer/assignment as soon as possible. The form in Figure 7.2 may facilitate such approval.

FIGURE 7.2 Landlord's Intent to Lease

LANDLORD'S INTENT TO LEASE

The undersigned landlord, hereafter known as lessor, for the business known as

_____ located

at _____ hereby

announces his intent to lease the real property on which the business is situated under the terms and circumstances described below:

  A. The lease will be subject to satisfactory sale of the business.

  B. The buyer of the business, hereafter known as the lessee, will meet all normal credit requirements of the lessor.

  C. The monthly rent for the property will be ($_____) per month for _____ months.

  D. The lessee will have an option to renew the lease for an additional _____ period(s) of _____ months each at the end of the original lease period.

  E. The lessee will sign a standard _____ County Business Property lease prepared by _____ for the transaction.

_____   _____

Witness   Lessor

_____   Dated _____

Witness

After the review of books and records has been completed, the purchaser is normally motivated to make application for and receive approval for lease changes. What we are dealing with is the relative bargaining strength of the landlord (lessor) versus the tenant (lessee). Landlord posturing may create anxiety, but in most cases the landlord has an obvious reason to accommodate the timely transfer/assignment of the lease—collecting rental payments!

As the incoming tenant, you can expect to fill out an application, pass a credit review, and turn over a personal and/or company financial statement. Be prepared to negotiate against an increase in the security deposit, emphasizing your operating strengths and experience in a positive, firm fashion. In worst case scenarios, you will be turned down because the landlord has a clause buried in the current lease that spells out how and why a transfer/assignment may be rejected. If landlords don't believe you are capable of making timely payments, they may exercise their right to reject even though the initial tenant (seller) will likely remain on the lease. Most landlords, however, do not want to deal with lawsuits and seek to accommodate transfers.

There are several options regarding passing of the leasehold interest, including a new lease, assignment/transfer of the existing lease or a sublease. The first option is unlikely until the original lease expires and the original tenant is released. Consult an experienced leasing consultant or attorney if the possibility for a new lease arises. The assignment/transfer option is by far the most common. The seller (original tenant) *assigns* or *transfers* all rights, privileges, and responsibilities to the new owner (new tenant). While the seller loses rights and privileges, the responsibility for payment will generally remain. The landlord might remove the seller after one year of timely payments by the new tenant coupled with an increase in the security deposit from one to three or four months. Review the following sample agreement in Figure 7.3, noting the provision for the original lessee (seller) to reenter the lease.

FIGURE 7.3   Assignment of Lease with Reassignment Provision

ASSIGNMENT OF LEASE WITH REASSIGNMENT PROVISION

FOR VALUE RECEIVED, I or We, The undersigned assignors: _____
_____ do hereby assign, sell, transfer, and convey unto: _____
_____, ASSIGNEES,
All of our rights, title, and interest in and to that certain Lease bearing date of

_____

By and Between,

_____, AS LESSORS,
and _____, AS LESSEES,
which said lease covers the property known as:

_____

It is understood and agreed that the herein assignees shall assume and pay the rent accruing under the terms of said Lease commencing with that rental payment due and payable _____

FIGURE 7.3   Assignment of Lease with Reassignment Provision, continued

and that the herein assignees shall be entitled to credit for all rent paid in advance on said Lease by the herein assignors or other persons that have held an interest as Lessee under the said Lease.

Assignor warrants and represents to Assignee that the Lease has not been amended or modified except as expressly set forth herein, that Assignor is not now and as of the Effective Date will not be in default or breach of any of the provisions of the Lease, and that Assignor has no knowledge of any claim by Lessor that Assignor is in default or breach of any of the provisions of the Lease.

Lessor now holds the sum of _____ Dollars ($_____) as a security deposit and the sum of _____ Dollars ($_____) as prepaid rent for _____. Assignor releases all claims to these sums, and said sums shall be held by Lessor for the benefit of Assignee, subject to the provisions of the Lease.

Lessor and Assignee shall have the right to amend, modify, terminate, extend, or renew the Lease without the consent of Assignor, provided, however, that no such amendment, modification, termination, extension, or renewal shall increase or alter Assignor's then existing liability or obligations under the Lease, unless Assignor shall have expressly consented thereto. In the event Assignee exercises any right provided by the Lease to expand the Premises or to extend or renew the term of the Lease, Assignor's obligations and liability shall remain as if such right had not been exercised.

It is further understood and agreed that concurrently with this Assignment of Lease the herein Assignees have executed a Note and Chattel Security Agreement to the herein Assignors for the purchase of certain personal property, more fully described in said Chattel Security Agreement, and that in the event the herein assignees, their heirs, assigns, or successors are in default in the terms of said Note, Chattel Security Agreement and/or Lease, then said Lease is reassigned to the herein assignors, their heirs, assigns, or successors, without recourse.

Dated this _____ day of _____, 19_____.

Assignor/Lessee: _____

Assignee: _____

An often ignored question is when and how the seller (original tenant) can re-enter the premises if the buyer defaults on the carry-back note. Unless specifically incorporated into the lease assignment provisions, the seller cannot normally reenter without landlord permission. The lease assignment form (Figure 7.3) includes such a useful provision. Without such a clause, the seller could end up taking the business back but losing the location, a potentially devastating state of affairs. It is critical that any such agreement between the buyer, seller, and landlord be properly worded and included in one or all of the following: the purchase agreement, lease assignment form, promissory note, or chattel security agreement. In almost all cases, *permission of the landlord will be required.* In this light, review the form in Figure 7.4.

FIGURE 7.4 Lessor's Consent to Assignment of Lease

LESSOR'S CONSENT TO ASSIGNMENT OF LEASE

The undersigned (Lessor), lessor under the Lease, hereby consents to the foregoing Assignment without waiver of any restriction in the Lease concerning further assignment or subletting. Lessor certifies that, as of the date of Lessor's execution hereof, Assignor is not in default or breach of any of the provisions of the Lease, that Lessor holds the prepaid rent and security deposit set forth in the foregoing Assignment, and that the Lease has not been amended or modified except as expressly set forth in the foregoing Assignment. Lessor agrees to send Assignor a copy of any notice of default or breach Lessor sends to or serves on Assignee, at the following address: _____

_____ or such other address as may be designated in writing from time to time by Assignor, and agrees that in the event Lessor fails to send a copy of any such notice of default to Assignor, Assignor shall have no liability to Lessor on account of such default or breach. Lessor further agrees that no amendment, modification, termination, extension, or renewal of the Lease entered into by Lessor and Assignee shall be effective to increase or alter Assignor's liability or obligations under the Lease, unless consented to by Assignor, and that in the event Assignee exercises any right provided by the Lease to expand the Premises or to extend or renew the term of the Lease, Assignor's obligations and liability shall remain as if such right had not been exercised.

Date: _____

Lessor:_____

By: _____

Title: _____

By: _____

Title: _____

A *reassignment of lease* clause will protect the seller by allowing reentry in the event of borrower default. The seller will be allowed to reenter and reclaim ownership to the property, fixtures, and equipment covered by said assignment. The seller will be obligated under such conditions to pay all past due amounts. Yet another possible means of entry for the new owner is through a sublease. If the landlord will allow the seller to sublease, the seller can control his ability to reenter directly, in effect becoming the landlord to the new owner, who will have no direct contact with the primary landlord (unless required as part of the seller's lease). *Obtaining permission to sublease is a rare occurrence for commercial leases.*

The best way to deal with landlords concerning lease transfers is to be friendly, cooperative, and a bit submissive. If landlords feel they are in control, they will normally respond in a fair manner. In the event that you find the need to amend an existing lease (e.g., a sublease), the form in Figure 7.5 will suffice:

FIGURE 7.5   Amendment to Lease

AMENDMENT TO LEASE

This Amendment made this _____ day of _____, 19_____.

By and between _____ (Lessor)

and _____ (Lessee),

on that certain Lease dated _____, 19_____,

Does hereby amend section # _____ entitled _____

to read:

_____

_____

_____

_____

_____   _____

Lessor: Lessee:

_____   _____

The second group of transfers/assignments/assumptions deals with operating assets (e.g., equipment and automobiles) or a variety of service-type contracts (e.g., maintenance, janitorial, security). The existence of all such commitments should be fully disclosed by the seller and addressed promptly because of processing delays on the part of lessors. They should occur between the time of agreement on price and terms and the scheduled closing date. Lack of timely disclosure will open the seller to legal battles or possibly destroy the deal. Even if the seller fails to disclose and the purchaser fails to locate an outstanding commitment such as leased equipment or a service contract, it may surface as part of the UCC search. Escrow companies will not (should not) close a sale and transfer ownership until all such "clouds" are satisfactorily addressed by the would-be owner. *If the seller resists use of an independent escrow company, this should serve as a "red flag." Sellers can make a convincing case that there is no compelling reason to spend the money for escrow services.* The incentive to cut out this expense is greater for smaller businesses and/or businesses sold with a low down payment.

As concerns the contingency for bank financing, there is great latitude in terms of both structure and term. *Some of the better offers made are based on securing a bank loan and offering, in effect, a large (up to 100 percent) cash down payment. On the other hand, the deal is at risk until the funding is actually received, which may be as late as the day of closing.* It is not uncommon for the closing date to be extended to accommodate the bank's ability (or lack thereof) to process the loan and supply the funds.

Opening and Closing of Escrow

Just as there are deadlines for removal of contingencies, there should be deadlines for opening *and* closing of escrow. A typical case would be that escrow must be opened within three days after removal of all contingencies and/or on or before a certain date and time (e.g., 6-30-97 at noon). There should also be a "drop-dead" date for the deal as a whole, commonly in the form of a closing date constraint. The contract may read that closing must occur on or before 6 PM of 7-31-97, unless otherwise agreed on in writing by both buyer and seller.

In addition to removal of major contingencies, there are a wide variety of "housecleaning" tasks to be completed prior to closing. Accordingly, I have prepared a comprehensive checklist as part of Step 9, which includes the major contingencies described previously. *For escrow to be opened, a fully executed purchase agreement, earnest deposit, and escrow instructions from broker are normally required.*

Step 9: Orchestrate Successful Closing

This is the climax of emotionally draining negotiations, compromises, and agreements. It is scary indeed to realize that all the hard work that leads to this fateful day may be for naught. All parties (i.e., buyer, seller, spouses, brokers, attorneys, and escrow agents) gather to execute the finalized documents, which serve to transfer ownership of the myriad assets involved with the sale/purchase, under intense pressure. I have sadly witnessed deals that disintegrated on the day of closing because one or more of the outstanding, unresolved issues was too sensitive to allow common ground! When personalities clash, the pressure of the closing can erode what goodwill exists and sabotage the deal's chances for closing. It is here, at the closing, that the conditions for change in ownership are met and substantial monies are irrevocably transferred. Typically, the closing occurs at the same time that the purchase contract is formally executed.

To minimize last-minute disputes/debates, it is recommended that the buyer and seller ask the escrow company to prepare documents (e.g., bill of sale, promissory note, chattel security agreement, closing worksheet), several days before closing so that the principals and their agents can review all paperwork. This should be done even if it means that costs will be incurred if the deal fails. The fees for these documents are small relative to the benefits of early and advanced discussion of their many details. It is *impossible* to review all this paperwork at the time of closing, which may only involve one to two hours.

Basically, a successful closing is one where the buyer and seller agree to complete the transaction. Because of the many problems that can develop during the preclosing period, it is wise to schedule a timely closing without jeopardizing the buyer's or seller's cautionary objectives. It is also wise to recognize extenuating circumstances that call for extension of the closing date. Once the contractual dropdead date is reached, it is normally possible for either party to walk away. If closing was unattainable because one of the parties was not acting in *good faith*, legal remedies may be available.

Another suggestion is to schedule the closing for the end of the month/payroll cycle, facilitating a smooth cutoff. It is also wise to schedule the closing for eight or nine in the morning instead of three or four in the afternoon in order to leave time for unexpected hurdles or delays.

Let's review this event from the point of view of the independent, third party escrow company. If you were to query these professionals as to what was required for a timely and productive closing, the following points would be made.

- Utilize complete names and addresses of buyers and sellers, for both home and business. Clearly specify relationships between parties (e.g., husband and wife).
- Make sure that the contract and its addendum/changes are legible and understandable. Type the contract if possible and give the escrow company sufficient time to process/incorporate any changes to the original purchase agreement, hopefully before the day of closing. All addendums should be ordered by date of occurrence. Clear, concise clauses are important.
- Both the earnest deposit and closing funds should be cashiered/certified if submitted within five to seven days of the closing. If money market checks are involved, allow extra time for clearing (especially out of state funds). Wire transfers should be sent the day prior to closing because same-day transfers may not be posted in time.
- UCC searches should be ordered no later than two days prior to the scheduled closing (preferably three to seven days prior). When listing creditors, make sure that all necessary information is included (e.g., name, address, phone number, account number, total amount, and current balance).
- Complete all lease/franchise assignments prior to closing.

- If the closing is to be postponed for any reason, let the escrow company know as soon as possible. Closings scheduled for the 1st or the 15th of a month are especially tight, and you must be on time to accommodate the multiple closings.
- Do not try to play attorney if you are not one. If you are unsure about any clause, issue, or part of law, check it out with your broker, escrow agent, and attorney.
- Last, but not least, it is wise to limit the negotiations that take place during the closing. Try to resolve all matters prior to closing, following the advice detailed in this section. If significant points of contention are left to the closing, the deal might be postponed or even ultimately canceled.

Use the checklist in Figure 7.5 to ensure that all critical pre-closing problem areas have been addressed. For proper tracking, after you have copied the following list, insert the name or initials of the party who is responsible for seeing it happen and an estimated completion date.

FIGURE 7.5   Things to Do

I. **Closing Date**
    A. Have buyer and seller sign paperwork authorizing closing (typically after all contingencies are removed in writing).
    B. Determine if buyer or seller will be represented by attorneys at closing or if paperwork needs to be reviewed before closing (request early completion of paperwork at agreed upon fee).
    C. Review the following escrow prepared documents:
        1. Additional escrow terms and conditions
        2. Bill of sale
        3. Bulk sales notification/affidavit
        4. Chattel security agreement
        5. Closing statement (watch for fees and prorations)
        6. Equipment list
        7. Pledge agreements
        8. Promissory note
    D. Establish preliminary closing date with escrow company.
    E. Remind each other of date and time of closing, remind buyer to bring certified funds. If buyer is out of state, have bank send cashiered funds to in-state bank to avoid delay.
    F. If closing date must be extended, notify all parties (including escrow company) as soon as possible.

II. **Lease**
    A. Confirm details of new lease or lease assignment with landlord or seller (new, assignment/transfer, or sublease).
    B. Verify if lease to be transferred inside or outside of escrow (determining whether or not lease deposits will be transferred).
    C. If rent is in arrears, bring current or make acceptable arrangements.
    D. If equipment is leased, confirm details of new equipment lease or lease assignment/assumption with leasing company or seller (obtain current payoff balance and next due date). All leases should be assigned prior to or at closing.

FIGURE 7.5 Things to Do, continued

E. If liquor permit transfer is required, have landlord sign Certificate of Tenancy Rights.

III. Bulk Sales Act

A. Determine if Bulk Sales Act applies (consult with broker, attorney, escrow company).

B. If applicable, determine if buyer will waive. Have Bulk Sales Waiver signed. Include as addendum to purchase contract.

C. If Bulk Sales Law not waived, send letter to seller to obtain list of suppliers. Arrange notification letters to be sent out to creditors (signed by buyer and typically mailed 45 days prior to closing). Consult attorney for advice.

D. Regardless of bulk sales status, determine if and how all creditors are to be paid prior to or at closing.

IV. Assumption/Retirement of Liabilities

A. Determine if buyer is assuming any liabilities (e.g., equipment, seller carry-back notes, existing bank loans, credit card services processing contracts, auto leases, phone system, supplier debts, postage meter, maintenance and janitorial contracts, sign lease).

B. Determine employee wages, including payroll taxes, to be accrued to date of closing.

C. Accrue any miscellaneous expenses (e.g., utilities, personal property taxes).

D. For all assumed obligations, list due dates, date of last payment, interest rates, and obtain copies of notes, if possible, for review.

E. Obtain formal, signed assumption/retirement documentation. If equipment acquired by buyer is paid off with funds obtained by seller at closing, ask for a copy of the appropriate UCC lien removal documentation.

V. Taxes

A. Verify status of federal withholdings: FICA, FUTA, income, medicare.

B. Verify status with county/state auditor: state unemployment taxes, state sales taxes, workers' compensation taxes, local personal property taxes.

C. Determine amount of sales tax on furniture, fixtures, and equipment (check with accountant or tax professional).

D. Capital gains tax payable by seller (versus ordinary income) as calculated per Allocation of Purchase Price Form (IRS Form 8594).

E. If real property is involved, verify payment of all real estate property taxes.

VI. List of Furniture, Fixtures, and Equipment

A. Verify equipment list is current and accurate (with serial numbers).

B. Have buyer inspect and approve equipment list: sign furniture, fixture, and equipment list (to be attached to promissory note and bill of sale).

C. Prepare and sign Allocation of Purchase Price form (IRS Form 8594) on or before closing (both parties must sign).

D. Legally prepare and sign title transfer forms for all vehicles at closing.

E. Legally prepare and sign separately required transfer documentation, such as for computer software and other intangible assets.

VII. Inventory

A. Determine who will take inventory and at what time (typically as described in purchase offer).

B. If necessary, obtain estimated inventory level for closing worksheet.

C. Prepare addendum to purchase contract if inventory amount changes (this will change either the down payment or the balance on a promissory note).

FIGURE 7.5   Things to Do, continued

VIII.   Insurance

    A. Contact existing business property/casualty insurance agent to notify of pending changes in ownership.

    B. Provide for transfer of policy and proration at closing.

    C. Obtain necessary insurance binders.

IX.   Utilities

    A. Create complete list of all utility companies (with phone numbers) for buyer and seller to contact prior to closing.

    B. Check with utility companies to verify prior bills have been paid in full to help ensure a smooth transfer of service (also inquire as to required deposits).

X.   Miscellaneous

    A. Be certain all parties have complete, signed copies of purchase agreement and all addendums/amendments.

    B. Have copies of all paperwork ready for escrow company/attorney.

    C. Complete the escrow instructions for the escrow company/attorney (consult escrow company for instructions on how to prepare this information).

    D. If corporation is involved, prepare and notarize corporate resolution to buy or sell, normally signed by secretary and other officers. Consult your attorney.

    E. Have contingency removal forms and closing authorization forms signed.

    F. Prepare and obtain signature for seller's disclosure statements (business and real property) and/or certificate of warranties and representations.

    G. Prepare and confirm validity of noncompete agreement and tax implications of consulting agreements (if applicable).

    H. Clarify status and disposal of cash, receivables, and work in progress prior to close of escrow.

    I. Prepare detailed instructions regarding mutual release of escrow funds (in the event deal falls apart after escrow is opened).

    J. Ensure that any last minute changes signed by both parties are added as addendum/amendment to purchase contract.

    K. Address thoroughly any liens or encumbrances found by escrow company during lien search (UCC filings, tax liens, and judgments). Allow three to five days for this search and one to three days to resolve.

    L. Verify buyer's source of funds and remind buyer that escrow funds must be certified (or wire transfered).

    M. Ensure buyer fills out paperwork and pays requested fees for transfer of business trade name and/or patents, copyrights, or trademarks.

    N. Transfer any distributorship/supplier agreements and/or outstanding contracts with customers or employees (as needed).

    O. Obtain insurance binder if necessary (temporary insurance coverage).

    P. Assist each other with processing/obtaining bank financing.

XII.   Licenses/Permits

    A. Obtain city and state sales tax licenses for new owner.

    B. Obtain business permits (transaction privileges), e.g., health, food service and licenses (FDA, EPA, liquor, DEA, etc.).

    C. Obtain formal transfer approval from franchiser, if applicable.

FIGURE 7.5 Things to Do, continued

D. Obtain formal transfer/assignment of liquor license.

E. Obtain other required licenses/permits.

XII. **Real Property**

A. Have seller prepare and sign seller's disclosure statement.

B. Conduct necessary environmental inspection and/or tests (e.g., Phase I or Phase II).

C. Prepare contract and other required paperwork for closing (consult attorney for these matters).

D. Verify current payment of taxes and insurance.

XIII. **Prorations**

A. When investigating exact balances, determine if vendor bills are in advance or in arrears and document content of conversations and other parties' names.

B. Accounting fees

C. Alarm/security

D. Answering service

E. Appraisal fees

F. Attorney fees

G. Automobiles

H. Computers

I. Copier

J. Credit card service contracts

K. Employee wages/taxes/vacation days

L. Escrow fees (e.g., document preparation, lien search, cancellation, mutual release)

M. Franchise assignment fees

N. Ice machine and vending machines

O. Insurance

P. Miscellaneous advertising expense

Q. Miscellaneous equipment

R. Personal property taxes (per escrow search)

S. Property lease and deposit

T. Property lease and deposit (include provision for handling upcoming year-end CAM charges)

U. Utilities (e.g., gas, electric, phone, water)

Y. Yellow Pages ad

Note: Make sure that all the above prorations are either handled outside of escrow or inside of escrow (if inside, these amounts should be reflected in the closing worksheet prepared by the escrow company).

Step 10: Deal with Transition Issues

There are six key areas that extend across the time spectrum from pre-closing to post-closing, but should be fully addressed and negotiated prior to closing. To varying degrees, their relevance survives the closing and carries forward for long periods of time.

1. Covenant not to compete
2. Training/familiarization agreements
3. Employment/consulting contracts
4. Earn-out provisions—right to inspect books
5. Early possession
6. Operational transition and management of acquisition

Of these six issues, numbers one and two are almost always either included in purchase contracts or exist as supplements thereto. Less frequently, numbers three and four are negotiated as part of the overall purchase or sale. Number five is uniquely risky, quite uncommon, and not normally recommended (requires great care and confidence in application). Number six is not a clause but a series of activities designed to ensure success for the new owner.

Before proceeding into the specifics, allow me to preach the virtue of genuine cooperation and trust. Better, stronger, longer lasting quality deals result from such open and honest cooperation. *Full disclosure, dealing with problems openly and head-on, coupled with genuine trust are the lasting hallmarks of the most successful deals.* Even in the most open and honest relationship, there will be inevitable tension, disagreement, and negotiations. These six issues are often as troublesome as price and terms when it comes to reaching a meeting of the minds as each of them involve the time and/or money of the buyer and/or seller! These areas will be more or less important to each buyer and each seller in each deal. The same issue that the seller is completely indifferent to will be *the* "hot button" for the buyer that jeopardizes a deal. It is often impossible to predict what these hot buttons will be, unless you have the advantage of working with a broker who has been down the trail before with a particular buyer or seller.

If any of these six issues are important to the buyer, they should be addressed in the first offer. It may be the case that the seller has already signaled his or her position concerning one or more of these areas in the offering package (e.g., purchase price includes two weeks full-time training). More common is the situation where none of these issues have been presented or discussed by the seller in any detailed way and the buyer must present an offer as he or she feels fit. The seller, as part of a counteroffer, may respond to these areas in detail. What is unacceptable to one side presently may become acceptable two weeks later. Clearly, the negotiation process can be dynamic, arduous, and complex. Accepting this dynamic interplay and never-ending give and take, we can proceed to discuss these six extremely important areas in detail. Don't skimp on getting help with these issues (i.e., hiring brokers, attorneys, etc.)—they can make or break a successful deal.

1. Covenant Not to Compete

Rare is the deal where the buyer is not at least moderately concerned about this topic. These covenants generally restrict the seller from competing with the business being sold for an agreed-upon duration, geographical proximity, and range of activities or products. It is not rare to end up negotiating with great fervor the precise components of the covenant, also called a *noncompete agreement*.

For example, the purchaser of an accounting practice had made a generous offer with a heavy cash down payment that was accepted by the seller, subject to numerous contingencies. One of these contingencies was reaching agreement on the precise terms of the noncompete clause. This case is an excellent example of how easy it is to misunderstand the other party and create perceptions that are simply not true. The problem revolved around establishing exactly what the seller would be doing after the sale. Two specific events clouded this deal and ultimately destroyed it. First, the seller was not clear about his post-sale desires. He was considering a completely different line of business with a friend at the same time he was considering working for another accountant. Second, the buyer had previously purchased a practice that was severely harmed by the seller, who intentionally drew his previous customers back, to the great chagrin of the buyer.

These two unrelated facts coalesced into a dead end for the deal. The buyer was overly cautious going into the deal because of his previous experience, which cost him a lot of time and grief (he did recover partially through a successful lawsuit). The fact that the present seller was wavering about his future plans was quite discomforting to the buyer. Even though the seller was only being honest, the fact that he moderately resisted the buyer's offered geographic constraint of 25 miles (seller would not set up a new practice within 25 miles of the current location) set the buyer down a path of negativity. The buyer quickly was thinking in terms of worst case scenarios, and the deal disintegrated. Consider the many ironies here. One, the seller truly did not want to reenter the accounting world with a new practice of his own. He was selling precisely to leave this behind. Two, if the seller would have preliminarily agreed to the 25 mile constraint, he knew that it would probably be unenforceable in a court of law as unreasonable (as long as he didn't solicit his previous customers). Three, the seller actually would have preferred to work with/for the buyer for the indefinite future, presenting an excellent opportunity to foster a trusting relationship, which would reduce the likelihood of violations to the noncompete.

Two insights remain with me long offer this deal dissipated. First, *it is important that the seller credibly present all components of his business to the buyer, including plans for work subsequent to the sale!* Wavering in this area can needlessly harm the progress of a deal. Second, *do not hold out for terms that ultimately will have little or no impact on your well-being.* The seller knew that 25 miles was probably unreasonable and unenforceable. If he would have agreed to this condition, the deal might have closed. When a business is purchased (whether stock sale or asset sale), the buyer is obtaining all tangible and intangible assets, unless specifically excluded. The noncompete clause enhances the value of all assets by prohibiting the seller from reentering the same line of business and taking customers. Many a buyer has spent a sleepless night contemplating the nightmarish scenario of the seller opening up across the street.

Here are the pertinent issues/concerns surrounding these important clauses.

Key Issues/Concerns:

- What are duration of covenant (years), geographical area, and product/service restrictions?
- Which parties (i.e., spouses, family members, other shareholders, other relatives, former business associates, hired assistants) are covered?
- Will a judge interpret the covenant as reasonable? Are disputes subject to arbitration?
- Is the covenant executed separately from the purchase agreement?
- What portion of the purchase price is allocated to the covenant not to compete?
- Are there specific procedures outlined regarding possible breaches of the covenant (e.g., how are damages calculated and paid, can buyer offset remaining note payment to seller in the event of breach by seller, is written notice required)?
- If there is an employment or consulting agreement involved, how is it related to the covenant (e.g., are new clients generated as part of consulting efforts by seller property of seller or buyer)?
- Does the covenant carry over to third parties?

Simple concepts are greatly complicated by reality. Covenants not to compete are no exception. Different buyers, sellers, and circumstances will dictate the wide ranging possible outcomes regarding actual clauses. The noncompete covenant found in the purchase agreement (see Figure 5.1) is clear and serves as a good starting point.

> Seller agrees not to compete, directly or indirectly or in any manner, or engage in the _____ business within _____ (miles or area) of the business purchased; nor aid or assist anyone else, except the buyer, to do so within these limits; nor solicit in any manner any past accounts or employees of the business; nor have any interest, directly or indirectly, in such a business excepting as an employee of the buyer, for a period of ____ consecutive years from the close of this sale.

This particular covenant is contained inside the formal purchase contract. Prior to recent changes in tax laws, which currently allow amortization of *all* intangible assets over a fixed, 15-year period, the importance of the covenant not to compete was greater due to quicker write-offs. Given the important tax shield of noncompete agreements, they were often executed separately from (in conjunction with) the purchase contract to reinforce their tax deductibility. Note also that this covenant extends beyond customers (past accounts) to employees and other third parties. Particular restrictions on family members, past and present business associates, and even suppliers could also be added. The ultimate constraint is that covenants cannot be so harsh as to restrict the ability of the seller to earn a living. Additionally, they must contain a definite duration and scope and be associated with sufficient consideration. Acceptable durations will vary depending on the nature of the business. For example, the quantity of customers and how frequently they change companies will impact this figure. The longer the customers stay with a given owner in a particular industry, the longer the duration might be. Finally, the noncompete agreement cannot be for life or forever. Uncle Sam has a measurable distaste for such restrictions (anticompetitive). Here is another example:

> Seller agrees not to operate or to assist in operation, of any landscape maintenance or installation business within _____ County, State of ____, for a period of five years following Close of Escrow. Seller agrees not to solicit employees of the Company for employment in any business in which Seller is employed or in which seller holds any interest. Seller agrees not to solicit the Company's present landscaping customers to obtain their business for any competitive purpose.

Short, but sweet! This next covenant is placed into the section of the purchase contract that deals also with the training period and employment subsequent to closing. Note the breach provisions and arbitration procedures as well.

a) Seller hereby agrees to be available, without charge, during normal business hours during the month of _____ to perform such services for Buyer that are designed to facilitate the transition of the BUSINESS from Seller to Buyer.

b) As from the date of closing and for a period of five years thereafter, Seller agrees and covenants not to compete with the business, either by performing services for existing clients, or soliciting work from existing clients, or opening an office offering such services anywhere in _____ County, State of _____.

c) Should Seller breach aforesaid covenant not to compete by performing services for clients, or establishing an office within the defined area and offering competitive services, in addition to such other remedies as may be available to Buyer, any receipts realized from such breach shall be for the account of Buyer, and the same amount shall be offset dollar for dollar against any amounts still owing under aforesaid promissory note. If there is money still owed, then Seller shall pay such amount directly to buyer.

d) Notwithstanding the provisions of this paragraph, Seller may perform services for and at the behest of Buyer in any aspect of the business and in such event shall be compensated therefore at the rate of $_____ per hour.

e) This agreement is drawn in accordance with the laws of the State of _____ and is to be interpreted accordingly.

f) In the event of a dispute arising from any part of this agreement, the parties agree to submit such dispute for final and binding resolution to and by the American Arbitration Association, for adjudication in its offices in accordance with its rules and procedures. The prevailing party to such dispute may be awarded its reasonable attorneys' fees and costs.

The following covenant explicitly covers cooperative activities between buyer and seller and the ongoing validity of the covenant upon resale by the purchaser.

Seller agrees that neither it nor any of its officers or directors, including especially _____, will not for a period of five consecutive years from the close of escrow within the state of _____ or on any present or past accounts of the company outside the state of _____ and one year following the close of escrow within the United States of America, directly or indirectly compete with Buyer in any of the following activities: (a) engage in the manufacturing and/or sales of _____; (b) have any interest, directly or indirectly, in any business engaged in the foregoing activities; (c) aid or assist anyone else in engaging in such a business; or (d) solicit any past or present accounts or customers of the Company with respect to any of the foregoing activities. _____ further agree that accounts secured by the company during employment with the company shall become property of the company and shall be included in this covenant not to compete. Seller and _____ reserve the right under this covenant not to compete to market their own designs for national retail consumption and agree for one year following the close of escrow to hire the company to silk screen any of seller's designs that are silk screened provided however the company's quality and prices are reasonably competitive. Buyer understands the majority of seller marketed lines shall be embroidered and buyer gives seller and _____ consent to use an outside manufacturer to embroider such items. If during the covenant not to compete buyer shall resell the company to a subsequent purchaser, seller agrees to continue to be bound by the covenant not to compete for the remainder of the covenant.

2. Training/Familiarization Agreements

Now we move on to the second major transition issue, training, where the precise details are often subject to heated negotiations. If the seller is willing to offer extended training, the buyer may be willing to pay a higher price (and vice versa). Occasionally the seller is under great pressure to sell and leave the area immediately, which naturally influences the outcome. Chapter 5 contained a basic training/familiarization clause:

Seller, without compensation, shall familiarize and acquaint buyer with all material aspects of the business from the close of escrow for a period of _____.

Training periods are typically provided without charge and serve primarily to accomplish a

- complete, timely education of the new owner regarding basic/peculiar operations of the business;
- smooth and cooperative introduction to employees, suppliers, and customers.

The overall importance depends on the complexity of the business and the experience of the buyer. There may be only one day of training. For a more complex business and a relatively inexperienced buyer, 30 days or more of full-time assistance may be required. If extensive training is necessary, there may be additional compensation. A common question posed by buyers when they hear the asking price is, "What am I paying for?" My response often includes a reference to training, particularly when speaking to first-time buyers. *The practical matter is that many buyers find it difficult to admit that they need help and most sellers are adamant that their help is mandatory for future success.*

The buyer should be prepared to get the most out of the seller that he can. Even open-ended questions (e.g., what can we do to improve the sales and cash flow?) are worthwhile. It is typically only the seller that has the intimate knowledge of a particular business that can best answer such questions.

The seller, on the other hand, should seek to fulfill his or her obligations by openly and honestly giving the best advice possible. Realize, however, that the buyer may not seek your assistance or agree with your business philosophy. This is quite difficult for many sellers to accept while they are still going to work every day.

A few final points. When drafting the clause, be precise regarding future commitments of time, possibly incorporating a sliding scale to reflect the buyer's growing confidence. The buyer might agree to release the seller prematurely if the need for his or her help diminishes (quite comforting to the seller). Finally, consider placing funds into an escrow account to be released only after completion of training.

3. Employment/Consulting Agreements

The end result of many deals is an ongoing relationship between buyer and seller beyond the purchase contract and closing. They often become "partners," whether through a formal/legal partnership agreement or a long-term earn-out provision (as described in the next section). These agreements accomplish many things, including

- allowing buyer continued access to the owner;
- offering a more favorable, overall package to seller;
- buyer advantage of immediate tax deductions for payments to seller; and
- delaying/extending large payments from buyer over the life of the agreement.

The most important reason for engaging the seller past closing is access to the irreplaceable knowledge, skills, and contacts. There are cooperative and forceful ways to keep the seller active. A consulting contract would be cooperative. After determining what training is part of the original purchase price, you can evaluate the scope and amount of additional work that the seller is willing to perform and at what cost. Another important reason to keep the seller active is to reassure the employees, customers, and suppliers that although ownership may be changing hands, the new company is even better, a synergistic combination of the old and the new. Presenting this image is critical for service companies, where "rocking the boat" can be devastating. The sale of accounting or tax practices is commonly accomplished with the assistance of joint correspondence from the new owner and the previous owner to all customers. This correspondence occurs whether or not there is a formal post-closing, consulting arrangement. The logic behind such "partner-oriented" correspondence without a formal partnership arrangement is based on the fact that the buyer still owes the seller money, the final sum being dependent on the actual revenues earned over the first year (earn-out arrangement) When such a payment scheme exists, the buyer and seller are truly partners until the final payment is made.

Let's look at the major issues to be addressed:

- Is the deal contingent on concluding a satisfactory consulting/employment contract?
- What exact types of activity will the seller perform? Not perform?
- Is the seller comfortable as an employee, manager, or independent contractor? Buyer's preference?
- Are any of the buyer's funds at risk pending satisfactory training?
- Are buyer and seller aware of key factors that determine independent contractor status?
- What is the nature of the compensation package? Per hour, day, week, month, or flat fee, etc.?
- Are there minimum/maximum payments to be made? Will seller have expense account?
- What is the overall relationship between the covenant not to compete, training period, and consulting contract? Are they consistent with one another?
- Does breach for one constitute breach for the others and vice versa?
- Under what circumstances may the contract be terminated? Are conflicts subject to arbitration?

Consider the following:

Seller agrees to consult with and assist buyer with normal operating procedures, including customer interface, for as many as _____ hours per week over the next _____ months, beginning after close of escrow. Buyer will compensate seller $_____ per hour, payable under independent contractor status (buyer to pay no payroll taxes, which will be the sole responsibility of the seller).

This clause highlights the tax advantage of employment contracts. To the extent that payments made to the seller are considered part of the overall purchase price, they are made from pretax dollars rather than the aftertax dollars utilized to finance the down payment. Scrutiny of employment contracts by your CPA or tax attorney will ensure that you play by the rules. It is *illegal* to structure a deal whereby the buyer compensates the seller with inflated consulting fees simply to enjoy tax savings. The seller can only be paid a fair compensation (market wages). The seller must be aware that payments received as an independent contractor are subject to self-employment taxes (i.e., social security, medicare and medicaid, income taxes) and can easily rise above the tax liability associated with capital gains.

Attorney assistance is recommended. Make sure that the seller signs a nondisclosure agreement (in addition to the noncompete covenant), spelling out clearly any termination provisions and describing the options available to both parties in the event of a breach (e.g., arbitration clause). *Different types of contracts include independent contractor status, consultancy agreements, or employment contracts.* Consider purchasing *The Upstart Small Business Legal Guide*, by Robert Friedman (Upstart Publishing Company, 312-836-4400).

Here is one last comprehensive agreement:

Understanding that buyer _____ desires to acquire certain assets from the seller and his corporation with a scheduled closing date of _____, the buyer wishes to avail himself of future consulting services of the seller (consultant) and seller (consultant) wishes to provide such services, over and beyond the initial, one-month, full-time familiarization period to be provided by seller to buyer as part of the purchase price and as outlined in said purchase agreement. Furthermore, buyer seeks to obtain an agreement not to compete with seller, as described below:

In consideration of all promises, mutual covenants, and other commitments between buyer and seller, the buyer and seller hereby further agree that:

I. Beginning _____ and ending _____, (the duration) the seller (consultant) shall be available to buyer (the company) to perform consulting services and refrain from competing as described below:

A. For the duration, consultant agrees to respond to requests by seller to perform miscellaneous advisory/consulting services related to the normal day-to-day operations of the company. Such services will be provided subject to reasonable notice being provided to consultant and subject to prior commitments of consultant. Consultant agrees to be available a total number of hours equal to a minimum of 30 hours per week for the first six months after closing, 20 hours per week for the next six months and 10 hours per week thereafter. Additionally, the buyer agrees to reimburse consultant for any reasonable, out-of-pocket expenses incurred as a result of providing these services.

B. For the duration and one more additional year, consultant agrees not to compete, directly or indirectly, with the business in any part of _____. Compete hereby refers to any material contact as agent, principal, shareholder, employee, consultant, partner or director, etc., in buying, selling, investing, advising, etc., relating to the manufacturing, distribution or sale of _____ products that are deemed to be in competition with the buyer's new business. Consultant may purchase up to 3 percent of the outstanding stock of any publicly traded competitor's securities.

II. Consultant to be paid $5,000 per month on the last workday of each month subject to fulfilling all obligations. Such services rendered by consultant are to be of an outstanding character and beneficial to the financial health of the company.

III. In the event of breach, both parties may seek any and all appropriate legal remedies, with written notice being given (registered mail) for any claim of breach. All the consultant's rights and obligations are nonassignable and nontransferable, unless agreed to in writing.

Other clauses could be included concerning modifications, amendments, entire agreement, invalidity of particular provisions, relevance of state laws, etc. *Attorney guidance is highly recommended.*

4. Earn-Out Provisions—Right to Inspect Books

One of the most dynamic, troublesome, yet potentially useful transition-related issues is the *earn-out* clause. The exact terms of an earn-out, which is nothing more than a type of creative seller financing, are limited only by one's imagination. They have been known to resurrect otherwise dead deals. Also referred to as a *contingent price*, the business is sold for a guaranteed amount (down payment plus other fixed payments) and a contingent amount (contingent upon some measure of actual performance subsequent to closing). The contingent, or earn-out, amounts become payable at mutually agreed on intervals. A particular formula (e.g., 10 percent of operating income [EBIT]) is spelled out and future payments are made accordingly. There will often be minimum and/or maximum payments agreed on in addition to the fixed component of the purchase price. It is essential that the formula be clear (examples should be spelled out as part of the agreement), and the seller must retain the right to audit the buyer's books. Entering into deals based on earn-out provisions is risky and will often lead to anger and disappointment. Review the following key issues/concerns:

- Is the earn-out formula precise and easily understood? Are examples included to support the formula?
- What rights does the seller have to audit the buyer's books?
- Will company be changed (e.g., merged) after the purchase from seller? (Affects formula payments.)
- Will the seller remain involved in the day-to-day activities of the business?
- How are depreciation, nonrecurring, extraordinary, and capital expenses being handled?

- Is there an acceptable degree of good faith between buyer and seller to ensure success?
- Is cash being placed in escrow to assure seller that earn-out obligations will be met?
- Why do the buyer and seller disagree on the current value and projected profitability of the business?

Earn-outs have historically been the domain of larger companies. Today, even the smallest of businesses are being sold on this basis. An earn-out is useful when the parties differ greatly on their perception of current value and expected profitability, regardless of company size. Not all buyers and sellers are interested in this type of arrangement, for reasons such as difficulty in establishing and proving sales and profits; great expenses involved in settling disputes; buyers are hesitant to share in future profits; and sellers are hesitant to rely on the efforts of buyer to determine their final payments.

Buyers often require an earn-out because the seller has been a major factor in the success of the business, lessening its value to the buyer. It may also be that the business has two or three major customers who could leave at any time (no contract). Buyers seeks to pay for only the business that is generated under their ownership. In each case, there is a risk to the seller that the buyer will not perform to capacity and the actual, final sales price will suffer. Consider the following simple earn-out clause:

> The purchase price for the assets shall be paid as provided in this paragraph. Subject to all other provisions of this agreement, within 60 days after the end of each of the next five years after the effective date of this agreement, purchaser shall pay seller the greater of (a) 20 percent of net income from purchaser's business operations that year and (b) $500,000, provided that in no event shall purchaser be obligated to make payments to seller that cause the total purchase price to exceed $400,000. (For example, assume that the effective date of this agreement is 12-31-98. Assume that on 12-31-99, purchaser's net income for the calendar year 1999 equals $300,000. Within 60 days after 12-31-99, purchaser shall pay seller $60,000. Assume further that on 12-31-00, purchaser's net income for the calendar year equals $100,000. Within 60 days after 12-31-00, purchaser shall pay seller $50,000. Suppose that by 12-31-02, purchaser has paid seller payments equaling $400,000. Regardless of purchaser's net income for the year ending 12-31-02, purchaser shall have no further obligations regarding this earn-out provision. Net income for purposes of this paragraph shall be determined by purchaser using generally accepted accounting principles (GAAP) consistently applied to the accounts and records of purchaser.

A pertinent question is what precisely is meant by net income and what components or expenses are relevant to this calculation. Want to see a higher net income? Recognize sales quicker and delay recognition of expenses. Choose to capitalize assets that you would normally expense. Reduce your estimates for bad debt expense this year. Fail to reduce the carrying value of assets that have fallen substantially in value. Want to see a lower net income? Do all of these things in reverse! Although most of these accounting changes are based on timing and will reverse themselves eventually, sophisticated accounting users can manipulate as needed, engaging in what is referred to as *earnings management*. What about one-time, nonrecurring revenues and expenses? Should net income be adjusted accordingly? The point is that for these earn-out structures to work, they must be clear, concise, and difficult to manipulate. Total sales is a better (less manipulative) figure than net income (which includes sales and old expenses). Furthermore, gross sales is preferred to net sales, which can be manipulated via sales returns and allowances. Alas, even gross sales can be manipulated through changes in recognition criteria (e.g., sales are recognized at the time of taking the order, at the time of shipping, at the time of receipt by customer, at the time of collection of cash). The second major problem is that there appears to be no specific clarification as to how the seller can access the buyer's books and records.

Many larger transactions are based on operating earnings or EBIT (earnings before interest and taxes). This measure of earnings is attractive in that it excludes taxes and interest, both of which are subject to the unique situations of the owner and can be quite easily manipulated. Let's say the buyer and seller have agreed to the following formula:

In addition to a cash down payment of $100,000, annual payments will be made to seller subject to the formula below:

Year 1	*Years 2 to 4*	*Years 5 to 7*
25% of EBIT	33% of EBIT	20% of EBIT

Annual payments will be at least $20,000, but no more than $50,000 with a cumulative total of $300,000. Buyer agrees to place $100,000 in a separate interest-bearing escrow account opened at the close of escrow, from which annual payments will be made if buyer fails to make them on his own accord. If all required payments are made by buyer, the $100,000 plus interest will be returned. Seller to inspect buyer's books and records at any time to verify reported sales and EBIT. EBIT to be calculated exclusively based upon GAAP with any disputes settled through binding arbitration (American Arbitration Association).

Note that requiring GAAP would seem to solidify the requirements for calculating EBIT. It does not! For example, GAAP allows many different schemes for depreciation of fixed assets (e.g., straight-line versus accelerated methods), each of which has an important effect on EBIT. Only detailed, precise descriptions of numerous accounting issues will eliminate these possible disputes. Please note that earn-outs are initially presented and discussed in Chapter 4.

5. Early Possession

A controversial aspect of buying or selling a business is the granting of early possession to the buyer. Perhaps the buyer, who is anxious to begin a new pursuit and earn enough money to repay debts, wants to move in as soon as possible, despite the fact that the closing cannot officially occur for another two weeks (buyer will not be funded until then). Maybe the seller, who is ecstatic about selling the business for what he or she believes is a fair price, is all too ready to turn over the reins. Perhaps the seller is terribly ill and the business is falling apart, causing the buyer to want to move in quickly. It is possible, if properly handled, to agree on a date of possession that differs from the closing date.

However, *be careful! This is risky business.* The greatest risk is to the seller, who may be faced with an occupant unable to close the transaction. This increases the likelihood of damaged or stolen equipment, lost sales, irritated customers, or missing cash! Yet another risk for the seller is that the buyer might change his mind about the business after the reality of spending long days and long nights at the business (employees fail to show up, suppliers hassle for prompt payment, and customers complain bitterly)! If you choose this option, *get it in writing!* Essentially, this amounts to obtaining a lease (sublease) from the buyer (tenant), which unfortunately probably requires the permission of the landlord. It would be extremely risky (foolish) to proceed without the landlord's knowledge and consent. Given that a prepossession agreement is essentially a lease, it should address the following issues:

- Will the buyer pay all rent (including CAM) for the period of early possession?
- What are the buyer's responsibilities regarding maintenance of the property?
- What are the buyer's rights if the sale does not close as planned?
- Does the seller's property/liability insurance transfer to buyer?
- How will ongoing expenses and sales be split between buyer and seller?

Most business brokers will resist this arrangement. They will ask the buyer and seller to sign a disclaimer advising against early possession. At a minimum, they will advise you to complete all other aspects of the transaction before early possession is granted. They will want to ensure that the UCC search is completed satisfactorily, the lease assignment has been formally approved and all or most of the funds required for closing have been deposited in escrow. Consider the following sample clauses and make sure you obtain qualified legal assistance before agreeing to early possession.

In exchange for granting of early possession (prior to legal close of escrow) of business premises located at _____, buyer acknowledges and agrees that he will personally assume all new debts incurred during the period of early possession. Seller acknowledges and agrees that granting said early possession might result in harmful consequences to the business and that there is no guarantee that granting of early possession will lead to a successful, legal closing. Buyer and seller agree to hold broker harmless and fully indemnify him from any and all possible liabilities/have occurring as a result of such early possession.

6. Operational Transition Issues and Management of Acquisition

Optimally managing an acquisition is equally challenging for the individual owner-operator taking over a smaller business and the corporate management team taking over a larger business. Entire books have been written on running and operating a business successfully in general and managing an acquisition specifically, both of which are beyond the scope of this guide. See the suggested reading choices at the end of this chapter for further guidance. Now we consider a few important ideas regarding the operational transition period.

Operational transition—prior to closing. Almost every deal contains at least a minimal training/familiarization period, which takes place immediately after closing (averaging one to two weeks, full-time). Somewhere between early possession, where the buyer takes over the business prior to closing, and a formalized familiarization commitment from the seller lies the common situation wherein the buyer, by virtue of due diligence efforts and completion of pre-closing tasks, spends more and more time with the seller. What may begin as "after hours," formal discussions tend to evolve into anytime, informal chats about all facets of the business (assuming the deal is progressing nicely). Ideally, the buyer and seller *will* develop a close, cooperative, trusting relationship that also survives the closing. However, it is not wise for the seller to fully familiarize and train a buyer in the operation of a business, particularly if there is any chance that the buyer will back out. There is no way for sellers to know for sure what a buyer's true intentions are, so they will tend to act on the conservative side and limit the buyer's exposure until after closing has occurred. There is, therefore, a tendency for many sellers to isolate themselves and their businesses from even qualified buyers out of fear that too many of the company secrets will be divulged or out of (often irrational) fear that the buyer may not like what he sees if he sees too much!

Most purchase contracts will detail specific activities that the seller agrees to undertake or not undertake between the time the contract is signed and closing (covenants). Considerate and timely communications with the buyer will go a long way toward firming the buyer/seller relationship. Once the contract is signed both ways, the seller probably should not commit the firm contractually to anything unless discussed with the buyer. On the other hand, the seller should do everything possible to keep the business profitable and the customers and employees happy. The more likely it appears that closing will occur, the more important this open line of communication is. Other ideas worthy of discussion include:

- Substantial purchase of new inventory or equipment
- Any new debt obligations or substantial new orders, contracts, or bids

- Plans to hire/fire personnel
- New product lines to be inherited by purchaser or planned changes in pricing/terms

Some discussions cut both ways, meaning that the seller needs to know if the buyer has any particular plans regarding personnel, new product lines, desired levels of inventory, etc.

Operational transition—post closing. After the closing, the buyer and seller will likely continue working closely together during the familiarization period. Key aspects of the training commitment once again are:

- Introduction to employees, suppliers, key customers, bankers
- Discussions covering all material operational and financial aspects of the business; possible changes
- Collection of seller's receivables and payment of overlooked payables
- Follow through on unfinished transition issues (e.g., lease assignment, contract assumptions, asset transfers, insurance binders)

Tapping the collective knowledge of the seller and key employees is a vital component of long-range planning and will hopefully create positive feelings within the company regarding its future. As a rule, it is not normally wise to undertake wholesale changes in operations, no matter how great the urge to do so might be. Meeting with employees soon after closing is important in order to stem the tide of rumors and uncertainty that will inevitably develop. Any actions that you do take regarding hiring/firing should be done carefully—especially the firing. If this is new territory for you, you should consult yet another legal expert—the labor attorney!

Go to your local library or bookstore to locate one of the literally hundreds of books written about successfully owning and operating a small business. Consider the following books:

Larger Acquisitions
- *Making Mergers Work: A Guide to Managing Mergers and Acquisitions*, by Price Pritchett (McGraw-Hill)
- *Managing Acquisitions: Creating Value Through Corporate Renewal*, by Philippe Haspeslagh and David Jemison (Free Press)
- *Managing the Merger: Making It Work*, by Philip Mirvis and Mitchell Marks (Prentice Hall Trade)
- *Mergers and Acquisitions: The Human Factor*, by Sue Cartwright and Cary Cooper (Butterworth-Heinemann)

- *Mergers: Growth in the Fast Lane: A Field Manual for Management*, by Price Pritchett and Robert Galbreath (Pritchett Publishing)

Smaller Purchases (available from Dearborn/Upstart Publishing Company, 800-245-2665)
- *Owning and Managing Series*, by various authors. Call for a list of specific businesses covered in this series (e.g., bar and tavern, florist, travel service, desktop publishing).
- *The Language of Small Business*, by Carl O. Trautmann
- *The Ted Nicholas Small Business Course*, by Ted Nicholas
- *The Small Business Survival Kit*, by John Ventura
- *Secrets of Entrepreneurial Leadership*, by Ted Nicholas

CHAPTER 8

Introduction to Business Valuation Techniques

Perhaps the most misunderstood aspect of buying or selling a business is the valuation process. Valuing a business is in reality an art as much as it is a science. What is a business worth? To whom and at what time? What is meant by *goodwill* or *blue sky*, and how much do you pay for it? If you ask five different professionals (e.g., brokers, business appraisers, attorneys, CPAs) to place a value on a going concern, they would undoubtedly return five different results! Valuation must be considered a matter of perception.

Valuation results will differ from person to person and over time for three reasons. (1) The purpose and timing of the valuation will have an impact on the range. (2) Sellers and their agents typically believe that a business is worth more than it is, while buyers and their agents believe that the business is worth less than it is. (3) Sellers will even occasionally adjust what they think the business is worth depending on who the buyer is. For example, the seller of a niche manufacturing business may require a higher price from a large, well capitalized corporate purchaser (strategic buyer) than from a working couple utilizing retirement funds to buy a job (financial buyer).

The sales process begins with the seller evaluating the market value and incorporating this figure into an asking price, which is almost always higher than what the seller believes the business is worth or what the seller would accept to reach agreement. The buyer tours the business and performs numerous analyses to determine the desirability and value of the opportunity at hand. Of course, the buyer's perception of value will normally differ from that of the seller, and both sides will experience changes in their understanding of the value as time passes. The seller will monitor his or her feelings about the value of the business as current and expected sales and profits rise or fall, while the buyer will be perfecting his or her knowledge of the operation as he or she spends more time at the business and with the seller before and during due diligence. Coming to agreement on price and terms is one of the most critical points in the sales and negotiation process. Acceptable prices for the buyer and seller are greatly influenced by the results of the valuation processes prepared by all parties and are subject to changing perceptions.

Another important facet of valuation relates to the differences between an all-cash offer and an offer with terms. For the sale of real property, the general assumption is that the valuation results are based on an all-cash offer. There are no concrete rules for business sales relating to cash discounts, but the typical range is between 10 and 25 percent. One theory holds that all-cash terms should be the basis for valuation as it is for most other assets. Another theory finds its roots in the majority of business sales that do occur with seller financing. Many sellers will offer their business for sale with two separate prices, one all-cash and the other with terms.

The pertinent question is how does the presence of terms affect the valuation process. The most widely accepted answer would be that the valuation results obtained are for businesses that will be offered with financing terms of about 33 percent down and the balance carried over approximately five years at going market rates. For seller financing, these rates will hover around the prime rate (plus or minus one to two points). The following relationships tend to hold in practice: *higher down payment, lower price; shorter repayment term, lower price; higher interest rate, lower price; more collateral, lower price.*

In addition to these four factors, the method by which the business will be sold (asset sale versus stock sale) affects the value. A buyer will normally pay a higher price for an asset purchase, owing to the ability to redepreciate the fixed assets and enjoy a reduced taxable income. On the other hand, a stock purchase might be more valuable if there are prior period net operating losses that can be used to shield future taxable income.

Concepts of Value

- Fair Market Value (FMV)
- Book Value (BV)
- Liquidation Value (LV)

Fair Market Value

The most important concept is *fair market value* (FMV), represented by the price that a willing buyer with complete information, not under unusual stress, will pay a willing seller not experiencing undue pressure to sell. This is also referred to as an *arm's-length* transaction. The FMVs of today's transactions will become tomorrow's *comparable sales* to be used by brokers, buyers, and sellers to stay abreast of market conditions. Sources of comparable sales statistics are presented later in Chapter 10. Note that comparable sales figures include a number of sales that were made under duress (liquidation values), skewing the averages and lessening their usefulness.

The FMV of a business is a function of internal and external factors. Internal factors are those that are unique to the particular firm, such as the strength of the existing lease, quality of employees, appeal of the products, availability of low-cost inventory, etc. External factors are related to the competition, various government taxes and regulations, and the overall economy. As a brief example, a business associated with the following characteristics will tend to have a higher FMV:

- Below-market lease with long term options
- Skilled employees who intend to stay with new ownership
- Few competitors for a "niche" product (high profit margins)
- Strong local and national economy, with growth continuing

The many factors affecting business value will be covered in a variety of scenarios later in this chapter. There are several methods used under varying conditions by different practitioners. FMV is a fluid and dynamic concept that is difficult to pinpoint precisely. The methods introduced in this chapter are attempts to quantify the FMV of a going concern within the context of buying or selling the ownership rights to such a business.

Book Value

Although this measure of value is less important than FMV overall, it still plays a useful role in facilitating understanding of the financial condition and value of a business. When referring to the concept of *book value* (BV), there are two general applications (the BV of a particular asset and the BV of an entire business). The major similarity between the two is that they represent accounting figures subject to variation and even manipulation through different accounting procedures. The accounting concept of book value plays an integral part in the application of the asset-based valuation methods discussed in Chapter 9.

Consider the effects of different assumptions regarding the useful life and depreciation method for fixed assets. A shorter useful life increases the current period's depreciation expense, reducing current net income. Note that whether depreciation expense is $3,000 or $6,000, it is added back to net income (non-cash expense) to arrive at adjusted cash flow (ACF). However, depreciation expense does affect reported net income, which is an important bottom-line figure. Greater depreciation deductions not only reduce reported income, but also led to lower reported book values. As you analyze this area, *remember that there are almost always differences between book accounting and tax accounting*. For example, depreciation methods and schedules will often differ between the two. For tax purposes, accelerated depreciation is preferred, owing to the benefit of lower tax liabilities and the use of those tax savings in the current period. For book purposes, if importance is placed on reported net income or book values of assets, lower and slower depreciation is preferred.

Now we turn to the many interesting concepts, ideas, and applications of BV relating to an entire business. The BV of a company is equal to Assets minus

Liabilities (BV = A − L). If you have taken accounting coursework, you will recognize the above as the accounting equation, which is more commonly written as: Assets minus Liabilities equals Owner's Equity (A − L = OE). In this sense, the BV of a company is equal to the owner's equity. Note that BV, owner's equity, and net worth all denote similar concepts. *The difference between what a company owns (assets) and what it owes (liabilities) is what the firm is worth (owner's equity).* BV always differs from market value, and the valuation technique known as the *Adjusted BV Approach* attempts to reconcile this difference.

Liquidation Value

This concept brings fear to the hearts of sellers as buyers rejoice. *Liquidation value* represents *the price that would be received if the assets were sold today in an auction-like format* or a one-day sale advertised in the classified section of the Sunday newspaper. The concept of liquidation value highlights the value of goodwill. Basically, the value of assets combined for the production of goods and services (going concern value) is greater than the value of the parts valued separately (liquidation value). The difference between the two is goodwill. Liquidation values can be as low as 10 percent of what might be received as part of a package deal, complete with customers, suppliers, employees, and a location.

I have witnessed numerous unnecessary business liquidations because sellers price their businesses at unrealistic levels, thereby discouraging serious buyers. If a business is priced too high, otherwise interested buyers will choose other options. Rather than overcome their pride associated with years of blood, sweat, and tears, and reduce the asking price to a reasonable level, sellers often persist at the higher level, wasting time and buyers. For various reasons, sellers then shut down and receive as little as nothing for their business! This is truly frustrating for a business broker.

Buyers should look beyond asking prices and make offers for any business they find attractive. Make an offer based upon what you believe the business is worth and you might be surprised! If the seller is unsatisfied, he *will* let you know. If the offer is properly written, you can obtain a risk-free look at the business, allowing proper time to make your final decision. See the section on distressed businesses in Chapter 1 for additional insights.

As a guide to liquidation values for general categories of assets, consider the following approximate percentages for two different levels of liquidation, planned and forced.

Asset Types	Forced	Planned
Cash (CDs, checking, savings)	95 to 100%	100 %
Marketable Securities	MV less commissions	MV less commissions
Accounts Receivable	Less than 90 days (50 to 60%)	Less than 90 days (up to 85%)

Asset Types	Forced	Planned
Accounts Receivable	More than 90 days (0 to 20%)	More than 90 days (0 to 33%)
Inventory		
Raw Materials	30 to 40%	40 to 60%
Work in Progress	0 to 30%	0 to 30%
Finished Products	30 to 40%	40 to 60%
Prepaid Assets	75%	75 to 90%
Land	30 to 45% of FMV	60 to 75% of FMV
Buildings	20 to 30 % of FMV	30 to 40% of FMV
Equipment	30 to 40%	33 to 50%
Furniture	0 to 10%	10 to 25%
Fixtures	0 to 10%	10 to 25%
Intangibles	Varies widely by type	Varies widely by type

Warning: The above percentages are only *averages* and must be cautiously applied to particular circumstances with the aid of professional appraisers.

Valuation Categories

Valuation techniques can be categorized in many ways. One useful categorization addresses the purpose of the valuation, including transaction-based, litigation-based, tax-based, and miscellaneous.

Transaction-based appraisals/valuations are made by business brokers or business owners, who will typically use cash-flow based formulas and/or rules of thumb. They will be tempered by current market values to a greater degree than the tax or litigation-based methods. Other transaction-based appraisals occur for initial public offerings, funding of ESOPs and writing of buy/sell agreements.

Litigation-based appraisals/valuations are utilized for divorce, bankruptcy, partnership dissolutions, shareholder disputes, regulatory issues and determination of damages. These are specialized applications to be completed by qualified brokers, attorneys, CPAs, or appraisers.

Tax-based valuations occur for many different purposes as well, including estate planning, gifting, recapitalizations, Subchapter S conversions, casualty losses, and Charitable Remainder Trusts. These also require professional assistance. Their essence is the establishment of the taxable basis of a group of assets (company) against which a tax deduction or tax liability is to be computed. Other reasons for professional valuations include attempting to obtain bank financing, analyzing a merger or joint venture, purchasing insurance, and satisfying the owner's curiosity.

Ultimately, all valuation approaches are a function of the elements of value. Specific techniques revolve around assets, cash flow, gross revenues, or other industry specific features, such as the number of accounts. While there are a host of elements that impact value, here is a short list:

- Market value of tangible and intangible assets (e.g., rights, patents, know-how)
- History, stability, and certainty of future operations and cash flow
- Overall appeal of business (i.e., difficulty, ease of operation, hours)

Before we can understand and interpret specific techniques, four points must be stressed: (1) Proper and consistent calculation of adjusted cash flow (ACF) is critical to the valuation of businesses. Review Chapter 3 for an introduction to the basics and Chapters 9 and 11 for sample calculations. (2) Different techniques will be used by different professionals. Being educated will improve your credibility as a buyer, seller, or intermediary. (3) For compiled statements, it will be necessary for the purchaser to verify that the presented financial data are accurate. The adage "garbage in, garbage out" applies here. (4) Note the material differences listed below between smaller (non-Fortune 5000) and larger (Fortune 5000) businesses and how they might impact valuation.

Smaller	*Larger*
1. Compiled statements	1. Audited statements
2. Cash basis accounting	2. Accrual basis accounting
3. S-Corporations, Partnerships, Sole Proprietors, Limited Liability Companies	3. C Corporations
4. Shorter track records	4. Longer histories
5. Asset sale	5. Stock sale
6. Purchased with cash plus seller carry-back	6. Purchased with stock, cash, or assumption of debt
7. Owner is active day to day	7. Owners are shareholders, may not be active or even present
8. Financial statements lead to minimal taxable income	8. Financial statements clearly separate from tax statements
9. Comps with credible statements difficult to find	9. Information publicly available through SEC or firm's accountant

As you can see, there are great differences between "mom and pop" stores and middle-market or larger companies. Small business owners wear many hats and tend to *do* rather than *delegate*. Larger companies require seemingly exorbitant investments (down payments and working capital infusions), more complicated organizational structures (more levels and delegation), and more employees. A medium-sized business or larger is properly viewed as a capital investment rather than an investment of time, blood, sweat, and tears. You must carefully evaluate all of these characteristics when attempting to value a business.

CHAPTER 9

Review of Valuation Techniques

Valuation techniques can be classified as cash flow-based, asset-based, revenue-based, or some combination thereof (including the many rules of thumb). Review the following list and then turn to the appropriate pages to continue your analysis:

Cash Flow/Earnings-Based Methods
- Discounted cash flow method
- Excess earnings method
- Capitalization of earnings method
- Ability to pay method

Asset-Based Methods
- Adjusted book value method
- Individual asset method

Revenue-Based Methods
- Industry specific method

Market-Based and Miscellaneous Methods
- Comparable sales with available market prices
- Comparable sales without market prices

Rules of Thumb
The many industry specific methods and multipliers used by business brokers are essentially what are termed *rules of thumb*. They are highly prevalent in the small business arena, but are also used for larger, publicly traded firms, as explained later.

Cash Flow–Based Methods

Capitalization versus Discount Rates

Sophisticated valuation approaches rely on cash flows and the use of discount and/or capitalization rates. Notably, these include the discounted cash flow (DCF) method, the excess earnings method, and the capitalization of earnings method. Each must be used with caution, as the results hinge on selecting of an arbitrary discount or capitalization rate. Financial theory teaches that the value of any asset (including a collection of assets such as a business) is determined by discounting and summing the assets' future net cash flows into present value. There are three important variables here: net cash flows, discount rates, and present value. Fully understanding these concepts is mandatory if you choose to apply these techniques.

Net cash flow is essentially the same thing as ACF, which represents the cash equivalent benefits accruing to a single owner-operator. Present value revolves around the concept of the time-value of money. Simply put, $100 received today is worth more than $100 received five years from today. A present dollar is worth more and a future dollar will be worth less because of inflation and because it could be invested risk-free for the five years in a bank CD, earning 6 percent annually (causing the $100 to grow in value to approximately $133.80 after compounding).

To then discount these future cash flows, you must select a *discount rate*. This selection process is both art and science. Next, we must clear up the difference between discount rates and capitalization rates, which tend to be used interchangeably. According to the American Society of Business Appraisers, the following distinction exists: A *discount rate* is the rate of return used to convert a monetary sum, payable or receivable in the *future*, into present value, whereas a *capitalization rate* is a divisor that is used to convert *current* income into present value. Entire textbooks and treatises have been written on these concepts.

Discounting is more commonly used for business valuation and is essentially the opposite of compounding. It involves conversion of a series of expected future returns into *present value*. According to the various methods that rely on the discounting of future cash flows, there are different choices regarding what figure to use as cash flow. We can use our familiar ACF for smaller businesses or net free cash flow or net income for larger businesses. The discount rate is applied to these future anticipated cash flows to reduce their nominal values into *real* values (adjusted for inflation, risk, and the time value of money).

Capitalization rates, on the other hand, are applied to historic or present period cash flows or earnings to establish value. In this regard, the value of a business is equal to the capitalized value of the last year's or the current period's earnings or cash flow. See Figure 9.1.

FIGURE 9.1 Discount Rates versus Capitalization Rates

	Discount Rate	**Capitalization Rate**
Time Horizon	Many Periods	One Period, Recent
	Future Periods	One Period, Current
Composition	Risk-free rate (includes inflation premium) plus risk premiums	
Primary Valuation Methods	Discounted Cash Flow (DCF)	Capitalization of Earnings

Discounted Cash Flow Method

The discounted cash flow (DCF) method is also referred to as an *income-based* approach. *The first income-based category relies on discount rates and future cash flows while the second category relies on capitalization rates of current period cash flows.* To the extent that the value of a firm is based on its earnings or cash flow generating ability, DCF is the purest of valuation techniques. It is not frequently used for valuing smaller businesses, but nonetheless provides valuable insights into the concept of firm value. Affordable software packages such as custom designed **Cashé** and **@Risk** and flexible **Excel** and **Lotus** should increase the usage of these tools. *One reason they are not used for smaller businesses is the need for precise estimation of all future cash flows (e.g., sales, cost of goods, operating expenses, capital expenditures, interest expense, tax rate).* This is difficult, time-consuming, and subject to wide-ranging results even for seasoned professionals.

Use of the second category of historical, income-based methods (capitalization methods) avoids these arbitrary projections. A *second reason* is that smaller businesses are highly dependent on the skills of the owner as opposed to larger operations staffed with management teams likely to transcend new ownership. The basic difficulty is the degree of speculation required. Despite these complications, it is worthwhile to grapple with the diverse accounting, tax, and finance concepts that permeate this method. They will generate invaluable insights into the following areas by forcing credible assumptions and projections (planning):

- Gross sales, net sales, taxes, and net sales
- Cost of goods sold, gross profits, operating expenses, and operating profit (EBIT)
- Depreciation, amortization, and interest expenses
- Investment tax credits, Section 179 deductions, and federal/state income taxes
- Future capital expenditures and other mandatory payments
- Working capital needs at various sales levels
- Riskiness of future cash flows (ACF)

There is great diversity in approaches within this category of valuation techniques. However, certain basic steps are required for all versions. Let's begin with these general steps:

Step 1: Determine the length of time for projections. This should be at least as long as you intend to own the business or as long as the acquisition-related debt service continues. Since you will be *summing* values, more years of positive cash flows will increase the value. In most cases, this value will include the value that will accrue to the new owner of the business when ultimately sold, less taxes and broker's commissions. *When evaluating various opportunities, credible and consistent application is mandatory.*

Step 2: Project sales, gross profits, and operating expenses. When preparing projections, be as realistic as possible. Credibility to outside parties is critical. All these assumptions and projections, which should be questioned by unbiased outsiders, can be utilized in preparing a business plan. Avoid overestimating sales and underestimating expenses. If you project rising sales, justify your estimate (e.g., increased advertising, expanded distributorships, additional locations).

Determining gross profit and operating profit can be difficult, depending upon the type of product or service involved. Variability in cost of goods, labor, and operating expenses is often greater than that of overall sales. To project these margins, you must prepare an adjusted income statement. If gross profit has been 50 percent and operating profit 10 percent historically, use these as starting points (weighted averages might be appropriate). Justify and document any changes from historical percentages. Realize also that the results depend on who the new owner will be. A new owner will incur different cost of goods sold, labor rates, and will perhaps utilize different suppliers, all of which will impact gross and net profits as well as cash flow (ACF).

Regardless of who the owner is or will be, remain credible and conservative in your estimates. Calculating operating profit requires accounting for projected depreciation and amortization charges. Under an asset sale, the new owner will redepreciate all tangible, fixed assets based on their FMV. The precise redepreciation is a function of an allocation of purchase price, as determined by buyer and seller on IRS Form 8594. The IRS provides write-off schedules for different classes of assets based on their "useful lives." Remember once again that depreciation for book purposes (GAAP) will not necessarily correspond to depreciation for tax purposes. Also, if real property is involved, remember that land is *not* depreciable.

Before looking at a detailed example, let's review the concept of present value once again. The value of the firm is the sum of all the expected net cash benefits accruing to the new owner over the life of the investment, discounted back to present value. *Under the DCF approaches, the four main factors are: the amount of future cash flows, the likelihood (risk) of the future cash flows, the timing of the cash flows, and the discount rate applied to the future cash flows.* The typical case involves the summation of discounted cash flows that accrue to an owner-operator (or shareholders for larger businesses), typically in unequal amounts over several years. Use of present value interest factors greatly simplifies the process.

PVIF(d,p) = the factor used to discount a future cash flow from period p using the discount rate d (**present value interest factors**)

Turning to the table in Appendix I, each of the future ACFs can be multiplied by the appropriate PVIF to obtain the present value figure to be added to all other periods. Imagine that a company is being analyzed for purchase and you intend to hold the business for five years, as introduced in Figure 9.2.

FIGURE 9.2 Present Value Analysis

Period	ACF ($)	PVIF	PV ($)
One	50,000	.806	40,300
Two	80,000	.650	52,000
Three	50,000	.524	26,200
Four	100,000	.423	42,300
Five	200,000	.341	68,200
	480,000		229,000

The assumption that the cash flows are received at the end of the period simplifies the process without compromising the results (as opposed to uneven cash flows occurring throughout the period). The discount rate has been established (built-up) to be 24 percent, which includes a risk and inflation component. We will present methods for determining the appropriate discount rate later in this section. According to the figures above, the anticipated $480,000 in nominal cash flows have a net present value of $229,000. Therefore, we can estimate the value of the business at $229,000. (Note that the receipt of the $200,000 at the time of sale should be net of taxes, commissions, and other closing fees). *From this level, complications may be introduced to match the user's needs.* For example, a weighted average basis could be used to refine the anticipated and discounted ACFs.

A second complication would be to account completely for the initial cash outflows (down payment toward purchase price). This makes sense if you are also counting the dollars when the business is sold. In our example in Figure 9.2, we included the dollars received at year five and discounted it to present value. *If you include the sales price received as an inflow, logically you should include the down payment toward the purchase price and other cash infusions as an outflow.* If we assume an initial cash down payment of $80,000 and additional working capital infusions of $30,000, the net present value must be adjusted. Adding the final cash inflow and the initial and secondary cash flows provides the most realistic valuation. *There is nothing more important than remaining consistent from one valuation to the next.* The ACF figures arrived at for each year may or may not already account for additional infusions of cash for working capital and fixed asset replacements or acquisitions. As detailed later, consideration of taxes and other mandatory cash payments is also required to correctly implement these techniques. A clear advantage to using software packages is that these issues are automatically addressed.

There are many different names attached to the basic DCF approaches, including the discounted future benefits method, the discounted future earnings method, and the free cash flow method. Major differences involve the precise calculation of cash flows, the period of time for which the cash flows are discounted, and the approach taken to determine the discount rate. Consider the following five measures regarding cash flows:

1. **ACF** = Net Income
   + Noncash charges
   + Interest expenses
   + Owner's reasonable salary
   + Owner's benefits
   + Unusual, nonrecurring expenses
   − One-time, nonrecurring revenues
   − Wages necessary to replace uncompensated work
2. **Net income before interest and taxes** (per GAAP), also called earnings before interest and taxes (EBIT) or operating income
3. **Net income after taxes** (per GAAP), also called earnings after taxes (EAT)
4. **Net free cash flow** (ACF minus anticipated capital expenditures minus increases in working capital)
5. **Net income before depreciation, interest, and taxes**, referred to as earnings before interest, taxes, and depreciation (EBITD)

Each of these streams can be based on historic numbers (current period or weighted average) or projected, pro forma numbers (e.g., the last 12 months or calendar year versus a pro forma forecast for 12 months under new ownership). Once again, the key is consistency in application.

Depending upon the business and year involved, required adjustments for determining the proper cash flow may be immaterial or substantial. Adjustments will be minimal for publicly traded firms that are often valued using multiples of pretax or after tax earnings (similar to the use of price-earnings [PE] ratios). On the other hand, adjustments made for the typical, closely held "mom and pop" business can total to an amount greater than the firm's net income. These firms are not as concerned with net income as the publicly traded firm and normally seek to minimize taxable income.

When establishing a firm's FMV, each business must be considered a unique collection of assets with unique streams of revenues and expenses. To the confoundment of many, no two businesses are alike—not even McDonald's franchises! Numerous adjustments to the income statement and balance sheet accounts are necessary to accurately establish value. When adjusting the income statement, there are certain routine steps. The fact is, however, that even professionals will disagree on a number of adjustments that can be made. *Remember the goal: to obtain a figure that represents a normalized reasonably expected cash flow figure (e.g., ACF), which will be available to the new owners to do with as they wish.* We are seeking what has also been called the owner's *discretionary* cash flow. Each adjustment made toward this end must be justified. Don't forget to compare the key calculations to industry averages (e.g., Robert Morris Associates), which can supply valuable insights into the proper functioning of a business and its untapped value. Consider the list in Figure 9.3.

FIGURE 9.3   Standard Income Statement Adjustments

Area	Specific Adjustments
Sales/Revenues	1. Increase reflecting additional products/advertising/price increases
	2. Decrease due to mature products, expiration of patents, new competition, etc.
	3. Decrease reflecting percent of reported sales deemed uncollectable
	4. Decrease reflecting any one-time/nonrecurring sales of a material size
	5. Decrease by amount of sales tax counted as sales revenue
	6. Decrease reflecting sales returns and allowances
	7. Decrease for lawsuits/insurance settlements received
	8. Increase or decrease for any one time losses or gains on sale of assets
Cost of Goods Sold	1. Decrease if LIFO caused excessive CGS/reduced profit (adjust from LIFO to FIFO)
	2. Decrease if excessive write-off of inventory occurred (reducing taxable income).
	3. Decrease if transportation charges are double-counted as operating expense
	4. Decrease if manufacturing costs are expected to decline with experience
	5. Decrease if supplier costs will fall (new owner advantage)
Operating Expenses	1. Increase or decrease to reflect fair market salary for owner/operator (if no salary is taken as operating expense, add reasonable salary; if salary is excessive, subtract excessive payments)
	2. Decrease for all personal expenses (perks) incurred for owner's benefit (e.g., health, auto, and life insurance; auto expense; travel and entertainment beyond normal business needs; membership fees; boats, bonuses, etc.)

FIGURE 9.3 Standard Income Statement Adjustments, continued

	3. Decrease for any one-time, unusual, and nonrecurring expenses (e.g., hurricane, earthquake, freeze, advertising expenditures that failed, strike, street repairs, illness, loss of financing, etc.)
	4. Decrease for all non-cash expenses (e.g., depreciation, amortization)
	5. Decrease for all interest expenses/increase for all interest revenues
	6. Increase/decrease for any expenses that are not at market rates (arm's length) (e.g., favorable lease rate for one year only or from rich uncle)
Other Expenses	1. Increase for annual expenditures to replace/maintain current productive equipment.
	2. Increase for accrued expenses (incurred but not yet paid) for cash basis companies
	3. Increase or decrease for expected changes in all lease payments (e.g., if equipment lease expires, subtract this expense; if rent is increasing, adjust accordingly)
	4. Increase or decrease reflecting future tax brackets and tax rates

You may notice that many of these adjustments are future-oriented (pro forma), highlighting the difference between historical cash flows (cap rates) and projected cash flows (discount rates). After all adjustments have been made, the results can be utilized as part of the DCF methods (see the analysis earlier in chapter). Larger, corporate acquisitions will be based on calculations similar to net free cash flow, which will be fully presented shortly.

Despite the variety in cash flow concepts, there is one primary objective in valuing a business. What will a willing and able buyer pay a willing and able seller to transfer ownership of the business? *Being able to justify your price to the other side is the primary reason you take the time to perform a valuation.* You (and your broker) must decide which approach is most applicable and decide which measure of cash flow (i.e., ACF versus EBIT versus NFCF) is appropriate before you can effectively utilize and discuss the results. We now turn to a sample valuation utilizing the DCF method.

FIGURE 9.4   Sample Company Income Statement

Company A Income Statement ($)

Sales	1,907,799
– Cost of Goods Sold	858,753
Gross Profit	1,049,046
– Operating Expenses	477,975
Earnings Before Taxes	571,071
– Income Taxes	207,971
Earnings After Taxes	363,100

When performing a DCF valuation, several decisions must be made. For example, will the cash flow figure be before taxes (ACF) or after taxes (NFCF)? In the sample income statement in Figure 9.4 for Company A, with nearly $2 million in sales, the NFCF figure seems appropriate. Accurate and credible estimates must be made for future sales, expenses, working capital infusions, replacements and additions to capital equipment, and future corporate tax rates. This is no easy task, but it is the approach of choice for sophisticated professionals. "Guesstimating" the effective tax burden in future periods alone is a daunting process. Projections must be made based on an assessment of the target's product lines, management team, distribution networks, age of facilities, debt capacity, reputation, etc. In the case of a merger, consideration of how the two companies will meld together (e.g., reducing overhead, increasing market share) is as difficult as it is necessary.

Regarding Company A, let's look at a few rules of thumb to get an idea where we might be heading. We have determined that Company A is a service business with an asset value (fair market value) of $121,313, pre-tax income (earnings before taxes) of $571,071 and after-tax income (earnings after taxes [net income]) of $363,100. A common rule of thumb that utilizes pre-tax income is based on a multiple of ACF. A preliminary review of recent market comparables shows that this type and size of business (low asset base) has been selling for 2.4 times ACF. Assuming an ACF of $573,100 (net income plus owner's benefits plus depreciation, etc.), a simple rule of thumb gives us a "guesstimate" of $1,375,440 ($573,100 times 2.4). A more conservative estimate, based on the common rule of thumb that combines asset values and ACF, would be $980,963 (1.5 times ACF plus the value of the assets). *As a general rule, the greater the cash flow, the larger the multiple up to a certain point.* Larger businesses lend themselves to absentee or semiabsentee ownership if qualified management teams are in place. An absentee-based cash flow is normally worth more than an active participation based cash flow.

When it comes to valuation methods based on after-tax income (net income or earnings after taxes), the most common technique is PE ratio. Of course, the information required for this calculation is only available for publicly traded companies. It is possible to use the PE ratio of similar publicly traded businesses, but great care must be exercised. A similar service company might be selling for ten times after-tax earnings, giving us an estimated value of $3,631,000. Determining exactly how similar the two companies are is fraught with complications, as discussed in the section on market comps in Chapter 10. Furthermore, considering that the average PE ratio is about 15 for all stocks, you can see that the valuation results here are widely different than the ACF-based rules of thumb. Another possible after-tax valuation rule for service businesses is four to seven times net income, giving us an approximate value of $1,997,050 (363,100 times 5.5). *Our quick scan has generated results of between $980,963 and $3,631,000. This wide gulf must be addressed head-on through careful analysis of the specific features of the subject company, the use of valid market comparables, and ideally a weighted average of all methods.*

Net Free Cash Flow

We are now ready to estimate the value of this business using a DCF method based on the net free cash flow (NFCF) concept. The NFCF measure to determine the firm's value is preferred in that it recognizes that portions of the cash flow generated by the company must be reinvested into capital enhancements and additional working capital to sustain projected growth. For calculating net free cash flow refer to Figure 9.5 and the explanation following it.

FIGURE 9.5 Net Free Cash Flow

NFCF = ACF – R – P – D – PS – O – T – WC

- **R:** interest payments
- **P:** net additions to property and plant (fixed assets)
- **D:** principal payments on outstanding debt
- **PS:** payments to preferred shareholders (if any)
- **O:** other mandatory fixed payments such as sinking funds, ESOPs, etc.
- **T:** state and federal income tax payments
- **WC:** working capital infusions

Net free cash flow (**NFCF**) is a comprehensive measure of cash flow that accounts for all the components of the traditional ACF plus much more. First, the component **R** is included because interest expense was originally added back into ACF and must be backed out to obtain a figure representing cash left over to be paid to the owners (shareholders). **P** represents all required payments to replace or expand the plant and equipment. Realistic expenditures must be accounted for to place faith in future cash flows. This figure can be calculated as the net increase in fixed assets shown on the balance sheet plus the amount of depreciation claimed for the period. **D** is a measure of the firm's debt payments that go to reduce the principal. Principal payments do not show up on the income statement as deductions (only interest is deducted). Principal payments will be found by looking to the firm's statement of cash flows if there has been one prepared. If not, this information must be obtained. Remember that the focus of the DCF method is to look toward future cash flows, not historical cash flows. The present serves as a springboard into the future. **PS** represents preferred dividends payable to preferred shareholders. Preferred stock, while nonvoting, carries varying degrees of fixed payments that are either cumulative (preferred shareholders must be paid all unpaid dividends from prior years before common shareholders are paid) or noncumulative (if the board of directors chooses not to pay any dividends in a given year, the liability does not exist in future periods to pay for previous unpaid periods). **O** represents other mandatory payments, including sinking fund payments to retire a bond or payments into an employee stock ownership program (ESOP), bonus payments to managers and employees, satisfaction of stock options exercised by management, and cash payments/withdrawals to or from underfunded or overfunded pension plans. **T** represents all tax payments including state and federal income taxes (sales taxes were deducted to get to ACF).

Guidance is needed to accurately project tax obligations as a result of dynamic tax laws. Furthermore, material differences exist between income taxes on an accrual basis and a cash basis. For valuation purposes, tax payments incorporated should be stated on a cash basis through adjusting the firm's accumulated deferred income taxes found on the balance sheet. Finally, **WC** reflects the fact that a growing business requires additional cash infusions to support growing payrolls, inventory, and customer credit. Properly funding this area can damage short-run profitability while building long-term value.

There are many variations of NFCF, each possessing unique complexity and credibility. Our formula will generate accurate valuation results if used in conjunction with market comparables and other valuation approaches. For a detailed analysis of another free cash flow concept, consider purchasing the book *Valuation: Measuring and Managing the Value of Companies*, by Tom Copeland,

Tim Koller, and Jack Murrin (McKinsey and Company, Inc., a highly reputable consulting firm in New York). They explore issues such as investments in unconsolidated subsidiaries, multibusiness firms, minority interests, and foreign currency implications.

To summarize, *NFCF is the amount of cash available to the new owners (shareholders) after debt is serviced, equipment is maintained/upgraded/expanded, working capital is supplied, taxes are paid, and all other required obligations are met.* This concept is most applicable to broad-based ownership (as opposed to a small, owner operated business). If you utilize this approach for a single owner-operator, you must properly calculate the ACF figure, capturing all cash benefits (perks) to the owner. These perks are not as material for larger businesses with layered management teams, but if they do exist, they should also be included in ACF or NFCF.

For Company A, we have projected the future NFCF based on an assumed purchase price of $1,500,000 with $750,000 down and $750,000 in bank financing at 10 percent over ten years. One drawback of the DCF approach is that the anticipated cash flows are based on an anticipated sales price, which should be based on anticipated cash flows, etc. This interdependence is a problem, but by utilizing several rules of thumb, it is possible to estimate a value to use as part of the future cash flow projections. I chose the $1,500,000 price on the basis of these rules of thumb. As you scan the income statement in Figure 9.6, note the difference between principal and interest payments.

Our example generates the NFCF figure for an active owner-operator drawing a salary and other perks from the business. If it were a typical corporate acquisition, the NFCF would not include compensation to the manager or chief executive officer because these costs would have to be paid before arriving at free cash flow available to the acquiring company's shareholders. *Larger businesses with broad ownership and layered management will sell for higher multiples of earnings and/or cash flow* because cash flows associated with a single owner are generally riskier than cash flows associated with broad-based management. A secondary reason is that a firm with established management does not require the full-time effort of the new owner(s). This is no different than the idea that an absentee-run franchise hair salon would sell for a higher multiple of net income than one that is heavily dependent upon the skills and relationships of an active owner-operator.

After reviewing the pro forma projections for sales, expenses, taxes, and NFCF, it should be clear how fragile these estimates and related valuations are. For example, projections for sales and cash flows will be deflated by the estimate of the appropriate discount rate. The essence of the DCF approach, after all, is to project the cash flow accruing to the owners in future periods associated with the purchase of a business, and then discount them back into present value dollars. If you project cash flow

FIGURE 9.6 Income Statements ($), ACF, and NFCF for Company A

Years 1 to 10	Year 1	Year 2	Year 3	Years 4 through 10
Sales	1,907,799	2,098,437	2,308,437	Assume approximately
Cost of Goods Sold	858,753	944,486	1,029,091	constant growth in sales,
Gross Profit	1,049,046	1,153,951	1,279,346	cost of goods, operating
				expenses and income
Operating Expenses	477,975	524,782	577,261	taxes, with earnings after
				taxes growing as
Earnings Before Taxes	571,071	629,169	702,085	presented below with
				NFCF projections.
Income Taxes	207,971	226,501	252,750	
Earnings After Taxes	363,100	402,668	449,335	

NFCF, Years 1 to 10($)	Year 1	Year 2	Year 3	Years 4 through 10
Earnings after Taxes	363,100	402,668	449,335	Assume approximately
				constant growth rates in
				NFCF, as supported by
+ Addbacks*	210,000	231,000	254,100	notes below.
ACF	573,100	633,668	703,435	

NFCF, Years 1 to 10($)	Year 1	Year 2	Year 3	Years 4 through 10
Interest [R]	72,929	68,111	62,789	
Property replacements [P]	20,000	20,000	20,000	
Payment of principal [D]	46,006	50,823	56,145	
NFCF	**434,165**	**494,734**	**564,501**	
Addbacks*				
Depreciation	15,000	15,000	15,000	
Interest	72,929	68,111	68,111	
Owner's salary and perks	122,071	147,889	170,989	
Total Addbacks	210,000	231,000	254,100	

Notes:
1. Combined state and federal income tax rate is assumed to be a constant 36%.
2. Purchaser is single owner who will actively participate and draw salary and benefits.
3. P, R, and D are the only known, mandatory payments.
4. Discrepancy between net property increases and depreciation charges reflect choice in accounting methods.
5. Amortization of goodwill, which should be based on the difference between an assumed purchase price of $1,500,000 and $112,313 is ignored for simplicity (note that amortization expense would reduce earnings after taxes but would be added back to come up with NFCF).
6. Based on purchase price of $1,500,000 and a $750,000 cash down payment, payments of interest and principal at 10% for ten years are incorporated into the relevant calculations (e.g., $9,911 per month or $118,935 per year).
7. No additional working capital infusions are required.

to grow at 10 percent per annum while you discount these future cash flows at 20 percent, the valuation result will markedly differ from a growth rate of 30 percent and a discount rate of 20 percent. Growth in cash flow at a rate greater than the appropriate discount rate will obviously increase the valuation results. In our current example, we have estimated sales, expenses, net income, and NFCF to grow at an approximately constant rate of 14 percent, with the bottom-line results for NFCF (dollars per year) as follows:

NFCF-1	NFCF-2	NFCF-3	NFCF-4	NFCF-5
434,165	494,734	564,501	643,531	733,625

NFCF-6	NFCF-7	NFCF-8	NFCF-9	NFCF-10
836,333	953,419	1,086,898	1,239,064	1,412,533

The next step is to discount these expected NFCF figures into present value. Several decisions must be made, including the appropriate discount rate and whether or not to include the *terminal value* of the investment when the business is sold. If the terminal value is included, the initial cash down payment should also be included. Just add these two figures to the many important estimates that permeate the DCF methods. As concerns the discount rate, several approaches exist to establish this percentage. At this point, we will assume that this business is a "Category 3" from Schilt's Risk Premiums, giving us a discount rate of 24 percent, which is a 7 percent risk-free rate plus a 17 percent risk premium (flip ahead to the section in this chapter that outlines three approaches for establishing discount and capitalization rates if this process is unfamiliar). Accordingly, the NFCF figures from year one to year ten must be *discounted* back to present value. Assuming that the cash flow culminates at year-end, we can use the convenient PVIF numbers found in this guide. The present values are therefore:

	PV-1	PV-2	PV-3	PV-4	PV-5
	349,937	321,577	295,799	272,214	250,166
PVIF	.806	.650	.524	.423	.341

	PV-6	PV-7	PV-8	PV-9	PV-10
	229,992	211,659	194,555	178,425	163,854
PVIF	.275	.222	.179	.144	.116

Ignoring initial investments and terminal values, the present value of the future anticipated NFCFs from the next ten years is equal to $2,468,778. If a higher or lower discount rate were chosen (estimated), the present value of these cash flows would differ. If the chosen discount rate were 36 percent, the present value would fall to $1,641,509. If initial investments and terminal values are considered, we must reduce the present value of these cash flows by the amount of the cash down payment (e.g., $750,000) and estimate the sales price ten years hence and discount back to present value. For example, if the estimated sales price in ten years is approximately 2.4 times ACF, we can estimate the value in future dollars to be approximately $3 million. Believe it or not, *$3 million received in ten years, discounted back at a 36 percent discount rate is only $138,000!* Thus, the final estimated net present value ($) for this service business is:

PV of NFCFs	2,468,778
Less initial outlay	750,000
Plus terminal value	138,000
Net present value	1,856,778

In addition to providing an idea as to the value created by owning this business, you now have a figure that can be compared to alternative opportunities.

Concluding Remarks about the DCF Method

It should be clear that critical assumptions and choices in procedure must be made before reaching a final estimate of value. Differences from one practitioner to the next can be *Huge!*

Perhaps the most important attributes that can accompany these types of valuations are credibility and consistency. Being credible in your estimates makes the results of your valuation useful to outside parties. Being consistent in your procedures allows you to be true to yourself!

Excess Earnings Method

An easy to use process, the excess earnings method is not always well received by professionals. Also known as the formula approach, its origin is found in a 1920 IRS ruling. The IRS has subsequently ruled (Revenue Ruling 68-609) that this formula should be used only if there is "no better basis available for making the determination."

The essence of this historical-based approach is to combine the value of the tangible assets with a capitalized value of the intangible assets. *The key variables to be computed are net tangible assets; historic earnings to be capitalized; equivalent returns for similar risk investments; and capitalization rates applied to excess earnings.* First, a value must be placed on the net tangible assets. Most practitioners utilize an FMV basis. In addition to adjusting the accounts that are in the books, careful consideration of any assets or liabilities *off* the books should occur (e.g., contingent liabilities and prepaid assets). Review the balance sheet in Figure 9.7.

FIGURE 9.7 Balance Sheet

Assets		Liabilities	
Current Assets		*Current Liabilities*	
Cash	30,000	Accounts payable	130,200
Accounts receivable	84,000	Notes payable	150,000
Inventory	440,000	Wages payable	70,200
Prepaid expenses	20,000		
Fixed Assets		*Long-Term Liabilities*	
Equipment and furniture	720,500	Bank loan payable	70,150
Real estate	80,000		
Other assets	10,900	*Total Liabilities*	420,550
(accumulated depreciation)	(230,250)		
		Contributed and Retained Capital	
		Common stock	650,000
		Retained earnings	84,600
Total Assets:	1,155,150	**Total Liabilities and Equity**:	1,155,150

Consider the following adjustments that are required by the excess earnings method:

1) *Accounts Receivable* are adjusted downward based on review of an A/R aging schedule and historic bad debts.
2) *Inventories* are adjusted after a complete physical inventory has been taken. This adjustment often requires estimation, but the relevant value should be the lower of cost or market value. Obsolescence and LIFO accounting merit special attention. Remember that LIFO tends to overstate CGS and understate profits and ending inventory as it minimizes current period tax liabilities.
3) *Prepaid Assets* should be recorded as assets here even if they are not already on the books. Ask the seller if any items/expenses (e.g., rent, insurance supplies) have been prepaid and adjust accordingly.
4) *Fixed Assets* should be stated as a figure equaling replacement cost on a depreciated basis, which equals the current cost of a new asset minus an allowance for the useful life that has expired to date. If reliable, current market values are available; they should be utilized. Fixed assets include furniture, fixtures, and equipment. Real estate should be carried at current market values.
5) *Leasehold Improvements* also must be adjusted, unless the current lease is expiring soon without an extension. A good rule of thumb used here is to estimate the value as the difference between original cost and the current depreciated value.
6) *Intangible Asset* value determination is an art to itself. Since we are looking for the value of the tangible assets, however, they should normally be removed from the adjusted balance sheet. Readily marketable intangibles with liquid values can be included with the tangibles, such as a liquor license, patent, or proprietary software.
7) *Liabilities* are normally carried at their book values without any required adjustment. Areas that might need adjustment include mortgages payable, loans payable to shareholders, and expiring leases of all types. Importantly, verify the existence of any contingent or otherwise unrecorded liabilities such as pending lawsuits, warranty work payable, expected returns and allowances, etc. See the section on asset-based valuation method for further insights.

Second, the average earnings capacity of the firm must be determined based on analysis of preferably at least five years of operating history. The earnings should be reasonably expected to continue into the future. Using the income statement, the following types of adjustments need to be made. Review Figure 9.8, which illustrates these adjustments.

FIGURE 9.8 Calculation of Normalized Operating Profit

	1994	1995	1996	1997	1998
Net Income	xx	xx	xx	xx	128,800
+ Owner's salary	xx	xx	xx	xx	32,000
+ Owner's perks	xx	xx	xx	xx	18,800
+ Interest expense	xx	xx	xx	xx	15,000
+ Depreciation expense	xx	xx	xx	xx	82,500
+ One-time loss on sale of asset	xx	xx	xx	xx	12,000
ACF	198,000	210,300	214,800	229,200	289,100
Weighting	.10	.10	.10	.20	.50
Weighted Average ACF	$252,700				
Minus Fair Compensation to Manager	$(60,000)				
	$192,700				
Minus Future Annual Capital Outlays	$(30,000)				
Normalized Operating Profit	**$162,700**				

One distinction of this method is the subtraction of a fair salary to a manager after adding back the actual compensation to the current owners in reaching a normalized profit. Also, the anticipated annual expenditures toward fixed assets required to generate these future profits are deducted. Then, the normalized annual profit based on the previous five years must be allocated between that generated by tangible assets versus intangible assets. *We must calculate the return associated with the tangible assets and subtract this from the normalized profit figure to determine excess earnings.* It is these excess earnings that are associated with the intangible assets of the business. It is convenient to think of the intangible assets collectively as *goodwill*, representing the ability of the business to earn more than a *normal* return on its tangible assets.

When determining returns on tangible assets, they should be categorized according to risk. Investing in inventory is less risky than investing in equipment. Fixed assets such as equipment are not normally as liquid as inventory and their value is more dependent on the continued existence of the business. Examine the example in Figure 9.9.

FIGURE 9.9 Calculation of Excess Earnings

Normalized Operating Profit	$162,700
Allocations:	
Return on Current Assets ($574,000) x 6%	$(34,440)
Return on Fixed Assets ($581,150 x 15%)	$(87,173)
Excess Earnings	**$41,087**

The meaning of excess earnings should be clear now. The owner of the business has invested capital into tangible assets, and there is an opportunity cost associated with this. The $574,000 invested in current assets (working capital) could be invested elsewhere at say, a 6 percent return based on similar risk. The $581,150 invested into fixed assets could also have been invested elsewhere, with a higher, risk-adjusted return of 15 percent. Overall, the business is generating excess earnings of $41,087, derived from the intangible assets of the business. According to this method, a business is worth the value of the tangible assets plus the intangible assets. The final step is to *capitalize* (cap) these historic excess earnings. Note the cases in Figure 9.10.

FIGURE 9.10 Effect of Cap Rates on Business Value

Case 1

Excess Earnings	$100,000
Cap rate	15%
Value	$100,000 divided by 15% equals $666,667

Case 2

Excess earnings	$100,000
Cap rate	30%
Value	$100,000 divided by 30% equals $333,333

The IRS ruling written in 1968 suggests a capitalization rate of 8 to 10 percent for tangible assets and a 15 to 20 percent rate for intangible assets. Given that market rates are higher today than in 1968, these are not acceptable (guidelines for establishing discount/cap rates will be presented shortly). In our example, the excess earnings might be capitalized based on a 25 percent cap rate, giving a value of $164,348, as follows: $41,087 divided by 25 percent equals $164,348. *The final value is equal to the sum of the capitalized intangible assets ($164,348) plus the tangible assets ($1,155,150), or $1,319,498.*

It is not wise to rely on only one method. Compare these results with other methods and average them together. If the appropriate rule of thumb were between one and two times ACF for this type of business, an analysis should be conducted to analyze the unique characteristics that would determine the correct multiple. Using the ACF and weighted average ACF from Figure 9.8, if the correct multiple were two, the value of the business using this method could be estimated as $578,200 ($289,100 times two) or $505,400 ($252,700 times two). Many assumptions must be made, including the relatively simple choice between using last year's ACF ($289,100) or a weighted average of the past five years' ACF ($252,700). Once again, consistency in application is the key to useful valuation results. For optimal results, you should also locate and utilize recent comparable sales figures. Note that capitalization rates are directly related to multiples, as follows:

Capitalization Rate	Multiple
50%	Two
33%	Three
10%	Ten

As the capitalization rate increases, the multiple decreases. *Higher risk will mean a higher cap rate, which translates into a lower multiple.* Consider the following:

Business Type	Rule of Thumb
Landscaping companies	1 to 2 times ACF plus FF&E (minus vehicles)
Coin laundries	2 to 3 times ACF plus FF&E and inventory
Bowling centers	3 to 5 times ACF plus real estate and inventory

Many rules of thumb have an implied *capitalized earnings* component. If one assumes that the assets must, in effect, be purchased separately from the cash flow (ACF), what conclusions can be drawn about the relative earnings multiples for these businesses? Presumably, the cash flows are riskier for a landscaping company than a coin laundry operation. Similarly, the coin laundry cash flows are riskier than those of the bowling center. *It also appears that the more substantial the asset base, the higher the multiple.* For the landscaping business, the cash flow is dependent on the existing owner's relationship with customers, tends to be seasonal in nature, and competition is fierce (low barriers to entry). Compare these risk factors to the coin laundry business, where cash flow is less dependent on the existing owner's presence, is not as seasonal, and competition can be fierce, but entry requires substantial planning and financial capital. Finally, consider the bowling center, where cash flow is significantly independent of the owner, somewhat seasonal, but tends to be fairly consistent and competition is not normally fierce owing to significant entry costs.

The greater the asset requirements, the more difficult entry is. This difficulty in entering *protects the cash flows, enhancing their value.* Let's not forget that all generalizations are just that—generalizations. A landscaping business with high dollar commercial contracts, a highly efficient management team, and ten years of rising sales and cash flow will generate a higher multiple than one or even two times ACF. On the other hand, a bowling center with failing equipment, high crime, and rapid employee turnover experiencing falling sales will sell at a reduced multiple.

Capitalization of Earnings

The capitalization of earnings method also relies on the use of a cap rate against an historic earnings base. The major differences between the excess earnings method and the capitalization of earnings method are the measure of earnings and the use of asset values for the first, but not the latter, method. The first step is to calculate an earnings base (e.g., ACF, EBIT), preferably a weighted average of the past five years, to be capitalized (greater weight on recent years). A common debate between buyer and seller is the elusive future. A seller will tell the buyer that the future looks great and sales will increase dramatically next year! The buyer, on the other hand, will quickly remind the seller that he or she is not in the habit of paying for potential (or blue sky or the future or whatever else it might be called!). Feeling hard-earned optimism, the seller will tend to value a business higher than a buyer will.

The mechanism whereby the future is incorporated into this formula (using historical numbers) is the capitalization rate. A more optimistic sense of future earnings (less risk, more growth) will lead to a lower capitalization rate. Consider the following calculations.

$$\text{Market Value} = \frac{\text{Normalized ACF}}{\text{Cap Rate}} = \frac{\$100,000}{10\%} = \$1,000,000$$

$$= \frac{\$100,000}{25\%} = \$400,000$$

Determination of the Capitalization or Discount Rate

To consistently apply these rates, we need a reliable framework. A common option is the *build-up* approach, which begins with a risk-free rate of return, as typically found in yields for U.S. Government securities. Treasury bill yields are used for short terms and Treasury bonds for longer terms. These securities are used as a risk-free proxy because Uncle Sam has never defaulted. The risk-free rate is comprised of the *real rate* plus an inflation premium. The real rate is the rate of return required by investors to induce postponement of consumption into the future. The inflation premium accounts for the fact that future dollar cash flows will depreciate in value due to rising prices (lenders must be compensated for this loss in value). We will use 7 percent (recent long-term yields) as a springboard. Because every business is different, we must account for each one's unique risks. I will introduce two methods, an academic *build-up* approach and the *Schilt's risk premiums*, and let you decide which one is appropriate. *Most valuation experts will incorporate the following risks into their derived discount rate: overall market risk, industry risk, and company specific risk.* Beginning with the risk-free rate, additional percentages are added to reflect these risks, as described below.

Overall market risk. In computing a cap/discount rate for a small, privately held, mom and pop type of business, we lack fluid market statistics that could be used to calculate expected returns to owners of comparable companies. We must proceed, nonetheless, in establishing an appropriate discount rate. From this point forward, I will refer only to a discount rate, but the derivation process is similar for both discount and capitalization rates.

Common stocks for large publicly traded companies have yielded approximately 7 percent more than long term government bonds, which currently are yielding about 7 percent. Smaller sized publicly traded stocks have yielded approximately 12 percent more than long-term government bonds. So, in addition to the 7 percent risk-free rate, at least 12 percent more should be added as we build up to the appropriate level. Beyond this additional 12 percent, we should presumably add 3 to 4 percent more if the stock is not publicly traded (if a company has gone public, there has been rigorous due diligence performed by CPAs, attorneys and investment bankers). We have thus built our discount rate from 7 to 19 to 23 percent, as we have adjusted the market risk factors.

Industry risk. Now we consider risk from an industry perspective. The determination of this factor is even more subjective in nature. If the industry at hand is cyclical in nature (rises and falls with the overall business cycle), this calls for adjustment. Risk factors associated with governmental interventions (e.g., new taxes, regulations, tariffs), strengthening organized labor movements, or high industry failure rates due to obsolescence or overseas competition must be addressed. A fair range is approximately 2 to 5 percent, bringing the rate to between 25 and 30 percent.

Company risk. Isolating this risk factor is an important step for both valuing a business and understanding the future of the business. Key factors include:

- Long term profitability
- Years in business
- Degree of competition
- Importance of original owners
- Speed of product life cycles

- Employee skills and loyalty
- Historical collections difficulty
- Percent of sales from top customer(s)
- Degree of deferred maintenance
- Extent of sales outside U.S.

These factors can add 5 to 20 percent to the discount rate. Finally, we add each of the risk factors together to come up with our built-up discount rate, as shown below:

Risk-free rate	7%
Market risk	15%
Industry risk	4%
Company risk	<u>14%</u>
Discount Rate	40%

Our finalized rate using this approach is 40 percent, which could be used to capitalize the current period's income (capitalization of earnings) or discount future expected cash flows (DCF).

A second approach for establishing a discount rate is based on Schilt's risk premiums. This user-friendly approach is widely used by valuation professionals to discount expected future cash flows into present value. It offers proven guidelines for establishing the discount rate used to value businesses. The results obtained from the table in Figure 9.11 are added to the risk-free rate to obtain the final discount or cap rate.

FIGURE 9.11 Schilt's Risk Premiums

Category One

Established businesses with a strong trade position, well financed, depth in management, past earnings have been stable and future performance is highly predictable. Risk premium of 6 to 10 percent.

Category Two

Established businesses in a more competitive industry, well financed, depth in management, stable past earnings, future is fairly predictable. Risk premium of 11 to 15 percent.

Category Three

Businesses in a highly competitive industry, requires minimal capital to enter, lack of management depth, element of risk is high, although past record may be good. Risk premium of 16 to 20 percent.

Category Four

Small businesses that depend on the special skill of one or two people and larger established businesses that are highly cyclical in nature. In both cases, future earnings may be expected to deviate widely from projections. Risk premium of 21 to 25 percent.

Category Five

Small, one-person businesses of a personal services nature, where the transferability of the income stream is in question. Risk premium of 26 to 30 percent.

Ability to Pay/Payback Methods

The ability to pay/payback method is based on the buyer's need for income, not on the traditional concept of cash flow. This method is generally utilized only for small businesses where the owner will be active day to day. It serves as a reality check to determine what price and terms (debt service) are supported by the existing or anticipated cash flow of the business. If the business cannot pay for itself over a reasonable period of time, it might be a poor choice.

First, calculate ACF as done for other methods (net income + owner's salary + owner's perks + non-cash expenses, etc.). Second, subtract the owner's required salary and other expenditures necessary to sustain the cash flow of the business over the first year of new ownership, including estimated taxes. This gives us cash flow available to satisfy the new debt service.

The third step requires assumptions regarding the seller's carry-back note. Different businesses and different sellers are associated with varying payback periods. While most sellers prefer a quick payback, they realize that they cannot "choke" the new owner with debt payments that jeopardize the owner's salary, standard of living, or overall sanity. Many sellers will accept a longer payback period from qualified purchasers as a type of retirement plan (e.g., steady monthly payments for ten years). Tax advantages may exist as well. There are no standard guidelines, but the following seems to hold:

Payback Periods

Accounting practice	1 to 3 years
Small business	2 to 4 years
Larger business	3 to 10 years
Service business	2 to 5 years
Manufacturing business	3 to 10 years

For our example in Figure 9.12, we assume an ACF of $100,000 with a reasonable salary to the owner of $40,000 and an annual requirement of $15,000 to replace and upgrade existing furniture, fixtures, and equipment.

FIGURE 9.12 Sample Payback Valuation

Seller's ACF	$100,000
Minus salary and required expenditures	$ 55,000
Amount available to service debt	$ 45,000
Utilize a three-year payback period	$135,000
($45,000 times 3 years)	
Add down payment amount to obtain	$ 65,000
Purchase price	**$200,000**

Note that the $45,000 available for debt service must satisfy principal and interest. Also note that the value of $200,000 associated with an ACF of $100,000 amounts to a simple multiplier of two or a cap rate of 50 percent. *The appeal of this method is that it brings the desired price and terms into the light of day, linking them to the amount of debt service the business can support.* An integral part of this method is the concept of payback periods. When calculating the payback period, it is necessary to establish the appropriate measure of cash flow. For example, ACF, earnings before interest and taxes (EBIT), or variations thereof could be utilized. It is wise to use a variation of ACF for smaller businesses. If we seek to equate future net cash inflows with current outflows, we should adjust ACF to account for expenditures toward replacing or expanding fixed assets or for building up inventory and expanding credit in order to grow the cash flow. The goal is to determine how long it will take to get your cash investment back. Finally, payment of income and payroll taxes must also be addressed. *Cash out is to be measured honestly against cash in.*

Another idea involves what is considered a safe level of debt relative to the anticipated cash flow. The amount of cash flow required to safely service the debt is a function of the riskiness of the anticipated cash flows. The riskier the future cash flows are, the greater the required coverage should be. Commercial bankers look to a financial statement ratio (referred to as a fixed charge coverage ratio) to analyze a customer's credit capability, calculated as:

$$\text{Total fixed (mandatory) payments} \div \text{ACF or EBIT}$$

This ratio is important enough to bankers that it will find its way into commercial loan agreements as a restrictive covenant. *Acceptable ratios will vary, ranging from 25 to 50 percent of estimated after tax cash flow.* Debt service payments equaling 50 percent of the total available cash flow might be considered a maximum exposure.

Asset-Based Methods

If you have perused the rules of thumb, you may have noticed that asset values play an important role in determining the value of a business. Second only to cash flow (ACF), asset values are an integral factor in almost every case. A useful way to view any business is as a *collection* of assets (i.e., cash, accounts receivable, inventory, equipment, real property) that must be financed through either liabilities (i.e., accounts payable, wages payable, notes payable, seller carry-back obligations, etc.) or owner's equity (i.e., capital stock or retained earnings). *A common rule of thumb leads to results equal to some multiple of cash flow plus the value of the firm's assets* (with the noteworthy exceptions of cash and accounts receivable, which normally remain the property of the seller). The typical case might be one times ACF plus the value of inventory, equipment, furniture and fixtures, and real estate, if applicable.

I have seen buyers salivate at the realization that large dollar value assets are associated with firms that they are evaluating. This reaction increases if buyers feel they can be "had" for less cash down than their market value. The reasons for this excitement are both rational and irrational.

First, hard assets are real and tangible, and they have a fair market value (in the worst of situations, they have a liquidation value). Second, financing options are better with verifiable, hard assets than without. Finally, equipment and real estate in particular offer tax shields in the form of annual deductions against income and potential appreciation in market value. The irrational component arises when buyers experience "tunnel vision" and cannot appreciate a solid opportunity because there is a lack of high dollar assets. *Buyers miss the forest (cash flow) because of the trees (assets).* They feel that if a business lacks these assets, it is less desirable. While this may be true (all other things equal), it must not be forgotten that *service businesses* (e.g., a trade show, software development company, landscaping business) *generate high dollar sales and cash flow without high dollar assets.*

Asset-based methods (beyond simple rules of thumb) are complex and often challenging to utilize. Contrary to first impression, these methods are related to the concepts of book value and owner's equity, involving more than the simple addition of asset values. The various methods involved in this category revolve around restatement of the firm's assets and liabilities. Specifically, the following must be completed: (1) establish current FMV of all assets being sold (tangible assets and intangible assets); (2) reduce the amount determined above by the FMV of all liabilities to be assumed as part of the sale. *These methods involve the restatement of a firm's entire asset and liability structure, including those assets that may not be presently recognized on the balance sheet.* The starting point should be a balance sheet prepared in accordance with GAAP. The required changes involve adjusting the balance sheet from historical costs (both assets and liabilities) to some approximation of FMV. There are several different versions of this technique, including: the net asset value method, adjusted book value method, and the asset accumulation method. Whatever the name, the types of adjustments in Figure 9.13 are made.

FIGURE 9.13 Balance Sheet Adjustments

1. **Identify and value all liquid assets,** such as cash, certificates of deposit, accounts receivable, and marketable securities included in the sale. Of these assets, accounts receivable represent the most difficult assessment as they must be adjusted to their net realizable value based on historical collections experience.
2. **Identify and value all hard assets,** such as inventory, equipment, furniture, fixtures, and real property such as buildings and land. Deciding whether to use fair market value or a type of liquidation value is a key issue. Normally, a business that will remain a going concern should be valued utilizing fair market values.
3. **Identify and value all intangible assets** on and off the firm's balance sheet. This includes patents, trademarks, leasehold interests, going-concern value, software, easements, mineral rights, liquor licenses, etc.
4. **Identify and value all short-term liabilities** (e.g., accounts payable, current portion of long-term payables). Just as assets can and do have a fair market value, liabilities do as well. Short-term payables are valued at close to or exactly at their carrying value. Precisely measured, in the same fashion that future cash inflows are worth less than present period cash inflows (time value of money), future payments are "worth" less (cost less?) than present period payments. In practice, most short-term liabilities will be valued at their historical or book amounts.
5. **Identify and value all long-term liabilities** (over one year), such as notes payable, bonds payable, mortgages payable, etc. Valuation of longer-term obligations requires a departure from carrying or book (historical) values. For example, a face value bond payable of $100,000, due lump sum in five years, represents a "real" obligation of less than $100,000 in today's dollars (calculate the present value of these future payments). Besides the time value of money factor, consider the following. A mortgage with a remaining term of, say, 20 years, which was

FIGURE 9.13 Balance Sheet Adjustments

financed when interest rates were significantly higher than current rates, could be refinanced at today's lower rates, which would reduce the carrying value and the fair market value of this debt. Conversely, if a mortgage were financed at lower rates than current market levels, it could possibly be paid off at a discount, with the bank's permission, of course.

6. **Identify and quantify any off-balance sheet liabilities**. These are generally contingent liabilities, ranging from a certain obligation to repair or replace goods sold under warranty (estimated warranties payable) to a less certain obligation concerning pending lawsuits. Establishing a FMV for these liabilities involves estimates and should be handled conservatively and consistently. Other examples include ESOP related obligations, stock repurchase plans, owed vacation amounts, expected returns and allowances, and outstanding tax disputes. The greater these off-balance sheet obligations are, the less valuable a company is.

The bottom line is that the value of the firm is equal to the difference between the adjusted FMV of its assets and the adjusted FMV of its liabilities. Consistent and credible application of all methods will be helpful in your business evaluation efforts (a weighted average of several methods is ideal). Be aware that *asset-based methods will typically result in lower values than cash flow-based methods, particularly for businesses that are fully operational.*

Revenue-Based Methods

Some businesses rely almost exclusively on gross revenues as the key determinant of value, most commonly for professional practices, restaurants and other food establishments, and certain small businesses. There is nothing more charming than the use of a simple multiple of sales to value a business. Sales figures can typically be easily verified, and use of a multiple requires only one simple calculation. Unfortunately, this opens the door for abuse as well.

Using a multiple of one times gross revenues assumes that the subject business fits a profile as to general profitability and risk. *Companies within an industry that are less profitable and/or riskier should receive lower multiples.* Additionally, overall asset values, lease quality, ease of operation, current trends in cash flow, and other factors must be considered. Despite these difficulties, users must know when "custom" calls their application. Just as there is great discretion in choosing multiples of ACF, there is room to maneuver with these multiples. In every case, averages (market comps) should be reviewed for the particular type of business at hand.

A key attraction to this method for small businesses such as restaurants is that great efforts are taken to minimize taxable income—to the point where P&Ls are often meaningless. Even if all sales are reported, more times than not expenses will be exaggerated to reduce the tax bill. *Total sales can be reconstructed with less difficulty than total profits.* Accordingly, it is common to see restaurants, deli's, etc. valued at 30 to 40 percent of annual gross sales. From a given sales level, average profitability can be computed using averages for cost of goods sold, labor, and overhead.

CHAPTER 10

Market Comps
and Rules of Thumb

Market Comparables

Blind reliance on formulas is as unacceptable as blind reliance on market comparables for businesses that are only of the same category and type while differing in key aspects such as years of operation, trends of cash flow, and value of assets. *A better approach is to rely on a variety of methods, with each one serving as a balance to the other.* Professionals know to search for current data and incorporate these findings into their analyses. Unlike real estate transactions, however, there is not always a requirement to report the sales figures to local public officials. For private companies, this information remains in private hands and may not be readily available.

Larger Businesses

We begin our analysis with larger companies. Market data for publicly traded companies (larger businesses) is readily available, coming from many sources. Regardless of the source, the primary statistic you are looking for is a multiple of the price paid per share to earnings (after taxes) per share, commonly referred to as a PE ratio. Current values may be found for specific companies or by industry. Consider, for example, the following statistics obtained from the Corporate Growth Report (805-964-7841), which discloses PE ratios for public transactions by Standard Industrial Classification (SIC) code.

SIC Number	Industry	PE Ratio	
		1995	1997
2700	Publishing	36.1	31.1
3900	Miscellaneous Manufacturing	18.5	34.4
5900	Miscellaneous Retail Sales	26.2	32.4
7300	Computer and Data Services	38.9	56.5

Valuing publicly traded companies through the use of market comparables is difficult for the same reason that it is difficult to compare small, privately held companies. Namely, *few businesses can really be considered similar, when you account for varying sales, expenses, debt levels, operating histories, management teams, competition, geographic location, etc.* Even McDonald's restaurants will differ in terms of sales and profitability. Whether publicly traded or not, this approach is the only one based on data from actual sales, keeping subjectivity to a minimum. DCF and capitalization of earnings methods require estimates for discount and capitalization rates. Even rules of thumb require estimation of the proper multiple. Asset-based methods require appraisals, which can also be highly subjective. *The difficulty lies in the reality that no two businesses are exactly alike.* To say that a business is comparable is to say that it is not only similar, but suited for comparisons. A first step in this approach is to narrow down the business by SIC code. The more precise the code, the better, for both privately held and publicly traded companies. Even the IRS places emphasis on market comparables as a guide to valuation. According to Revenue Ruling 59-60:

> When a stock is closely held, some other measure of value must be used. In many instances, the best measure may be found in the prices at which the stocks of companies engaged in the same or similar line of business are selling in a free and open market.

Conducting this SIC-based search will require flexibility, but the results will be worth the effort. When comparing privately held companies to publicly traded ones, differences in risk must be acknowledged. As discussed earlier, privately held companies have not typically been through the same review as publicly traded businesses. Their financials are not audited, nor are quarterly reports sent to the SEC. Once you have determined the SIC code, you must search for information regarding similar companies. Sources listed in Figure 10.1 range from information regarding future industry sales (*Predicast*) to articles from business periodicals (*Business Periodicals Index*) to recently completed mergers and acquisitions (SDC Database and Mergerstat).

FIGURE 10.1 Market Comparables Source Data

S&P Register and Compustat (800-525-8640)*
Market Guide Database (516-327-2400)*
U.S. Equities Database (800-554-5501)*
Moody's Manuals
U.S. Public Database (800-554-5501)*
SEC Directory
Disclosure SEC Database (800-945-3647)*
The Wall Street Journal* (use *The Wall Street Journal* Index for efficient searches)
National Monthly Stock Summary*
Barron's*
Value Line*
SEC Reports (10Q and 10K)
Annual Reports
Mergers and Acquisitions Digest*
Corporate Growth Report (805-964-7841)
Mergers and Acquisitions Sourcebook
Mergerstat Review* (800-455-8871)
National Review of Corporate Aquisitions*
Consulstat*
Predicast (sales forecasts)
Business Periodicals Index (company-related articles)
Dun and Bradstreet Reports (800-223-0141 for credit and UCC data)
Dun and Bradstreet MarketPlace Database (800-590-0065)
Thomas Register (lists key firms in each manufacturing sector)
Encyclopedia of Associations
SDC M&A Database (201-622-3100)*

* Contains information on recent mergers and acquisitions, useful for generating comparable sales figures for business valuation; **bold = highly recommended**.

After the SIC code leads you to comparable companies, you must apply current information to reach your goal of determining a market value. Ratios should be analyzed, including price per share to earnings per share ratio, price per share to ACF per share ratio (or other measure of cash flow) dividend yield, price per share to book value per share, and price per share to sales per share.

Standard financial statement analysis should also be conducted to find the most similar businesses. A thorough review of all areas (qualitative and quantitative) within these companies will lead to the most similar candidates. A company presumed to be similar by product lines may be totally unacceptable for use as a *market comp*. The key differences between seemingly similar companies follow:

- Company has greater international exposure
- Financial and operational information is limited
- Recently merged with key supplier

- Sales and assets are significantly greater and newer
- Company lost money last year
- Entered joint venture with major competitor
- Received financial assistance from minority shareholder
- Capital structure is different (e.g., higher debt to equity ratio)
- Considering filing for bankruptcy protection
- Sold large subsidiary last year

The fact that different companies will use widely differing accounting procedures also complicates matters. Conducting the proper analysis to find suitable comps is easier said than done.

Smaller Businesses

Finding market comps for smaller businesses requires a different approach. Generally, you must turn to one of several databases maintained nationwide by various organizations. Many of these databases are proprietary and can only be tapped in limited fashions. As a business broker for VR Business Brokers, which has operated nationwide since 1979, I am fortunate to have access to thousands of comps representing virtually every type, category, and size of business in existence. There is no other database as large and complete as VR's (800-377-8722).

There are also local or regional firms/organizations that have gathered useful, current market statistics. For example, as a member of the Valley Board of Business Brokers (VBBB) in Phoenix, Ariz., I am privileged to have market statistics for businesses sold by the 65 members throughout the Phoenix area. Local firms with many years of experience will also maintain a database of past sales that may also be useful as comps. Besides the nationwide VR statistics and the Phoenix area VBBB results, I can recommend two other sources of market comps.

BIZCOMPS and the Institute of Business Appraisers

Compiled since 1990 by Jack Sanders (Certified Business Appraiser) in San Diego, California, BIZCOMPS (619-457-0366) has accumulated sales data for thousands of transactions across the country. The stated objective of BIZCOMPS is to accumulate reliable comparable business sale information for entrepreneurs, investors, and advisers trying to estimate the fair market value of small businesses. It provides regional breakdowns (western, central, and eastern). Data is also provided for businesses sold for all cash, with terms, for more than $500,000, for less than $500,000, for more than two times ACF, and for less than two times ACF.

Professionals willing to pay for access to other reliagle comps may consider contacting the Institute of Business Appraisers (561-732-3202). They also compile sales statistics from across the country by SIC code.

Rules of Thumb

These methods are the most utilized, cursed, and varied valuation processes that exist. They cannot be dismissed out of hand as some "sophisticates" would recommend, nor should they be used blindly without comparing the results of other methods. This broad category is comprised of formulas that are based on many factors, including adjusted cash flow (ACF) or some derivative thereof, assets of all types, gross revenues, and many other interesting, industry-specific components.

Please review the presented formulas, noting how they change from one category to the next. The reality is that their application will differ not only across categories but across the country and over time (depending on local conditions and customs). Valuation formulas for retail businesses rely heavily on inventory whereas manufacturing formulas place a greater emphasis on total assets. Many service business rules of thumb rely on the number of accounts or sales per account. The value of automotive repair businesses will depend on the number of bays, whereas accounting practice valuation is a function of the quality of repetitive accounts (as opposed to one-time services). Travel agencies tend to be valued based on gross commissions and restaurants on gross sales receipts. The fact that they are market-driven helps provide a useful range of values against which the specifics of a given company can be evaluated. For a comprehensive collection and an analysis of rules of thumb and industry association and publication phone numbers, call 602-509-6995 (or send $5 check or money order to 7201 E. Camelback Rd., #335, Scottsdale, AZ 85251).

Collection of Actual Rules of Thumb

The following rules of thumb have been collected in an entirely unscientific fashion from various business brokers, CPAs, attorneys, and other sources. Clearly, there are many factors that ultimately determine the value of a business. As you review the following rules, you will note substantial ranges within which each rule can be applied. The determining factors for each category and type of business are unique and include the following:

- Location, location, location
- Rent options?
- Years in business
- Gross sales and ACF expenses history/trends
- General appearance of business
- Lifestyle of owners. Long hours? Low stress?
- Recent sales prices of comparable businesses
- Reputation, goodwill, proprietary products
- Amount of inventory, accounts receivable, and/or real estate included in sale

- Reliability of business records and financial statements
- What is the owner's function? Any special skills required?
- What percent of sales comes from each of the top five and ten customers?

Before looking at the extensive list of specific rules of thumb in Figure 10.2, consider the following general after-tax, income-based averages that are "bandied about" by brokers and mergers and acquisitions specialists. *Whereas the following after-tax multiples are more commonly used for larger businesses, almost all the rules of thumb or multiples utilized by business brokers for smaller companies are based on some figure similar to our ACF, which is a pre-tax quantity.*

FIGURE 10.2 Common After-Tax Multiples

Manufacturing Companies	
• with proprietary/patented products	4 to 10 times net income (after corporate taxes)
• with nonproprietary products	3 to 8 times net income (after corporate taxes)
Retail Stores	3 to 6 times net income (after corporate taxes) (plus inventory at cost plus accounts receivable if included in sale)
Service Businesses	4 to 7 times net income (after corporate taxes) *or* adjusted book value*
Wholesale/Distribution Companies	2 to 5 times net income (after taxes) (plus inventory at cost)

* *Adjusted book value*: This method requires adjustments to be made for all assets in order to determine their true economic value. For example, fixed assets are appraised at their fair market value. Similar adjustments are made for other asset types to reach adjusted book value.

The rules of thumb in Figure 10.2 are more applicable for larger companies (sales more than $3 million and net incomes of greater than $300,000). The difference between net income and ACF can be quite large for smaller companies.

What follows now is a cursory compilation of the rules of thumb used by business brokers. In each case, the user must carefully consider and weigh the many factors that will tend to increase or decrease the appropriate multiple. Look to Chapter 1 for more detailed discussions of the general business categories and types (e.g., retail versus manufacturing). Typical averages for each category will tend to be in the middle of the presented ranges. General SIC codes are provided for analytical purposes and to lead you to other, similar types of businesses. Finally, phone numbers for trade publications and trade associations have been provided to guide you to additional industry-specific information.

Automotive Repair

Variation in automotive repair exists in terms of specialization (e.g., brakes, radiators, tire-ups, transmission). Most purchasers in this category are able to determine value based on monthly sales, from which they will calculate a breakeven amount based on standard parts and labor expenses. See Chapter 1 for more details regarding automotive businesses.

Range 1: 2 to 3 times monthly gross revenues plus inventory
Range 2: 1.5 times assets (inventory, e.g., fixtures) plus owner's salary
Range 3: 1 to 2.5 times ACF plus inventory
SIC Code: 7530 (Automotive Repair Shops)

Coffee Shops/Diners/Deli's/Drive-Ins/Pizza Shops/Fast Food/Restaurants

These businesses feature cash sales and poor payroll records. A buyer should conduct a visual audit for a few days to help verify reported sales. Experienced participants look to gross sales, rent, and cost of food and labor as key variables. As always, high volume and short hours are attractive. Alcohol normally adds value. Complex menu, no stove or hood, and insufficient parking are also negatives. Franchising opportunities are extensive. Look for brokers who specialize in the restaurant and food area for the best inventory, knowledge of current market values, and experience with liquor licenses.

Range 1: 30 to 50 percent of annual sales plus inventory
Range 2: 1 to 2 times ACF plus inventory
Range 3: 35 percent of annual sales
Range 4: 4 to 6 times monthly gross sales
SIC Code: 5200–5900 (Retail Trade), 5810 (Eating and Drinking Places)

Trade Associations and Publications:
National Restaurant Association (202-331-5900)
Restaurant News (212-986-4800)

Computer Repair/Service Companies

Computer repair and service is truly a growth industry. Reputable and experienced owner-operators offer a valuable collection of accounts. Unique personal characteristics, skills, and relationships will complicate the determination of value and future performance under new ownership. Long-term contracts are highly desirable. See the section on service companies in Chapter 1.

Range 1: 1 to 1.5 times ACF plus equipment, fixtures, and inventory
Range 2: 1 to 2 times ACF
SIC Code: 7000–8900 (Business Services), 7370 (Computer Services)

Trade Associations and Publications:
>   Computer Dealers & Lessors Association (202-333-0102)
>   Electronic Industries Association (202-457-4916)
>   *Electronic News* (212-741-4230)

Convenience Store

Convenience stores vary greatly in terms of amount, type, and availability of stock, gasoline, or alcohol. Gas and alcohol will increase value dramatically. Inventory is typically priced separately from the business and can be excluded from the purchase price used to calculate commission to broker. Short hours, high gross minimal payroll, and no assaults or robberies are favorable considerations as well. Convenience stores are quite attractive when combined with gas and auto repair. Look for high markups on gasoline and a successful full-service island. Be aware that the franchiser (oil company) may not own the property on which the station is located, increasing the difficulty of selling such a business. Check for up-to-date compliance with all EPA standards (conduct a Phase I or Phase II Environmental Audit).

Range 1:   1 to 2 times monthly sales
Range 2:   1.5 to 2.5 times ACF plus inventory
Range 3:   10 to 30 percent of annual sales revenues (lower end with no gas or alcohol)
Range 4:   3 to 4 times monthly gross sales
Range 5: $1 for each gallon sold monthly plus one year's net income on minimarket sales and repairs (if any)
SIC Code: 5200–5900 (Retail Trade) 5540 (Gasoline Stations)

Trade Associations and Publications:
>   National Association of Convenience Stores (703-684-3600)
>   *Convenience Store News* (212-594-4120)
>   Gasoline and Automotive Service Dealers Association (718-241-1111)
>   *Service Station Management* (708-296-0770)

Distributorships

Exclusivity and reputation of product line are key determinants of value for these businesses (location, products, or services). The use of distributors frees up capital for manufacturers and broadens exposure. Average inventory purchased is as high as $1 million. See section on wholesale/distribution in Chapter 1 for more details.

Range 1: 1 to 2.5 times ACF
Range 2: 25 to 40 percent of annual gross revenues
SIC Code: 5000–5100 (Wholesale Trade)

Manufacturing Businesses

Many different rules of thumb apply to this general category, including those that are pre-tax, after-tax, and based on ACF, total assets, or some combination thereof. Return to the beginning of the rules of thumb section for after-tax multipliers, used primarily for larger, publicly traded companies. Generally speaking, companies whose products are patented, sold for cash, nonperishable, nonunion, noncyclical, and spread out to dozens of customers around the world will sell for the highest multiples. Recently deteriorated relations with suppliers and distributors must be investigated. See the section on manufacturing businesses in Chapter 1 for detailed insights. Addressing work-in-progress can prevent unwanted difficulties regarding value during negotiations.

Range 1: 1 to 2 times ACF plus equipment, inventory, and fixtures
Range 2: 3 to 5 times ACF (larger business, more proprietary products—higher multiplier)
Range 3: provide a 20 to 35 percent return on investment (invested cash)
Range 4: price to earnings ratio of 4 to 12 (publicly traded, primarily)
Range 5: 1 to 1.5 times ACF plus equipment plus allowances for work-in-progress
SIC Code: 2000–3900 (Manufacturing)

Trade Associations and Publications:
National Association of Manufacturers (201-342-0700)

Print Shops/Copy Shops/Digital Imaging/Printers

There are many variations within this general category, including numerous successful (expensive) franchise opportunities. Opportunities range from storefront, quick-copy locations (high rent and high traffic) to major commercial printing companies located in industrial parks (low rent with minimal disturbances). State-of-the-art operations are heavily equipment and technology intensive. Valuable niches are available, but require the newest technology to ensure future success. High sales volumes increase profitability, multiples, and general value. Also important is a broad customer base, wide range of service offerings, and a skilled and reliable workforce.

Range 1: .5 to 3 times ACF plus equipment, inventory, fixtures, and trucks

Range 2: 2 to 4 years of taxable income plus all assets

Range 3: amortization of free cash flow (ACF) over predetermined period of time (e.g., eight years) at market rates (e.g., prime plus two percent)

SIC Code: 7000–8900 (Business Services), 7380 (Miscellaneous Business Services)

Trade Associations and Publications:
National Association of Quick Printers (312-644-6610)
Printing Industries of America, Inc. (703-519-8130)
American Printer (312-726-2802)

Retail Businesses

As indicated elsewhere, successful retail businesses depend primarily on location and traffic, lease terms, cost, variety, availability and desirability of inventory, and effective advertising efforts. See Chapter 1 for more descriptive insights into this category of business.

Range 1: 25 to 50 percent of annual gross sales
Range 2: .75 to 2 times ACF plus inventory, fixtures, and other assets
Range 3: 3 to 5 times monthly gross revenues
SIC Code: 5200–5900 (Retail Trade)

Trade Associations and Publications:
National Retail Merchants Association (212-244-8780)

Caveat Regarding Rules of Thumb

Rules of thumb are not to be used as the sole guide to establishing value. They should be in conjunction with other methods, such as the DCF and ability to pay approaches. There is wide variation in multiples across industries, regions of the country, and time. For example, car washes in California can sell for up to twice their selling price in Arizona. *Do not exclusively rely on these rules of thumb. Every business is different and must be carefully and realistically analyzed, using a combination of methods.*

Recommended Reading

Given the great importance of valuing a business, whether as a buyer or as a seller, I have accumulated a short list of excellent valuation related books, primers, guides, and texts that might be useful for smaller, larger, or both sizes of businesses. This list is supplemented by the sources presented in the bibliography.

Smaller Businesses
- *A Basic Guide to Valuing a Company*, by Wilbur Yegge (John Wiley and Sons, Inc.)
- *The Business Valuation Manual: An Understandable Step-By-Step Guide to Finding the Value of a Business*, by Thomas W. Horn (Charter Oak Press)
- *Buy the Right Business at the Right Price*, by Brian Knight and the Associates of Country Business (Upstart Publishing Company)

Larger Businesses
- *Valuation—Measuring and Managing the Value of Companies*, by Copeland, Koller, and Murrin (John Wiley and Sons, Inc.)
- *Cashing Out*, by David Silver (Enterprise/Dearborn)
- *Mergers and Acquisitions: A Valuation Handbook*, by Joseph H. Marren (Irwin Professional Publishing)

Both Smaller and Larger Businesses
- *Valuing a Business: The Analysis and Appraisal of Closely Held Companies*, by Shannon P. Pratt, Robert F. Reilly, and Robert P. Schweihs (Irwin Publishing)
- *Handbook of Business Valuation*, by Thomas L. West and Jeffrey D. Jones, editor (John Wiley and Sons)
- *Valuation of a Closely Held Business*, by the American Institute of Certified Public Accountants

CHAPTER 11

Valuation Analysis

To help clarify and expand on the valuation techniques introduced in Chapter 9 and 10 and the due diligence techniques presented in Chapters 6 and 7, the following analysis of a manufacturing or service company will provide additional insights into business valuation drawn from the real world. Small manufacturing businesses are in great demand—especially profitable ones. Buyers are looking for proprietary products or a niche that allows favorable pricing and long-term profits. They are also looking for substantial hard assets. The company we are analyzing here can be characterized as high-tech, service-oriented, and computer-related. Specifically, they manufacture, repair, and service test equipment (fixtures) for printed circuit boards (PCBs). From here on, we will refer to our subject business as *High-Tech*.

High-Tech's customers are manufacturers of PCBs or PCB assemblies. They require either test equipment or test services, both of which can be provided by our subject company. Their competitors are major PCB manufacturers with *in-house* capabilities. Even these large firms will often *farm out* to companies like High-Tech. Another set of competitors manufactures test designs, a different type of fixture growing in usage. High-Tech has been profitable for many years, after being founded in 1982. The company has been in the same location for several years, with lease payments of $2,800 per month for 5,000 square feet. The current term expires within a few months and must be renegotiated. Sales and cash flow were down in the most recent years, apparently because of illness, owner burn-out, and minimal attempts to obtain new customers. In the latest year, ACF was over $200,000 on sales of only $632,000, indicating the high value added of the manufacturing and service process. The business is asset rich with estimated equipment and leasehold improvements of more than $300,000 and inventory of $36,000. There are lease payments remaining on certain pieces of equipment as discussed later. Sales were more than $1,000,000 only two years ago with an associated ACF of $320,000. This is an important consideration. Sales and cash flow would appear to be trending downward, although ACF remains respectable at about $200,000. Thorough due diligence to explain why they are declining is *mandatory*.

The financial statements are prepared by a CPA, but are unaudited (compiled only). Balance sheet and income tax returns are available for the past 12 years. The company is a declared S-Corporation, with the husband (active) and wife (inactive) majority shareholders. The husband works full time as do six other employees, each with specialized roles and skills. One key employee is critical to the short run, undisturbed success of the business. If a new owner came in without this employee or these skills, time and sales would pass while the problem was remedied. An employment contract with this key employee would be ideal to firm up the transition.

Let's begin our financial analysis with a determination of the firm's ACF to a single owner-operator. Remember throughout our analysis that sales and ACF have been trending downward. Examine the following:

1997	ACF
Net Income	54,256
Owner's Salary	69,600
Owner's Payroll Taxes	10,440
Health, Life Insurance	10,318
Personal Auto Expense	22,458
Donations	90
Entertainment	2,056
Travel	11,840
Depreciation Expense	27,272
Interest Expense	11,522
Legal and Accounting Fees (excessive)	5,276
Total ACF	**225,128**

ACF is intended to represent the pre-tax cash benefits accruing to a single owner. It can also be considered *discretionary* cash flow, which will be available to a new owner to pay a salary, service debt, earn a return on investment, purchase additional inventory, or replace/expand equipment holdings. This important figure is used for comparison purposes from one company to the next and is used (in slightly varying forms) by practically all business brokers. It is also loosely referred to as *net* or *cash flow*. Many rules of thumb are multiples of ACF. From here, various adjustments could be made to turn these historic numbers into pro forma numbers reflecting the future. If the buyer were considering borrowing money from the bank (e.g., SBA loan), these projections for *at least* the first year would be required from both the current owner and the borrower (prospective owner). Additionally, preparation of a credible business plan will call for these pro forma preparations.

Before we turn to projections, let's attempt to value the business using historical data and the following methods: excess earnings, capitalization of earnings, ability to pay, and rules of thumb. As detailed in Chapter 9, each of these methods requires numerous assumptions and considerations. Consider the following key questions and how they might impact the determination of discount or cap rates:

- What is the pace of technological change? How long will current equipment serve to generate profits before large capital expenditures are required?
- What is the precise role of key employees? Can they be quickly and easily replaced?
- Can owner's relationship with customers and personal experience be replaced without great harm to sales and cash flows?
- Why are sales dropping? What are they currently (e.g., last quarter and last month)? Obtain assistance of CPA. What is the near-term prognosis?
- Does any one or two customers generate a large percentage of sales?

Excess Earnings Method

The essence of the excess earnings method is to add the value of the tangible assets to the capitalized value of the excess earnings associated with the intangible assets. Recall, however, that the IRS frowns on this method, recommending its usage only if no better approach is possible. Despite this bad review by the IRS, the formula is still widely used and intellectually appealing. First, the tangible assets must be valued (see balance sheet in Figure 11.1).

FIGURE 11.1 Balance Sheet ($)

		(Adjusted Values)	
Assets			
Current Assets			
Cash	39,602	0	(goes with seller)
A/R	12,634	11,366	(10% uncollectable)
Inventory	63,372	50,697	(lower of replacement cost or market value)
Total Current Assets	115,608	62,063	
Fixed Assets			
Furniture and Fixtures	220,438		
Equipment	226,038		
Leasehold Improvements	17,689		
	464,165	302,963	(value is estimated at halfway between original cost and depreciated value)
Less: Acc. Dep.	(322,404)		
	141,761		
Deposits	816	0	
Total Fixed Assets	142,577	302,963	
Total Assets	248,185	365,026	

The tangible assets have an estimated current value of $365,026. If the business is being sold as an asset sale, the $11,366 value for the receivables should be subtracted, giving us a total of $353,660. We will assume that the seller has agreed to include these minimal receivables with the sale and use the higher asset figure. The more significant the dollar value of the assets, the more important a professional appraisal would be. If bank financing is involved, it is likely that formal appraisals will be required.

Next we need to determine a normalized operating profit, as defined in Chapter 9. We will use only the current period's income statement to estimate a normalized figure, because of the fact that the business has been suffering from declining revenues and cash flows, leaving little reason to place a weight on these previously higher numbers. Note, however, that valuation transcends science and becomes an art precisely because of these types of decisions. *If the decline in sales is temporary and easily reversed, a higher figure for ACF could and should be utilized.* We will remain conservative in our valuation attempts.

Normalized Profit and Excess Earnings

ACF =	225,128
Fair Salary to Manager	45,000
	180,128
Anticipated Annual Capital Expenditures	35,000
Normalized Profits	145,128
Allocations:	
Return on Assets (12½% on $365,026)	45,444
Excess Earnings	99,684

There is a "method to this madness" as follows. A business is a collection of assets, tangible and intangible. There are opportunity costs of investing in these assets. The opportunity cost of investing in fixed assets is higher than investing in current assets, and a weighted average, risk-adjusted return must be estimated (we utilized 12½ percent in this example, which incorporates a weighted average, higher return for fixed assets and a lower return for current assets). In other words, if $365,026 were invested in similar assets, a return of $45,444 could be reasonably expected. The difference between the normalized profits of $145,128 and the estimated return of $45,444 is $99,684, or excess earnings, which must be attributed to the intangible assets of the business, such as the customer base, employee knowledge, trade name, and business reputation.

The final step requires "capitalization" of those excess earnings. The suggestions in Chapter 9 might lead us to a cap rate of approximately 25 percent, giving us:

$$99,684 \div 25\% = \$398,736$$

Note once again how the many assumptions made throughout this process have a material effect on the end result. If a cap rate of 33 percent were used, the value would fall to $302,073. Keep in mind that a weighted average "basket" of several valuation results will generate the most reliable estimates.

Rules of Thumb

Let's change course here and consider a popular rule of thumb for small manufacturing businesses. Rules of thumb will tend to be grounded in historic, comparable sales figures. A commonly utilized rule of thumb for *small*, privately held manufacturing operations is:

Value = 1 to 1.5 years ACF + MV of all assets included in sale

For *larger*, privately held, or publicly traded manufacturing companies, the following rule is used:

Value = 4 to 10 times profit after taxes (net income)

Given the declining state of affairs for our subject business, we will use one year's ACF ($225,128). As stated earlier, if there is a credible, realistic, believable reason why the business has recently declined and could be quickly turned around, a higher multiple could be justified. Turning to the assets, which have an adjusted value of $365,026, we calculate the value of the business as:

ACF	$225,128
+ Assets	$365,026
Total	$590,154

This result is more than 50 percent higher than the excess earnings method. Let's reconsider our work so far. Maybe we have overestimated the ACF. No, it looks solid. One important change could be made, however, to make the result above more in line with the excess earnings method. If it is necessary, as we assumed earlier, to devote $35,000 each year to replace the existing equipment in order to maintain the future cash flows, the ACF should be reduced accordingly. Most business brokers will not make this kind of adjustment (nor will they use the excess earnings method unless it is a larger small business), but the sophisticated, discounted cash flow techniques require precisely such an adjustment. In our case, the value would be changed to:

ACF (Adjusted for anticipated capital expenditures— $225,128 less $35,000)	$190,128
+ Assets	$365,026
Total	$555,154

Perhaps we have overestimated the asset values. Having relied on a single rule of thumb (halfway between original cost and depreciated book value), we might be off target. Let's assume that based on a more conservative analysis, the assets had a market value of only $293,000. As a result, the value based on our rule of thumb would fall to:

ACF	$225,128
+ Assets	$293,000
Total	$518,128

Another common rule of thumb is to simply take a straight multiple of the ACF without regard to asset values. Generally, a multiple of one to three will be used, depending on the many factors that make one business more attractive and secure versus another. Manufacturing businesses will normally enjoy higher multiples than service businesses because of their large asset base. Given the downward trend in sales and revenues, use of a multiple of only 2.5 might be justified:

$$Value = 2.5 \times 225,128 = \$562,820$$
$$Value = 2.5 \times 190,128 = \$475,320$$

Already we have values ranging from $302,069 to $590,154, and we are only warming up!

Capitalization of Earnings Method

The capitalization of earnings method also relies on historic earnings. The earnings base is different and the value of tangible assets is basically ignored. The first step is to calculate a normalized earnings base generated from the previous five years of financial results. A weighted average, with a greater weight on current years, is preferred, but we will once again rely solely on the last year. We have calculated historical ACF to be $225,128 (or $190,128 if we account for anticipated required capital expenditures). An accurate determination of ACF and the proper selection of a cap rate are the keys to useful results.

To determine our cap rate, we will rely on the use of Schilt's risk premiums (see Figure 9.11). Category Three seems most appropriate, with Category Four a close contender. The positive attributes that minimize the risk are a long history of profitability (over ten years), significant barriers to entry in the form of material capital costs (approximately $500,000) and the need for specialized skills to be successful. Ironically, this latter strength turns out to be a weakness (increasing risk) to the extent that if one or two key employees were to leave, business would suffer as the search for replacements took place. Assuming that the key employees would sign a long-term employment contract (minimum of six months with at least one month's notice required before leaving), this risk could be minimized, and Category Three would seem appropriate. Category Three requires the addition of 16 to 20 percent to the risk-free rate of 7 percent. We chose 20 percent, leaving a final rate of 27 percent. The valuation results from here are quite straightforward, as follows:

$$Value = 225,128 \div 27\% = \$833,807$$
$$Value = 190,128 \div 27\% = \$704,178$$

If employment contracts were not obtainable and the new owner did not have extensive skills in this area, Category Four or Five might apply. Consider the value based on cap rates of 31 or 34 percent.

$$Value = 225,128 \div 31\% = \$706,219$$
$$Value = 190,128 \div 31\% = \$613,316$$
$$Value = 225,128 \div 34\% = \$662,141$$
$$Value = 190,128 \div 34\% = \$559,200$$

This brings up an important and often overlooked point in business valuation. *Businesses have different values to different buyers.* Depending on buyer backgrounds, some business ventures will be extremely risky or extremely safe. There really is no single valuation figure that applies to a given business.

Ability to Pay Method

The ability to pay method is different from most others to the extent that you back into the purchase price based on the anticipated cash flow and the desired payback period. Beginning with our standard ACF ($225,128), we must subtract the owner's *required* salary ($50,000), the anticipated annual capital expenditures needed to maintain the cash flows ($35,000), and expected tax payments (varies from buyer to buyer depending on tax brackets) of, say $30,000. Consult your tax attorney or CPA to figure this one out. The result of $110,128 represents the amount of cash flow remaining to service the debt.

Next, you must assume (negotiate) the payback period, which is typically three to seven years. Let's assume a five year payback (seller's carry-back), which gives us a total of $550,640 ($110,128 x 5). Add the down payment required by the seller of $175,000 to get an approximate purchase price of $725,640. *Note how the results could differ dramatically with a higher or lower down payment or a longer or shorter payback period.* This is a very arbitrary method and should be used only as a reality check to determine what levels of debt the business can safely support.

ACF	$225,128
Minus Salary	(50,000)
Minus Capital Expenditures	(35,000)
Minus Taxes	(30,000)
Cash Flow Available to Service Debt	$110,128

Assume 5 Year Pay Back	$550,640
Assume $175,000 down payment	(175,000)
Purchase Price	**$725,640**

Before completing our valuation analysis (ACF and Adjusted Back Value approaches), let's determine the average of our results. Thus far, the average of all valuation results (14 calculations) is $586,205, which equals approximately 2.6 times ACF.

Discounted Cash Flow Method

Now we will attempt to value our business based on the discounted cash flow (DCF) method, which is forward-looking and *relies on material estimates regarding the amount, timing, and risk of the expected future cash flows*. Specifically, the following areas must be credibly forecasted (assuming the new owner is in control of the business):

- Sales, cost of goods sold, operating expenses (including owner's salary)
- Depreciation and amortization expense (including capital expenditures)
- Interest expense
- Additions to working capital
- Other future related events

It is one thing to understand the current health of a company (based on historical data) and quite another to predict the future under new ownership. Relevant historical data to be analyzed includes financial statements from the past five years, review of all product lines or services offered, summary of company history, complete listing of assets included in sale, breakdown of inventory, accounts receivable and accounts payable, important competitors, customers, suppliers and employees, strengths, weaknesses, opportunities and threats, all leases, contractual commitments, and other likely financial obligations such as returns and contingent liability.

This review is critical for understanding the business in general as well as trying to establish its value. Predicting or forecasting the future must be based in great part on understanding the past. *New ownership may lead to significant changes in both strategic and tactical plans, requiring adjustments to the pro forma financial statements* and careful consideration of a number of key areas, including plans to reduce costs, strategies to increase sales, potential acquisitions to spur growth, reduction of owner's compensation (salary plus benefits), adjustments in accounting methods (including redepreciation of fixed assets), and projections of future macroeconomic performance. All these areas must be credibly analyzed and incorporated into future period projections. *Recent court cases have placed greater reliance on this method as a preferred way to value businesses.*

The essence of this method, once again, is to calculate the present value of all future cash flows accruing to the owner. The specific approach that we will utilize here is to add the present value of the expected cash flows to the present value of the residual assets (assets minus liabilities) that will accrue to the owner at the time of sale several years into the future. For this particular valuation, I have been able to prepare the pro forma projections based on lengthy discussions with the seller and the buyer. The seller knows the intimacies of the business and the buyer has specific plans for the future regarding owner's compensation, advertising, purchasing, new equipment, etc. Note once again that the same business today will be worth differing amounts to different buyers with different experience and different plans. The important point to recognize is that you must carefully project the future sales and expenses, putting great effort into these calculations, which at the same time will help the new owner understand and optimally run the business.

What this means, of course, is that *you* must make numerous assumptions that will dramatically affect the outcome of the valuation. At a minimum, *you* must analyze and determine the following:

- What measure of cash flow will you use?
- Will you include initial investments, cash infusions into working capital, replacements and additions to fixed assets, and a terminal value on sale many years into the future as part of your bottom-line cash flow projections?
- How much will increased advertising expenditures increase projected sales and profits?
- How much will sales and operating expenses increase?
- How much will interest expense be (what is the expected down payment and total purchase price)?
- How risky are these anticipated cash flows (what discount rate is appropriate)?

You must address these questions in a consistent fashion. My analysis led to cash flow figures as follows for the next 10 years:

Year 1	Years 2 to 10
$212,000	8% growth each year

After the expected cash flows have been projected, they must be discounted back into present value. *I have slightly modified the previous discount rate to 30 percent, which was calculated using the build-up approach* instead of Schlit's risk premiums.

	1	*2*	*3*	*4*	*5*
ACF($)	212,000	228,960	247,277	267,059	288,424
PV ($)	163,077	135,480	112,553	93,505	77,681

	6	7	8	9	10
ACF($)	311,498	336,418	363,331	392,397	423,789
PV ($)	64,536	53,615	44,541	37,003	30,742

The present value of all future cash flows (utilizing the ACF concept and ignoring working capital infusions, capital replacements, and taxes) is: $812,733. If we accounted for capital replacements and taxes and/or raised the discount rate, the valuation results would decline. I've been intentionally "sloppy" during this case study to stress the point that there are many acceptable ways to proceed. This flexibility is not a problem unless it is blatantly abused within and across each of the valuation approaches *and* from one business to the next. *Be consistent and credible!*

Adjusted Book Value Approaches

Also referred to as the book value approach, the net tangible asset value approach, the asset accumulation method, or the economic value of assets method (to name four), the crux of these methods is to determine the net book value of the business. The idea that a business is worth its book value (A–L) is questionable due to the quirks of the accounting process and the diversion of book value from true market value. Accordingly, the adjusted book value approach calls for proper adjustments to be made for intangible assets such as goodwill and customer lists, the economic depreciation of fixed assets, appreciation in real estate values, and improperly stated inventory amounts. A critical choice to be made for most of these methods is whether to use market values or liquidation values for the assets. As presented in Chapter 9, liquidation values are well below market values and would lead to dramatically lower valuations.

A basket of valuation approaches is recommended for optimal results. Use of the adjusted book value approach above is not advisable, except for perhaps newly established businesses without a track record for sales and cash flow. This approach is also used in rare cases where the assets of the business will be liquidated piecemeal subsequent to acquisition (e.g., bankruptcy cases). This method will almost always tend to undervalue a business that is generating profits and cash flow.

As concerns our current business (High-Tech), the asset approaches do not seem to be worthwhile, given the ten-year history of positive earnings. If we were to apply this method, adjustments to all balance sheet accounts and a few amounts that do not show up on the balance sheet would be required (as per Chapter 9). The relevance of the liability amounts disappears if the buyer is purchasing the assets only (as opposed to a stock purchase). The practical point is that *almost every business, including companies that are losing money, is worth at least the value of its assets* (whether liquidation, market, or somewhere in between). Even companies that generate *negative* valuation results because of negative cash flow should be valued equal to their usable, marketable assets, both tangible and intangible.

Conclusion

Placing a 50 percent weighting on the average result figured earlier ($586,205) and a 50 percent weighting on the DCF approach ($812,733), we might be comfortable in stating that the current market value of this business is somewhere in between these two numbers, or approximately $700,000 (which amounts to a multiple of ACF of slightly more than 3). *When negotiating with the other side (e.g., buyer, seller, IRS, partner), you should clean up your presentation and compare these results with recent comparable sales figures*, if they are available. Clearly, there is no single correct way to value a business. Your goal should be to *credibly and consistently build your case when entering into negotiations and attempting to justify your listing price (seller) or your offered price (buyer).*

CHAPTER 12

Selling Your Business: The Basics

Selling a business is perhaps even more emotional than buying a business. Sellers have typically devoted a great deal of their blood, sweat, and tears to the running of and building up of their business. I have personally seen several sellers actually crying at the realization that they had finally secured a buyer who was ready, willing, and able to purchase their business. Deciding if, when, how, and for how much to sell a business requires significant analysis and emotional capital, as this chapter will clearly illustrate. The list of **reasons for selling** is quite long indeed:

- Retirement/illness/burnout/boredom
- Breakup of/disagreement between partners/shareholders
- Raising cash to focus on other businesses/going public
- Lack of working capital to grow/business is losing money
- Moving out of state/desire to spend time with family

Whatever your reasons, you must be able to credibly and fluently explain to a suitor exactly why you are willing to part with such a personal collection of assets. There are numerous factors to consider, trade-offs to make, and steps to take during this emotional roller coaster. The best advice I can give to you now, besides thoroughly reading this entire guide, is to *carefully select and rely on respected professionals* in your area. The money you spend on qualified business brokers, accountants, and attorneys will be well spent.

Preparing for Selling Your Business

All business owners should begin planning for the sale of their business from the time of acquisition or inception. Every business plan should include exit strategies describing the seller's preferences regarding his or her exit from the business (e.g., cashing out, selling on terms, gifting to children, plans for new ventures, or retirement). Regardless of the particular strategy, owner(s) will seek the highest return (down payment plus future payments) and the least amount of state and federal income, estate, and capital gains taxes with the greatest certainty and least hassle.

Obtaining top dollar from a qualified purchaser is *not* normally an easy task. It takes planning, hard work, and good negotiating skills to reach this goal. By understanding the determinants of value, you can plan your way to a favorable return. After you have figured out how much you think your business is worth (Chapters 8, 9, and 10), how do you convince suitors that your premium price is reasonable? When it is time to sell, you must be prepared to take the steps to make it worthwhile.

Properly and efficiently use professional help. Brokers have invaluable contacts, accountants can help in due diligence, and attorneys will ensure that your legal interests are protected. If their efforts result in safely receiving substantially more dollars from the purchaser, their cost of $10,000 to $15,000 dollars is worthwhile.

If you choose to sell the business without the aid of a broker, proper scrutiny of buyers will require that they sign nondisclosure agreements (Chapter 2), and provide resumes and sign personal financial statements (Chapter 2). References and credit reports should be requested as well. Discerning who is a "real" buyer is not easy. Brokers take many years to feel comfortable passing judgment on a prospect (even then they can be miserably mistaken!). This process is more art than science and can lead sellers down a path of wasted time and unnecessary distractions. Properly assessing motivation and qualifications is the core of the matter.

When dealing with a broker, retainer fees, exclusivity, commission, and contract duration must be addressed. These issues should be incorporated into the body of the contract between broker and seller, commonly referred to as a *listing agreement*. Specific instructions for the broker regarding handling of buyers (e.g., seller approval before release of company financials) or escrow funds (minimum of 10 percent of purchase price) should be placed directly into the listing contract. If you enter a *sole and exclusive* agreement and seek to terminate prior to the expiration date, ask the broker to sign and notarize a termination statement. You must also guard against multiple open agency and one-party listings, whereby two different brokers qualify and introduce the same buyer to your business. Upon termination, ask the broker to provide you with a list of all parties shown the business. Specifically, request a listing of "the names of any persons, corporations, or other entities to whom you or your affiliated agents have in any manner, shown, introduced, revealed, or made aware of my business being for sale."

Value your business properly. Valuation is also as much an art as it is science. Regardless, obtaining assistance will help ensure that you are not underpriced or overpriced. Also, having a credible third party conduct the valuation will help you market your business. The harm from undervaluing your business is obvious. The harm from overvaluing is that you may lose the opportunity to sell to qualified buyers. An astute purchaser can quickly determine the range within which a particular type of business should sell, simply based on your sales, cash flow, and asset values. If you are overpriced, buyers will lose interest quickly. Pricing your business based on how much money you have invested is a waste of time, and a qualified broker is your best bet to find fair market value. Brokers are preferred because they are involved in the valuation/sale of businesses full-time and can combine access to comparable sales with a good feel for the market. Brokers will normally be interested in getting the highest price the market will bear (maximizing their commission) without pricing it so high that good prospects, time, and advertising money are wasted.

Prepare and present complete, accurate, and neat financial statements, leases, and other supporting documents. If you want to sell quickly for top dollar without creating doubts on the purchaser's mind, have these documents readily available. Once an offer has been accepted and earnest money turned over to the broker, be prepared to work with the buyer toward removing contingencies and opening escrow.

Remember that all these tips relate to maximizing the purchase price that a buyer will agree to pay. By understanding the determinants of value and valuation techniques, you can better appreciate these recommendations. Review Chapters 8 through 11, focusing on the key determinants of value.

Most P&Ls are geared toward minimizing taxable income (a good strategy until you seek to sell your business). Remember this—every dollar of ACF will get you two to three dollars at the time of sale. If you earn an extra $50,000 profit and pay $15,000 in taxes, you will get a return of $30,000 to $45,000 (that's 200 to 300 percent). Obtaining top dollar normally means reporting all income. Also, if you show a trend of rising profitability, you can more easily sell the future profitability. Besides reporting all income, you need to reconstruct your income statement to reflect the true cash flow of the business, adjusting for bloated inventory, all personal expenses, travel and entertainment, donations, interest and depreciation, salary, uncollectible debts, promotional expenditures, and income tax to obtain a realistic measure of the firm's cash flow capability.

Next, have a copy of all leases (premises and equipment) available to assist in executing transfers or assignments. Deals fail because of undisclosed (forgotten) equipment leases or the inability to obtain a lease transfer. Before a buyer tours the business, you should prepare a list of all assets included and *not* included in the sale. Even small surprises near the closing can be insurmountable.

Next, consider spending time to improve your records regarding inventory, accounts receivable and customer lists by computerizing the inventory tracking system (e.g., point-of-sale software), preparing monthly accounts receivable, aging reports, and creating comprehensive customer files.

Report all income (revenues) despite higher tax liabilities. Not only should you report all income, you need to be able to match or explain any differences between your financial statements, your sales tax returns, and your federal tax returns. Complete and accurate reporting of sales will maximize the value of your business (not to mention your credibility). If you do not report all income, you are exposed to the serious risk of alienating the prospect. Buyers might have an ideological bent toward full payment of all taxes, maintaining that they have always paid their taxes. Although a great percentage of buyers will take this underreporting in stride and even expect it, some will take this personally and react in a deal-breaking fashion.

It is true that certain types of businesses are characterized (or plagued) by less than full reporting (skimming). These are typically cash intensive businesses such as restaurants, ice cream parlors, and water stores. If a business is described as a cash business, this is an indication that you will need to look long and hard to prove the total sales figures. These businesses will be sold as much on location, equipment, head counts, and visual inspections as on reported sales and cash flow. Buyers will recreate their own sales figures based on watching the traffic counts at different times of the day and imputing their own estimate of cost of goods. Buyers may request trial periods of ownership (or in-person monitoring) to verify reported sales.

Focus intently on maximizing sales and minimizing expenses for at least one year prior to sale. The last 12 months of financial data are probably the most frequently analyzed and highly scrutinized by buyers. Put in extra effort as you plan to sell and you will be nicely rewarded. Suggestions include selective *advertising increases*, even if it means additional work or overtime. Consider creating a homepage on the World Wide Web. Even if sales do not immediately increase, this will certainly impress the prospective purchaser. *Stay open additional hours* to boost sales. You might try to *book sales by the end of the tax year,* rather than postponing it to reduce your taxable income. Be more aggressive in your sales efforts, even if it means reduced margins.

Cut out the frills and reduce discretionary items, even if they are added back to cash flow. For example, *travel and entertainment expenses* are considered discretionary and would be included in a cash flow calculation (particularly if they are not fully business-related). Even though it will be considered cash flow, a dollar of net income is stronger in the eyes of many buyers. Clean up your income statement by reducing travel, entertainment, inflated family wages, and other discretionary items.

Pay close attention to *inventory purchases*. If you can find lower cost sources of the same quality, try it. Depending on your accountant, there may also be a timing issue. Higher cost of goods sold in the current year will reduce your taxable income, but will reduce net income and cash flow as well. If you are using the cash basis of accounting, postpone a large purchase of inventory into the next year. Gross margins will rise as will net income and cash flow. Note that this effect will be reversed in the next tax year, but more attention should be paid to the results of the year prior to sale of the business. *Higher ACF is more valuable than higher inventory values!* Reinvesting profits into inventory may not be optimal when it is time to sell.

Pay close attention to *payroll costs*. By working additional hours, you will put more money in your pocket now and again at the time of sale (higher ACF, higher value). You might also consider reducing your family-related payments, which cloud the true picture and can be the cause of much concern to a buyer.

Another area to examine is *utility expenses* (electricity and phone). Contact the American Council for Energy-Efficient Economy (202-429-8873) for answers to your utility-related questions. Consider hiring a commission-based auditor to review all your utilities.

Additional options for reducing expenses are more cumbersome. If nothing else, be prepared to discuss the following with prospects to show them how cash flow can be improved:

- Renegotiate your *lease* (i.e., lower payments, smaller increases, return of deposits)
- Renegotiate *debt payments* on bank loans, seller carry-backs, loans from shareholders, etc. (lower interest rate + longer payback = lower payments)
- Ask for more *favorable payment terms* to suppliers (but take advantage of cash discounts)
- Selectively accelerate *payments collections* from customers
- For property owners, consider appealing your *property taxes*
- Renegotiate your property, health, auto, and liability *insurance coverage*—be aggressive
- Review *advertising budgets*—cut expenditures that do not directly and obviously improve sales. Pay close attention to your Yellow Pages expenditures.
- Evaluate your *long distance telephone* charges. Competition in this industry has complicated matters, but you can save money after a thorough, careful analysis.

You might consider hiring a *management consultant* who will work on a commission basis (after a one-time introduction fee) to examine carefully your entire business. Consider shopping around for a *new attorney or accountant*. Look for the lowest bid, highest quality offer. Tempt your existing professionals to reduce their rates. Also investigate the use of prepared business forms and contracts. Two final areas to evaluate are *postage expenses* and *travel costs*. First, carefully evaluate overnight delivery services, packaging materials, and postage costs. If you are shipping frequently and are using direct mail for your advertising campaign, take the time to review these expenditures. Second, cut travel costs. It is very easy to spend thousands of dollars more than you should. You should look to not only save money, but also time (time is money!). If your travel expenses are $20,000 per year and you can save only 25 percent, you have saved $5,000 and increased the value of your business on average by $10,000. Consider gaining travel agent status.

Clean up your business for presentation. It might seem trivial, but sprucing up the appearance of your business is a high return step to increase its salability. A fresh coat of paint, new carpeting in selected areas, and careful attention to picking up debris are all guaranteed to pay for themselves. *First impressions are important when selling a business.* Dust on the inventory, clerks with overflowing ash trays, empty aspirin containers, and machinery held together with T-shirts do not help! During the period of time that buyers are touring your facility, assign each area of your business to one or more employees to keep all areas clean and presentable. If a qualified buyer is coming at a specific time, prepare accordingly. If your company owns the real estate and the business through two separate corporations, match the rental payments to the current market rates. Accurate, transparent, verifiable figures are normally ideal.

Consider selling to a strategic rather than a financial buyer. Strategic buyers are interested in the long-term value of the opportunity associated with a given company. They tend to be larger companies seeking to acquire market share or enter new niche markets. They pay more than financial buyers, who are buying the business primarily for immediate cash flow as they seek to leverage their limited cash into high profits. Financial buyers will seek out bank financing and seller financing to make the deal work and often end up strapped for working capital. Strategic buyers will have ample cash, but might move the operation and cut staff in half as they seek economies of scale. Financial buyers will pay less and need more help, but will offer incentives to key personnel. Financial buyers will focus on reducing overhead to meet the new debt payments. Above all else, you are selling the future and a large upside potential to strategic buyers, who have the cash and other resources to make it happen. Strategic buyers rely on projections of future cost savings and revenue increases via detailed, pro forma analyses (DCF analysis).

The real world, of course, operates in shades of black and white. Somewhere in between these two types of buyers we find the following candidates to purchase "larger" small businesses: small investment banks/companies/funds and venture capital firms.

Small investment banks are similar to financial buyers in their quest for leverage and are similar to strategic buyers in their respective industry expertise and experience. There are surprisingly dozens of these firms across the country that specialize in the buying and selling of equity interests in small companies. These companies vary in terms of geographic location and preferences, size of investments, preferred industries, and interest in turnaround situations. They will make higher down payments than individual financial buyers, but may seek lengthier payback periods with delayed balloon payments. A fairly lengthy compilation of such organizations is found in *Cashing Out*, by A. David Silver (Enterprise/Dearborn). Venture capital firms are discussed in Chapter 14.

Stress the future over past performance. The constraint here is that most people agree that realizing potential takes a lot of hard work. Buyers will therefore hesitate to make generous payments for future potential. Nonetheless, obtaining a higher price for your business based on future potential is not only possible, but common.

Make concrete suggestions for improvement, reminding the purchaser that you lacked sufficient funds to place all your ideas into action. Remind prospects that if they were to follow these ideas, they could dramatically increase the cash flow. Many buyers will have the confidence and ego to buy into the future, but only some will have the capital. Suggest to the prospective purchasers that they could franchise the company, open new marketing channels (e.g., the Internet), or bid on additional jobs. Use your imagination and be convincing.

As noted in Chapters 8 and 9, the valuation technique of choice for experts (and increasingly the IRS) is the future-oriented discounted cash flow technique (DCF), which holds that the value of any asset (or collection of assets) is the net present value of all associated cash inflows and outflows. If you choose to sell the future in conjunction with the past (as you properly should), you must document your assumptions. This means preparing a business plan that includes five-year projections of sales, expenses, and cash flows and plans outlining how to reach your targets. You must avoid making unjustifiable and noncredible claims. Placing a disclaimer into the business plan and in your purchase contract to the effect that you cannot, will not, and are not guaranteeing any level of future sales or profits is prudent. Beyond a minimal business plan, mission statements, value statements, marketing plans, and strategic plans can be quite useful. Have your employees read these documents if you take the time to prepare and discuss them with suitors.

Sell when the economy and your industry are strong. Having enjoyed three years of successive growth in sales and cash flow is also ideal. There is always the temptation to believe that next year will be even better. Near the end of recent expansions, business leaders and even trained economists have expressed their belief that perhaps the business cycle has been tamed once and for all. Don't count on it! As sure as the sun will rise tomorrow, there will be another recession, and it will impact the value of your business and the ease with which you can sell it.

Notify key employees of your decision to sell. This is a gray area and must be approached with caution. Many sellers do not want to tell their employees (including key employees) that the business is for sale out of fear that they will leave for a more stable position. Another reason is that they *will* talk! Customers, suppliers, competitors, neighbors, and friends will find out, sooner rather than later. The problem is, however, that by the time a suitor has met with you two or three times, after normal operating hours, they will want to interview key employees. There are also good reasons for informing key personnel right away. First, you might offer them the chance to buy the business. Second, you need their assistance in letting other employees, customers, and suppliers know what is transpiring. Basically, *they are the company* and must be treated with respect. You want them to speak favorably of the business, and you might even want to coach them about selling the future to prospects.

Other steps to consider, which do not involve informing the employees, include: create, maintain, and update employee files for all key personnel (background checks, resumes, confidentiality agreements, annual evaluations, etc., and calculate total cost per key employee; appeal your workers' compensation rating if you believe it is too high; create employee handbook; and document compliance with important personnel laws.

One final idea is to tie a bonus payable to key employees based on the price the business sells for. Higher sales price, higher bonus. Provisions guaranteeing continued employment in the event of sale for at least one to six months can also be reassuring (consult attorney for proper verbiage).

Avoid incurring excessive debt. Many business owners like to "have their cake and eat it too." They fail to report income to enjoy lower taxes, but expect the purchaser to believe that the sales are *really* more than what is on the books. Similarly, many owners believe that they can leverage the cash flow of a business and then sell it for more than its outstanding debt obligations. I have seen owners borrow thousands of dollars against the company's assets (personally guaranteed, of course) only to siphon these funds through bogus compensation. If the company owes you money, this will be considered an equity investment and you cannot expect to be compensated for this. If you owe the company money, this asset will have no value. Don't put yourself in the position of having debts greater than the fair market value of your business.

Turn verbal agreements into written agreements. A verbal understanding or contract is not enforceable; written agreements are. If properly addressed, this step will increase the marketability of your business. Suggestions include commission agreements with salespeople, manufacturer's reps, suppliers, and possibly key employees. A prospective owner will feel more confident if key suppliers are promising to deliver inventory for a definite period into the future. Remembering that key employees *are* the business, contracts for a minimum time period after sale will solidify the value. This process might be completed in conjunction with a comprehensive legal review of your business, ranging from analysis of your bylaws and their relationship to legally selling the business (corporate resolution to sell) to a thorough examination of all contractual commitments (e.g., leases, licenses, permits, loans and UCC filings).

Computerize your business. There is no excuse for not having your business fully computerized. Sales, inventory, A/R, A/P, cost of goods, fixed assets, taxes, etc. can all be tracked efficiently with computers. There are numerous accounting packages that are quite user-friendly. Notable examples include Peachtree (800-247-3224), QuickBooks Pro 4.0 (800-816-8025), and MAS 90 (800-854-3415). They are so user-friendly that many accountants are diversifying into other areas, such as securities and insurance sales, to make up for expected lost income from clients doing their own accounting. Don't forget the rising appeal of being on the Internet with your own home page on the World Wide Web. This is an indication of a progressive, attractive company.

Have key employees sign confidentiality/noncompete agreements. Without exception, all prospective purchasers must sign a confidentiality agreement prior to receiving the name, location, or financial and proprietary information. This is a *no exception* situation, whether your broker is introducing the business to prospects or you attempt to do it on your own. You might consider similar documentation for all key employees. Although it is difficult to prevent key employees from going to work for competitors, you certainly can try to prevent them from damaging your company for either yourself or a new owner. Consult your attorney for advice on this issue. Basic employment agreements should include clauses that restrict employees from revealing trade secrets to competitors or competing directly with the employer. The employees should be required to surrender all company paperwork prior to leaving the business. Including a provision for arbitration is also recommended. These non-compete agreements take on added importance during a transition period from one owner to the next as a result of wavering loyalties.

Obtain regulatory approvals. This is particularly relevant if your business has engaged in any type of manufacturing, processing, or distribution of toxic waste or any other environmentally unfriendly chemicals. Basically, if there are damages, they must be calculated and cleaned up with the approval of the federal EPA and similar state agencies. Look before you leap, and pay the money to have the appropriate environmental test performed by a credible company specializing in this area.

Notify landlord of possible sale. If your business operates subject to a lease, the value of your business is interwoven with the future of this agreement. If you surprise your landlord at the last minute, you might be rudely surprised. Bargaining power between landlords and tenants changes over the business cycle in different areas at different times. If your local economy is strong and occupancy and rents are rising, they feel this power and will not hesitate to flaunt it. The best advice is to notify land-lords or management companies early in the process, asking them to please remain quiet regarding your intentions to sell. It really is in their best interest to cooperate with you, but their egos can get in the way. By selling during a lease period that has several years remaining, you are creating an additional workload for them that will essentially create no income for them. Be prepared to remain on the lease until the original term expires. Let me stress the importance of obtaining renewal options. If you have a month-to-month lease, turn this into a period lease with options. The longer the cumulative option periods and the more fair the details regarding payment increases, the more valuable the business will be.

Renegotiate your lease. Before you notify your landlord of your intent to place the business for sale, consider evaluating your lease with a leasing consultant to make sure that you have not been overcharged (as compared to comparable rates in the area and in terms of year-end, common area maintenance adjustments). Also, you might attempt to renegotiate the terms of your lease toward lower payments and reduced security deposits. The ideal lease has minimal rent increases and multiple long-term options. Most bank loans to acquire established businesses will require lease terms at least equal to the repayment term.

Leasing consultants will often work on a commission basis and examine important issues such as paying for usable versus rentable space. The odds are that if you measure your space independently, it will be different than what the lease represents. The likelihood of being able to renegotiate your basic lease terms is a function of your negotiating skills and the current state of occupancy in the area. If the economy is growing and rents and occupancy are rising, your chances to obtain lower payments are slim. Adding an option or extending the lease are more likely and again will generally add value to your business. Excellent sources for information concerning commercial leases include: *Negotiating Commercial Real Estate Leases*, by Martin Zankel (Dearborn Financial Publishing, 800-982-2850) and the *Tenants Handbook of Office Leasing*, by Stanley Wolfson (McGraw-Hill, 800-262-4729). Chapters 6 and 7 contain more information on leases.

Increase role of key employees to reduce the business's dependence on owner for success. The goal here is to improve the chances for new owner success. A training provision and detailed transition arrangements will help, but allowing your current employees to assume greater responsibilities will strengthen the foundation and value of your business. Being able to confidently inform prospects that the business is not overly dependent on your skills is a major plus. Many would-be entrepreneurs are seeking opportunities where the business can run for long periods of time without their presence.

Continue to run the business as if you were remaining indefinitely. This seems contradictory to many of the preceding points. However, it might take six months to three years to consummate the sale, and you cannot lose focus of what it takes to keep your business profitable. The main problem occurs when the seller and buyer have reached agreement on price and terms and due diligence has begun. As the seller's confidence in the buyer and the probability of actually closing the sale grows, there is a tendency to lose control. This loss of control ranges from working fewer hours to avoiding important expenditures related to advertising, employee training, research and development, and other longer-term impact items. Maintain inventories, continue advertising, promote employee morale, and above all else keep your customers happy!

Prepare and sign a seller's disclosure statement. Refer to Figure 4.10. Full and upfront disclosure of all material facts, good and bad, will go a long way toward establishing your credibility and the quality of your operation. Take control of the situation and your credibility will lead to greater interest in you and your business.

Present a clear and credible reason for sale. One of the first questions asked by a prospective buyer is "Why is the owner selling?" The response to this question should be honest and consistent throughout the negotiating process. Buyers needs to know that there is a good reason for the sale as they begin to digest the facts related to your business. Their primary interest is to help establish the true financial health of the business. Obviously, there are many acceptable reasons for selling, including illness, breakup of partnership, retirement, and moving out of state. If your reason for sale changes from illness to lack of working capital as discussions unfold, your credibility is damaged and the buyer's faith in the business will be harmed.

Address work-in-progress balances in initial discussions with prospective buyers. In the rush to reach agreement, there is a tendency to overlook certain aspects of the sale. Normally, a certain dollar amount of inventory is included in the agreed on price, with either the down payment or the final price to be adjusted prior to closing. Also, all payables will be paid by seller and all receivables will belong to seller (unless otherwise agreed to). For manufacturing businesses, there is another asset that is often overlooked altogether or handled in a sloppy fashion. An accurately determined sales price should be adjusted for *work in progress* (WIP) just as it is adjusted for inventory in general. One reason that it tends to be avoided is that there is a degree of complexity in calculating this figure, requiring the use of subjective estimates. However, for some companies, work in progress (also referred to as work in process) can represent a notable percentage of current assets. If the decision is made on the part of the seller to seek payment for completed work in progress, it will most likely require an addition to the original offer (counteroffer) because most buyers will not include payment for work in progress as part of their original offers. Key issues include defining work in progress, determining overhead allocations, and accounting for a proper cutoff date. For inventory to be considered as work in progress, the following general conditions should apply:

- An order for a specific job at a specified price must have been received.
- A cash deposit equal to at least 40 percent must have been received.
- A majority percentage of the specific material used to complete the order must have been ordered, received, and paid for prior to close of escrow.
- Material must have been processed and labor utilized with the job well under way.

Special concerns include orders and deposits not yet considered WIP and outstanding warranty obligations. Address these issues head-on for durable results.

Consider terms. As described in the section covering promissory notes and chattel security agreements in Chapter 4, offering terms offers many distinct advantages to the seller, including quicker sale, higher price, and deferred taxes. If you agree to finance at least part of the purchase price for the buyer, you must exercise caution. Generally, the less cash purchasers put into the business, the easier it is for them to walk away when things "turn south." If you sell your business based on significant credit to the purchaser and the operating performance deteriorates, seller beware! Under these circumstances the following steps will strengthen your position:

- Review buyer's background and credit history as if you were a bank (obtain references).
- Consider arbitration as a means of settling disputes.
- Secure the seller's note with the assets of the business, the buyer's personal guarantee, and the pledging of specific assets.
- Include an evergreen, cross-default, and acceleration clause in the agreement.
- Prenegotiate right to reenter premises if buyer defaults on either the carry-back note or the lease (reassignment of lease clause).

Willful nonpayment is the most disappointing situation of all. The new owner has the money, the business is doing fine, but he chooses to delay or stop payments. He might claim that you, the seller, or the broker, misrepresented some material fact, over-stating the performance and value, basically saying "sue me" if you want your money. This is a lose-lose situation, but it happens. One solution is to rely on arbitration pro-ceedings to settle disputes, although this still entails costs (there must be a clause in the purchase agreement similar to the one in Chapter 5). There is another option that can give a strong signal to the buyer. Specifically, you can request that the deal include an *evergreen clause* and a *cross-default clause*. These are strongly worded provisions that protect the seller's interests. An *evergreen clause* requires that the new owner main-tain inventory and/or fixed assets at or above a certain dollar level. If this level is vio-lated, the seller's note is considered in default, with the outstanding balance immedi-ately due and payable. A *cross-default clause* stipulates that if the purchaser is in default on his or her lease, the carry-back note is also in default, and viceversa. This makes it easier for the seller to receive full payment, or if the new owner threatens harm to the business by neglecting lease payments, to reenter the business, assume the lease payments, and maintain the integrity of the operation. Carefully chosen words are required for maximum impact. A *reassignment of lease clause* is recommended to facilitate timely reentry by the seller. Attorney advice is mandatory.

Beware buyer tricks. Sellers must beware two buyer strategies that are highly unethical. They are the walk-away and straw man strategies, which can drastically improve a buyer's position via deceptive and unethical maneuverings. They are gen-erally difficult to detect, but if you are educated regarding their existence, you can exercise extra caution. The first case is that of *walk-away* artists. Their scheme is to negotiate a deal with the seller that appears to be credible and acceptable. They may appear to be savvy negotiators working to get every last concession from the seller. They are convincing enough that the seller is confident that the business will sell at the agreed on closing date. They will skillfully write the contract with at least one contingency that remains unresolved right up until closing. One such contingency involves financing. Although they might be bold enough to make a nonrefundable escrow deposit of $2,000 to $10,000, their offer and therefore the entire deal remains contingent on the buyer obtaining the stipulated financing. These buyers will consistently reassure the broker and seller that they will be getting the money (in certified funds) by the date of closing. All other steps that lead to a successful closing will proceed as expected. Due diligence is expeditiously completed and lease assignments are arranged. They may even purport to have hired a new manager or purchased a new product line, skillfully creating the appearance of real progress. The day before closing they regretfully inform the seller that their financing has fallen through. They state that they must call the deal off and are most apologetic. That is, until they call the seller early in the morning of the scheduled closing date (5 PM that afternoon) to share a brainstorm that might save the deal. If the seller will take an additional carry-back note for the down payment, they will not have to walk away. The buyers have been reassured by their lenders (maybe family members back home) that they will have the money within 45 days. Imagine the gravity of this predicament. At this point, the seller may have already made an offer to purchase a new business (nonrefundable escrow deposit) and bought tickets to tour Europe. This is besides the fact that the utilities have already been transferred, attorney and CPA fees of several thousand dollars have been paid, and most importantly, the seller is not in tune with running the business anymore. After powerful and emotional soul searching, the seller agrees to the additional temporary financing and the buyer walks into a quality business with virtually no money down.

The contingencies can be different, such as obtaining a favorable lease arrangement, hiring or retaining qualified managers under contract, etc. Or, the buyers can conduct a long, drawn-out due diligence period and prey on the seller's illness or other motivators by claiming that the business will not support the pre–due diligence price and terms. Either the seller agrees to a lower price, lower interest rate, longer payback, or any combination thereof, or the buyer might walk away. As a seller, you can protect yourself from this type of abuse by following some basic but often overlooked procedures. First of all, *insist on a definite and short period of time for due diligence to be completed.* If it is not completed within this period of time, the buyer better have a very good reason for an extension. Let the buyer know right up front that time is of the essence (in fact, this verbiage should be in the contract) and that you will provide all the necessary information on a timely basis. Second, request that the earnest money deposit be nonrefundable under certain conditions, such as after a certain period of time has passed. As described in Chapter 4, this is a delicate area in that buyers do not want to risk money on a business for which they have no verified information. On the other hand, sellers do not want just anybody who can write an earnest check (which after all is not usually deposited until the review is completed) to pry into the sacred details of the business. A possible solution for the seller is to request that the earnest check be nonrefundable after the original due diligence period has passed. If the buyer wants more time and the seller has been fully cooperative, the seller needs to be compensated, particularly if the business has been taken off the market. If a buyer will not agree to a nonrefundable deposit, the seller should have the right to continue showing the business and accept additional offers.

The *straw man* technique is not quite as risky for the buyer. The buyer sends in a relative, close friend, or trusted associate to evaluate the business as if they were genuinely interested and qualified to buy the operation. They discuss the finer points, evaluating the seller's "hot buttons" and motivations. It may even come to the presentation of an offer in search of the seller's reservation price, which is the bare minimum that he will accept, given a certain down payment. The seller can be tested as to his willingness to carry paper, precise terms of repayment, desired date of closing, etc. This straw man then withdraws and passes on all acquired insights to the buyer who is truly interested in the business if it can be had for the most favorable price and terms.

CHAPTER 13

Selling Your Business: Key Contractual Issues

Stock versus Asset Sale

An important decision to be made by owners of corporations (S or C) is whether to sell the company's stock or assets. In other words, should the mechanism for passing ownership be a *stock sale* or an *asset sale*. Motivations, advantages, and disadvantages differ greatly whether you are the buyer or the seller. The driving goal of most sellers is to receive as much cash as possible from the sale of the business. Part of reaching this goal involves careful consideration of tax implications, primarily capital gains. Accordingly, a seller (C Corporation) might prefer a stock sale to avoid double taxation (corporate and shareholder levels) of gain that accrues from an asset sale. Under the asset sale, liquidation leads to corporate taxes before shareholders receive their taxable income. Of course, electing S corporation status or LLC status can improve matters and should be carefully scrutinized. The primary problems associated with a stock sale (stock purchase for the buyer) are twofold. First, the *buyer assumes all liabilities, known and unknown.* Second, if the seller's assets are fully or near-fully depreciated, there are no substantial depreciation tax shields available for the new owner. This occurs because existing depreciation schedules are simply assumed by the new owners. *Lower depreciation means higher taxes and lower cash flow, which means less value.*

Tax Implications of a Stock Sale

The seller of a business under a stock sale will pay taxes based on the appreciation in value of the stock. The average investor in the stock investment is familiar with the concept. If you buy stock at $40 per share and sell at $60 per share, you have earned a capital gain of $20 per share and will be taxed accordingly. Currently, capital gains are taxed at a maximum of 28 percent, whether short term (stock held less than 12 months) or long term. Every buyer and seller should keep abreast of developments in all tax laws, with none being more important than the capital gains tax when it is time to sell. The actual calculation of the gain on a sale of stock for a small company is based on the difference between the amount received at closing (and over several years if there is seller financing) and the seller's taxable *basis* in the stock being sold. Basically, the seller's tax basis is affected by additional equity investments, accelerated depreciation deductions, use of investment tax credits, taxable dividends, liquidation of specific assets (tax is paid during the year of liquidation), and other factors. One important area of concern is what the IRS calls *depreciation recapture*, which basically amounts to an unwanted tax bill on the sale of most businesses. The calculation of this gain should be handled by tax professionals.

Tax Implications of an Asset Sale

The seller of a business for cash under an asset sale will generally be subject to taxation (capital gain or ordinary income) if the amount received is greater than the depreciated value or cost of the assets sold. The nature of the gain depends on the nature of the assets sold. This aspect of the sale requires careful scrutiny by your CPA or tax attorney and is dependent on the mutually agreed on allocation of purchase price as disclosed on IRS Form 8594 (Asset Acquisition Statement). The purchase price must be allocated among the various assets being sold, namely depreciable assets such as equipment and buildings, inventory, intangible assets other than goodwill, and goodwill. Agreement on allocation should be reached as part of the final sales document. For sellers who properly scrutinize this aspect of the sale, it is often sobering enough to deter the offering. The purchase price will be allocated among the acquired assets in proportion to their fair market values. The specific gain involved will depend on this allocation as follows:

- **Amounts allocated to fixed assets.** The seller will be taxed at either the corporate ordinary income tax rate or the capital gains rate, depending on such issues as depreciated tax basis, depreciation recapture, and prior year investment tax credits. Consult your CPA!
- **Amounts allocated to inventory.** This normally results in ordinary income to the seller. Consult your CPA!
- **Amounts allocated to other assets—intangible.** The gain here can be either ordinary or capital. Consult your CPA!
- **Amounts allocated to goodwill.** Gain on the sale of goodwill is a capital gain. Consult your CPA!

The way to look at this process is that when you sell your business under an asset sale, for tax purposes it is considered the sale of many separate assets. Basically, the chart in Figure 13.1 applies.

FIGURE 13.1 Asset Types and Tax Forms

Asset Type	IRS Form
1) Capital (fixed) assets such as equipment, buildings, land	Schedule D
2) Business—use Assets such as inventory	Form 4797
3) Other assets	Form 4797, Schedule C or F

For example, the sale of a retail business might consist of the sale of the building, land, shelves, displays, signs, inventory, and goodwill. The precise allocation must be agreed on, according to the IRS, under the so-called *residual* method. The purchase price will be allocated, in a prescribed fashion, to one of four classes as described below:

Class I.   Cash and cash equivalents (checking accounts)

Class II.   Near cash assets such as certificates of deposit, foreign currencies, U.S. government securities, and other highly liquid securities

Class III.   All assets that do not fit into the other three classes, including tangible and intangible assets (includes building, land, furniture, equipment, automobiles, and inventory).

Class IV.   Includes most intangible assets similar to what is commonly known as goodwill or going concern value.

The general procedure requires allocation first to Class I assets and then to Class II and III, in this order. The allocation must be based on fair market value at the time of sale. The residual amount is then allocated to Class IV.

Let's walk through the steps of such an allocation. A good place to begin is inventory, for which a value has probably been agreed to as part of the purchase contract, say $50,000, to be adjusted up or down near closing. If adjustments are made, the allocation is to be adjusted accordingly. Different buyers will proceed in various ways from here. Some are interested in obtaining a minimal allocation to inventory and a maximum allocation to fixed assets, in search of future tax deductions (depreciation) and a taxable gain on the sale of the business figured as a capital gain (which is presently less the ordinary income in most cases). On the other hand, certain buyers will look for a minimum allocation to inventory, in search of immediate, first-year write-offs against taxable income. The downside is that if the overallocation is extreme, the IRS might disallow the entire allocation and allocate as it sees fit! Second, this will certainly increase the seller's immediate tax burden, to the extent that the taxation of ordinary income is presently higher than capital gains taxes (remember that capital gains presently are taxed as ordinary income up to a maximum of 28 percent).

Next we move on to plant and equipment (FF&E). Motivations are fairly clear here. The buyer wants a large allocation for greater depreciation amounts each year in the future. One mitigating factor is the fact the buyer (in many states) will pay a personal property tax based to varying degrees on the allocated value of these assets. The seller ideally looks for a value close to the book value for tax purposes (depreciated tax basis), which is original cost less accumulated depreciation and adjusted for special accelerated deductions and/or investment tax credits. A special concern here for the seller is the *depreciation recapture*, which leads to taxation at ordinary income levels and payments, due immediately. If the allocation to fixed assets is greater than the seller's depreciated tax basis, the excess (up to the original cost) is taxable as depreciation recapture. If, by agreement, the allocation to these fixed assets is greater than the original cost, the excess would be a clear-cut capital gain. A worst case situation for the seller would be a generous allocation to fixed assets that were fully depreciated, coupled with a minimal down payment toward the purchase of the business (perhaps only enough to cover the broker's commission). This could be a real problem (deal-breaker?) if the seller doesn't have sufficient cash to meet the associated depreciation recapture tax. Most sellers are hesitant to pay for the sale of their business!

Another common category relevant for this type of allocation is leasehold improvements, which in many ways resemble intangible assets since the owner cannot take them when he leaves. Therefore, they are normally treated as a capital (fixed) asset for tax purposes, which means they are also subject to depreciation recapture taxes.

Thus far, we have discussed allocations to tangible assets only: inventory, equipment, and leasehold improvements. If the purchase price exceeds these allocated amounts and the cash and accounts receivables remain the property of the seller, the balance must be allocated to one or more intangible assets (Class IV on Form 8594). If there is a noncompete agreement, as normally there is, a fair amount should be allocated here. As previously mentioned, from a tax standpoint, it doesn't really matter how the excess of the purchase price is allocated among the intangibles given that they are all amortized over 15 years. You can still, apparently, find trouble if you overallocate to this covenant, which could be struck down as unreasonable (even if you go to the trouble of executing a noncompete agreement separate from the purchase contract), possibly harming the seller. *Consult your tax attorney or CPA as to what might be deemed reasonable in your situation.*

A slightly different situation exists for employment contracts and consulting agreements. Employment contracts are a useful mechanism for keeping the seller active in the business, hopefully to the benefit of the new owner. The problem for the seller is that these agreements will lead to ordinary income as opposed to capital gains, likely increasing the tax bill. Furthermore, the dreaded self-employment tax (approximately 15 percent) must be paid on any such earnings. My advice is to use these agreements only as supplements to a deal and not part of the deal (allocation).

Familiarization clauses (training agreements) are also quite common and will generate a quick deduction for the buyer, obviously at the expense of the seller. Once again, the seller is liable for the added ordinary income tax burden and the substantial self-employment tax. When the seller is forced to pay this extra tax as part of the deal, it will certainly appear less attractive. All in all (and most commonly), the training agreement is included as part of the sale and allocated a relatively minor amount.

Finally, everyone is familiar with the "mother of all intangible assets"—goodwill. Whether the allocation is made to goodwill specifically, customer lists, trade name, trade secrets, telephone number, or any other such intangible assets, the tax implication is the same—amortized over 15 years. As a final note, remember that if the actual final amount of consideration paid to the seller changes after the original allocation (due to earn-out provisions or an unpaid carry-back note), an amendment must be filed as described later in the section covering Form 8594.

If you present your business to a prospective buyer as an asset sale, you might receive an offer to buy the stock. If you present your business as a stock sale, you might receive an offer to purchase the assets. There are major differences between the two options and you must closely examine the repercussions of each. Consider the table in Figure 13.2 as a general guide to this issue.

FIGURE 13.2 Overview of Advantages and Disadvantages of Asset versus Stock Sale

Sale of Assets

Advantages to Seller
1. Seller maintains certain assets such as selected patents, trademarks, licenses.
2. Seller keeps corporate name (sells DBA and trade names only).
3. Seller preserves corporate status for further endeavors.

Disadvantages to Seller
1. Double taxation—corporately at time of liquidation, then individually as shareholders
2. Generally more involved as specific assets must be transferred
3. Calculation of gain/loss also more complicated, depending on asset category

Advantages to Buyer
1. Buyer allowed to redepreciate assets based on allocation of purchase price.
2. Buyer has flexibility to purchase only selected assets.
3. Buyer does not automatically assume known or unknown liabilities.
4. Buyer is free to handle employee insurance and other benefit plans as desired.

Disadvantages to Buyer
1. Buyer cannot utilize tax benefits of selling corporation, such as tax loss carry-forward.
2. Buyer might forego rights to corporate name and certain patents and licenses.
3. Buyer helps pay cost of transferring title to all assets.
4. Buyer may lose the benefits of the selling corporation's favorable insurance ratings (liability, unemployment, workers' compensation).

Sale of Stock

Advantages to Seller
1. Avoids double taxation of corporation and then shareholders (remember S corporations are exempt from double taxation).
2. All liabilities (except those arising from fraudulent behavior), known and unknown, pass to the new owner.
3. Calculation of capital gain on stock is less cumbersome than calculating capital gain on ordinary income for each asset category.
4. Allows a clean break.

Disadvantages to Seller
1. Can lose use of net operating losses against future income elsewhere.
2. Must generally sell all assets (cannot pick and choose).
3. Loss of use of corporate name.

Advantages to Buyer
1. Favorable tax attributes are obtained (net loss carry-forwards, unused investment tax credits, etc.).
2. Lower closing costs (stock certificates are signed)
3. May avoid sales tax.
4. Buyer maintains continuity of legal relationships with suppliers, customers, and employees.

Disadvantages to Buyer
1. Costlier due diligence efforts (must investigate all liabilities, known and unknown)
2. Fixed assets cannot be redepreciated (depreciation schedules continue).
3. All liabilities, known and unknown, are assumed.

Note: This table should be used only as a general overview of the important issues involved in stock and asset sales. Actual situations differ greatly and should be analyzed by tax and legal professionals. Consult your CPA or attorney for current insights and interpretations.

Seller's Proceeds

When you have moved along into a deal that appears to be acceptable in more ways than not (e.g., price, terms, training, date of closing, qualifications of buyer), you will naturally begin to think about the bottom line. There are several considerations to be made when calculating the actual cash flowing to a seller. For example, security deposits, commissions, and prorations must be addressed. A sample guideline is shown in Figure 13.3.

FIGURE 13.3 Guideline for Calculating Seller's Proceeds from Sale

Cash Inflows

Earnest Check Deposit
+ Additional down payment
+ Inventory (if sold separately)
+ Work-in-progress payments
+ Security deposits (property, utility, equipment leases)
+ Credit for prepaid expenses (utilities, insurance, service contracts)
+ Credit for prorated rent
+ Probable collections on accounts receivable
+ Inflows

Cash to seller at or near time of closing

– Commission
– Attorney, CPA fees
– Closing Costs (UCC search, document prep, filing and recording fees, note servicing)
– Payment of outstanding liabilities (suppliers, income, payroll and sales taxes, back rent, working capital loans, previous seller carry-back note, credit card loans, other bank loans)
– Costs incurred to replace/repair equipment and clean up business to meet terms of agreement
– Lease transfer fees and miscellaneous franchise-related fees, if applicable

Seller's net proceeds from sale after closing

From here, you must account for any future payments to be received on a carry-back note or as part of an employment contract. Realizing that each situation is different, you must think as precisely as possible to determine the true cash proceeds you will receive from the sale. For example, it is fairly common for a certain portion of the down payment to be held in escrow for 30 to 90 days after closing as insurance against any unexpected or overlooked liabilities of the seller. These monies are often referred to as set-aside funds. Additionally, it is fair to include assumptions of debt by the new owner under an asset sale as part of the purchase price and seller's proceeds. Finally, *the seller will probably owe a substantial capital gains tax as a result of the sale,* which will materially reduce the amount of seller's proceeds.

For larger corporate sales via stock, the calculations are basically the same as for asset sales of smaller businesses. One notable difference, of course, would be that under a stock sale, the purchase price includes assumption of all assets (including accounts receivable, work in progress, and occasionally cash) and all liabilities (including accrued payroll expenses and accounts payable).

Important Contract Provisions

When it comes time to actually writing the purchase agreement or counteroffer thereto, consider including one or more of the following pro-seller clauses no matter how favorable your impression of the buyer is. Remember that buyers are normally the first to move aggressively into a deal and will try to take control by slanting the offer in their favor. You must be prepared to request changes as well as make concessions. You must also be prepared to spend a few dollars to receive competent legal advice. *Before reviewing the following clauses, make sure you have a solid understanding, practical and theoretical, of the major components that make up a complete purchase contract (e.g., conditions, contingencies, warranties).* (See Chapters 4 and 5.)

Clause 1

Buyer agrees to provide the following information to the seller within five working days from date of signature below:
- Current personal financial statement (statement of net worth)
- Federal and state tax returns for past three years (preferably five)
- Current credit report from two leading agencies
- Any other materials/information reasonably required to evaluate purchaser's background and intent.

If purchaser does not provide the above information to the satisfaction of seller, seller may rescind this agreement by providing written notice (registered mail) to purchaser.

The tone and depth of this clause is subject to variation depending on the size of the deal and the particular relationship between buyer and seller. A more simple and inoffensive clause would be:

Clause 2

Acceptance is contingent upon favorable seller review of purchaser's credit and background.

Some form of broad *seller contingency* like the ones above should be included in the agreement. You will likely need to write your own clause (with your broker or attorney) into a counteroffer, since many purchasers do not include this pro-seller contingency in their offers to purchase.

In legal terms, counteroffers "run with the offer" in that only the terms that specifically differ from the original offer are deemed to be changed by the counter. In other words, all information included in the original offer will stand as is unless explicitly overridden by the counter (e.g., a higher price and down payment).

A second important type of clause addresses the topic of earnest money deposits. The amount should be large enough to give the buyer a strong incentive to close (once due diligence is completed) and to compensate the seller fairly with liquidated damages if the buyer breaches the contract. *The more contingencies there are and the longer until the scheduled closing, the more the escrow deposit should be.* You should not completely open your books to a buyer who has not written an earnest check either to be held by the broker or placed into escrow. There are many reasons why buyers might try to get a "free look" at your business, including to obtain access to proprietary company information, to evaluate financial data such as gross margin, break-even points, and pricing as they consider opening a similar business from scratch, to generate insights that might help buyers attract financing to purchase the business, or to learn more about key employees/suppliers/customers.

On the other hand, it is clear that buyers of a business should expect to be able to conduct a thorough due diligence without risking their money. Offers are made based on the unaudited presentation of data by the seller (only larger companies tend to have audited statements).

Most brokers will write an offer to purchase clearly stating the price, terms, conditions, and contingencies. The earnest deposit check ranges from a mere $500 up to 25 to 50 percent of the total price. The amount of the check should be large enough to serve two purposes: (1) *to give the purchaser incentive to close the deal,* (2) *to create a situation whereby the seller can be provided liquidated damages in the event that the buyer backs out.* Another option is to seek additional deposits throughout the sales process (e.g., on removal of all contingencies). Beyond consideration of a percent of the purchase price, the following additional factors should be looked at: duration of closing period, potential harm to seller if deal fails to materialize, and the chance that buyer will not close (i.e., excessive open-ended contingencies). In most cases, the earnest check is written to a separate, third party account (broker, attorney, or escrow company).

My preference is to see the *earnest check* written (for at least 10 percent of the purchase price) to the escrow company with directions in the purchase contract to the broker to hold the check, uncashed, until all contingencies are removed; and only then will it be placed into escrow, as follows:

Clause 3

Broker is directed to hold earnest check uncashed until all contingencies are removed. On signed removal of all contingencies by buyer and seller, the earnest deposit will be placed into escrow (escrow will be opened) and held there until closing.

Most formal offer forms will contain specific instructions as to how these escrow funds will be handled and when they become nonrefundable. The buyer may ask that the funds be returned on request if due diligence fails. If an offer includes a buyer contingency such as the "favorable review of books, records, and operations," any excuse for not proceeding will be sufficient to request return of the check. *The earnest check, under these conditions is in fact risk-free until the money is deposited into escrow.* In other words, the buyer could claim that the "carpet was stained" and call the deal off without loss of funds *unless* escrow has been opened. *Once escrow has been opened, the escrow money is normally at risk.* Escrow will not normally be opened until all contingencies are removed. When handling due diligence proceedings and escrow deposits, try to be as clear and precise as possible. Require registered mail to notify the seller that the due diligence results were unfavorable and that the earnest funds should be returned. Precise time constraints should be placed on all activities. Consider the following clause:

Clause 4

Earnest Funds: Purchaser and seller hereby instruct broker to hold buyer's earnest money funds uncashed until all the contingencies (buyer's and seller's) have been removed. In the event that they are not satisfied and removed, the earnest deposit shall be returned to purchaser in full and without penalty. Buyer's earnest deposit is accepted by broker subject to prior sale and seller's executed acceptance of buyer's offer. If buyer fails to perform after removal of contingencies and opening of escrow and prior to or on the closing date, the earnest deposit shall be considered liquidated damages and shall be paid to the seller (and broker, if agreed to in listing contract between broker and seller).

One term above requires further discussion: *prior sale.* When the phrase "subject to prior sale" is included in the contract, this implies that other offers will be considered until all contingencies are removed and escrow is opened. This is a polite way of informing the buyer that there is no deal until all contingencies are removed and escrow funds are placed at risk. There is no area as sensitive as *backup offers.* Consider the following clauses:

Clause 5

Escape Clause: It is agreed that in the event seller receives a bona fide, noncontingent offer on the assets of the subject business during the term of this agreement, seller agrees to give written notice of such an offer to purchaser and purchaser shall have ____ days from receipt of such notice to remove all buyer's contingencies contained herein. In the event buyer is unable to remove all said contingencies within ____ day period, this agreement shall be rendered null and void and earnest check shall be immediately returned to buyer.

Clause 6

One Backup Offer. It is agreed that seller has accepted a contingent offer from a third party for the purchase of subject business. In the event that seller and third party negotiate the removal of the contingencies contained in said offer within the time periods allowed, this agreement shall be rendered null and void and earnest funds returned to buyer. However, in the event that said contingencies are not removed within the time periods allowed, this agreement shall become effective immediately. For all purposes herein, the date of mutual acceptance shall be the date on which this agreement becomes effective as provided in this paragraph.

Please recognize that based on Clauses 5 and 6, there is no deal until acceptance is communicated to the buyer. In the event that counteroffers have been made on outstanding deals, the following clauses might be appropriate:

Clause 7

Executed Counteroffer. It is understood that seller has executed a counteroffer to a third party for the sale of subject business. In the event that said counteroffer is accepted and seller and said third party negotiate the removal of the contingencies contained in said counteroffer within the time periods allowed, this agreement shall be rendered null and void and earnest check returned to buyer. However, in the event that said counteroffer is not accepted nor the contingencies removed within the time periods allowed therein, this agreement shall become effective immediately on communication to buyer of such fact. For all purposes herein, the date of mutual acceptance shall be the date on which this agreement becomes effective and was so communicated as provided in this paragraph.

Clause 8

Approval of Third Party. This contract is contingent on written approval by _____ within ____ days from execution by buyer and seller. In the event that _____ does not notify buyer and seller in writing of said approval in the appropriate time frame, this agreement shall no longer be considered as valid and enforceable, i.e., it will be considered null and void.

Occasionally, *third parties* must approve the sale of a business. Chief among these interested parties are banks, or previous owners that have extended credit to the current owner, and occasionally landlords. In most cases, if the prospective buyer is capable of bringing sufficient cash to the closing that will retire in full the outstanding balance, there will be no problems in receiving this approval. Buyers must ask the sellers directly if there are any contractual prohibitions on the sale that must be formally addressed to allow a legal sale.

The following clause relates to *close of escrow*:

Clause 9

Closing of this transaction shall occur on or before 11-11-99 (herein referenced to as "Closing") unless mutually extended in writing by the parties hereto. The parties designate Honest Escrow, Inc. to act as escrow agent for this sale, and each party agrees to pay one-half of the escrow agent's fees and expenses in connection with its services. This Purchase Agreement, when fully executed by the applicable parties, shall constitute the escrow instructions, except in the event that escrow agent shall seek to draw up separate escrow instructions using the same terms and conditions herein, provided, however, that in the event of any discrepancy between the terms and conditions of such escrow instructions and the provision of this Purchase Contract, the latter shall control. Close of escrow shall be deemed to be the date of delivery of possession (unless otherwise agreed on between buyer and seller) of the business and assets to the buyer. This date shall also serve as date of proration of rent, taxes, assessments, insurance, utilities, and all other charges, payments, or prepaid expenses relating to the subject business, its assets and the operation of the company.

After contingencies are removed and escrow is opened, there are serious potential consequences to the buyer or seller backing out unilaterally. If either party backs out against the will of the other party, the harmed party can file legal suit or, if the purchase contract contains an arbitration clause, institute arbitration proceedings. Arbitration clauses were presented in Chapters 4 and 5.

We are presently analyzing the role of escrow deposits specifically and default generally. After the buyer has conducted a favorable review of books and records (due diligence), escrow is opened and the check is deposited by the broker. The buyer is making a good faith down payment toward the purchase of the subject business and, in turn, the seller is removing the business from the market and relying on the promise of the buyer to bring the necessary funds to the scheduled closing in certified funds. The fact that the seller is now relying on the buyer to perform in exchange for pulling the business off the market is the foundation for possible legal damages to either side.

The term *damages* in general refers to the loss of money (value) by one party as the result of another party's action (or inaction). These *wrongful acts* take many different forms, but the common link between them is that one party causes injury and another party is injured, leading to claims for reimbursement to be made *whole*. Remedies for buyer and seller include the following: specific performance (the court orders the buyer to buy or the seller to sell or some variation thereof or monetary damages), escrow deposits can be forfeited, or additional payments required by the court or arbitrator.

Once agreement has been reached on price and terms, contingencies have been removed, and escrow opened, the game is now "for real." The buyer might leave his or her current employment or the seller may make a down payment on another business. Both sides are relying on each other. Consider the following clause referring to *breach of contract* and damages:

Clause 10

In the event of any anticipatory or other breach of this agreement for sale by any party hereto, or on the failure of this transaction to close due to the wrongful actions or failures to act of either party hereto, this agreement shall be deemed to be in default. In that event, the nondefaulting or nonbreaching party may immediately cease performance and avail such breach or default, including, in the case of default by seller, buyer's right to specific performance and in the event of default by buyer, seller's retention of the earnest money deposit as liquidated damages. In the event of default by buyer, seller may at its option pursue any and all available remedies against buyer.

Most buyers expect the seller to cease marketing the business during the due diligence period. The seller should understand this and give the buyer time to move forward without being "bested" by another party. The seller knows that the earnest check is more or less fully refundable, reducing its significance greatly. If the buyer will agree to make a certain portion of the escrow deposit nonrefundable, it becomes quite reasonable to request that the seller take the business off the market. The buyer, in effect, can purchase the sole right to buy. Otherwise, the seller is justified to request the right to continue showing the business and accepting other offers. There are many possibilities between the extremes of "off the market completely" and "taking all offers," such as requesting the right to continue showing the business and accept *backup offers*, as follows:

Clause 11

Seller maintains right to continue showing the business and receive backup offers until closing.

Note that *receiving* backup offers may not be the same thing as *accepting* them. If the word accept replaced receive above, then it becomes possible that the owner intends not only to continue marketing and showing the business, but also to enter into contracts for sale. *It is critical that precise intentions be spelled out carefully.* If the seller accepts a subsequent backup offer, what does this mean? Is it truly only a backup, as in secondary, offer, or is it meant to replace the first offer if it is superior in price and terms. Consider this:

Clause 12

Seller maintains right to continue marketing, showing, and accepting offers until closing. Seller shall have the right to accept these subsequent offers at any time prior to purchaser formally removing all contingencies. Seller may rescind this agreement by providing written notice via registered mail within three working days of accepting second offer. Buyer has three working days from receipt of the registered notice to remove all remaining contingencies and formally notify seller and escrow agency via registered mail. If purchaser fails to remove outstanding contingencies and notify seller and escrow company on a timely basis, seller may, at own option, terminate this contract and return the earnest funds back to purchaser.

Clause 12 gives the original buyer what is known technically as *right of first refusal*. As the clause above is written, the buyer need not "meet or beat" the subsequent offer, but simply remove the remaining contingencies to his or her offer quickly and move forward on the deal. The seller could strengthen his or her position here by requiring the buyer to meet or beat the new offer, if it is superior. As always, you must be sensitive to the "big picture" (i.e., relative bargaining strengths) when you make demands on the other party that may be found objectionable. You must weigh the pluses and minuses of each clause in light of the particular circumstances at hand.

Another important clause that is often overlooked by sellers relates to the *future resale* of the business to another party. The best way to provide maximum protection for the seller is to include a clause such as the following, which will at a minimum make it clear to the new owners that they cannot legally sell the assets until all liabilities to the seller are satisfied:

Clause 13

Buyer may not resell the assets of the business as a whole or in parts, or allow reassignment or sublease of any lease obligations to a third party as part of the sale of the business as long as the seller is owed monies by the original buyer or is remaining liable in any fashion for lease payments of any kind associated with the business.

The seller does not want to take the risk of providing credit to a buyer who may be qualified to successfully run the business only to have this buyer sell, perhaps at a profit, to a third party that may not be as qualified in the eyes of the seller. Of course, if the seller is paid in full and is removed from all other obligations, such as lease and equipment payments, there should be no reason to disapprove the sale. Related to the right of the buyer to resell the business is the right of assignment. As a rule, it is wise to prevent the buyer from assigning the contract to third parties (e.g., assignees, successors) without written approval of the seller. Any such assignment could cause the seller to deal contractually with an unknown third party.

Three more clauses that serve to uniquely protect the seller's interest in the case of seller financing are the *evergreen clause*, *cross-default clause*, and *reassignment of lease clause*.

First, the evergreen clause requires the buyer to maintain inventory and/or fixed assets at or above a certain minimum dollar value (typically as measured by original cost), as follows:

Clause 14

Buyer agrees and covenants that the inventory items that make up the core of the seller's business, e.g., _____, shall be maintained subsequent to purchase of the business and up to the time when the entire seller carryback note is paid in full at a dollar amount greater than or equal to $_____, as measured by original, invoiced cost (after discounts). Furthermore, the existing leasehold improvements, furniture, fixtures, and equipment, as described on the asset list accompanying the purchase agreement, shall be maintained at a dollar amount greater than or equal to $_____, as measured subsequently by invoiced cost, up until the seller's note is paid in full. During such period, the seller shall have the right to inspect and audit the levels of such inventory and other assets as requested, but no more than four times per year. If the inventory or asset levels are determined to be below the acceptable levels by more than 10 percent, the promissory note shall be considered in default and the entire outstanding balance is immediately due and payable.

Clause 15

In the event that the promissory note between seller (creditor) and buyer (borrower) is deemed to be in default (as described in the terms and conditions of the note and the related chattel security agreement), immediately and at the same time the lease with the landlord shall be considered in default. If the property lease is deemed to be in default, immediately and at the same time the promissory note shall be deemed in default.

This cross-default clause will allow the seller to reenter the premises and assume the rental payments immediately to preserve the integrity of the going concern and to protect the seller's ongoing commitment and responsibility to make the required lease payments.

Clause 16

In the event of default on the promissory note by borrower (purchaser), seller will be allowed to reenter the location and reclaim ownership to the property, fixtures, and equipment secured by said note. The seller will be obligated under such conditions to pay all past due rents.

The above version of a reassignment of lease clause is between the seller (creditor and assignor) and the buyer (borrower and assignee). Normally, of course, the landlord will have some say in this matter, and preapproval of such a move is highly recommended. Consider the following:

Clause 17

The undersigned landlord hereby agrees to grant reentry by holder of promissory note referred to in above reassignment clause. This right of reentry shall become null and void when promissory note is paid in full. If the lease falls into default status, lessor agrees to give holder of promissory note 15 days after notice by certified mail to cure said default.

Any well-written offer to purchase will include numerous warranties and representations agreed to by the seller (as presented in Chapter 4 and 5). The seller can and should also require the buyer to agree to certain statements, warranties, and representations, protecting the seller's legal position. These items often relate to the buyer's understanding of the business and the fact that the *seller cannot promise future profits* in any meaningful fashion. Consider the following:

Clause 18

> After a careful and thorough due diligence review related to this business, the purchaser is satisfied that the books and records are materially accurate, that the buyer is capable of successfully operating the business, and that all profits in the future are dependent solely on the buyer's efforts and knowledge.

Business brokers will try to avoid any responsibility regarding claims of past, present, and future business performance. The seller will sign a listing contract, which states that the broker is relying on the truthfulness of the seller regarding any and all operational or financial data. Furthermore, the broker will require the buyer to sign a nondisclosure form that contains a protective clause releasing the broker from any responsibility regarding the seller's claims. *Although the broker cannot fraudulently mislead anyone, the burden is firmly on the seller to be truthful and the buyer to be careful and thorough in terms of due diligence.*

For a company being presented as an asset sale, there is a chance that legal counsel for the buyer or seller might feel that the optimal structure for the sale could be a sale of stock (securities). An informed seller and experienced business broker will agree to include a provision or clause similar the one that follows here in order to clarify the broker's right to a commission or finder's fee:

Clause 19

> Seller agrees that in the event that the broker is the procuring cause for the sale of the company's assets via a stock sale, the broker will have earned and will be owed the total commission/finder's fee as agreed on for the sale of assets only.

As a practical matter, Clause 19 may be found either in the listing contract or in the purchase contract. The major difference, of course, is that the buyer must also sign off on such a clause if it is in the purchase agreement.

If you are selling your business under *distressed conditions*, there are unique clauses to be inserted into the agreement. Every purchase agreement should include an acknowledgment by the purchaser that the seller cannot and is not guaranteeing any level of future sales or profits. It is one thing to warrant that the historical earnings are accurate and quite another thing to guarantee future success. A simple clause like the following is a good start:

Clause 20

> After a thorough review of the books, records, and operations, buyer has satisfied himself that he has the financial resources and business acumen to

successfully run this business. Buyer also acknowledges and understands that future profits from the operation of this company are in no way guaranteed by the seller.

Another area of concern that can be easily addressed involves the *condition of equipment* and other fixed assets. Consider this clause:

Clause 21

Purchaser is buying this business, including the furniture, fixtures, equipment, and other assets, as described on the attached equipment list, Exhibit X, "AS IS," and with all faults. Any and all implied warranties, including the implied warranties of merchantibility and fitness for a particular purpose, are hereby disclaimed. Seller has made and will make no express warranty of any kind in connection with these assets. Accordingly, purchaser acknowledges that he/she has had ample opportunity to inspect all such assets to his/her complete and irrevocable satisfaction.

Closing

This is the place to be. Whether you are buying, selling, advising, or brokering, this is the final destination. A successful deal requires a successful closing. Closing can occur anywhere—at the seller's location, at the buyer's attorney's office, or an independent third party location such as an escrow company. As a business broker, I recommend that closing for almost all small companies take place with the help of an escrow company. The escrow company provides an element of independence and lack of bias to the process. The company will try to ensure that the transfer of ownership occurs legally and smoothly. Many buyers believe that paying closing fees to an escrow company is an avoidable, unnecessary cost. If attorneys and brokers have been actively involved in creating, reviewing, and approving the sales documents (bill of sale, promissory note, contract for sale, bulk sales waiver, lease assignment), perhaps it is overkill to pay the closing costs. However, an escrow company specializing in business sales offers extensive experience and neutral advice, both of which may be lacking for a given deal. The escrow company will prepare all the necessary documents, conduct a lien search, prorate and allocate closing-related adjustments such as rents, payroll taxes, insurance, etc., and for a nominal fee they will handle future payments made against a seller carry-back note. The company has notary publics who can witness the signing of documents. The escrow company will process the payments from buyer to seller. Chapter 4 presented several escrow-related clauses.

A sample sole and exclusive agreement is provided in Figure 13.4.

FIGURE 13.4 Sample Sole and Exclusive Agreement

LISTING CONTRACT
SOLE AND EXCLUSIVE RIGHT TO SELL

SUBJECT BUSINESS: Legal Business Name/dba: _____

_____

Address (street, city, state, zip):

_____

County and Phone Number :

_____

Type/Category of Business:

_____

Owner(s) (as shown on business/liquor license): _____

Ownership Structure: ( ) Individual ( ) Partnership ( ) Limited Liability Company
( ) Corporation

Key Contact/Title : _____ Personal Telephone Number: _____

If corporation, names of President _____ and Secretary _____

Name of Partnership, LLC, or Corporation if different from dba listed above:

_____

Seller's Estimates of: Annual Sales Volume _____ Adjusted Cash Flow _____

Asset Value _____

Listing Terms and Provisions

Based on the mutual promises set forth below, _____ (Broker) and
_____ (Seller) hereby agree as follows:

1. Seller hereby appoints _____ as seller's agent (broker),
   granting to broker the sole, exclusive, and irrevocable right to sell, exchange,
   lease, trade, or otherwise dispose of all or any portion of the business
   described above, including but not limited to its tangible and intangible assets,
   including furniture, fixtures, equipment, inventory, trademarks, trade names,
   customer lists, telephone number and listing, customer deposits, goodwill,
   licenses, and franchises on the proposed terms set forth herein or for any other
   terms to which seller agrees during the sole and exclusive period beginning on
   _____ and ending _____.

2. Broker hereby pledges to use its best efforts as part of broker's ordinary course
   of business to offer for sale and to procure a ready, willing, and able purchaser
   for the business. If required by seller, broker agrees to perform the specific
   marketing procedures as outlined in Addendum A to this contract. Broker is
   authorized to present any and all offers broker may receive in writing, until

FIGURE 13.4 Sample Sole and Exclusive Agreement, continued

such time as seller accept(s) an offer to purchase. Seller agrees to advise broker as to how to handle backup offers. Further, seller(s) grants to broker the right to show the business during normal business hours and the right to generically advertise the business. Finally, seller(s) agrees to review and respond to all offers to purchase in a timely fashion.

3. Broker is entitled to and seller agrees to pay a commission equal to _____ percent of the total purchase price (which includes cash and all other consideration furnished by buyer, including without limitation, the purchase price of the assets plus any obligations assumed by buyer or the purchase price of corporate stock plus all liabilities assumed by buyer in conjunction with purchase of said stock) *or* a minimum of $_____, whichever is more, on or before closing, if any of the following occur:

   A. Broker procures a ready, willing, and, able buyer during the sole and exclusive period on the proposed terms set forth below, or as otherwise mutually agreed on between buyer and seller, *or*

   B. Seller sells, exchanges, leases, trades, or otherwise transfers any portion of the business during the sole and exclusive period, regardless of whether or not the broker was involved in or responsible for such transfer, or seller enters into a contract for sale without broker's assistance, accepts a deposit and/or opens escrow or formally gives notice of intent to sell, e.g. filing for bankruptcy reorganization/liquidation, *or*

   C. Seller unilaterally takes business off the market during the term of this agreement or intentionally hinders or refuses to complete a sale, exchange, lease, or trade after contractually agreeing to do so with buyer, *or*

   D. Seller sells, exchanges, leases, trades, or otherwise disposes of all or any part of the business within (2) years after expiration of this agreement (inclusive of amendments to extend this agreement) to any person(s), firm, or entity found by or registered with broker, or who became aware of business through broker's endeavors during listing period.

Broker may agree to waive compliance with any of the above conditions, but only with written, notarized notice signed by broker.

4. Seller represents and warrants that seller and the business are now and shall remain, in full compliance with all local, state, and federal laws, rules, and regulations regarding the operation and sale of the business.

5. Broker and seller hereby acknowledge that the transfer or other disposition of the lease (if applicable) for the above referenced business premises is only incidental to the sale of the business. No part of the broker's fee payable hereunder is consideration for services rendered, if any, in connection to the

FIGURE 13.4 Sample Sole and Exclusive Agreement, *continued*

lease transfer. In the event that a new lease is to be negotiated and executed, broker is entitled to a commission equal to _____ percent of gross rental payments over the entire duration of said lease. Broker is hereby given permission to contact landlord as soon as deemed necessary.

6. Seller understands and hereby acknowledges that all facts, figures, and all additional supporting documentation pertaining to the business, has been provided to broker by seller, and that broker will rely on seller's representation of such facts, figures, and other information when describing and promoting the business to potential purchasers without an investigation into the accuracy of such representations by seller. Therefore, seller hereby represents and warrants that all such facts, figures, and all additional supporting documents are true and accurate. Seller hereby agrees to indemnify and hold harmless broker against any all claims, demands, causes for actions, losses, damages, cost, and expenses including reasonable attorney's fees and fees on appeals arising out of breach of the warranty, and further agrees that the county in which broker's office is located, designated above, is proper venue for any dispute.

7. Seller will reimburse the broker for reasonable attorney's fees and all other cost and expenses incurred by broker in enforcing this agreement. Seller hereby grants broker a lien on all the assets and properties of the business to secure the payment to broker of all amounts payable by seller to broker under this contract, and seller appoints broker its attorney-in-fact to prepare on behalf of seller and to file the necessary documents to evidence and perfect said lien.

8. As agent for seller(s), broker, cooperating brokers (cobroker) and/or selected escrow agents are authorized to accept and hold all monies paid or deposited toward purchase of said business (with instructions explicitly described in relevant purchase offer/contract). In the event that buyer must forfeit said deposit (in accordance with instructions in relevant purchase offer/contract), broker is entitled to one-half of said amount, while not exceeding the amount of broker's commission as described above, as compensation for broker's efforts.

9. Seller understands that by this agreement broker does not guarantee the sale of the above business, but that broker will make an earnest and continued effort to sell the business during the sole and exclusive period.

10. If real property is available for sale along with this business, a separate listing contract will be executed and attached hereto.

11. This contract constitutes the entire agreement between the parties hereto, supersedes all previous agreements and understandings between them, and shall not be modified except in writing executed by the parties. No representations or promises are made other than as expressly set forth herein. Seller expressly acknowledges reading, understanding, and receiving a copy of this contract.

FIGURE 13.4 Sample Sole and Exclusive Agreement, continued

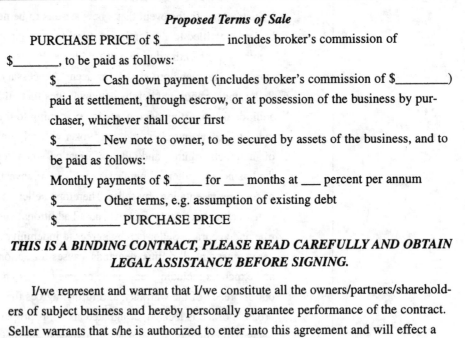

> ***Proposed Terms of Sale***
>
> PURCHASE PRICE of $_____ includes broker's commission of
> $_____, to be paid as follows:
>
> $_____ Cash down payment (includes broker's commission of $_____)
> paid at settlement, through escrow, or at possession of the business by pur-
> chaser, whichever shall occur first
>
> $_____ New note to owner, to be secured by assets of the business, and to
> be paid as follows:
>
> Monthly payments of $_____ for ___ months at ___ percent per annum
>
> $_____ Other terms, e.g. assumption of existing debt
>
> $_____ PURCHASE PRICE
>
> ***THIS IS A BINDING CONTRACT, PLEASE READ CAREFULLY AND OBTAIN
> LEGAL ASSISTANCE BEFORE SIGNING.***
>
> I/we represent and warrant that I/we constitute all the owners/partners/sharehold-
> ers of subject business and hereby personally guarantee performance of the contract.
> Seller warrants that s/he is authorized to enter into this agreement and will effect a
> notarized corporate resolution to sell if necessary.
>
> Dated _____ At _____ ❑ AM ❑ PM Dated _____ At _____ ❑ AM ❑ PM
>
> _____ _____
> Seller   Phone   Seller   Phone
>
> _____ _____
> Address   Address
>
> _____ _____
> City   State Zip   City   State Zip
>
>   Employment accepted by _____
>   (agent for broker)

Note: The contract terms in Figure 13.4 could be easily modified if other commitment levels were sought by seller and broker. For example, by striking out "sole
and exclusive" and replacing it with "open," the force and effect of this agreement
is changed dramatically. Exclusive agency or one-party listings can be created via
this document as well. Clarity should be sought in every case. For example, if the
seller wishes to proceed with an exclusive agency arrangement, verbiage should be
included (either in the body of this contract or as a signed addendum) to the effect that
the seller maintains the right to locate buyers and sell the business without obligation
of a commission. If one-party or multiple-party contracts are desired, complete names
and addresses of the covered parties should obviously be included as part of the contract. As always, obtaining the go-ahead from your attorney is mandatory whether you
make any changes to the above agreement or not. This particular contract is clearly
pro-broker, as evidenced by paragraphs 3, 6, and 7. Everything (almost) is negotiable!

CHAPTER 14

Financing Issues

No guide to buying and selling businesses would be complete without ample attention paid to financing. As it relates specifically to the purchase or sale of a business, the most important, relevant, and useful form of financing is the *seller carry-back* or seller financing. This common tool was fully addressed in Chapter 4, where a comprehensive review of important promissory note provisions and relevant UCC laws were presented. This chapter will focus on the following:

- Capital structure of the firm (debt versus equity)
- Small Business Administration (SBA) programs/requirements
- Creative financing options/techniques
- Financing via the Internet

Financing concerns the many types of lending by creditors (debt) and investing by investors (equity). Proper understanding requires familiarity with the accounting equation, which holds that assets = liabilities + owner's equity. *Every business is comprised of assets (e.g., cash, receivables, inventory, equipment) that must be financed, or paid for*, by either the incurrence of liabilities or the receipt of owner's capital. The point is that every firm has a capital structure (combination of debt and equity financing) associated with different levels of cost and risk.

When comparing the two options (debt versus equity financing), it becomes clear that most types of debt are riskier than equity financing, as evidenced by the possibility of bankruptcy. This risk, however, is at least partially offset by the fact that all interest payments made by a business are 100 percent tax deductible. A company can either borrow money and pay $100,000 in interest or attract equity investments and pay $100,000 in dividends. Assuming a 30 percent tax rate, the interest payments will reduce taxable income by the full $100,000 and reduce the tax liability by $30,000. No such treatment for dividends exists. Lower taxes will increase both the firm's after-tax cash flow and value. On the other hand, payment of dividends are at the discretion of the board of directors. When the economy or the firm is suffering, the board may postpone dividend payments. Interest payments may not be postponed without the full cooperation of the lender. Even with such cooperation, the borrower suffers a deteriorating credit history, making future debt financing costlier and more difficult to obtain.

Financing takes many forms and is available from many different sources. The term *credit* normally refers to debt financing whereas the term *investment* refers to equity financing. With debt financing, the lender taps into the future cash flows of the borrower to service the interest and principal obligations. With equity financing, the investor shares in the future profits and dividends.

Debt Financing

Seller Financing

Most small business acquisitions are financed partially with the help of seller financing. Typically, a buyer will give the seller 30 to 60 percent down, with the balance paid off at an agreed on interest rate and term. In addition to seller financing, other attractive options exist.

Asset-Based Lenders

Asset-based lenders generally require that the market value of collateral (typically equipment, buildings, inventory, or receivables) be greater than the loan amount. These fully secured loans are risky for the borrower in that default may force the lender to seize the collateral, which could obviously damage the business. As a result of the strong collateral, these loans are available at relatively attractive interest rates.

As illustrated later in this chapter in the section on creative financing, it is possible for the purchaser (with the cooperation of the seller) to utilize the acquired assets as a source of cash subsequent to the closing. The difficulty is that if the seller has already provided financing for the purchase, he or she will have filed a lien against the assets of the business. Without the release of this lien, lenders will not be able to use these assets as collateral. In fact, I will occasionally find a buyer who places a clause into the purchase contract that specifically allows the new owner to utilize these assets as collateral for future funding. This is a material concession by the seller and cannot always be obtained. *The seller must be willing to subordinate his or her interest to the asset-based lender.*

Suppliers

For many businesses, financing by suppliers is the key to ongoing profitability. Good cash management requires quick collection of accounts receivable from customers and flexible payment of accounts payable to vendors. Receiving inventory (either raw materials for a manufacturer or finished goods for a retailer) on terms (e.g., "2/10 net 30") creates a window of 30 days to sell the products before payment is required. Under these terms, if you pay within 10 days, you will receive a 2 percent discount against the total purchase price. Otherwise, the entire balance is due at the end of the 30-day period. If you are able to negotiate, net 45 or net 90 will improve your cash flow accordingly. However, *passing up the 2 percent discount for early payment under terms of "2/10 net 30" carries an implicit interest cost of around 28 percent!* If a company has a strong income statement and a solid cash account, all discounts should be taken. When evaluating acquisitions, a legitimate *add-back* to ACF is the money saved if cash discounts could have been taken. If you can borrow money at 15 percent, taking the discounts is worth the effort.

On certain occasions, it is possible for the purchaser of a business to negotiate new terms with suppliers near closing. A new owner can use the leverage of uncertainty when dealing with the established suppliers, hinting that other options are being considered. It is even possible for the prospective owner to borrow money from a major supplier (to help finance the purchase of the business) in exchange for a contractual commitment to continue buying goods.

Commercial Banks

Depository institutions such as Citibank and Wells Fargo, and commercial banks provide credit in a variety of fashions. They will loan money toward the purchase of a business, either through SBA-backed programs or independently. They will also make equipment loans and loans for working capital needs. These loans will always require a personal guarantee, even if the loan documents are executed in the corporate name. *Loans based on your signature only are possible, but collateral of some sort will improve the interest rate and your chances of being funded.* Home equity loans are an attractive source of cash, and banks are currently eager to make these loans (particularly when property values are rising). When you receive a business loan from a commercial bank, be prepared to "bare your soul" and your records, as the bank will routinely monitor (audit) the financial condition of your operation. If your credit rating is marginal or deteriorating, consider using a third party to cosign your application. Commercial banks are historically the most conservative lenders of all, but this is changing to a certain degree.

Nonbank Banks (Commercial Finance Companies)

The Money Store and AT&T Capital have led the so-called nonbank banks in making aggressive SBA-guaranteed loans during the past few years. Many are approved SBA lenders, reducing the time required for loan approval. They often work harder to structure a loan so that it can be approved. They will tend to be more interested in the liquidity and quality of the assets, while commercial banks will be more interested in cash flow. However, as recently as spring 1997, one of these major lenders was facilitating deals with only 10 percent down from the buyer, based almost exclusively on cash flow (the seller participated with another 10 percent in the form of a second position carry-back note). When dealing with banks or non-banks, *don't let a "no" response get you down. Maybe the answer was really a qualified "yes."* Politely inquire as to why you were turned down before moving on to the next lender.

If you obtain preapproval (loan commitment), be prepared to negotiate interest, repayment periods, and collateral. You may receive interest rate concessions anywhere from ½ to 3 percent if your plan is well documented. Always seek the longest repayment period possible (assuming that there are no prepayment penalties), but note that SBA loans are made normally for a term matching the remaining life of the property lease (options to renew count). Try to limit the collateral to the assets of the business only. If the finance company asks for a lien against your home, you should initially refuse. Although you will be required to sign a personal guarantee, it is wise to have the corporation borrow the money.

Equity Financing

Partners

Finding trustworthy individuals to share the financial burden and/or work load is a potential source of cash. Partners can be passive (not working the business) or active (involved in the day-to-day operations). Passive partners will receive a lower return, obviously, than active partners.

Negotiating the precise conditions of a partnership arrangement is both challenging and necessary. Expectations of a partner's performance will be markedly different from the unfolding reality. Partnership breakups are one of the most frequent reasons for the sale of a business. The favorable results of partnering, whether through a formal partnership or corporation, include more initial capital to invest, greater capability to tap working capital funds, flexibility in work hours, two perspectives instead of one, and synergies of distinct skills.

I have seen exceptional partnerships where there was mutual trust, respect, and the capacity to get along. However, partners come in many forms from many backgrounds, and the dynamism of such a working relationship cannot normally be pretested. The possibilities extend from small, minority-interest, "silent" partners

(1 to 20 percent equity share) to majority-interest, active investors (51 percent and above), with relationships begun by mutual interest or arising out of desperation by one of the parties for additional cash.

Try to "put a lid" on the payback amounts. Receipt of $50,000 from an investor that allows you to increase cash flow annually by the same amount should not necessarily entitle the investor to an "eternal stream" of payments. Offer a return commensurate with the risk and high enough to attract the funds, but do not give away your hard-earned profits (particularly to a silent, nonactive partner).

If you are attempting to solicit a working partner, check his or her financial strength by asking to see personal tax returns. Also, run a credit check to verify his or her willingness and ability to live up to financial commitments. If you did not know the person beforehand, you had better check references and/or former employers, being up front about your need to check references and credit reports. Surprise checks might be unnecessarily offensive.

My advice is to seek legal assistance before proceeding too far into a partnership arrangement. Partnerships may be formed as a formal partnership, evidenced by a partnership agreement, or they may arise out of equity investments (minority or majority) into a corporation or limited liability company (LLC). Technically speaking, a partnership is defined as an association of two or more persons carrying on as co-owners of a business for profit. Legally speaking, a partnership may even be implied by the conduct and acts of the purported partners. Partnerships are often referred to as *conduits*, owing to the fact that even though persons have banded together to generate profits, it is not considered a legal entity separate from the partners. This differs, of course, from a corporation, which is a separate legal entity and may, for example, be the target of a lawsuit. Under such arrangements, each partner shares potential joint and several liability. There are two types of partnerships, general and limited. Under a general partnership, each partner shares equally (or as otherwise agreed) in the profits and losses. General partners will typically assume full personal liability, whereas limited partners can avoid this potential risk. Partnership agreements will normally address the following key areas: name, location and purpose, division of profits/losses, duration of agreement, authority/titles, amounts of contributed capital, additions, changes and amendments, retirement/buyouts/exit strategies, arbitration, books and records, and contractual authority.

An important and relevant area of partnership agreements deals with exit strategies. If one or more parties exit the business, by choice or by death, proper planning can ensure a smooth transition. Typically, *buy-sell agreements must be created and incorporated into the partnership agreement.* Buy-sell agreements serve to present a working formula by which one or more partners, under predetermined conditions, can buy out one or more existing partners.

Venture Capital Firms

If traditional bank financing (which requires fixed, periodic payments), or investments from friends and family members (which present unique practical challenges), do not appeal to you, then becoming involved with venture capital firms is another option. They are located throughout the United States and can offer substantial equity financing to appealing, growth-oriented firms.

Venture capital firms have a very unique culture that should be fully understood before entering. Beware their nature! If your business is growing, well documented (hopefully with audited financial statements), and presented via a professionally prepared business plan, you might get their full attention. They are seeking a very high return (high risk, high return) as well as significant if not complete, control of your operations until their return objectives are met. Also known as risk capital, funding is provided for start-up, turnaround, and other risky types of investments. Funding is provided at different junctures in a company's development, beginning with *seed capital*, followed by first and second round phases, and then what is referred to as mezzanine level financing that hopefully leads to an initial public offering (IPO). Before you become too excited, realize that only about 1,500 firms receive this type of funding each year. The end of this chapter contains a comprehensive list of venture capital firms and clubs for your consideration, as well as a current list of Internet-based venture capital leads. Ask your broker, accountant, and attorney for local leads as well.

Historically, venture capital funding has been associated with investments into high-tech, start-up corporations. There is presently a trend toward investing in a wider range of companies, such as service businesses and fast-food concepts that are already successful. They are looking for a proven concept that is beyond the start-up phase, has a solid and committed management team, current revenues of between $5 million and $15 million, and an upside potential of $100 million. In exchange for the required capital, they seek equity ownership ranging from passively influential to outright control. They will commonly seek one or more seats on the board of directors.

The desired outcome for the venture capitalist is either a successful merger or IPO, where the return on investment can reach stratospheric levels. A rule of thumb is that venture capitalists will try to recoup between 5 and 10 times their initial investment over a three to six year period. The majority of firms that receive venture capital investments wind up participating in mergers rather than IPOs . On the other hand, firms that receive venture capital funding are five times more likely to go public than other companies, proving the value that venture capitalists bring to the table. In effect, companies are "professionalized" by the scrutiny and advice given by the venture capitalists.

Although the strategies and goals of venture capital firms vary greatly and have evolved over time, the following list describes several potentially attractive scenarios involving these providers of risk capital:

- Ground-breaking technology, patented processes, or rapid growth service companies
- Significant control in management of business, where counsel of venture capital principals is expected to add value
- Relatively quick culmination in the form of an IPO/merger
- Synergistic relationship between venture capital firm and competent, current management team

A newly prominent source of venture capital is the *venture capital club*, which consists of wealthy, accredited entrepreneurial investors. These clubs allow companies in need of funding to speak directly to the investors, forging a more personal bond and relationship. Traditional venture capital firms are much more demanding than venture capital clubs in terms of requiring several classes of stock and seats on the board. The firms are also stingier when it comes to releasing funds. The clubs have filled a void left by the traditional firms, namely that of the smaller deal. Wealthy individual investors formed clubs to share their knowledge and risks with the hope of picking tomorrow's superstar companies.

Even Uncle Sam is involved in the risk capital arena. The SBA promotes venture capital programs through the licensing and financing of small business investment corporations (SBICs). Specifically, they are licensed to make both equity and debt investments in small businesses. They raise their capital by borrowing from the SBA and other sources. Typically, they will take an equity position in companies that they loan funds to, hoping to profit from the anticipated higher than average growth and prosperity.

As indicated earlier, venture capital companies will vary significantly in many different aspects. *Areas of specialization, type of financing, manner of participation, industry preferences, size of portfolio, characteristics of preferred clients, preferred holding periods, minimum return on investment, controlling interest requirement, and the average time from initial contact to closing* differ widely from one firm to the next.

Typical investments will involve the purchase of the company's senior securities, both debt (bonds) and equity (preferred stock), which are convertible into common stock. Using debt financing (convertible bonds) has the major benefit of tax deductible interest. However, if there is significant uncertainty as to the future of the company's cash flow, the need for greater flexibility might lead to the equity preference (preferred stock). Use of preferred stock (convertible) has the advantage of keeping the firm's debt-to-equity ratio low, which will improve the chances for additional financing in later periods. It will also allow the investor to defer the income tax on the associated capital gain. Concerns relating to the use of preferred stock include establishing the appropriate coupon rate for the preferred dividend, priority rights in the event of liquidation, redemption rights, and registration rights. The venture capital firm may also impose certain restrictions on future financings or other major decisions without full consent. Less common is the right of the venture capitalist to veto the sale of additional stock and/or the sale of the business.

If you feel that your company is in the position to possibly benefit from the use of a venture capital firm, three important steps must be taken immediately: (1) Select, interview, and hire a consultant with the right experience to help guide you through the process (a qualified attorney and CPA are also required); (2) Prepare a comprehensive, quality business plan, covering at least five years into the future; and (3) Check references thoroughly for the venture capital firm, financial consultant, and attorney.

"Angels"

Somewhere in between passive investments made by personal friends and high dollar venture capital lies the funding available from so-called *angels*. Many of these investors are retired businesspeople who do not wish to devote themselves full-time to a business, but nonetheless want to remain active and earn above-normal returns. Angels will provide needed financing in exchange for a stake of the company. If you are not prepared to give up an equity stake, this is not the financing option for you. Angels like to see a formal business plan, strong management teams, and either current or likely profitability. Angels can be found via online financial forums, such as Capital Quest (http://www.usbusiness.com/capquest/home.html), and other networks, such as the Southwest Venture Capital Network (602-263-2390).

Small Business Administration Related Funding

The federal government plays an active role in funding the growth of small business. Several different programs exist, covering both equity (small business investment corporations) and debt options (SBA loan guarantees). The most important programs supported by the SBA are aimed at providing loans to worthy entrepreneurs to assist them with their "growing pains," including loans for working capital, new equipment, buildings, and land and export financing (as well as the purchase of ongoing concerns).

The number of loans recently guaranteed by the SBA has dramatically increased as a result of increased budgets, an improving economy, and a record number of new small business formations. Despite lingering perceptions of overwhelming paperwork requirements, these loans are available to those who are willing to "jump through hoops," most of which are quite reasonable. As a result of the popular LowDoc program (discussed later in this chapter), the quantity of guaranteed loans doubled between 1993 and 1995 from about 26,000 to 55,000. Hundreds of financial institutions across the nation participate in these increasingly attractive programs. The two leading SBA lenders during the 1996 to 1997 period were national firms with offices in most major metropolitan areas. The Money Store (800-768-6340) and AT&T Small Business Lending Corporation (800-221-7252).

Look to the business section of your local newspaper for advertisements of active lenders in your area. The bank that you conduct your normal banking business with might be your best chance, but there are certain institutions that are simply more eager to make SBA-guaranteed loans. Call your local SBA office and ask for a current list of the leading SBA lenders in your area.

Contrary to common perception, the SBA rarely provides funds directly for small business loans. Primarily, it will guarantee a portion (up to 80 percent) of the loan made by the financial institution, thus encouraging lending. Approval is normally required by both the bank and the SBA. Experienced institutions may be designated as *preferred lenders*, which means they are able to approve certain loans without waiting for official SBA approval. As a borrower, working with a preferred lender can prove invaluable. When dealing with impatient sellers, assuring them that loan approval will be quickly forthcoming can be quite comforting.

The 7(a) loan program is the workhorse of the SBA, accounting for approximately 75 percent of all loans. This program features fully amortized loans (no balloon payments), long repayment periods (up to 25 years), and high loan-to-value ratios (low down payment). There are no prepayment penalties or annual processing fees. Loans are guaranteed by the SBA for up to 80 percent of the total loan amount and may be used for equipment, working capital, business acquisitions, franchise financing, buildings and land, and tenant improvements.

Up to $750,000 will be guaranteed by the SBA, although banks will often make larger loans of up to, say, $1,500,000. Borrowers must pay a loan guarantee fee of normally between 1 and 2 percent of the guaranteed amount, which is either paid from the cash down payment or is financed with the principal amount of the loan. Interest rates are variable (floating at prime plus 2¼ to 2¾ percent). Loans of less than $50,000 may have slightly higher rates. The actual interest rate, to a certain extent, is negotiable. You won't know about a lower rate unless you ask for it. In an improving economy, record numbers of new small businesses, and record profit levels, banks are more aggressive. Take advantage of this situation while it lasts!

Let's focus now on the relevance of the SBA program for business acquisitions. Why would a buyer consider using bank financing? Primarily, it allows the buyer to offer the seller an attractive amount of cash at closing. Furthermore, the greater the percent of cash offered in the down payment, the lower the total purchase price will be. Most buyers expect and most sellers will grant a material discount for a heavy cash offer, ranging from 10 percent to as high as 33 percent. Sellers are normally happy to receive this cash to reduce the constant worry about collections that will accompany note payments.

In reality, however, there are often compelling reasons why the buyer and the seller do not want an all cash offer. The buyer may not feel as confident about the transition period and future performance of the business under new ownership if the seller is completely removed from the picture. If the seller has financed a portion of the sales price, there is a great incentive for him or her to stay in touch with the buyer and help with the continued success of the business. On the other hand, the seller may not want the entire purchase price paid at one time, primarily due to tax liabilities. By extending payment over at least two periods, effective marginal tax rates on the capital gain will be reduced. Additionally, many sellers look at the future note payments as a type of retirement plan. Equal monthly payments coming from a party that is trusted and financially secure can be quite appealing. One final reason concerns interest rates. Generally speaking, bank rates will be 2 to 4 percent higher than seller rates. Many factors must be considered by both sides in determining the appeal and likelihood of bank financing, but in many cases this will be an attractive option for all parties.

If you are interested in obtaining SBA-guaranteed bank financing for the purchase of an ongoing concern, the following five primary conditions must be met satisfactorily in the eyes of the bank and the SBA: (1) satisfactory credit record, (2) similar management experience, (3) sufficient cash flow, (4) adequate equity investment, and (5) a proper mix of assets and working capital. Let's look at each of these requirements in detail.

1. Satisfactory credit record. The bank will require that you can demonstrate creditworthiness. Carefully examine your credit report before you turn in your loan application so that you can address any shortcomings or remove any mistakes. Call Equifax (800-685-5000 [$8]), Trans-Union at (800-680-7289 [$15]), or TRW at (800-682-7654), or call your local credit reporting agency found in the Yellow Pages for a current copy and current fees. Different lenders utilize different credit reports, so you should obtain copies from each of these major agencies. They process literally millions of entries every year, so they will make mistakes. It is your responsibility to make sure that your report is accurate. Check the reports every six months whether you need credit or not. Your personal balance sheet, resume, and personal presentation will also be important considerations.

Bear in mind that your credit report does not need to be perfect, as long as problems are minor, infrequent, and easily clarified. One or two late payments can be overlooked with a reasonable explanation. It is difficult, however, to overcome personal bankruptcy. A priority is often placed by the lender on the most recent 12-month period, which should be as near perfect as possible. Not surprisingly, *honesty is the best policy*. Your loan officer is evaluating both your creditworthiness and your credibility. The main question bank loan officers are asking themselves is whether or not you are likely to repay the loan. If you are able to alert the lender to problems that will surface on your credit report, you will improve your chances. If you have the opportunity to "fess up" and do not, including your predictions of future sales, expenses, and cash flows, you have given the loan officer good reason to doubt any claims that you might make.

2. Similar management experience.
Preferably, you will already have substantial management experience in a similar industry. If your background is not in the same industry or category of business, general management experience can be sufficient to convince the lender that you are *operationally qualified*. Resumes, letters of recommendation, or performance evaluations can bolster your chances as well. You are selling yourself as much as you are selling the viability of the business.

Of all the criteria analyzed by the lender, this area is the most flexible. You must be able to convince the financial institution that you will live up to your commitment. For example, if you are trying to obtain funding for the purchase of an automotive repair business, it is not always necessary that you have had experience as a mechanic or a manager of such an operation. Possessing significant management experience in the fast-food industry (i.e., hiring, firing, purchasing, customer service) might suffice. *Convince the lender that you can make it happen.*

Sell yourself in terms of experience and commitment. If your family will be involved, make this convincingly clear as well. Having said this, bankers are notorious for their quantitative nature. There is a reason why banks have loan committees that never actually meet the borrower. They seek to focus exclusively on financial data and to avoid being persuaded by the artful narrator!

3. Sufficient cash flow.
You must document that the business you are purchasing is capable of servicing the debt that will arise from the new loan. To substantiate such a claim, you will need to create monthly, pro forma cash flow analyses for at least

the first year subsequent to closing and preferably for several years. The more detail you present, if it is credible and favorable, the better your chances. Either five years of projections or a period that matches the life of the loan is optimal.

Genuine effort should be placed into both the creation of these projections and the firm's business plan. Even the LowDoc loans (discussed later in this chapter) require a one-page business plan and one-year projections made by both the current and future owner.

Many lenders have established internal criteria relating to cash flow, as measured by something similar to our adjusted cash flow figure (ACF). The Money Store requires a verifiable (normally per tax returns) cash flow ratio of 1.2 to 1 over a two-year period. Recall that cash flow is calculated in such a way as to establish the amount of cash benefits accruing to a single owner-operator over a period of one year. This cash flow figure also represents the cash available to owners to pay themselves a salary, service debt, and hopefully earn a return on investment. Cash benefits (ACF) are found by adding: net income; owner's salary and benefits; depreciation expense; interest expense; and one-time, nonrecurring expenses (see Chapters 3, 9, and 11).

The Money Store ratio is based on an important adjustment to the ACF figure above. The new owner's compensation (salary and benefits) is subtracted, whatever it may be, to arrive at a figure representing cash available to service the debt. The amount of cash available to service the debt must be 1.2 times greater than the cash required to service the debt under the proposed financing terms.

Example: Money Store Calculation

ACF – Owner's compensation = Cash available to service debt

It should be clear that if the new owner/borrower is able to live off a relatively small salary, perhaps because the other spouse continues to work, this ratio can be improved (manipulated). Bankers like to see the borrower willing to forego a plush salary the first few years to create a safety barrier for the repayment of debt. Every bank will have its own unique measure of *cash flow cushion* or *debt service coverage* that it utilizes to evaluate loans. Many brokers will request that debt service not exceed 25 to 33 percent of projected cash flow (ACF).

4. Adequate equity investment. Most buyers seek to obtain the most assets and greatest cash flow they can for a given down payment. Leverage is an important tool utilized by the most savvy investors in the world. Bankers, on the other hand, would like to see substantial equity investments (cash down payment) into the businesses that they finance. One common percentage is 30 percent (SBA requirement), requiring that the borrower place personal funds at risk equal to at least 30 percent of the purchase price. The more capital that the borrower has placed into the business, the more likely there will be a profitable outcome.

Many aggressive lenders (find out who they are!) will finance acquisitions for as little as 20 percent down. Surprisingly, many bankers will presently consider a seller carry-back as part of the equity or risk capital. In other words, it is possible to buy a business for 10 percent cash down if the seller will carry back at least an additional 10 percent of the purchase price! The difficulty is getting the seller to go along with this, once he or she realizes that the carry-back is in "second place" behind the lender's note, leaving little chance of collecting this money in the event of bankruptcy. Depending on how the purchase agreement is structured, the seller may lose the ability to move back into the business if the new owner experiences difficulty and stops making payments. To protect the seller's interest in these situations, he or she may require the buyer to allow the seller (in the event of buyer default on seller note) to secure his or her own financing to pay off the bank loan and reenter the business. Consult your broker or attorney for professional guidance.

5. Proper mix of assets and working capital. Most SBA programs require that the loan amount be either fully collateralized by assets or made for working capital needs. In other words, care must be taken to structure the allocation of the loan proceeds in such a way that it meets government and bank requirements. For example, a business being sold for $200,000 can normally be financed only to the extent of the firm's hard assets (i.e., inventory, equipment, leasehold improvements, buildings, and land) plus an appropriate amount for working capital. The SBA 7(a) program rules are quite specific in this regard and must be carefully understood as you present your loan application. You must present a schedule allocating the purchase price among the different asset categories and a schedule allocating the loan proceeds. Either your business broker or a financing consultant can help you understand this requirement. Keep in mind that different banks will have different guidelines for different types of loans.

Miscellaneous Loan Programs

LowDoc program. One of the most successful SBA programs ever has been the LowDoc Program, which features a one-page SBA loan application and quick turnaround once the buyer has met the lender requirements. According to the SBA, 56 percent of the 55,600 loans made in 1995 were through the LowDoc Program. More LowDoc loans were made in one year than the total number of SBA loans made since 1993. The key constraint on this program is the $100,000 limit on loan size, of which 80 percent is guaranteed by the SBA. The fact that banks have historically resisted making loans of this size has magnified the importance of the program. Funds may be used for any purpose available under the 7(a) program, except for certain restrictions on loan repayments of existing debt. Pertinent requirements include company sales volume of less than $5 million per year and 100 or fewer employees. Fees, maturities, and interest rates are also similar to the 7(a) program. This loan program is tapped extensively for business acquisitions and should be seriously considered if the required funding is $100,000 or less. Responses from the SBA are typically received within a few days!

Fastrak program. This program also limits the loan size to $100,000, but approval is based solely on the lending institution (no additional paperwork for the SBA). Because the SBA guarantees only 50 percent of the principal amount of this loan, it is more difficult to obtain. Purpose, fees, rates, and maturities are similar to the 7(a) program. You should specifically ask your lender if your loan would qualify for either the LowDoc or Fastrak programs.

Creative Financing

For purchasers with an open mind, there are many different ways to creatively finance the purchase of a business. You must be both clever and bold to ask for and implement these unconventional strategies. *In most cases, you will not get what you are asking for, but you will never know unless you try!* The goal is to purchase a business for as little cash down as possible. Note, however, that no cash down does not necessarily imply that the seller will receive no cash at closing. You are trying to find outside sources of cash to purchase the business and facilitate a successful operation after ownership passes.

Your need for cash will not end after the seller has received a down payment and closing has occurred. Carefully analyzing your *working capital* needs is critical. Your subsequent needs for cash are not likely to be met from profits alone, particularly if you plan on growing the business. It is absolutely pointless to work so hard at creatively financing the purchase of a business if you will not have sufficient cash to sustain profits and growth. Your needs for additional cash will stem from the following: growing inventory, increased financing of sales (accounts receivable), replacing and improving fixed assets, additional advertising, and additional payroll costs.

You must be painfully realistic as you implement these creative strategies. As you pursue such options, you are basically attempting what investment bankers refer to as leveraged buyouts (LBOs, or 100 percent debt-financed acquisitions). If your management skills coupled with the strength of the business and the economy are sufficient, leveraging your purchase in general is not a problem. The obvious difficulty arises from the fact that all debt payments are legal, obligatory payments. If payments to creditors are missed, the creditors have the ability to force your company into bankruptcy.

Seller Financing

First and most common is seller financing. Most small businesses are sold with at least a small portion of the purchase price financed by the seller. These take-back notes are the most convenient and often the most favorable in terms of interest rates and other repayment terms. An average transaction might entail a down payment of one-third with most deals falling within the 20 to 50 percent down range. Although this financing tool is analyzed thoroughly in Chapter 4, a good review here is warranted because it is likely to be at the center of any successful creative financing scheme. The eight basic reasons to consider seller financing follow:

1. Below market interest rates
2. Longer repayment period
3. No loan processing/guarantee fees
4. No invasive audits by lender
5. Reduction of capital gains tax immediately due by seller
6. Seller remains involved in the business, contributing to smooth transition
7. Cash requirements of purchaser reduced, freeing funds for working capital
8. More forgiving lender than financial institutions.

Any one of these reasons might be sufficient to push for seller financing. Numbers one and two, for example, are quite tangible advantages. Longer repayment periods without prepayment penalties provide the new owner much needed flexibility. To appreciate the significance of lower interest rates, consider the following example. The purchaser of a business could either obtain bank financing for $200,000 at 16 percent over a five-year term or seller financing for the same term at 10 percent. The savings in interest payments over the five year period is approximately $30,000! As always, many factors must be considered when comparing seller financing with bank financing. In this case, if the purchaser borrowed the money from the bank, he or she would be offering much more cash down to the seller and is likely to receive a much better price. Number eight, on the other hand, is an intangible factor that could prove invaluable. People who have sold their businesses are generally more understanding and cooperative than financial institutions and will be more interested in seeing the new owner succeed. Accordingly, they are more likely to work with the buyer (borrower) in the event of cash flow problems. Additionally, sellers are less skilled at and less likely to pursue the option of foreclosing on a promissory note.

The final determination of the availability and extent of seller financing is a function of many variables, including the following: the degree of seller motivation; persistence, affability, and credibility of the purchaser; and quality of overall deal.

The first factor, *degree of seller motivation*, is often difficult to decipher. I have encountered a whole spectrum of seller motivations, ranging from sellers who state undeniably that they must sell, only to reject a solid offer, to those that say over and over again they are not really interested in selling but take the first offer that comes their way. Asking sellers why they are selling is a first step toward analyzing the situation. Common reasons for sale are listed at the beginning of Chapter 12. They are all legitimate reasons to sell, but should be analyzed carefully by the purchaser. A degree in psychology might be useful in this regard!

A common problem is that the seller is using an illness as an excuse to cover up the real motivation for sale—the business is suffering. Make sure that you receive updated financial information and attempt to audit the presented numbers as best you can. A business can show strong results for a calendar year, say 1997, while the business slumps steadily into early 1998. Assuming the decline began in September, this could mean falling sales and cash flow for more than six months, a fact that could not be determined by looking at the full year 1997 numbers alone. The illusion might even be that the business is improving, if the total 1997 sales and cash flow were greater than the total for 1996. Once again, make sure you have a solid understanding of current sales and expenses, asking the seller specifically if business has deteriorated recently and requesting updated financial statements. Revisit the section on due diligence proceedings in Chapter 6. The fact is that illness or retirement is often the secondary motivation for selling. As you can easily understand, a poorly performing business is a good reason to retire! In any case, the degree of motivation will influence greatly the willingness of the seller to consider seller financing and other creative types of arrangements.

The second set of factors, *persistence, affability, and credibility of the purchaser*, are also important. If the seller has the impression that you are the kind of person that gets things done, your chances of winning his or her cooperation improve greatly. Also, if the seller has the feeling that you really want his or her business in particular, you are more likely to win important concessions. When negotiating the sale of a business worth thousands of dollars, it is difficult to focus on being nice, but the fact seems to be that if the seller likes you personally, your chances for negotiating a solid deal increase dramatically.

The third factor, *quality of the overall deal*, is somewhat of a catchall. Depending on the seller's true motivating circumstances and the credibility and even affability of the purchaser, the deal must make sense to the seller. For example, if the purchaser offers a credible upside potential to the seller in the form of an earn-out, this can prove to be a significant enticement. An earn-out allows the seller to share in the future success of the business beyond the cash received at closing and the future note payments from the purchaser. The point here is that earn-outs can improve the overall attractiveness of a deal and improve the buyer's chances of structuring and implementing creative deals (see Chapter 7 for details).

Other sources of creative financing exist in the form of bank loans, investments by silent partners, personal loans, assumption of seller's existing debts, cash raised by the sale of company assets, supplier financing, funds tapped from future cash flows, and loans from business brokers! We are trying to clarify the many tools available to buyers of ongoing concerns that can reduce the cash needed to complete a deal. Given that most buyers will express the need or desire to conserve their use of cash, these options are worthy of consideration. Situations range from inexperienced buyers who truly have very little cash and are looking for businesses where they can "take over the payments" to seasoned veterans who are always trying to leverage their cash to the fullest extent possible. These experienced buyers have established criteria for return on cash investment, payback periods, or some other measure of success related to the cash placed into the business. This obsession with limiting cash investments and maximizing leverage can backfire if proper attention is not paid to the need for working capital subsequent to the purchase. You do not want to lose your business in a few months because you run out of cash.

The attempt to minimize the amount of cash put into the purchase of a business is a basic example of financial leverage. Advanced financial theory taught at leading business schools across the nation proves that leverage is a worthwhile tactic (i.e., it can be shown to increase shareholder value [the value of the firm]). By using borrowed money at a cost of between 10 and 15 percent and earning a return of between 15 and 20 percent, wealth can be created. So, if you can purchase a business for $200,000 with $20,000 of your own money, you hope that the cash flow generated by the business will not only pay the creditors and/or investors for the other $180,000, but also pay a respectable salary to you and a return on your cash investment. Consider the financial structures relating to the purchase of a hypothetical, $200,000 retail business in Figure 14.1.

FIGURE 14.1 Deal Structures

Deal #1

$40,000	cash down payment
$160,000	seller financing

Deal #2

$40,000	cash down payment
$60,000	bank financing—SBA guaranteed
$100,000	seller financing

Deal #3

$20,000	cash down payment
$40,000	investment by silent partners
$60,000	bank financing—SBA guaranteed
$80,000	seller financing

Deal #4

$10,000	cash down payment
$15,000	sale of company assets
$15,000	personal loan
$20,000	assumption of seller's existing debt
$70,000	bank financing—conventional
$70,000	seller financing

Deal #5

$5,000	cash down payment
$5,000	borrowed against future cash flow
$10,000	personal loan
$10,000	supplier financing
$10,000	loan from business broker
$15,000	investment by silent partners
$15,000	sale of company assets
$20,000	assumption of seller's existing debt
$20,000	bank financing—conventional
$90,000	seller financing

As you analyze these varying structures, it should be clear that they will be increasingly difficult to obtain as you move down the list (less cash, more creativity). There are numerous complications to working out deal #5. For example, most banks will not loan money for business acquisitions unless their lien against the assets of the business is in first place, forcing the seller to subordinate his or her interest. This is not always obtainable, particularly when the seller is carrying a substantial note such as the one in deal #5. There are also timing issues. When will the assets be sold? Before or after closing? If these assets are sold, will they harm the firm's ability to make sales and generate the necessary cash flow to service the various debt obligations incurred as part of the deal? Will the bank and suppliers agree to the sale of these assets? The task of obtaining supplier financing alone requires a particular set of circumstances, fancy footwork, and even luck!

As awkward and time-consuming as deal #5 appears, it is theoretically possible (possible, yes; probable, no). It would certainly require a motivated and cooperative seller or perhaps an upside potential allowing the seller to share in future profits beyond the initial $200,000 purchase price (earn-out). Another concern is that one or all these lenders will require that the purchaser or borrower personally guarantee the debts, which means that the personal assets of the buyer (assuming there are some) are at risk in the event of default. Most states have homestead laws, which will protect a predetermined amount of equity in a borrower's personal residence, but all other assets would be targets for the lenders as they attempt to recoup their investments. Consult your attorney in order to "keep your ducks in a row"!

Supplier Financing

As you have probably realized by now, there are two separate types of supplier financing. The first type is the standard credit offered by manufacturers and wholesalers as alluded to briefly earlier in this chapter. The second type is by far the most creative, aggressive, and unlikely form of financing for a low cash down business acquisition. The reality here is that the key suppliers of every business make attractive profits from the sale of their inventory. Within the framework of purchasing a business with minimal cash down, suppliers will have valid reasons for assisting with the acquisition. In particular, assuming that the seller is motivated to sell and there are quality, reasonably priced substitute products (suppliers) available on the market, the buyer should be able to get the attention of such a major supplier, and request a modest cash advance to assist in the acquisition.

Clearly, this type of financing will not work for every type and category of business. A business with large amounts of inventory purchased from one primary supplier that is family-owned and for which there are readily available substitutes is the ideal candidate. This approach would be virtually impossible for a day-care center or a residential cleaning business. In addition to meeting the criteria listed in this paragraph, the actual request for a cash advance must be boldly and skillfully presented and the promissory note thoroughly and legally perfected. Execution of this interesting technique requires a special mix of knowledge in psychology, finance, and business acquisition strategies. Without a doubt, presentation of a professionally prepared, credible business plan that projects steadily rising sales and cash flows will greatly support your cause. As concerns the specific terms and conditions, there are two primary, distinct issues to be addressed.

First, you must accurately calculate the *value* of your account to the supplier, based on a determination of the net present value of these earnings. As explained in Chapter 9, the concept of net present value is the foundation of modern financial theory. Specifically, your calculation of net present value should be based on the suppliers gross profit margin, ignoring their operating expenses. In other words, you must determine what the average markup is for the sale of the particular product being sold. If you do not know and the supplier will not tell you (this information might be considered proprietary), you can ask around your industry or you can look up common-sized financial statement data in a number of sources, such as Robert Morris Associates or the Almanac of Business and Financial Ratios. These common-sized financial statements include average gross margins (sales minus cost of goods sold) for different sized businesses within hundreds of different industries, arranged by SIC codes. For example, if the gross margin is 50 percent and the total purchases made through a given supplier are $250,000, the value of your account in the present year to the supplier is 50 percent of the total sales or $125,000. If projected purchases are greater in future years, this must be accounted for and then the results must be discounted back to present value. The total value is based on all projected sales into future periods. The relevant time period should be based on the length of time you are willing to commit to purchasing your inventory from this supplier.

The second area is the terms and conditions contained in the promissory note. The term of repayment, interest rate, and collateral must be formalized. Expect to be asked to personally guarantee the loan and be prepared to handle requests for collateral, ranging from the provided inventory to your personal residence. Don't forget that if you are being truly creative in your financing, you will have multiple lenders. The assistance of a qualified attorney is normally required. Finally, you will be asked to sign a commitment letter of some sort, pledging you and/or your company to purchase certain minimum amounts of inventory over a stipulated period of time.

Financing via the Internet

Most modern day entrepreneurs (existing or potential) have found that computer literacy is helpful, if not essential, for maximum profits and cash flow. Whether it means computerized accounting packages and inventory tracking systems or instant and direct access to current information such as industry reviews, airfares, or credit reports on new customers, computers are increasingly integral to remaining profitable into the 21st century.

Even the task of obtaining financing for the small business has taken a turn toward computerized access. Yes, it remains true that you still need to meet prospective lenders and investors in person and shake their hands before a deal can be struck.

Increasingly, however, initial contacts or matches are being made over the Internet for a wide variety of situations, ranging from accounts receivable financing to venture capital funding. Although it is easy to get lost on the Net, as you refine your searching capabilities, this hurdle can be easily overcome. When executing a search for financing sources, many excellent avenues exist, including the following:

Alta Vista
Description: state by state listings of major banks' web sites
Address: http://www.altavista.digital.com/

Bank Web
Description: state by state listings of major banks' web sites
Address: http://www.bankweb.com

Campbell-Becker, Inc.
Description: venture capital financing for high-tech companies with average investments of more than $100,000
Address: http://www-dev.cecase.ukans.edu/cambell-becker/html/cbi-home.html/

Capital Quest
Description: a forum where business plans are exposed in search of finding "angels" and other private investors
Address: http://www.usbusiness.com/capquest/home.html

Falcon Financial
Description: high-tech businesses of the future (telecommunications, health care, and the environment) capture their attention and money
Address: http://www.webthread.com/falcon.html/

Finance Hub
Description: comprehensive linkages to both venture capitalists and commercial banks; allows business proposals to be presented for a small fee
Address: http://www.financehub.com/vc/vctab.html

Galaxy
Description: allows searching of entire World Wide Web
Address: http://galaxy.einet.net/

Olympic Venture Partners
Description: also interested in high-tech, future oriented products and businesses
Address: http://info.product.com/olympic/

Price Waterhouse LLP National Venture Capital Survey
Description: tracks the pulse of venture capital deals across the country, presenting interesting statistics and trends
Address: http://www.pw.com/vc/~somerset/

Somerset Capital Corporation
Description: venture capital firm offering a variety financing options to qualified parties
Address: http://rampages.onramp.net/

Venture Capital Analysis
Description: interactive site to help you determine whether or not venture capital is a good option for your firm and how to find it
Address: http://www.kcilink.com/brc/financing/ventcap.html

Venture Capital World
Description: new forum where investors of all types can meet and discuss financing options
Address: http://www.ccpartner.se/

Web Crawler
Description: well known, fast, and thorough search engine
Address: http://www.webcrawler.com

Yahoo
Description: another well-known search engine, with categories such as small business information and venture capital
Address: http://www.yahoo.com/

Appendix A
Present Value Interest Factors

Present Value Interest Factor

PERIOD, n	1%	2%	3%	4%	5%	6%	7%	8%	9%	10%	11%	12%	13%
0	1.000	1.000	1.000	1.000	1.000	1.000	1.000	1.000	1.000	1.000	1.000	1.000	1.000
1	0.990	0.980	0.971	0.962	0.952	0.943	0.935	0.926	0.917	0.909	0.901	0.893	0.885
2	0.980	0.961	0.943	0.925	0.907	0.890	0.873	0.857	0.842	0.826	0.812	0.797	0.783
3	0.971	0.942	0.915	0.889	0.864	0.840	0.816	0.794	0.772	0.751	0.731	0.712	0.693
4	0.961	0.924	0.888	0.855	0.823	0.792	0.763	0.735	0.708	0.683	0.659	0.636	0.613
5	0.951	0.906	0.863	0.822	0.784	0.747	0.713	0.681	0.650	0.621	0.593	0.567	0.543
6	0.942	0.888	0.837	0.790	0.746	0.705	0.666	0.630	0.596	0.564	0.535	0.507	0.480
7	0.933	0.871	0.813	0.760	0.711	0.665	0.623	0.583	0.547	0.513	0.482	0.452	0.425
8	0.923	0.853	0.789	0.731	0.677	0.627	0.582	0.540	0.502	0.467	0.434	0.404	0.376
9	0.914	0.837	0.766	0.703	0.645	0.592	0.544	0.500	0.460	0.424	0.391	0.361	0.333
10	0.905	0.820	0.744	0.676	0.614	0.558	0.508	0.463	0.422	0.386	0.352	0.322	0.295
11	0.896	0.804	0.722	0.650	0.585	0.527	0.475	0.429	0.388	0.350	0.317	0.287	0.261
12	0.887	0.788	0.701	0.625	0.557	0.497	0.444	0.397	0.356	0.319	0.286	0.257	0.231
13	0.879	0.773	0.681	0.601	0.530	0.469	0.415	0.368	0.326	0.290	0.258	0.229	0.204
14	0.870	0.758	0.661	0.577	0.505	0.442	0.388	0.340	0.299	0.263	0.232	0.205	0.181
15	0.861	0.743	0.642	0.555	0.481	0.417	0.362	0.315	0.275	0.239	0.209	0.183	0.160
16	0.853	0.728	0.623	0.534	0.458	0.394	0.339	0.292	0.252	0.218	0.188	0.163	0.141
17	0.844	0.714	0.605	0.513	0.436	0.371	0.317	0.270	0.231	0.198	0.170	0.146	0.125
18	0.836	0.700	0.587	0.494	0.416	0.350	0.296	0.250	0.212	0.180	0.153	0.130	0.111
19	0.828	0.686	0.570	0.475	0.396	0.331	0.277	0.232	0.194	0.164	0.138	0.116	0.098
20	0.820	0.673	0.554	0.456	0.377	0.312	0.258	0.215	0.178	0.149	0.124	0.104	0.087
24	0.788	0.622	0.492	0.390	0.310	0.247	0.197	0.158	0.126	0.102	0.082	0.066	0.053
25	0.780	0.610	0.478	0.375	0.295	0.233	0.184	0.146	0.116	0.092	0.074	0.059	0.047
30	0.742	0.552	0.412	0.308	0.231	0.174	0.131	0.099	0.075	0.057	0.044	0.033	0.026
40	0.672	0.453	0.307	0.208	0.142	0.097	0.067	0.046	0.032	0.022	0.015	0.011	0.008
50	0.608	0.372	0.228	0.141	0.087	0.054	0.034	0.021	0.013	0.009	0.005	0.003	0.002
60	0.550	0.305	0.170	0.095	0.054	0.030	0.017	0.010	0.006	0.003	0.002	0.001	0.000

Present Value Interest Factor, continued

PERIOD, n	14%	15%	16%	17%	18%	19%	20%	24%	28%	32%	36%	40%
0	1.000	1.000	1.000	1.000	1.000	1.000	1.000	1.000	1.000	1.000	1.000	1.000
1	0.877	0.870	0.862	0.855	0.847	0.840	0.833	0.806	0.781	0.758	0.735	0.714
2	0.769	0.756	0.743	0.731	0.718	0.706	0.694	0.650	0.610	0.574	0.541	0.510
3	0.675	0.658	0.641	0.624	0.609	0.593	0.579	0.524	0.477	0.435	0.398	0.364
4	0.592	0.572	0.552	0.534	0.516	0.499	0.482	0.423	0.373	0.329	0.292	0.260
5	0.519	0.497	0.476	0.456	0.437	0.419	0.402	0.341	0.291	0.250	0.215	0.186
6	0.456	0.432	0.410	0.390	0.370	0.352	0.335	0.275	0.227	0.189	0.158	0.133
7	0.400	0.376	0.354	0.333	0.314	0.296	0.279	0.222	0.178	0.143	0.116	0.095
8	0.351	0.327	0.305	0.285	0.266	0.249	0.233	0.179	0.139	0.108	0.085	0.068
9	0.308	0.284	0.263	0.243	0.225	0.209	0.194	0.144	0.108	0.082	0.063	0.048
10	0.270	0.247	0.227	0.208	0.191	0.176	0.162	0.116	0.085	0.062	0.046	0.035
11	0.237	0.215	0.195	0.178	0.162	0.148	0.135	0.094	0.066	0.047	0.034	0.025
12	0.208	0.187	0.168	0.152	0.137	0.124	0.112	0.076	0.052	0.036	0.025	0.018
13	0.182	0.163	0.145	0.130	0.116	0.104	0.093	0.061	0.040	0.027	0.018	0.013
14	0.160	0.141	0.125	0.111	0.099	0.088	0.078	0.049	0.032	0.021	0.014	0.009
15	0.140	0.123	0.108	0.095	0.084	0.074	0.065	0.040	0.025	0.016	0.010	0.006
16	0.123	0.107	0.093	0.081	0.071	0.062	0.054	0.032	0.019	0.012	0.007	0.005
17	0.108	0.093	0.080	0.069	0.060	0.052	0.045	0.026	0.015	0.009	0.005	0.003
18	0.095	0.081	0.069	0.059	0.051	0.044	0.038	0.021	0.012	0.007	0.004	0.002
19	0.083	0.070	0.060	0.051	0.043	0.037	0.031	0.017	0.009	0.005	0.003	0.002
20	0.073	0.061	0.051	0.043	0.037	0.031	0.026	0.014	0.007	0.004	0.002	0.001
24	0.043	0.035	0.028	0.023	0.019	0.015	0.013	0.006	0.003	0.001	0.000	0.000
25	0.038	0.030	0.024	0.020	0.016	0.013	0.010	0.005	0.002	0.000	0.000	0.000
30	0.020	0.015	0.012	0.009	0.007	0.005	0.004	0.002	0.000	0.000	0.000	0.000
40	0.005	0.004	0.003	0.002	0.001	0.000	0.000	0.000	0.000	0.000	0.000	0.000
50	0.001	0.000	0.000	0.000	0.000	0.000	0.000	0.000	0.000	0.000	0.000	0.000
60	0.000	0.000	0.000	0.000	0.000	0.000	0.000	0.000	0.000	0.000	0.000	0.000

Appendix B
Useful Web Sites for Buying, Valuing, and Selling Businesses

The following Web sites (URLs) were located after extensive searching via numerous search engines/keyword combinations through Compuserve and America Online. To find local business brokers, the best approach is to enter the name of your state (and/or city) along with the words "business" and "broker." The sites selected below are all considered credible and are broken down into three categories: nationwide brokerage networks, businesses for sale, and general information.

Most applicable URLs begin with "http://www." followed by the address information below presented in bold print (note that it may or may not be necessary to enter the www designation, depending on your mode of search).

Nationwide Brokerage Sites
1. VR Business Brokers—national (vrbusinessbrokers.com)
2. VR Business Brokers—Arizona (az-vr-businessbrokers.com)
3. Immigration Network (bizbuy.com/)
4. California Association of Business Brokers (cabb.org)
5. American Motel/Hotel Brokers (primenet.com/~amhb/)
6. M&A Source (masource.org/default.asp)

Businesses for Sale
1. The Internet Business Multiple Listing Site (bbn-net.com)
2. The Relocatable Business Newsletter (relocatable.com)
3. The Central Business Opportunity Exchange (c-box.com)
4. The Business Broker Web (business-broker.com)
5. BizBuySell (bizbuysell.com/)
6. M&A Marketplace (webcom.com/cfnet/)
7. Business Net (kudonet.com/index.html)
8. Americanet (americanet.com)
9. National Business Exchange (nbe.com)
10. BusOp Search Newsletter (worldprofit.com)
11. Business Opportunities (busopps.com)
12. BIZQUEST (bizmart.com/index.html)
13. SLO For Sale (sloforsale.com/)
14. Nationwide Commercial Directory (enet.ca/ncd/)
15. Business Locator (207.67.226.117/abls/)
16. Web Directory of Businesses For Sale (tbzweb.com/estbus.htm)

General Search Information

1. The Business/Finance Library (web.idirect.com)
2. BankNet (bank.net)
3. Entrepreneurs on the Web (eotw.com)
4. Amazon Bookstore (amazon.com)
5. Business Services, Inc. (busserv.com/)
6. Home Based Business Bookstore (advgroup.com)
7. Shannon Pratt's Homepage (transport.com/~shannonp/)
8. SEC Edgar Database (sec.gov/edgarhp.htm)
9. LSU/US Government Federal Agencies Page (lib.lsu.edu/gov/fedgov.html)
10. Small Business Note Acquisitions (sbna.com/)
11. Bizquest (bizquest.com/)

Glossary

ability to pay valuation method This is an interesting method that serves as a reality check on the other valuation results. The practical "ceiling" on the price of the typical small business is dependent on the company's ability to pay the owner a salary, provide a return on the owner's down payment and working capital investments, and finally service the debt associated with the purchase on credit.

absentee or semiabsentee ownership If a business can be run near capacity and optimal profitability without the owner present (absentee-run), its value is significantly increased. From a standard valuation point of view, multiples are higher or capitalization/discount rates are lower for such a business. Most small businesses are valued based on the cash flow accruing to a single, active owner.

acceleration clause An important provision in a promissory note that gives the seller (lender) the right to declare the entire amount immediately due and payable upon violation of a loan provision, such as late payments. In each case, default should be clearly defined to prevent misunderstandings.

accounts payable (A/P) Balances owed to creditors on open account for the purchases of goods and services. As concerns the purchase of a business via an asset sale, the buyer should expect all A/P to be paid in full at or before closing. Under a stock purchase, unless otherwise agreed, all liabilities pass to the new owner. This requires careful review on the part of the purchaser for what these amounts are and the maximum amounts to be assumed by purchaser should be mutually agreed on before closing with any debts beyond these discussed and agreed to being paid from cash balances set aside from the purchaser's down payment. All such assumed liabilities should be listed and attached to the purchase contract per addendum or attachment. Buyers may request a formal "set-aside" account be established with the escrow company to satisfy any unknown or undisclosed payables that surface subsequent to the closing.

accounts receivable (A/R) Amounts owed to a business for product or services sold on account. Under an asset sale of a business, A/R will typically belong to the seller. Under stock purchases, ownership of the receivables passes to the new owner and should be carefully considered in terms of the actual final purchase price. The purchaser should ask to see an "aging schedule" of A/R, indicating amounts owing and the age of the accounts (e.g., 0–30 days, 30–60 days). Also investigate historical write-offs of bad debt, specifically noting if there are any significant current problems. It is possible to overstate net income by failing to formally recognize bad debt expenses.

accrual basis   A method of accounting (as opposed to cash basis) whereby revenues and expenses are recognized as they are earned, regardless of when cash is received or spent. There may also be different procedures used for book as opposed to tax purposes. When evaluating the cash flow of a target business, adjustments must be made to account for accrual based entries (e.g., sales made on credit).

adjusted cash flow (ACF)   This important concept underlies much of the business valuation process. It represents the actual cash benefits (before income taxes) accruing to a single owner-operator and is calculated by adding non-cash expenses, such as depreciation and amortization; personal or discretionary expenses, such as travel, entertainment, and personal automobile expenses; interest expense and one-time or nonrecurring expenses such as start-up advertising campaigns to the net income for the period. Depreciation is added back because it represents a non-cash expense and interest is added back to arrive at a cash flow figure available to a new owner to do with as he or she pleases (e.g., salary, debt service, and a return on investment).

agency   The legal relationship between a principal and an agent arising from a contract (e.g., listing contract) in which the principal hires the agent to perform certain duties on his or her behalf. Brokers and their agents may represent the seller, the buyer (buyer broker), or both (dual agency). Agency must be disclosed to all parties in a timely fashion.

amortization   The periodic write-off of costs associated with the acquisition of intangible assets, such as patents, goodwill, and organization expenses. For tax purposes, all intangible assets must currently be amortized over 15 years. Amortization expense is a type of non-cash expense that is added to net income in determining the annual cash flow (ACF) of a business.

asset sale   One of two general choices faced by buyers and sellers in the sale of a business (see stock sale for the other alternative). There are advantages and disadvantages to buyer and seller with each option. Consult your broker, CPA, or tax attorney for a thorough analysis. Most sales of small businesses are asset sales. The advantages to the buyer are significant. First, by purchasing the assets, all equipment and fixtures may be fully "redepreciated," allowing a significant tax benefit. Secondly, an asset purchase does not carry the same "baggage" as a purchase of stock. A stock purchase brings all liabilities (known and unknown!) to the new owner. There are possible benefits to a stock sale as well, such as a speedier closing process, that should be considered.

assignment of lease   A critical buyer contingency for businesses with a property lease. Most offers to purchase such a business are subject to the satisfactory assignment/transfer of the existing lease.

assumption of liability   A common occurrence in the purchase of a business. Typical assumptions relate to equipment leases, credit card processing arrangements, and several types of bank loans, all of which can be considered part of the purchase price.

backup contract   A contract to buy a business that becomes effective if a prior contract falls through. A seller's best interest is served by allowing backup offers, but the buyer with the first contract will often request that the seller accept no further offers until the first deal is completed or aborted (the buyer does not want the seller to continue searching for a more favorable deal).

better business bureau (BBB) A useful due diligence tool, the BBB is a system of more than 200 independent offices serving their respective communities in resolving disputes and building trust for more than 100 years.

bill of sale A written instrument given at closing to pass title of personal property from a seller to a buyer. Related closing documents include a promissory note, UCC-1 financing statement, and chattel security agreement. The escrow company will hold on to the original bill of sale until the promissory note is paid in full.

binder As concerns insurance, this is a contract for temporary insurance coverage. When purchasing a business, you should attempt to ensure constant coverage for both property and liability, and obtain a binder receipt as evidence of an application to extend the existing coverage of the seller.

books and records clause An important contingency placed into purchase offers, it allows the buyer ample opportunity to review the books, records, and operations of a company before placing money at risk.

book value This has two primary applications. Concerning a business, the book value is the difference between total assets (net of depreciation, amortization) and total liabilities as they appear on the balance sheet. This is the same thing as net worth and owner's equity. Concerning specific assets, book value is the original cost (capitalized value) less accumulated depreciation and amortization as it appears on the balance sheet.

capitalization Refers to the process whereby income or cash flow is converted to a value. An income stream can be capitalized into a numerical dollar value. For example, an expected "stream" of $100,000 for five years, discounted with a 12 percent capitalization rate (cap rate) yields a value of $404,410.

cash business When a business is described to a buyer as a cash business, the primary implication is that this business completes a great deal of its transactions for payment in cash, as opposed to checks or credit cards.

certified funds Bank certified monies, required by escrow company for closing process and transfer of business ownership interest. Out-of-state funds require extra time for processing and can unnecessarily delay the closing.

closing Technically, the act of transferring ownership of a business from seller to buyer in accordance with a purchase agreement. After all contingencies relating to the contract (e.g., books and records review, lease assignment) are removed, escrow is opened and an earnest deposit is made. Unless the closing occurs at an attorney's office, it will normally occur at the offices of a qualified escrow company (specializing in business closings as opposed to real property closings). The escrow company will typically prepare all closing-related paperwork (closing documents), including the bill of sale, promissory note, chattel security agreement, bulk sales waiver, broker disclaimer, closing statement, etc., at the same time it is conducting a thorough review of the public records for any existing liens, attachments, judgments, or other encumbrances affecting the ownership of the business and its assets.

compiled statements These are commonly used by smaller "mom and pop" businesses. Essentially, they are compilations of account balances calculated based on information supplied to the CPA by the firm. They are not audited or reviewed and lack any assurances from the CPA as to their fairness, or conformity with GAAP. Remember, garbage-in, garbage-out. Caveat emptor!

contingencies   These are events that must or must not occur before a certain time. Offers written to purchase a business almost always are contingent on the occurrence/nonoccurrence of certain events. If an offer is accepted by the seller, so are the contingencies contained therein. Once there is this agreement on price and terms, contingencies must be removed. There can be both buyer and seller contingencies, with buyers typically including several in their offer.

contingent liability   Pending litigation, disputed customer claims, court decisions under appeal, or any other negative event representing possible future financial liability. Purchasers should ask the seller to comment on any such contingent liabilities (seller's disclosure form) and warrant that they either do not exist or have been properly disclosed and/or addressed.

cross-default clause   This clause is a condition of sale that ties default on the property lease with default on the seller's carry-back note. In other words, if the new owner defaults on property lease payments, the note to the seller is considered in default and subject to payment in full (acceleration clause). Importantly, this clause may also state that default on the note to the seller will be considered as a default on the property lease, allowing quicker reentry into the business by the seller. This clause protects the seller's interest in the business, which would be severely damaged if the new owner defaulted on the lease and was evicted. The seller should also try to work out a separate arrangement with the landlord to facilitate reentry if the need arises (reassignment of lease clause).

distress sales   Businesses that are experiencing financial difficulties (illiquidity and insolvency) and are in or near bankruptcy. Favorable terms can be secured for these turnaround opportunities. Local auctioneers, bankruptcy attorneys, credits rating agencies, and the local public records are all excellent sources of prospective acquisition. Extra care during due diligence is required.

due diligence   This term represents all the steps taken by the prospective purchaser of a business to verify that the information presented by the seller is accurate and that the purchaser is fully convinced of his or her choice. Due diligence is completed when contingencies are removed and the purchaser is ready to open escrow and schedule closing. In addition to hiring an accountant, consider calling the better business bureau for an inexpensive look at the company's public record and Dun & Bradstreet for a minimal cost look at its financial history.

earnest money deposit   This is a deposit of funds by a purchaser that serves as evidence of the buyer's serious intentions. In many cases, this earnest check will be held by the business broker, uncashed, until all contingencies are removed, and then placed into an escrow account (escrow is opened). The escrow check will normally be at risk only after escrow is opened.

earn-out clause   This creative financing option can resuscitate a deal and lead to closing. The premise is to tie the final payments made to the seller to the actual future performance of the business subsequent to closing. They can give the buyer courage to take on a dying or damaged business while allowing the seller to potentially receive top dollar upon sale. Exact details and possibilities are limited only by the imagination. The payments can be based on sales (dollars or units), net income, or ACF.

employer identification number Every new business and most businesses changing hands need to obtain this number, which is used by the IRS to identify taxpayers. Call 800-829-1040 or your local IRS office for the proper forms and instructions. Many IRS forms are also available by fax at 703-487-4160 or through the World Wide Web at http://www.irs.ustreas.gov or at its previous online service at 703-321-8020.

evergreen clause This is another clause that protects the seller's remaining interest in the business after sale on terms. This clause requires the new owner to maintain inventory (can also address equipment) at or above a certain threshold or default on the note will occur. This condition of sale is intended to prevent the new owner from liquidating inventory to the point of damaging the long run stability of the business. If a business is sold on terms with a low down payment, the seller should seek to prevent the possibility of the new owner liquidating the inventory, equipment, and fixtures for amounts more than the original down payment and destroying the business.

fair market value The amount at which a business would change hands between a willing buyer and seller when both sides are acting with reasonable knowledge and a lack of excessive compulsion. What a willing buyer will pay a willing seller under normal conditions.

full disclosure This concept applies equally for the sale of a publicly traded security and a privately held company. All licensed business brokers, for example, are legally mandated to disclose all material facts and treat all parties fairly, regardless of their particular agency allegiance. This full disclosure applies to physical, financial, and economic conditions relating to the subject business. See the sample seller's disclosure form (in Chapter 4) for precise inquiries to make.

generally accepted accounting principles (GAAP) Generally accepted accounting principles are the backbone of financial statements. The value of these principles lies in the resulting ability of users to accurately and consistently compare one firm's financial performance with another firm's performance over time. Financial statements prepared for most small businesses are compiled (as opposed to audited) and are not prepared in full accordance with GAAP.

gold card visa Officially known as employment creation visas, foreign residents may obtain permanent residency by maintaining certain investment and employment levels in U.S. firms. Generally, an amount of $1 million must be invested and ten jobs created or maintained. Numerous specific requirements and exemptions exist, so attorney assistance is mandatory.

goodwill Technically, goodwill represents the dollar amount paid for a business that exceeds the market value of the assets. A business purchased for $200,000 with only $120,000 of "hard," tangible assets (machinery, fixtures, inventory) contains $80,000 of goodwill. This basically means that the business, complete with customers, suppliers, and procedures, is worth more than simply the value of the assets.

indemnification A type of representation or warranty made by buyer or seller in a purchase agreement signed by both parties. Basically, an indemnification serves to protect the buyer or seller from clearly specified liabilities, known or unknown. In the purchase/sale of a business, both the buyer and seller will indemnify the other party to one extent or another (cross-indemnification). For example, sellers will typically indemnify buyers against any unknown or contingent liabilities and the buyers will indemnify the sellers against future claims, made by lenders, other creditors, or shareholders.

intellectual property Intangible assets that must be protected through proper application and filing with state and federal agencies. Intellectual property includes trademarks, service marks, patents, and copyrights, and are considered intangible assets. Continued protection of a newly acquired trade name is critical.

inventory The most important asset for retail businesses (percent of total assets) and a significant asset for manufacturing businesses. When evaluating a business for purchase, important investigations include:

- How much of the inventory is unsalable, obsolete, or damaged? Pay only for salable goods.
- Has the owner paid suppliers on a timely basis? Ask directly and check Dun & Bradstreet.
- Is the bulk sales law applicable (requires certified letters to all creditors from prior two years)? Do parties agree to waive bulk sales law? Consult your attorney.

letter of intent An instrument for purchasing a business whereby the prospect states an interest in furthering discussions and negotiations without being legally bound to do so. It is an expression of desire to enter into an agreement without actually doing so, and is a weaker expression of interest than a standard offer to purchase.

lien search The escrow company or attorney will conduct an independent search of municipal, state, and federal recorded judgments, liens, attachments, or other encumbrances affecting the business being sold. If any are found, they should be satisfactorily addressed before the closing can occur. The seller is generally warranting that the business is being sold free and clear of any liens, attachments, or encumbrances.

liquidation value Cash value received as a result of a forced sale of assets, typically as a business is closing down. Liquidation values of assets can be as low as 5 to 10 percent of original cost. A seller of a business is almost always better off selling the whole of his or her operation at what seems like an unfavorable price as opposed to waiting too long and receiving only a liquidated value for the assets.

listing agreement or contract This is the formal agreement between the seller and a business broker regarding the marketing and sale of a business. It must contain an asking price, terms (if any), commission amount, and beginning and ending dates. There are four general types of listing contracts: sole and exclusive, exclusive agency, agency, and one-party. Brokers will prefer a sole and exclusive listing, which gives them the right to collect a commission regardless of who locates the buyer, whereas the seller may prefer an agency listing, which allows them the right to locate a buyer either on their own or with the assistance of another broker without obligation of commission.

market basket approach to valuation   If you seek to obtain an accurate estimate of a company's current fair market value, consider valuing the business using a collection of valuation methods (three or four different methods) and averaging their results. This approach is surprisingly accurate in most circumstances.

misrepresentation   A buyer's worst nightmare. This is the making of untrue statements, either deliberate or unintentional. If there is misrepresentation of a material fact, the injured party can sue for damages or seek recision of the contract. Generally, buyers should take all necessary and precautionary steps to independently verify any claims.

net present value (NPV)   The core of modern financial theory, this concept holds that the attractiveness of any investment (including into a business) is measured by the net present value associated with the relevant cash outflows and inflows. The DCF technique for valuing businesses is growing in popularity.

noncompete agreement   Also referred to as covenant not to compete, this clause is a legal promise by the seller not to compete with the purchaser for a certain number of years in a certain geographical area in a certain service or product line. It must be reasonable in order to be enforceable.

no-shop clause   An agreement between buyer and seller in either a letter of intent or formal purchase offer that restricts the seller's marketing efforts after signatures are obtained from both sides. This clause prohibits the seller, to varying degrees, from soliciting or engaging in negotiations or other communications with other potential buyers for a stipulated period of time, typically ranging from one to four months.

promissory note   A written instrument signed by a creditor (purchaser of a business) acknowledging a debt and a promise to pay. Promissory notes may be signed individually or by a corporation, but most sellers will require the note to be personally guaranteed. Regarding the sale of a business (personal property), promissory notes will be secured by the assets of the subject business through an executed chattel security agreement, with a corresponding UCC-1 financing statement recorded at the appropriate local and state agencies.

right of first refusal   The right, but not obligation, of a party to match the price and terms of a proposed sale of a business before the contract is executed. Oftentimes a contract will be signed between purchaser and seller allowing the business to continue to be shown to other interested parties during the due diligence period. Until all contingencies are removed, escrow is opened, and the deal closed, an outside party could come forth and offer to close the sale at a better price. Under these conditions, the original purchaser could ask for a right of first refusal against forthcoming offers.

right of offset (aka holdback or set-aside)   This contractual clause leads to an agreed on amount of the buyer's down payment being placed into an escrow account (preferably interest-bearing) at closing, to be disbursed on certain events occurring, such as the discovery of overlooked or intentionally ignored liabilities of the seller. The undefinable risk to the seller is that the buyer can concoct reasons for tapping these funds that may or may not be legitimate.

rules of thumb　A collection of formulas utilized to value both small, privately held and larger, publicly traded businesses. They are based on annual or monthly sales, adjusted cash flow, net income, earnings before interest and taxes, asset values, number of accounts, or any combination thereof. Purists reject the usefulness of rules of thumb, but they must be properly understood. Their usefulness revolves around decades-long development based on historical sales of similar businesses.

Schilt's risk premiums　Sound procedure (empirically proven) for establishing discount and capitalization rates used to value small businesses. These risk premiums range from 6 to 30 percent and are added to a risk-free discount rate of approximately 7 to 8 percent (includes inflation premium).

Section 179 expense　This IRS provision allows business owners to expense up to $25,000 of business personal property, rather than capitalizing and depreciating the assets over their useful lives. From a due diligence perspective, this means that a company might have thousands of dollars worth of equipment that has been expensed and therefore excluded from the balance sheet.

seller's disclosure form or statement　Important document utilized by the buyer to obtain pertinent, material information about the business (personal property) and/or the building (real property). There should be separate disclosure forms for both the business and for the real property.

SIC (Standard Industrial Classification) Codes　General SIC Codes are provided for each sector of our economy in an attempt to categorize the many sections of our economic system. Numerous invaluable sources of data are categorized, presented, and analyzed by SIC Code, including financial statement ratio analysis (e.g., Robert Morris Associates).

skimming　This controversial behavior involves underreporting of income by small business owners. There is great incentive to underreport sales for the purpose of minimizing income tax payments. Most buyers find it difficult to give credit to the seller for unreported sales. In some types of businesses, skimming is the rule rather than the exception. Buyers may conduct a visual audit, with the seller's permission, to help verify the claimed amount of sales, or actually watch the seller account for the sales of the day.

start-up business　One of two general choices facing an individual seeking to be a self-employed business owner. As opposed to purchasing an ongoing business, a start-up operation might require less up-front financial outlays. However, buying an existing business offers a proven product and a proven location with customers and cash flow.

stock sale　As opposed to an asset sale, a stock sale involves the purchase and transfer of ownership through shares of common stock. A stock sale generally provides more benefits to the seller than the buyer. The actual outcome depends on the type of corporation utilized by the owner, "C" or "S." There are significant differences between the two. Again, you need to consult a CPA or tax professional for current interpretations. For a C corporation, gains on asset sales will be taxed twice, once at the corporate rate and again at the shareholder (individual) rate. Also, there are currently (as of 1993) significant tax benefits to stock sales of small C corporations (up to 50 percent of the gain excluded from taxation, if stock was held for at least five years). A buyer might want to purchase the stock of a company because it can be procedurally quicker, given that the buyer is agreeing to assume all liabilities, whatever they are.

Subchapter S Corporation   A popular type of incorporation chosen by small business owners. Besides the general benefits of incorporating, such as limited liability for shareholders, there are favorable tax implications. Specifically, income is taxed only once as direct income to the shareholders, avoiding the double taxation that occurs for C corporations (corporate profits are taxed and then dividend distributions from after-tax profits are taxed again as ordinary income to shareholders). A limited liability company (LLC) enjoys the same pass-through benefits, but is less restrictive on the number and type of shareholders.

training agreement   Most business sales include a provision regarding training to be received by the buyer from the seller, typically included as part of the purchase price. This provision can be brief and general or substantial and detailed. The basic components of a training agreement include areas and length of training and additional compensation to seller (if any).

Uniform Commercial Code (UCC)   A group of laws adopted by most states in an effort to standardize state laws dealing with commercial transactions. UCC laws are relevant for chattel security agreements, promissory notes, and bulk transfers. Particularly relevant to the sale of businesses is the bulk sales law, which serves to protect the unsecured creditors of the business being sold.

valuation methods   Wide-ranging tools utilized by professionals to establish the value of going concerns. The type of method utilized depends on the size and type of the business and the sophistication of the preparer and the audience. They are generally asset-based, cash flow–based, or some combination of the two.

venture capital   A form of investment that entails sacrificing ownership and control in exchange for cash that may or may not be returned to the investors. It basically provides capital and expertise in exchange for an equity stake. The common forms of financing include preferred stock, convertible bonds, or warrants. Consult *Pratt's Guide to Venture Capital Sources*.

warranties and representations   Multifaceted statements, claims, and inferences that are binding components of legal contracts, particularly for purchase contracts. Both sides (buyers and sellers) make a number of such claims. Examples include statements regarding the buyer's ability to consummate the deal and the seller's ability to substantiate claims related to earnings and asset values. Warranties tend to be based on current or future facts while representations tend to be apply only to existing facts.

working capital   This area of investment is often overlooked and even subconsciously ignored. After the close of escrow, working capital is needed to support the daily operation of the business, including payroll obligations, inventory purchases, utilities, and other necessary expenditures. Some businesses will immediately generate sufficient cash flow to sustain these commitments, but most will not (particularly if the business is providing credit and growing).

Bibliography and Recommended Reading

General Business

A Basic Guide to Exporting. U.S. Government Printing Office. 202-512-1800.

American Arbitration Association. 1730 Rhode Island Avenue NW, Suite 512, Washington, DC 20036-3169. 212-484-4000.

American Demographics. Dow Jones. 800-828-1133.

Baker, Hoyt L. *Copyrights, Patents and Trademarks.* New York: Liberty Press, McGraw-Hill. 800-262-4729.

Brooks, Julie K., and Barry A. Stevens. *How to Write a Successful Business Plan.* New York: American Management Association.

Census and You—Demographic Information. (Free copy available) DVDS, Bureau of the Census, Washington, DC 20233.

Clifford, Denise, and Ralph Warner. *The Partnership Book: How to Write a Partnership Agreement.* Berkeley, Calif.: Nolo Press. 800-992-6656.

Cohen, William A. *Entrepreneur and Small Business Problem Solver: An Encyclopedia and Reference Guide.* 2d ed. New York: Wiley.

Commerce Business Daily. U.S. Government Printing Office. The source for government contract leads. 202-783-3238.

Corporate Statistics of Industrial and Office Real Estate Markets. Society of Industrial and Office Realtors. 202-737-1150.

The Copyright Handbook. Berkeley, Calif.: Nolo Press. 800-992-6656. 510-549-1976.

Diamond, Michael R., and Julie L. Williams. *How to Incorporate: A Handbook for Entrepreneurs and Professionals.* New York: Wiley.

Directory of Franchising Organizations. New York: Pilot Books.

Dorgan, Charity Anne, ed. *Small Business Sourcebook.* 3d ed. 3 vols. 1989. Detroit, Mich: Gale Research.

Elias, Stephen, and Susan Levinkind. *Legal Research: How to Find and Understand the Law.* Berkeley, Calif.: Nolo Press. 800-992-6656.

Encyclopedia of Associations. Detroit, Mich: Gale Research. 800-877-4253, ext. 1538.

EPA Public Information Center. 401 M Street SW, Washington, DC 20460. 202-260-7751.

Government Printing Office Bulletin Board. Many federal government related annual reports, policy changes, etc. 202-512-1387. 202-512-1524.

Guidebook to Fair Employment Practices. Commerce Clearing House. 800-835-5224.

The Human Resources Yearbook. Upper Saddle River, N.J.: Prentice-Hall. 800-223-1360.

Incorporation Consultants: Corporation Agents. P.O. Box 1281, Wilmington, Del. 19899. 800-877-4224. 302-998-0598.

Industry and Trade Administration. *U.S. Industrial Outlook.* Washington, D.C.: U.S. Government Printing Office.

Infolink Research Services. 914-736-1565.

Insuring Your Business. Insurance Information Institute, 110 William St., New York, NY 10038. 212-669-9200.

Jones, Seymour, M. Bruce Cohen, and Victor V. Coppola. *Coopers and Lybrand Guide to Growing Your Business.* New York: Wiley.

Lashbrooke, E.C., and Michael I. Swygart. *The Legal Handbook of Business Transactions.* New York: Quorum Books.

Lavin, Michael R. *Business Information: How to Find It, How to Use It.* Phoenix, Ariz.: Onyx Press.

Lifestyle Market Analyst, The. Current ed. Wilmette, Ill.: Standard Rate and Data Service.

Manufacturing USA: Industry Analyses, Statistics and Leading Companies. Detroit, Mich.: Gale Research.

Marketer's Guide to Media. Ad Week. 800-468-2395.

Martindale-Hubbell Law Directory. New York: Martindale-Hubbell, Inc. Profiles thousands of lawyers by specialty, across the country. 800-521-8110.

NAFTA Implementation Line. 202-482-0305.

National Association of Small Business Investment Companies (SBICs). 703-683-1601.

1997 Business Reference Guide. Boston, Mass.: Business Brokerage Press. 508-369-5254.

Office of Management and Budget Standard Industrial Classification Manual. Washington, D.C.: U.S. Government Printing Office.

Predicast's Forecasts. Cleveland, Ohio: Predicasts, Inc.

Simmons Market Research Bureau, Media Ad Research, 420 Lexington Avenue, New York, NY 10170. 212-916-8958.

Standard and Poor's Industry Surveys. New York: Standard & Poor's Corporation.

Standard Legal Forms and Agreements for Small Business. Self-Counsel Press. 800-663-3007. 206-676-4530.

Steingold, Fred. *The Legal Guide for Starting and Running a Small Business.* Berkeley, Calif.: Nolo Press. 800-992-6656. 510-549-1976.

Tax Guide for Small Business. Washington, D.C.: U.S. Department of the Treasury (IRS).

ULI Market Profiles. Urban Land Institute, Washington DC 20005. 800-321-5011.

Wolfson, Stacey. *Tenant's Handbook of Office Leasing.* New York: McGraw-Hill. 800-262-4729.

Zankel, Martin I. *Negotiating Commercial Real Estate Leases.* Chicago: Dearborn Financial Planning. 800-982-2850.

Negotiations/Marketing/Selling

Business Trend Analysts Market Research, 2171 Jericho Turnpike, Suite 200, Cormac, NY 11725. 516-462-5454.

Cohen, Herb. *You Can Negotiate Anything.* Secaucus, N.J.: Carol Publishing Group. 800-447-BOOK.

Girard, Joe. *How to Sell Anything to Anybody.* New York: Simon & Schuster.

The Idea-a-Day Guide to Super Selling and Customer Service. Chicago: Dartnell. 800-621-5463.

Mail Order Business Directory. B. Klein Publications. 305-752-1708.

Manufacturers' Agents National Association, P.O. Box 3467, Laguna Hills, CA 92654. 714-859-4040.

Thomas Register of American Manufacturers. New York: Thomas Publishing. 212-290-7277.

Trade Show & Convention Guide. Amusement Business. 615-321-4250.

U.S. Industrial Directory. New Providence, N.J.: Reed Elsevier Publishing. 708-574-7081.

Buying/Selling a Business

Baron, Paul B., *When You Buy or Sell a Company.* Stoney Creek, Conn.: Center for Business Information, Inc., 1986.

The Directory of M&A Professionals. New York: Dealer's Digest, Inc.

Goldstein, Arnold S., *The Complete Guide to Buying and Selling a Business.* New York: Wiley. 800-225-5945.

Hansen, James M. *Guide to Buying or Selling a Business.* Mercer Island, Wash.: Grenadier Press.

Joseph, Richard A., Anna M. Nekoranec, and Carl H. Steffens. *How to Buy a Business.* Chicago: Dearborn Financial Publishing. 800-245-2665.

Knight, Brian and Associates. *Buy the Right Business—At the Right Price.* Chicago: Upstart Publishing Company. 800-235-8866.

Mancuso, Joseph R. *Buying a Business (For Very Little Cash).* Upper Saddle River, N.J.: Prentice-Hall, 1990.

Mergers and Acquisitions. New York: Investment Dealer's Digest, 212-227-1200.

Ryan, Charles R. *Cashing in Your Chips.* Burr Ridge, Ill.: Dow Jones-Irwin.

Scharf, Charles A., Edward E. Shea, and George C. Beck. *Acquisitions, Mergers, Sales, Buyouts and Takeovers.* Upper Saddle River, N.J.: Prentice-Hall.

Sperry, Paul S., and Beatrice H. Mitchell. *The Complete Guide to Selling Your Business.* Chicago: Dearborn/Enterprise. 800-245-2665.

Valiulis, Anthony C. *Covenants Not to Compete: Forms, Tactics, and the Law.* New York: Wiley Law Publications.

Business Valuation

Desmond, Glenn M., and John Marcello. Current ed. *Handbook of Small Business Valuation Formulas.* Los Angeles, Calif.: Valuation Press.

Desmond, Glenn M., and Sandra Storm, ed. *Handbook of Small Business Formulas.* 3d ed. Culver City, Calif.: Valuation Press.

Horn, Thomas W. *Business Valuation Manual.* Lancaster, Pa.: Charter Oak Press.

A Practical Guide to Business Valuation. New York: McGraw Hill, 1986.

West, Thomas L., and Jeffrey O. Jones, eds. *Handbook of Business Valuation.* New York: Wiley, 1992.

Yegge, Wilbur M. *A Basic Guide for Valuing a Company.* New York: Wiley, 1996.

Financial/Accounting/Banking

Annual Statement Studies. Robert Morris Associates. 215-446-4000.

Association of Venture Capitalists, 265 E. 100th S., #300, P.O. Box 3358, Salt Lake City, UT 84110. 801-364-1100.

Bernstein, Leopold A. *Financial Statement Analysis: Theory, Application and Interpretation.* Burr Ridge, Ill.: Richard D. Irwin, 1989.

Business Capital Sources: More Than 1,500 Lenders of Money for Real Estate, Business or Capital Needs. Dun and Bradstreet, Small Business Services. 800-274-6454.

Cost of Doing Business Survey. National Association of Retail Dealers of America. 708-953-8950.

Emerson's Directory of Leading U.S. Accounting Firms. Redmond, Wash.: Big Eight Review, 1988.

Ernst and Young Tax Guide. New York: Wiley. 212-850-6000.

Financial Statement Data. Financial Research Associates. 941-299-3969.

Hayes, Rich Stephen. *Business Loans.* Revised and updated. New York: Wiley.

Industry Norms and Key Business Ratios. D&B Credit Services. 800-223-0141.

Kerwin, Christine, managing ed. *The Corporate Finance Sourcebook.* New Providence, N.J. : National Register Publishing. 800-521-8110, ext. 5745.

O'Hara, Patrick D. *SBA Loans: A Step-by-Step Guide.* New York: Wiley.

Pratt's Guide to Venture Capital Services. Wellesley Hills, Mass.: Capital Publications.

Profitability Analysis Report. Industrial Distribution Association. 404-325-2776.

Restaurant Industry Operations Report. National Restaurant Association. 202-331-5900.

Securities Data (merger and financing data), 1180 Raymond Blvd., Newark, NJ 07102. 201-622-3100.

Silver, A. David. *Who's Who in Venture Capital.* New York: Wiley, 1987.

Tracy, J.A. *How to Read a Financial Report: Wringing Cash Flow and Other Vital Signs Out of the Numbers.* 2d ed. New York: Wiley, 1985.

TRW Business Credit Services Hotline. 800-344-0603.

U.S. Securities and Exchange Commission, 450 Fifth St. NW, Washington, DC 20549. 202-272-3100. 202-272-7460.

Government Sources

Department of Commerce. 202-482-2000. This department is available at the state and federal levels. Federally, the Office of Business Liaison provides information on all federal business assistance programs. States also maintain aggressive small business assistance programs. Check your phone book or call directory assistance.

International Trade Administration. 202-482-0543. Can provide excellent contacts and leads for exporting and importing. Call for details.

Publications from the U.S. Department of Commerce. 800-854-8407.

Service Corps of Retired Executives (SCORE). 202-205-6762. Look in your local White Pages or call directory assistance to find seasoned veterans offering free training and consulting.

Small Business Answer Desk. 800-827-5722. Provided by the SBA's Office of Advocacy, this is a good information and referral service. Ask for a list of free SBA publications. Also ask for the telephone number of the local SBDC, which offers access to inexpensive counselors.

Index

removal deadlines, 160–62
seller, 97–98
Contingency release clause, 105
Contingency removal, 93, 108–9, 126, 141
Contract
breach of, 38
changes to, 79
standardized, 66
timelines, 39
wording of, 76–77
Convenience store, 228
Convenience Store News, 228
Cooling off period, 14
Cooper, Cary, 187
Copeland, Tom, 205
Copy shops, 229
Corporate Growth Report, 221
Corporate purchase, 102–3
Corporate resolution, 40, 44, 52–53
Corporate stock sales agreement, 68–76
Corporate veil, 77
Cost of goods sold, 201
Costs
fixed, 27–28
start-up, 4–6, 10, 13, 27
variable, 28
Couch, Reuel, 25
Counteroffer
deal-breaker, 138
purchase agreement provisions, 102, 126
sample, 135
seller contingency, 264, 266
Covenants, 73, 74, 104–5
Creative financing, 289–96
Credit agencies, 10
Credit record, 285–86
Credit reports, 11
Credit statement, 122
Crisham, Stephen, 31, 57
Cross-default clause, 82, 254, 270
Customer contact, 103

D

Damages, 267
Davis, Will, 6
Deal-breakers, 136, 137–45
Debt
assumption of, 125
excessive, 250
financing, 278–80, 283
payments, 205, 247
service coverage, 287
Default, 89
notice of, 44
provisions, 81, 83
remedies, 103, 131
Demand, 2
Depreciation
asset sale, 198
recapture, 258, 260
tax basis, 260

useful life, 191
Digital imaging, 229
Directory of M&A Professionals, 31
Disclaimer, 249
Disclosure, 30, 31
franchise, 14
importance of, 174
lease commitments, 167–68
statements, 113–20, 252
Discounted cash flow valuation technique, 197–209, 239–41, 249
Discounting, 77
Discount rates
capitalization rates versus, 196–97
determination of, 214–16, 234
Discretionary cash flow, 233
Disputes, 78
Distressed companies, 10–11
Distressed sale, 271–72
Distributorship. *See* Wholesale/distribution business
Dividends, 60
Double Lehman Index, 35
Down payment, 79–80
Dual agency, 30, 31
Due diligence, 145–46
accountants and, 41
business evaluation procedures, 145
deal-breaker, 138–39
document checklist, 146–47
procedures, 13–19
quantitative analysis, 147
timelines, 125–26, 255
Due on sale clause, 82, 83
Dun and Bradstreet, 10, 11

E

Early possession, 185–86
Earnest money deposits, 40, 264–65
Earnest receipt. *See* Purchase agreement
Earnings
after-tax, 60–61, 200
base, 237
before interest and taxes, 182, 184
before interest/taxes/depreciation, 200
capacity, 211
claims, 15
management, 184
Earn-out arrangement, 22
assignment restrictions and, 77
consulting agreement and, 180
issues, 182–83
price and, 79–80, 125
sample clause, 183
use of, 183
valuation and, 24
Economics, 2
Electronic Industries Association, 228
Employees, 103
business sale and, 249–50
confidentiality agreement, 251
noncompete agreement, 251
role of, 252

Employment agreements, 179–82, 237–38, 260
Encumbrances, 30, 44, 100
Entertainment expenses, 246
Equifax, 286
Equipment
mobile, 87
pre-closing issues, 171
purchase agreement provisions, 131
Equity financing, 280–89
Equity investment, 287–88
Escape clause, 101, 266
Escrow
agent, 128
cancellation of, 123
company, 43–45, 123
deadlines, 168
deposit, 66, 94, 125
documents, 121–23
instructions, 121–22
nonrefundable deposits, 40
Evergreen clause, 254, 270
Excess earnings valuation technique, 209–14, 234–36
Exhibits, 121
Exit strategy, 244, 281
Expenditures, 205
Expenses, 89
adjustments, 202
analysis worksheet, 158–59
purchase agreement provisions, 133
reduction of, 246–47
verification of, 41
Export business, 21

F

Fair market value, 190–91, 200–201
Falcon Financial, 295
Familiarization clause, 74, 129, 178–79, 260
Family members, 61, 62
Fastrak program, 289
Fax broadcast company, 2
Federal Filings, Inc., 11
Federal Trade Commission, 15
Fees
business broker, 35–36
closing, 44
franchise, 13, 15, 23
purchase agreement provisions, 133
Finance Hub, 295
Financial buyer, 189, 248
Financial statements
business sale and, 245
of buyer, 263–64
ratio, 218
Financing, 277–78
angels, 283–84
asset-based lenders, 278
bank, 95, 125, 168
bill of sale, 85
carry-back, 77, 80
chattel security agreement, 86–90

How to Install
and Use the Software

To Install the Application for Windows

- Insert the disk in drive A: (or B:).
- From Program Manager or the Start menu select Run.
- Enter A:\Setup.exe.
- Follow prompts on screen.

How To Use This Application

The forms processing application provides a minimized word processor to allow you to customize, revise, and change the forms and letters contained on this disk. We've provided it to allow you to be productive immediately with the forms and/or letters contained in this guide. To open the application from Program Manager or the Start menu, select the Dearborn program group and click on the icon. The basic commands and features of the application are described below.

To Select a Form to Edit

Select the **File** and **Open Form** command to access the forms available with this application. The Open Form command presents the forms dialog box where you can select a form to customize. To select a form, click on a title in the list on the left side of the dialog box. The form title and a brief description of the form appear on the right side of the dialog box. If this is the form you want to edit, select **Open**.

Editing the Form

To edit the form and customize it for your use, select the **Find** button in the toolbar at the top of the form window to automatically locate fields in the form where you need to enter information. These fields are noted with a ">". Of course, you may change or revise any of the text in the form at will.

The menu at the top of the form provides you with several controls. These are as follows:

- **Edit**: You can cut, copy, and paste segments of text.
- **Style**: You can bold, italicize, and underline text, as well as select a font and type size for selected text.

Many of the functions available as menu selections are also available as button commands in the toolbar. These are:

- **Font**: Select from the fonts available on your system by pressing the down arrow and clicking on the font name.
- **Size**: Select the font size by clicking the down arrow and highlighting the font size.
- **Bold (B), Italic (I), Underline (U)**: Select the text you want to change and press the button to change the format.
- **Justification**: You may change the text to flush right, left, centered, or justified by selecting the text and pressing the appropriate button.

Note: Save any edited forms under a different or new file name.

Favorites

If you are like most people, you'll likely use a few forms repeatedly. This application allows you to save forms as "favorites" to provide quick access to those forms frequently used. **To add a form to Favorites:**

- Open a form as you normally would.
- Choose **Favorites** from the File menu and select **Add to Favorites**.
- Enter a name for the file and choose Save.
- To reselect the form, select Favorites from the menu, and select Open Favorite Files. Select the file and press Open.

Help

To learn more about the forms application and the commands available to you, select **Help** from the menu.

If You Already Have a Word Processor . . .

If you have and are already familiar with one or more of the word processing applications available to you, you can use the functionality available in those programs to work with these forms. Select and edit any one of the forms directly from the forms subdirectory created on your hard drive during installation. The files are unformatted ASCII text files that work with all current applications. Text that you need to enter in order to complete a form is preceded by a ">" character. Using your word processor's search function to locate these areas will allow you to quickly customize the forms/letters to suit your needs.

Another way to use the forms in this application with other word processors is to save the file as either a text file (txt) or rich text file (rtf). To do this, select **File** and **Open** from the menu. Open the file you wish to edit and choose **Save As**. Select or enter the name of the file and choose the location where you want it to go. Select **OK**. Open the file in your word processor as you would any other file and edit. (Keep in mind that once you work on a file in another word processor and save it, it probably won't work in the forms processor application without conversion back to a standard text or ASCII file.)

TECHNICAL SUPPORT IS NOT AVAILABLE ON THE ENCLOSED COMPUTER DISK. Please read the installation and operating instructions carefully before attempting to use the disk.

LICENSE AGREEMENT

OPENING ENVELOPE VOIDS RETURNABILITY OR MONEY-BACK GUARANTEES
PLEASE READ THIS DOCUMENT CAREFULLY BEFORE BREAKING THIS SEAL

By breaking this sealed envelope, you agree to become bound by the terms of this license. If you do not agree to the terms of this license do not use the software and promptly return the unopened package within thirty (30) days to the place where you obtained it for a refund.

This Software is licensed, not sold to you by DEARBORN FINANCIAL PUBLISHING, INC. owner of the product for use only under the terms of this License, and DEARBORN FINANCIAL PUBLISHING, INC. reserves any rights not expressly granted to you.

1. **LICENSE:** This License allows you to:

(a) Use the Software only on a single microcomputer at a time, except the Software may be executed from a common disk shared by multiple CPU's provided that one authorized copy of the Software has been licensed from DEARBORN FINANCIAL PUBLISHING, INC. for each CPU executing the Software. DEARBORN FINANCIAL PUBLISHING, INC. does not, however, guarantee that the Software will function properly in your multiple CPU, multi-user environment. The Software may not be used with any gateways, bridges, modems, and/or network extenders that allow the software to be used on multiple CPU's unless one authorized copy of the Software has been licensed from DEARBORN FINANCIAL PUBLISHING, INC. for each CPU executing the Software.

(b) The Software can be loaded to the harddrive and the disk kept solely for backup purposes. The Software is protected by United States copyright law. You must reproduce on each copy the copyright notice and any other proprietary legends that were on the original copy supplied by DEARBORN FINANCIAL PUBLISHING, INC.

(c) Configure the Software for your own use by adding or removing fonts, desk accessories, and/or device drivers.

2. **RESTRICTION:** You may not distribute copies of the Software to others or electronically transfer the Software from one computer to another over a network and/or zone. The Software contains trade secrets and to protect them you may not de-compile, reverse engineer, disassemble, cross assemble or otherwise change and/or reduce the Software to any other form. You may not modify, adapt, translate, rent, lease, loan, resell for profit, distribute, network, or create derivative works based upon the Software or any part thereof.

3. **TERMINATION:** This License is effective unless terminated. This License will terminate immediately without notice from DEARBORN FINANCIAL PUBLISHING, INC. if you fail to comply with any provision of this License. Upon termination you must destroy the Software and all copies thereof. You may terminate the License at any time by destroying the Software and all copies thereof.

4. **EXPORT LAW ASSURANCES:** You agree that the Software will not be shipped, transferred or exported into any country prohibited by the United States Export Administration Act and the regulations thereunder nor will be used for any purpose prohibited by the Act.

5. **LIMITED WARRANTY, DISCLAIMER, LIMITATION OF REMEDIES AND DAMAGES:** The information in this software (Materials) is sold with the understanding that the author, publisher, developer and distributor are not engaged in rendering legal, accounting, banking, security or other professional advice. If legal advice, accounting advice, security investment advice, bank or tax advice or other expert professional assistance is required, the services of a competent professional with expertise in that field should be sought. These materials have been developed using ideas from experience and survey information from various research, lectures and publications. The information contained in these materials is believed to be reliable only at the time of publication and it cannot be guaranteed as it is applied to any particular individual or situation. The author, publisher, developer and distributor specifically disclaim any liability, or risk, personal or otherwise, incurred directly or indirectly as a consequence of the use an application of the information contained in these materials or the live lectures that could accompany their distribution. In no event will the author, publisher, developer or distributor be liable to the purchaser for any amount greater that the purchase price of these materials.

DEARBORN FINANCIAL PUBLISHING, INC.'S warranty on the media, including any implied warranty of merchant ability or fitness for a particular purpose, is limited in duration to thirty (30) days from the date of the original retail. If a disk fails to work or if a disk becomes damaged, you may obtain a replacement disk by returning the original disk and a check or money order for $5.00, for each replacement disk, together with a brief explanation note and a dated sales receipt to:

DEARBORN FINANCIAL PUBLISHING, INC.
155 NORTH WACKER DRIVE
CHICAGO, IL 60606-1719

The replacement warranty set forth above is the sole and exclusive remedy against DEARBORN FINANCIAL PUBLISHING, INC. for breach of warrant, express or implied or for any default whatsoever relating to condition of the software. DEARBORN FINANCIAL PUBLISHING, INC. makes no other warranties or representation, either expressed or implied, with respect to this software or documentation, quality, merchantability performance or fitness for a particular purpose as a result. This software is sold with only the limited warranty with respect to diskette replacement as provided above, and you, the Licensee, are assuming all other risks as to its quality and performance. In no event will DEARBORN FINANCIAL PUBLISHING, INC. or its developers, directors, officers, employees, or affiliates be liable for direct , incidental, indirect, special or consequential damages (including damages for loss of business profits, business interruption, loss of business information and the like) resulting from any defect in this software or its documentation or arising out of the use of or inability to use the software or accompanying documentation even if DEARBORN FINANCIAL PUBLISHING, INC. an authorized DEARBORN FINANCIAL PUBLISHING, INC. representative, or a DEARBORN FINANCIAL PUBLISHING, INC. affiliate has been advised of the possibility of such damage.

DEARBORN FINANCIAL PUBLISHING, INC. MAKES NO REPRESENTATION OR WARRANTY REGARDING THE RESULTS OBTAINABLE THROUGH USE OF THE SOFTWARE.

No oral or written information or advice given by DEARBORN FINANCIAL PUBLISHING, INC. its dealers, distributors, agents, affiliates, developers, officers, directors, or employees shall create a warranty or in any way increase the scope of this warranty.

Some states do not allow the exclusion or limitation of implied warranties or liabilities for incidental or consequential, damages, so the above limitation or exclusion may not apply to you. This warranty gives you specific legal rights, and you may also have other rights which vary from state to state.

COPYRIGHT NOTICE: This software and accompanying manual are copyrighted with all rights reserved by DEARBORN FINANCIAL PUBLISHING, INC. Under United States copyright laws. the software and its accompanying documentation may not be copied in whole or in part except in normal use of the software or the reproduction of a backup copy for archival purpose only. Any other copying, selling or otherwise distributing this software or manual is hereby expressly forbidden.

SIGNATURE_____
SIGN IF BEING RETURNED UNOPENED FOR REFUND